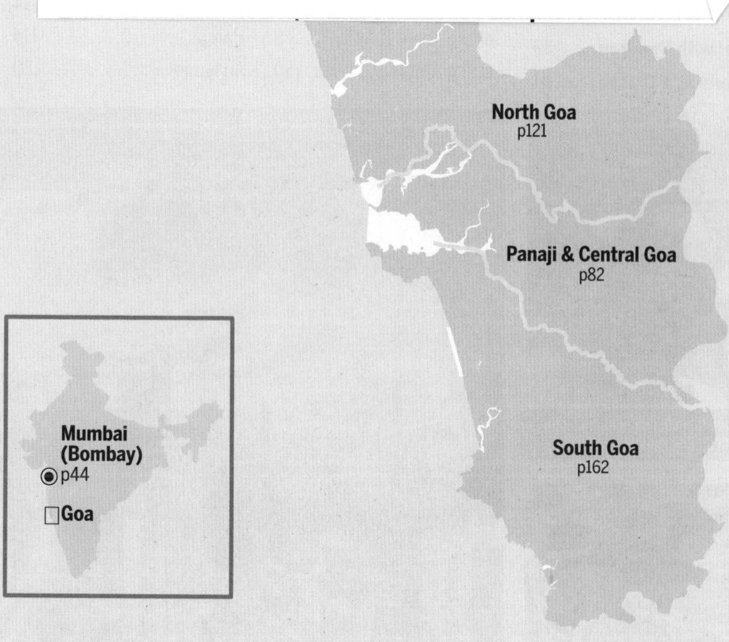
North Goa
p121
Panaji & Central Goa
p82
South Goa
p162
Mumbai (Bombay)
p44
Goa

PLAN YOUR TRIP

ON THE ROAD

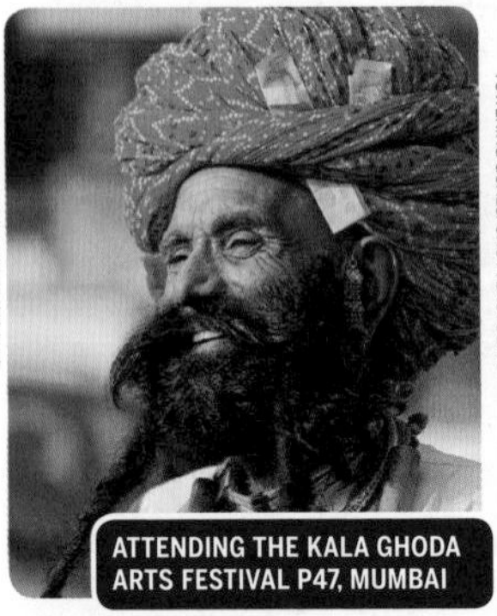
TUKARAM.KARVE/SHUTTERSTOCK ©
ATTENDING THE KALA GHODA ARTS FESTIVAL P47, MUMBAI

PIKOSO.KZ/SHUTTERSTOCK ©
STALL, ANJUNA FLEA MARKET P140

TOWERING GOALS/SHUTTERSTOCK ©

Contents

MUMBAI P44

UNDERSTAND

SURVIVAL GUIDE

SPECIAL FEATURES

Welcome to Goa & Mumbai

A kaleidoscopic blend of Indian and Portuguese cultures, sweetened with sun, sea, sand, seafood, susegad and spirituality, Goa is India's pocket-sized paradise.

Beach Bounty

Goa's biggest draw is undoubtedly its virtually uninterrupted string of golden-sand beaches. This coastline stretches along the Arabian Sea from the tip to the toe of the state, and each beach community has developed its own personality and reputation since the hippie days of the '60s. They cater to every tropical whim: choose from backpacker Arambol or bolder, brasher Baga; the palm-fringed sands of Palolem, hippie market bliss at Anjuna or lovely, laid-back Mandrem; expansive groomed sands in front of fancy five-star resorts or hidden crescent coves, where the only footprints will be the scuttling crabs' and your own.

Spiritual Sanctuary

Want to top up your Zen as well as your tan? Welcome to winter in Goa where yoga is king and the crop of spiritual activities grows more bountiful each year: sunrise yoga sessions on the beach, reiki healing courses, meditation, and just about every other form of spiritual exploration, are all practised freely. Many travellers come here for a serious yoga experience and you'll find everything from drop-in classes to teaching training courses and spiritual retreats.

The Spice of Life

Food is enjoyed fully in Goa and Mumbai, as it is throughout India. The scents, spices and flavours of Goa's cuisine will surprise and tantalise even seasoned travellers: whether it's a classic fish curry rice, a morning *bhali-pau* (bread roll dipped in curry), a piquant vindaloo, with its infusions of wine vinegar and garlic, or a spicy *xacuti* sauce, the Indian-Portuguese influence is a treat for the taste buds. While you're here, visit a back-country spice farm to learn why the Portuguese were so excited about Goa.

Cultural Crockpot

Goa stands out in India for its Portuguese colonial architecture and heritage, while Mumbai boasts the finest Victorian-era colonial architecture in India. The Portuguese arrived in Goa in 1510, lured by the exotic East and the promise of lucrative spice routes, before being booted out in 1961. Their indelible mark is still evident in the state's baroque architecture, whitewashed churches, crumbling forts, colourful Catholic ceremonies, mournful fado music and the stunning cathedrals of Old Goa.

Why I Love Goa

By Paul Harding, Writer

After travelling overland from Delhi through central India and Mumbai to Goa back in the '90s, the beaches, all-night parties and laid-back tropical vibe came as a blissful surprise. Over many return visits a lot of things have changed, but the essence of Goa remains the same. I love the omnipresence of the beach, cruising through impossibly green countryside on two wheels, and the evening ritual of watching the sun melt into the Arabian Sea with a cold beer and a fish thali. And the Goan people – hard-working, optimistic, witty, quick with a smile and always happy to chat.

For more about our writers, see p256

Above: Goan beach

Goa & Mumbai

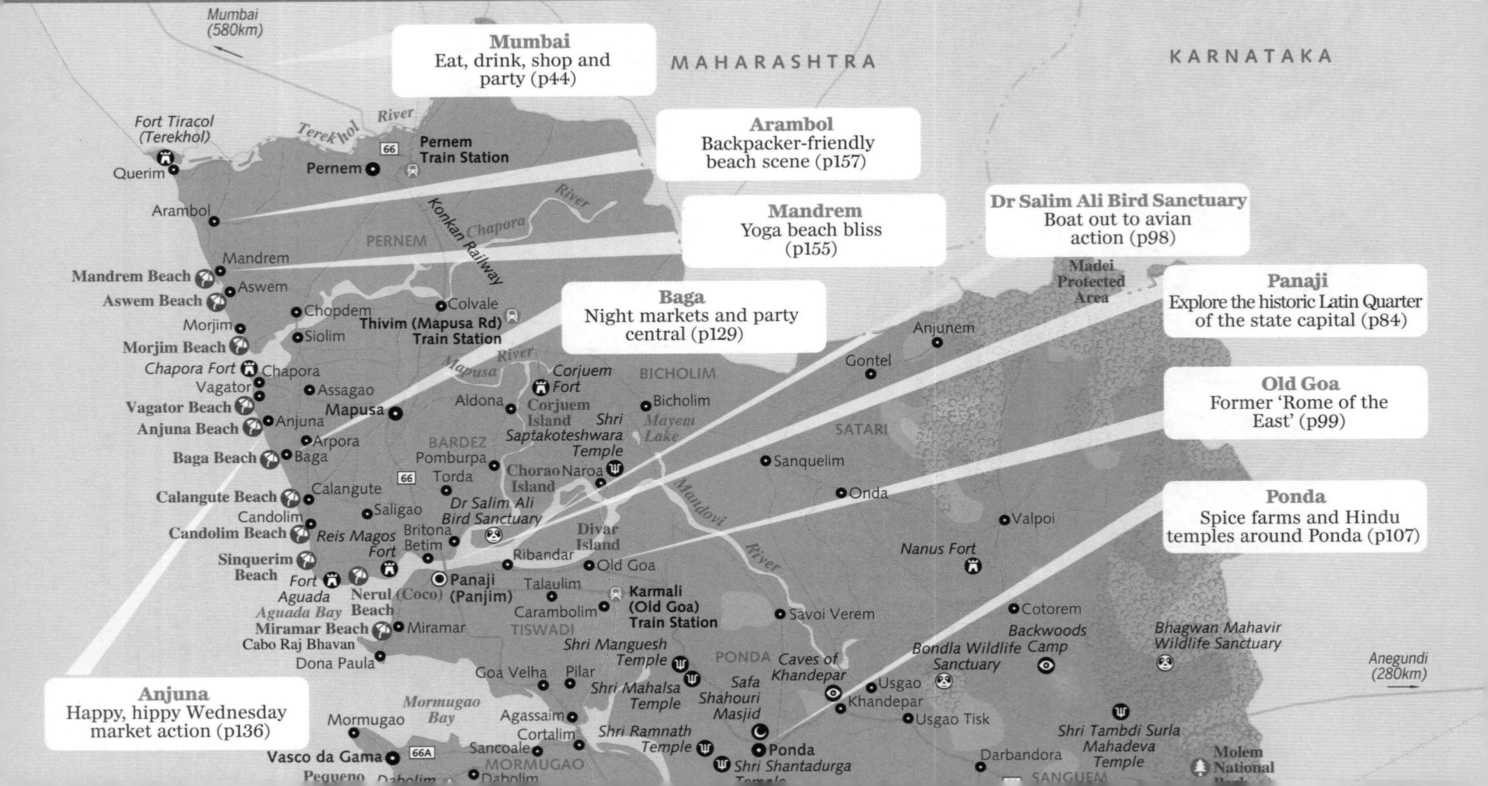

0 10 km
0 5 miles
Mumbai
Eat, drink, shop and party (p44)
Arambol
Backpacker-friendly beach scene (p157)
Mandrem
Yoga beach bliss (p155)
Baga
Night markets and party central (p129)
Dr Salim Ali Bird Sanctuary
Boat out to avian action (p98)
Panaji
Explore the historic Latin Quarter of the state capital (p84)
Old Goa
Former 'Rome of the East' (p99)
Ponda
Spice farms and Hindu temples around Ponda (p107)
Anjuna
Happy, hippy Wednesday market action (p136)
MAHARASHTRA
KARNATAKA
Mumbai (580km)
Anegundi (280km)
Fort Tiracol (Terekhol)
Querim
Terekhol River
Pernem
Pernem Train Station
Arambol
PERNEM
Chapora River
Konkan Railway
Mandrem
Mandrem Beach
Aswem
Aswem Beach
Chopdem
Colvale
Thivim (Mapusa Rd) Train Station
Morjim
Siolim
Morjim Beach
Chapora Fort
Chapora
Vagator
Assagao
Vagator Beach
Mapusa
Anjuna Beach
Anjuna
Arpora
Baga Beach
Baga
Mapusa River
Corjuem Fort
Aldona
Corjuem Island
BICHOLIM
Bicholim
Mayem Lake
Shri Saptakoteshwara Temple
BARDEZ
Pomburpa
Chorao Island
Naroa
Torda
Calangute Beach
Calangute
Candolim
Saligao
Dr Salim Ali Bird Sanctuary
Candolim Beach
Reis Magos Fort
Britona
Betim
Divar Island
Sinquerim Beach
Fort Aguada
Aguada Bay
Nerul (Coco) Beach
Panaji (Panjim)
Ribandar
Old Goa
Talaulim
Karmali (Old Goa) Train Station
Carambolim
Miramar Beach
Miramar
TISWADI
Cabo Raj Bhavan
Dona Paula
Shri Manguesh Temple
Goa Velha
Pilar
Shri Mahalsa Temple
PONDA
Caves of Khandepar
Safa Shahouri Masjid
Mormugao Bay
Agassaim
Mormugao
Cortalim
Shri Ramnath Temple
Ponda
Sancoale
Shri Shantadurga
Vasco da Gama
MORMUGAO
Dabolim
Mandovi River
Madei Protected Area
Anjunem
Gontel
SATARI
Sanquelim
Onda
Valpoi
Nanus Fort
Savoi Verem
Cotorem
Backwoods Camp
Bondla Wildlife Sanctuary
Bhagwan Mahavir Wildlife Sanctuary
Usgao
Khandepar
Usgao Tisk
Shri Tambdi Surla Mahadeva Temple
Darbandora
SANGUEM
Molem National

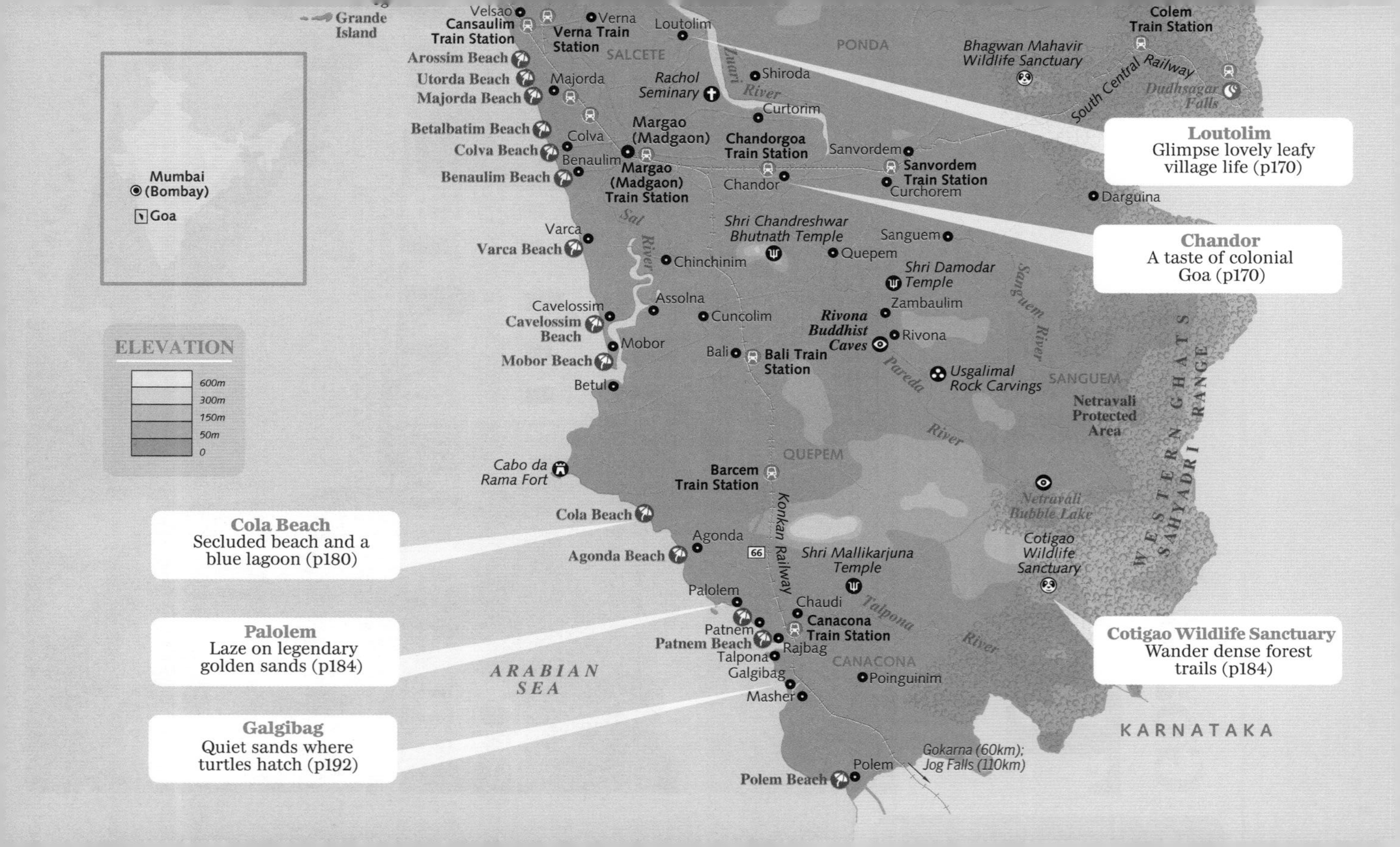

Loutolim
Glimpse lovely leafy village life (p170)
Chandor
A taste of colonial Goa (p170)
Cotigao Wildlife Sanctuary
Wander dense forest trails (p184)
Cola Beach
Secluded beach and a blue lagoon (p180)
Palolem
Laze on legendary golden sands (p184)
Galgibag
Quiet sands where turtles hatch (p192)
ELEVATION
600m
300m
150m
50m
0
Mumbai (Bombay)
Goa
Grande Island
Velsao
Cansaulim Train Station
Verna
Verna Train Station
Loutolim
SALCETE
PONDA
Arossim Beach
Utorda Beach
Majorda
Majorda Beach
Rachol Seminary
Zuari River
Shiroda
Curtorim
Betalbatim Beach
Colva
Colva Beach
Benaulim
Benaulim Beach
Margao (Madgaon)
Margao (Madgaon) Train Station
Chandorgoa Train Station
Chandor
Sanvordem
Sanvordem Train Station
Curchorem
Darguina
Colem Train Station
Bhagwan Mahavir Wildlife Sanctuary
South Central Railway
Dudhsagar Falls
Sal River
Varca
Varca Beach
Chinchinim
Shri Chandreshwar Bhutnath Temple
Quepem
Sanguem
Shri Damodar Temple
Sanguem River
Cavelossim
Cavelossim Beach
Assolna
Cuncolim
Zambaulim
Rivona Buddhist Caves
Rivona
Mobor
Mobor Beach
Bali
Bali Train Station
Pareda River
Usgalimal Rock Carvings
SANGUEM
Netravali Protected Area
WESTERN GHATS
SAHYADRI RANGE
Betul
QUEPEM
Cabo da Rama Fort
Barcem Train Station
Netravali Bubble Lake
Cola Beach
Agonda
Agonda Beach
66
Konkan Railway
Shri Mallikarjuna Temple
Cotigao Wildlife Sanctuary
Palolem
Chaudi
Canacona Train Station
Talpona River
Patnem
Patnem Beach
Rajbag
Talpona
CANACONA
Galgibag
Poinguinim
ARABIAN SEA
Masher
KARNATAKA
Gokarna (60km); Jog Falls (110km)
Polem
Polem Beach

Goa & Mumbai's Top 14

1

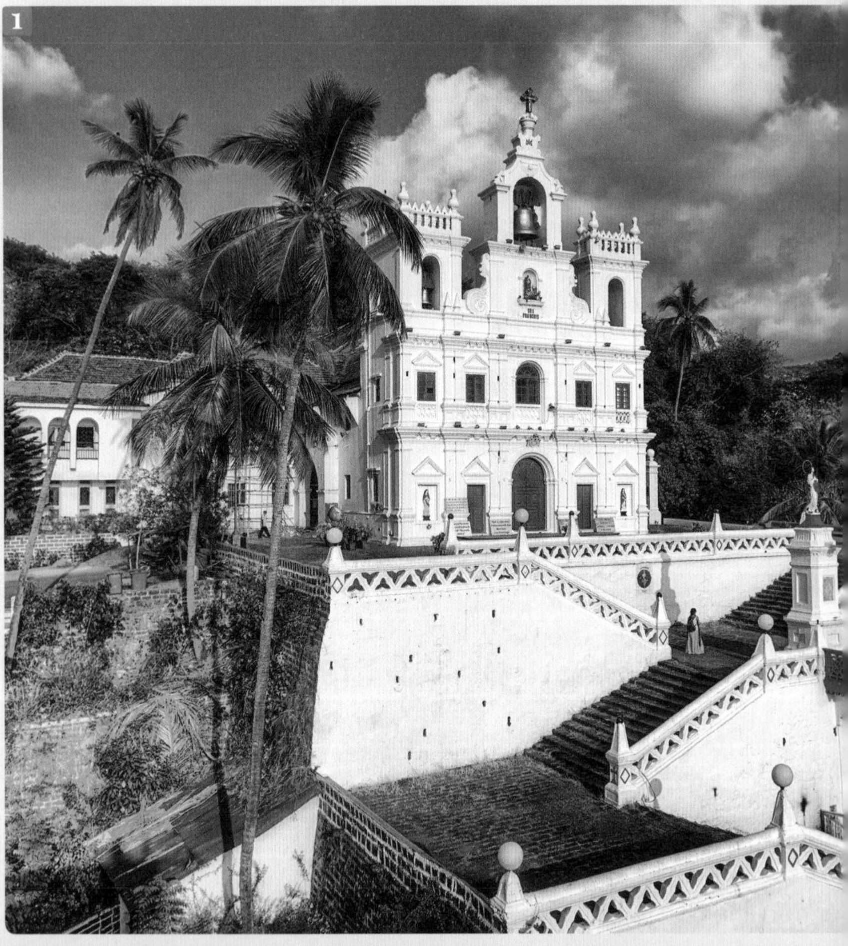

Panaji (Panjim)

1 Slung along the banks of the broad Mandovi River, Panaji (p84) is an easygoing city with the delightful old Portuguese districts of Fontainhas and Sao Tomé the perfect setting for a lazy afternoon of wandering. Sip firewater feni with locals in a hole-in-the-wall bar, gamble the night away on a floating luxury casino, clamber up to the wedding-cake-white Church of Our Lady of the Immaculate Conception or poke about in boutiques and book shops. You'll probably find you're not missing the beach one bit. Church of Our Lady of the Immaculate Conception (p84)

Historic Goa

2 The 17th-century Portuguese capital of Old Goa (p99) once rivalled Lisbon and London in size and importance and was widely known as the 'Rome of the East'. Today all that remains of the once-great city is a handful of amazingly well-preserved churches and cathedrals – but what a sight! The Basilica de Bom Jesus contains the grizzly 'incorrupt' body of St Francis Xavier, while Se Cathedral is the largest in Asia. Stop by for Mass on a Sunday morning, marvel at the intricately carved altars, and imagine religious life here four centuries ago. Basilica de Bom Jesus (p101)

PORAS CHAUDHARY/GETTY IMAGES ©

2

IMAGESOFINDIA/SHUTTERSTOCK ©

3

4

5

Mumbai to Goa by Train

3 The Konkan Railway (p233; pictured), linking Mumbai with Mangaluru (Mangalore) and passing right through Goa, is one of India's great railway journeys. It may be quicker to fly, but the romance of the rails is still alive here. Today the rails cross rivers and valleys, with some 2000 bridges and more than 90 tunnels. Whether you're riding in a 2nd-class sleeper or fancy air-con carriage, on the 12-hour Konkan Kanya Express or nine-hour Jan Shatabdi Express, make sure you sit near the window to watch the best show in town roll past.

Dudhsagar Falls

4 Frothy Dudhsagar (p111) – the name translates as 'Sea of Milk' – is the second-highest waterfall in India (after Jog Falls in Karnataka) and is a great day-trip adventure. Located deep in the Western Ghats on Goa's central border with Karnataka, the 300m-high tiered waterfall can be reached from Colem by a bumpy 4WD ride through stunning jungle scenery. Take a dip in the soothing pool or climb the rocky path to the head of the falls for great views. Start early and book your jeep in advance.

Palolem Beach

5 A blissful crescent of golden sand, balmy seas, gently swaying palm trees, good food, beach huts galore and a colourful backpacker-oriented beach bar scene make Palolem (p184) a favourite with travellers from across the globe. Though some say it's too crowded in season, there are few better all-round beaches in Goa for yoga, kayaking, swimming or just lazing in your beachfront hammock, and the quieter beaches of Patnem and Agonda are just a short ride away. Palolem's distance from the northern beaches keeps it off many travellers' radars.

Mellow Mandrem

6 Downward-dog the days away in lovely, laid-back Mandrem (p155), where an early morning yoga class, followed by a refreshing swim, an afternoon on a sun lounge with a good book and perhaps an ayurvedic massage are perfect for your spiritual soul. This is one of Goa's most alluring beach strips and an ideal base for accessing Asvem and Morjim to the south and backpacker-friendly Arambol to the north – all with their own impressive beach huts and activities from surfing to paragliding. Ashiyana Retreat Centre (p156)

Mumbai's Colonial Architecture

7 Mumbai's magnificent Victorian-era Gothic and Indo-Saracenic architecture is typified by the gloriously imposing Chhatrapati Shivaji Maharaj Terminus (p49) – the city's central train station – and the equally spectacular Taj Mahal Palace (p47), Mumbai's most famous landmark and one of India's most iconic hotels. Head down to Mumbai's harbour at Colaba to see the latter, with its fairy-tale blend of Islamic and Renaissance styles, all facing the grand Gateway of India (p48; pictured).

Anjuna Market

8 Whether you're in the market for some serious souvenirs or simply looking for an injection of local life, Goa's many markets are a must. The most famous is Anjuna's flea market (p140), held every Wednesday in season since the 1970s. It's a curious blend of traders and stalls from all over India, backpackers, day trippers and the odd dreadlocked hippie, but it's not to be missed. For more local flavour, head to Mapusa for its mammoth Friday market day, where you'll find fresh produce, spices and textiles.

Biking the Byways

9 Cruising Goa's back lanes and beach villages on two-wheels (p234) is practically de rigueur in Goa. For just a few dollars a day you can hire a moped or a thumping Royal Enfield motorbike at any of Goa's beach resorts, and head out into the hinterland to experience a slower, pastoral pace of life in the countryside. Cruise out to villages (p181) such as Chandor and Quepem, protected forest areas such as Netravali and cross rivers on old flat-bottomed vehicle ferries to see how rural Goans really live.

Fabulous Festivals

10 Goans love a good festival (p23) and the calendar here is packed with cultural events, religious feasts, street parades and music festivals. Among the biggest Catholic festivals are Panaji's Carnival, the Feast of St Francis Xavier in Old Goa and the Feast of Our Lady of the Immaculate Conception in Panaji. Major Hindu festivals include Shantadurga in January and Diwali in October/November. India's biggest international film festival is held in Panaji in November. Christmas, New Year and Easter are all big celebrations, too. Holi festival

Partying in Goa

11 Goa has long been a place for partying (p149), from the Portuguese sailors to the hippie freaks of the 1960s to the modern-day trance clubs and techno scene. These days it seems the rest of India has discovered Goa's beachside charms and cheap booze so resorts, clubs and even neighbourhood bars are packed in the peak December to February season. Finding the right party is a matter of luck and talking to locals, travellers and taxi drivers. Head to Curlies in Anjuna, Hilltop in Vagator and almost anywhere in Morjim for a party fix.

10

11

KIEVVICTOR/SHUTTERSTOCK ©

ALEX EROFEENKOV/SHUTTERSTOCK ©

Elephanta Island

12 Take a harbour boat from Mumbai's Gateway of India to the Unesco World Heritage–listed rock-cut temples on Gharapuri, better known as Elephanta Island (p54). Representing some of India's finest temple carving, the cave temples date to AD 450. The main Shiva temple contains a 6m-tall statue of Sadhashiva, depicting a three-faced Shiva. The hour-long boat trip gives a good harbour-view of southern Mumbai. Hindu statue, Elephanta Island

Spice Farms

13 South Indian spices – black pepper, cloves, cardamom, tamarind – were a major attraction for the seafaring Portuguese and today a fun day trip away from the beach is to one of several commercial spice plantations (p110) orbiting around Ponda or down south at the Tanshikar Spice Farm (p194). They can be a little touristy, especially on weekends, but the plantation tours are fascinating and aromatic. Most offer a delicious buffet thali lunch served up on a banana leaf, and sell spices and other plantation produce. Black pepper plant

Watching Wildlife

14 Goa's forests and wildlife reserves offer plenty for nature lovers, though most large animals are elusive. Birdwatchers will enjoy Dr Salim Ali Bird Sanctuary (p98), Bondla Wildlife Sanctuary (p111) or Goa's many other prime locations. Goa's most easily accessible wildlife watching is at Cotigao Wildlife Sanctuary (p184), about 9km southeast of Palolem, where you can stay overnight and rise early to spot various species of monkeys, deer and, if you're lucky, a leopard. Goa's rivers provide another highlight: spot dolphins playing offshore or mugger crocodiles basking in the estuaries. Monkey

Need to Know

For more information, see Survival Guide (p221)

Currency
Indian Rupee (₹)

Languages
Konkani, Hindi, English

Visas
Almost everyone, except nationals of Nepal and Bhutan, needs a visa before arriving in India. Note that your passport should be valid for at least six months beyond your intended stay, and have two blank pages.

Money
International ATMs are available in towns and at beach resorts. Credit cards are accepted at travel agents, in most midrange hotels and all top-end places, and an increasing number of restaurants.

Mobile Phones
Local SIM cards can be used on most smart phones, or phones can be set to (expensive) roaming.

Time
Indian Standard Time (GMT/UTC plus 5½ hours).

When to Go

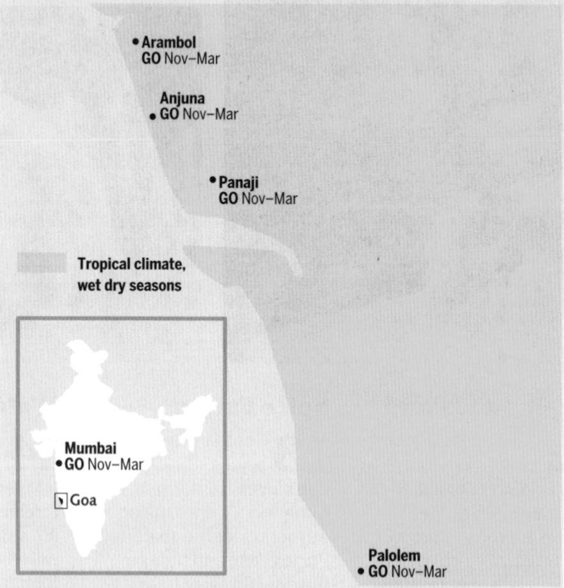

High Season
(Nov–Mar)

➡ Warm, sunny weather, with balmy but cool evenings.

➡ Calm seas perfect for diving, boat trips and swimming.

➡ Peak tourist numbers and prices, especially over frenetic Christmas and New Year.

Shoulder
(Apr & Oct)

➡ Quiet beaches, hotel bargains, but just a few beach shack restaurants and huts open.

➡ Seas may be too rough for swimming or boat trips.

➡ April can be hot and very humid.

Low Season
(May–Sep)

➡ Most tourist operations close.

➡ The monsoon brings rain, humidity, green countryside and local celebrations.

➡ Fewer tourists so the perfect time to experience 'real' Goan life.

Useful Websites

Lonely Planet (www.lonelyplanet.com/india/goa) A great first go-to point for information.

Goa Tourism (www.goa-tourism.com) Goa's state tourism body.

Goacom (www.goacom.com) Listings, information and recipes.

What's Up Goa (www.whatsupgoa.com) Listings, events and more.

Goa Streets (www.goastreets.com) News and entertainment weekly.

Important Numbers

From outside India, dial the international access code (00), India's country code (91), then the number you want, minus the initial '0'.

Country code	91
Police	100
Fire	101
Ambulance	102
General emergencies	108

Exchange Rates

Australia	A$1	₹51
Canada	C$1	₹53
Euro zone	€1	₹80
Japan	¥100	₹65
New Zealand	NZ$1	₹48
UK	UK£1	₹90
US	US$1	₹70

For current exchange rates see www.xe.com.

Daily Costs

Budget: Less than ₹3000

- Beach hut or hostel: ₹500–1500
- Local restaurants or self-catering: ₹500
- Kingfisher at liquor store: ₹50
- Local bus: ₹30
- Taxi/autorickshaw: ₹100–500

Midrange: ₹3000–12,000

- Midrange beach hut or air-con guesthouse: ₹1500–5000
- Meal in beach shack restaurant or cafe: ₹500–1000
- Rent a scooter/motorbike: ₹300/500
- Drink in shacks or bars: ₹500

Top End: More than ₹12,000

- Boutique heritage hotel or top beach hut: ₹5000–8000
- Hire car with driver: ₹1500
- Top restaurant: ₹1000–2000
- Ayurvedic spa treatment: ₹1000–5000

Opening Hours

Many tourist-oriented shops, restaurants and services may be closed completely outside high season (November to March). Other businesses may stay open with reduced services or shorter hours during the low season (May to September). Hours listed here are for high season.

Banks 10am to 2pm Monday to Friday, to noon Saturday

Bars noon to midnight

Clubs 10pm to 5am

Restaurants & cafes 8am to 11pm

Shops 10am to 6pm

Arriving in Goa

Dabolim Airport (Goa) Prepaid taxi booth to all Goan destinations; many hotels offer pick up. Airport bus between airport and Calangute via Panaji.

Madgaon Railway Station (Margao) Main stop on Konkan Railway; prepaid taxi booth to all Goan destinations.

Karmali Railway Station (Old Goa) Closest to Panaji; reservations at Panaji Kadamba Bus Stand.

Kadamba Bus Stand (Panaji) Long-distance and local buses; private long-distance bus companies have ticket booths here, but depart from the interstate bus stand.

Thivim Station and Mapusa Bus Stand Closest rail and bus services to Calangute and Anjuna.

Getting Around

Car & motorcycle Many travellers hire a scooter or motorbike for their trip; self-drive cars are less common but car and driver services are affordable for groups.

Taxi & autorickshaw Good for short hops around and between towns and beach resorts. Taxis will also take you on longer trips – agree on a fare beforehand.

Bus Extremely cheap, slow but fun local way of getting between towns and villages.

Train There are two rail lines in the state but it's not a particularly quick or convenient way of getting around.

For much more on **getting around**, see p234

First Time Goa

For more information, see Survival Guide (p221)

Checklist

- Make sure your passport has six months validation past your arrival date and two blank pages.
- Apply for an e-tourist visa (eTV; www.indianvisaonline.gov.in), if required, a minimum of four and maximum of 30 days before you are due to travel.
- Inform your debit/credit-card company you're heading to India to avoid security blocks.
- Arrange for appropriate travel insurance and vaccinations.

What to Pack

- A reliable padlock.
- A torch (flashlight) to navigate poorly lit streets and negotiate frequent power cuts.
- Driver's licence and International Driving Permit.
- Your bankcard/credit card.
- Something long-sleeved to throw on when visiting churches, temples and mosques.

Top Tips for Your Trip

- Unless you're here specifically for Christmas and New Year's Eve parties, avoid the overpriced peak season (22 December to 3 January).
- If hiring a moped/motorbike/car, make sure you have an International Driving Permit as well as your home licence. And always wear a helmet.
- Swim on patrolled beaches – undertows can be deadly.
- Don't get stuck on one beach or in one village all holiday – explore neighbouring beaches or further afield.
- Even if you're not a Christian, visit one of Goa's beautiful churches.
- Dress respectfully away from the beach. Topless or nude sunbathing is illegal on Goa's beaches.
- Try using the Goa Miles ride app for cheap taxi rides.
- Shop for produce or street food snacks at local markets and buy alcohol at liquor stores.

What to Wear

Goa is generally hot and humid, though it can get cool at night over the winter months. Light cotton fabrics are best. Being a beach state, shorts and skirts are acceptable attire but always pack a lightweight pair of trousers or an ankle-length skirt for evening wear or for visiting churches or temples. Likewise, T-shirts and strappy tops (for women) are generally fine but it pays to have a long-sleeve top. A wide-brimmed hat works wonders as well.

Some smarter Goan bars/restaurants/clubs may impose a dress code (eg no sandals or shorts).

Any type of clothing you might need, including shawls or dupattas, *salwar kameez* (traditional dresslike tunic and trouser combination) or kurtas (long shirts) with trousers, can be purchased cheaply in Goa.

Bargaining

Bargaining is certainly possible – and expected – at Goa's tourist markets, where the first price offered is usually inflated. Some gentle bargaining at local markets is also fine, but most shops work on a fixed-price basis.

Tipping

There's no official policy on tipping in India, though it's always appreciated, especially in holiday-friendly Goa: 10% of a bill is acceptable.

Hotels In five-star international hotels, tipping hotel porters and maids is the norm (at least ₹50).

Waiters Low-paid hospitality staff, including waiters and bar staff, expect a tip from tourists more so than elsewhere in India, even at beach shacks.

Taxis Taxi drivers don't need to be tipped for short trips, but if you've hired the driver for the day, adding 10% is fair.

Baksheesh This is a form of tipping in India, generally defined as a small gratuity paid to someone in order to have a little extra service delivered, or to pay someone off for turning a blind eye (authorities, guards etc).

Coconut stalls, Panaji (p84)

Etiquette

Cover up Cover shoulders and legs in churches and cathedrals.

Sunbathing Don't sunbathe nude or topless – it's illegal and unwelcome in Goa.

Footwear Remove shoes before entering local Goan homes.

Dress Don't wear bikinis or skimpy attire outside beach resorts; it's not considered appropriate.

Photographs Ask before snapping photos of people, sacred sites or ceremonies.

Eating The right hand is for eating and shaking hands, the left is the 'toilet' hand.

Sleeping

Goa's accommodation ranges from basic beach huts to opulent five-star resorts. Throughout Goa's coastal belt there are also private rooms and whole houses to let.

Beach huts From basic bamboo and palm thatch to more sophisticated midrange versions.

Backpacker hostels Good deal for solo travellers with dorms and some private rooms.

Heritage & boutique hotels Often in restored Portuguese homes.

Resorts Four- or five-star beachfront properties with pools, spas, high-end restaurants.

Rooms & houses to let Those staying from a week to six months should consider renting a local house or room(s) in a house.

What's New

Mumbai to Goa ferry

This luxury cruise ship ferry between Mumbai and Goa (p234) launched in 2018. It sails three times a week, leaving either end at 4pm and arriving at around 9am. See the sunset and sunrise and party the night away on board.

Mopa Airport

The new international airport at Mopa, North Goa, is expected to be operational by mid-2020. As well as being one of the largest 'greenfield' airports in India, it will bring international flights direct to North Goa. Dabolim Airport will remain in operation.

Highway Upgrades

Massive new road infrastructure projects are nearing fruition with the north–south highway being widened to four lanes combined with new bypass sections, overpasses and bridges over the Mandovi and Zuari rivers. The first stage is expected to be completed in late 2019. The highway from Panaji to Molem in the east of the state is also being upgraded.

Craft Beers

Given the Goan love of beer, it's unsurprising that the craft beer movement is beginning to take off. Two microbreweries have opened since 2017: the Goa Brewing Co and Susegado Brewing. Mumbai also has a burgeoning craft-beer scene: check out Independence Brewing Company (p71) or Toit Tap Room (p70).

Hop on Hop off Bus

This new sightseeing bus (p96) run by Goa Tourism plies two routes around Panaji and North Goa, stopping at major sights along the way. Get on and off at anytime.

Serendipity Arts Festival

Started in 2016, this visual and performing arts festival (p26) spans eight days across multiple venues in Panaji.

Fort Tiracol Heritage Hotel

This boutique hotel (p159) was refurbished and reopened in 2017 at this stunningly located North Goa fort.

Backpacker Hostels

Backpacker hostels with mostly dorm beds are popping up like mushrooms in traveller centres like Anjuna, Arambol, Vagator, Palolem and Mumbai. Great news for solo travellers.

Goa Miles

Goa Tourism's version of Uber (p236) could revolutionise taxi travel in Goa – if it works. In Mumbai, Uber and Ola (p81) are increasingly popular.

Beach Reception Centres

As part of its tourism infrastructure development, the government has been busy building 'reception centres' – car and bus parking, modern toilets and tourist offices – at a number of beach entrances including Candolim, Baga, Anjuna and Morjim.

For more recommendations and reviews, see lonelyplanet.com/goa

If You Like...

Good Food

No matter what your culinary persuasion, you'll satisfy your cravings in Goa and Mumbai.

Candolim, Calangute & Baga Dress up (or down) and head to one of the many sophisticated world cuisine restaurants. (p127)

Cooking courses Learn to cook like a local with Goan and Indian culinary courses in family kitchens. (p37)

Panaji Enjoy local food in the fabulously atmospheric Old Quarter or animated city centre of the mellow state capital. (p91)

Beach shacks The highlight is fresh seafood, often displayed on ice and barbecued by your table. (p33)

Mumbai A city of spectacular eateries, from a humble *bhelpuri* street stall to the fanciest Mughal feast. (p62)

History & Architecture

Goa's colonial heritage is most visible in its Portuguese-style mansions, churches and forts.

Basilica de Bom Jesus, Old Goa Visit a saint's desiccated relics at this splendid laterite basilica dripping with ecclesiastical glory. (p101)

Church of Our Lady of the Immaculate Conception Clamber the steps to Panaji's church, where sailors once celebrated their safe arrival from Portugal. (p84)

Braganza House, Chandor The split-personality Braganza House is a fascinating insight into how the aristocratic Goan other half once lived. (p170)

Palaćio do Deão, Quepem You can take tea on the terrace of this stunning *palaćio,* marvelling at the wealth of painstakingly renovated detail. (p168)

Goan forts The atmospheric remnants of a once mighty seafaring nation. (p193)

Colonial Mumbai The city's Victoria-era architecture can be seen in the High Court, Taj Mahal Palace hotel and Chhatrapati Shivaji Terminus. (p47)

Pampering

Luxury is done well in Goa but the best of the spas are housed in boutique hotels and five-star resorts and come with a healthy price tag. You can enjoy a traditional ayurvedic massage at many places for around ₹1000, a Thai foot massage in Calangute or Candolim for around the same, or a full-day spa treatment for up to US$600.

Kaya Kalp Royal Spa The spa at the ITC Grand Goa in Arossim is one of Goa's best. (p174)

Humming Bird Spa A good place for pampering on Palolem Beach is this spa at Ciarans. (p187)

Quan Spa Deluxe pampering at the Goa Marriott in Miramar. (p91)

Nilaya Hermitage Boutique luxury in Arpora. (p133)

Rejuve Spa At Rajbag's Lalit Golf & Spa Resort. (p192)

Niramaya Spa Ayurvedic spa at La La Land Resort, Colomb Bay. (p187)

Shopping & Markets

Goa's shops, markets and street stalls are full of handicrafts and souvenirs from all over India, while Mumbai has some of India's best shopping.

Anjuna Flea Market Hang out with backpackers and hippies at this venerable open-air market institution. (p140)

Golden Heart Emporium Vending classics, new releases and harder-to-find Goan titles, this book store is a treasure trove for bibliophiles. (p167)

Mapusa Market Browse fresh produce, spices, clothes and knick-knacks with droves of locals at Mapusa's Friday market. (p144)

Panaji The capital has a lively municipal market in the centre and some excellent boutiques in the Old Quarter. (p94)

Mumbai Delve into Mumbai's fascinating market district at Chor Bazaar, Crawford Market and Bhuleshwar. (p73)

Drinking & Nightlife

Goa is notorious for a good party: dance to trance or simply enjoy a cold beer at any beach shack or local bar.

Anjuna's Beach Bars Anjuna knows how to party, especially at the southern end of the beach where Curlies, Cafe Lilliput and Shiva Valley regularly fire up. (p139)

Tito's Baga's original clubbing strip gets lively with Club Mambo and Cafe San Francisco among the best. (p135)

LPK Waterfront This giant club looking over the Nerul River is whimsical in design and pumping in attitude. (p128)

Floating Casinos, Panaji Offering an entertaining night out with free drinks, buffet food and floor show – and gambling of course. (p94)

Silent Discos, Palolem Dance the night away in outward silence at one of Palolem's headphone parties. (p22)

Mumbai From dive bar to sky bar, craft-beer brewery to sophisticated club, Mumbai is a city that knows how to party. (p69)

Top: Indian meal (p210)

Bottom: Fort Aguada (p125)

Month by Month

TOP EVENTS

Shantadurga, January

Shigmotsav (Shigmo), March

Carnival, March

Feast of St Francis Xavier, December

January

The prime time for visiting Goa, January means blue skies and warm weather, making it perfect for hitting the beach but not too hot for the state's cities and wildlife sanctuaries.

Feast of the Three Kings

Held at Reis Magos, Chandor and Cansaulim on 6 January, this festival sees a re-enactment of the journey of the Three Wise Men to Bethlehem, with young boys playing the Magi. (p170)

Shantadurga

Also known as the 'Procession of the Umbrellas', this is one of Goa's most attended festivals, wherein a solid silver statue of Hindu goddess Shantadurga from the Kunkalikarin Temple is carried between the villages of Fatorpa and Cuncolim, fronted by 12 umbrella-carrying young men.

Festa das Bandeiras

Migrant working men return home to Divar Island in mid-January to celebrate their local saint's day by waving the flags of the countries in which they're currently working and, more bizarrely, firing dozens of peashooters at each other.

Republic Day

The celebration of India's 1950 establishment as a republic is a public holiday, held every 26 January.

February

Another reliably warm and sunny month for lazing on the beach or seeing the sights, February sees fewer crowds than January and a few festivals.

Hanuman Festival

In February, this festival lasting ten days sees the Hindu monkey god Hanuman celebrated at Panaji's Maruti Temple. (p88)

Shivratri

To celebrate the traditional anniversary of the God Shiva's wedding day, large-scale religious celebrations are held at the many Shiva temples across Goa on the 14th (moonless) night of the new moon, in the Hindu month of Phalgun, which falls in either February or March. Upcoming dates: 21 February 2020, 11 March 2021.

Kala Ghoda Festival

Getting bigger and more sophisticated each year, this two-week-long art fest sees tons of performances and exhibitions.

March

Things are starting to heat up considerably by now, but it's still high season in Goa – good for beach lounging, swimming and Easter celebrations.

Carnival

Four days of mirth and mayhem characterise Panaji's annual Carnival, held on the days prior to Lent. Festivities begin with Sabado Gordo (Fat Saturday), when you'll see a procession of floats through the city's packed streets. (p89)

Procession of All Saints

Held in Goa Velha on the fifth Monday during Lent,

this is the only procession of its sort outside Rome, where dozens of huge statues of the saints are paraded throughout the village. (p105)

Shigmotsav (Shigmo)

Goa's take on the Hindu festival of Holi marks the onset of spring over the full moon period with statewide parades, processions, and revellers flinging huge quantities of water and coloured tikka powder with wild abandon.

April

Most tourists have departed Goa, and temperatures begin rising in anticipation of the monsoon, still over a month away. If you can stand the heat, it's quiet and calm, with great deals on accommodation.

Feast of Our Lady of Miracles

Held in Mapusa 16 days after Easter, this cheerful festival, also known as a *tamasha,* is famously celebrated by both Hindus and Christians at Mapusa's Church of Our Lady of Miracles. (p144)

Easter

Churches fill up over the Christian festival of Easter, with plenty of solemn High Masses and family feasts. The biggest church services are in Panaji and Old Goa.

Ramadan (Ramazan)

Marked by 30 days of dawn-to-dusk fasting, the ninth month of the Islamic calendar is when Muslims traditionally turn their attention to God, with a focus on prayer, purification and charitable giving. Ramadan begins around 24 April 2020 and 13 April 2021.

May

May is perhaps the most uncomfortable month in Goa, with heat, humidity, and everyone awaiting the coming of the rains. Most tourist operators have closed for the season.

Igitun Chalne

Igitun Chalne is one of Goa's most distinctive festivals, specific to the temple in Sirigao (near Corjuem Fort). *Igitun chalne* means 'fire-walking', and the high point comes when devotees of the goddess Lairaya traverse a pit of burning coals.

Eid al-Fitr

Muslims celebrate the end of Ramadan with three days of festivities, beginning 30 days after the start of the fast. Upcoming dates: 24 May 2020, 13 May 2021.

June

It's here! The monsoon's arrival sparks a host of celebrations, and the land turns miraculously green overnight. Water buffalo bask, children dance in the showers, and frogs croak out elated choruses.

Feast of St Anthony

This feast on 13 June in honour of Portugal's patron saint takes on particular significance if the monsoon is late in appearing, whereupon each Goan family must lower a statue of the saint into its family well to hasten the onset of the rains and pray for bountiful crops.

Sanjuan

The Feast of St John (Sanjuan) on 24 June sees young men diving dangerously into wells to celebrate the monsoon's arrival, and torching straw dummies of the saint to represent John's baptism and, consequently, the death of sin.

Sangodd

The annual Feast of St Peter and St Paul on 29 June marks another monsoonal celebration, and is particularly ebullient in Candolim, where boats are tied together to form floating stages and costumed actors play out *tiatrs* (Konkani dramas) to vast crowds.

August

Though the monsoon is slowly receding, the rains are still a-coming; fishermen await calmer waters and local life goes on, almost tourist-free.

Nariyal Poornima

In both Goa and Mumbai, a coconut offering is made to Lord Varuna, god of the sea, to mark the start of the post-monsoon fishing season; fisherman pray for a bountiful harvest before hitting the first choppy waves of the August seas.

Independence Day

India's 1947 independence from Britain is celebrated with an annual public holiday on 15 August.

Top: Ganesh Chaturthi, Mumbai

Bottom: Carnival (p89), Panaji

Feast of the Chapel

Cabo Raj Bhavan draws scores of visitors each 15 August to a special church service in honour of its 500-year-old chapel's feast day, which long pre-dates Independence Day. (p96)

Bonderam

Celebrated annually on the fourth Saturday in August on sleepy Divar Island. Locals take part in processions and mock battles to commemorate historical disputes that took place over island property.

September

The rains have all but subsided, leaving a scoured, green Goa just ripe for the upcoming tourist season. Local businesses begin building the season's first beach shacks. Popular time for domestic tourists.

Ganesh Chaturthi

Mumbai gets totally swept up by the 10- to 12-day celebration of the elephant-headed Hindu god Ganesh. On the festival's first, third, fifth, seventh and 11th days, families and communities take their Ganesh statues to the seashore and auspiciously submerge them.

October

Though not all beach businesses are in full swing, October's warm days tempt a trickle of in-the-know travellers, who benefit from the widest choice in long-stay accommodation.

Feast of the Menino Jesus

On October's second Sunday, coastal Colva's village church sees its small and allegedly miracle-working statue of the Infant Jesus dressed up and paraded before scores of devoted pilgrims at this important village festival. (p171)

Dusshera

This nine-day Hindu festival celebrates the god Rama's victory over Ravana in the Hindu epic Ramayana, and the goddess Durga's victory over Mahishasura. It's celebrated with bonfires and school-children's performances of scenes from the life of Rama. Upcoming dates: 25 October 2020, 14 October 2021.

Diwali

Held in October or November, the five-day Hindu 'festival of lights' celebrates the victory of good over evil with the lighting of oil and butter lamps around the home, lots of family celebration and loads of firecrackers. Upcoming dates: 14 November 2020, 4 November 2021.

Gandhi's Birthday

The national holiday of Gandhi Jayanti is a solemn celebration of Mohandas Gandhi's birth, on 2 October.

November

High season really kicks off in November, when the countryside remains post-monsoon green, and Goans gear up for the tourist onslaught. This is one of the best times to visit.

Feast of Our Lady of Livrament

Each mid-November sees a cheerful saint's day street fair set up in Panaji, outside the tiny Chapel of St Sebastian, in the Goan capital's atmospheric old Portuguese-infused Fontainhas district. (p85)

International Film Festival of India

This annual film festival – the country's largest – graces Panaji's big screens with a gaggle of Bollywood's finest glitterati jetting in for premieres, parties, ceremonies and screenings. (p89)

December

Packed with parties, December is the wildest, busiest and most expensive month to be in Goa, especially between Christmas and New Year.

Feast of St Francis Xavier

Thousands upon thousands of pilgrims file past the shrivelled remains of St Francis Xavier in Old Goa every 3 December, opening a week-long festival and fair, complete with large-scale open-air Masses. (p105)

Feast of Our Lady of the Immaculate Conception

Panaji's wedding-cake Church of Our Lady of the Immaculate Conception plays host to this feast and large, joyful fair on 8 December. (p89)

Liberation Day

This unusually sober celebration on 17 December marks Goa's 'liberation' from Portugal by India in 1961 with military parades.

Goa Arts & Literacy Festival

Inaugurated in 2010, this is one of Goa's premier literary and arts festivals (www.goaartlitfest.com), attracting writers, poets, artists, musicians, speakers and performers to Panaji (Dona Paula) over four days in early December.

Serendipity Arts Festival

Launched in 2016, this eight-day arts festival (www.serendipityartsfestival.com) features visual and performance arts at multiple venues in Panaji, as well as street exhibitions and events.

Christmas

Midnight Masses abound in Goa on 24 December, traditionally known as *Misa de Galo* (Cock's Crow) since they often stretch on far into the wee hours, while the following day is celebrated with feasting, fireworks and festivities.

Siolim Zagor

Siolim's multifaith Zagor, which takes place on the first Sunday after Christmas, involves a procession, folk plays, music and celebrations.

New Year's Eve

This is the party night many travellers have been waiting for. Fireworks displays erupt up and down the coast and dance parties take over the beaches. Book ahead for dining or club venues.

Itineraries

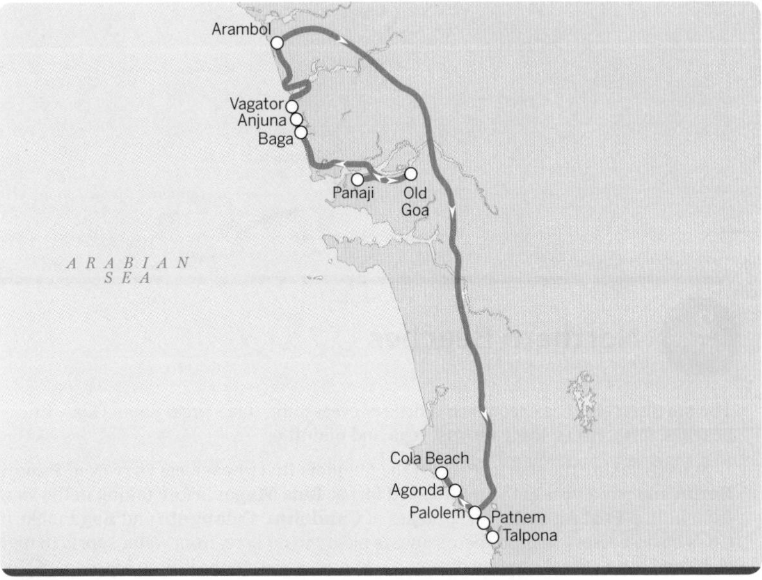

2 WEEKS Goa's Greatest Hits

If you have a two-week holiday in Goa you'll probably spend it at one or two beach locations, but if you want to explore the best of the whole state, consider this path.

Start in the capital, **Panaji**, preferably staying in the Fontainhas area, cruising on the Mandovi River and spending a morning exploring the churches of **Old Goa** and the region's spice farms. Next head up to the beaches of North Goa: depending on your taste you could base yourself at busy **Baga**, backpacker-friendly **Anjuna** or **Vagator**, or further north at the mellow yoga-friendly beach strip between Asvem and **Arambol**. Wherever you stay, most beaches are close enough to easily explore by motorbike or taxi. Spend a week here checking out the party scene (Anjuna, Vagator and Morjim), markets (Saturday night bazaars near Baga, Wednesday market at Anjuna, Friday market at Baga), water sports (surfing at Asvem), yoga (everywhere) or just chilling at beach shacks and backstreet cafes.

Next, head to the deep south of Goa, taking the highway all the way to beautiful **Palolem**. From here you can explore the surrounding beaches of **Patnem**, **Agonda**, **Cola** and **Talpona**. This is a place for lazing on the beach and staying in Goa's best beach huts.

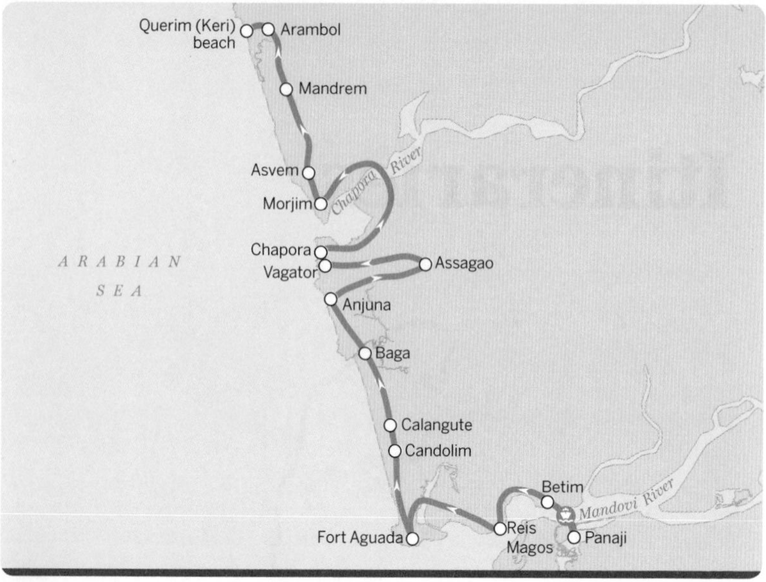

2 WEEKS Northern Beaches

The northern beaches encompass a little of everything that's great about Goa – fine beaches, forts, rivers, lively resorts, yoga and nightlife.

Start by taking the shortcut across the Mandovi River by vehicle ferry from **Panaji** to **Betim** and pay a visit to the refurbished fort at **Reis Magos** before taking in the views from hilltop **Fort Aguada**. The beaches of **Candolim**, **Calangute** and **Baga** make up Goa's busiest resort strip so there's always plenty to do here, from water sports to nightclubs and beach shacks to fine dining. Don't miss a visit to the hilltop Museum of Goa and (in season) one of the Saturday night markets in Baga or Arpora.

Head north of the Baga River to **Anjuna**, where the hippie trance days all began. It's a good place to join a yoga class, party at one of the beachfront clubs or browse the Wednesday flea market. Head inland to the country lanes and Portuguese villas of villagey **Assagao**, where you'll find a number of excellent restaurants. If it's Friday, head into Mapusa for the fabulous local market. Back near the beach, **Vagator** and **Chapora** are easy-going coastal villages with a relaxed party vibe: climb Chapora Fort for great sunset views or dine at one of the clifftop restaurants. Vagator's Hilltop music club is still the place for a Sunday session.

Across the Chapora River is Russian-flavoured **Morjim**, with a growing number of EDM clubs and fancy resorts. Further north are mellow **Asvem** and **Mandrem**, with upmarket hut villages, a lovely clean beach, good yoga retreats and watersports such as standup paddleboarding, kitesurfing and surfing. Then it's on to **Arambol**, a popular backpacker and family beach with a Bob Marley vibe, a surf club, paragliding from the northern headland and budget accommodation along the cliffs. Although Arambol is the last proper beach resort in the north, you can continue further to the peaceful **Querim (Keri) beach** and cross by vehicle ferry over the Terekhol River to Terekhol (Tiracol) Fort, a former Portuguese stronghold that's now a heritage hotel and restaurant.

Top: Church of St Francis of Assisi (p103), Old Goa
Bottom: Beach, Calangute (p129)

IMAGESOFINDIA/SHUTTERSTOCK ©

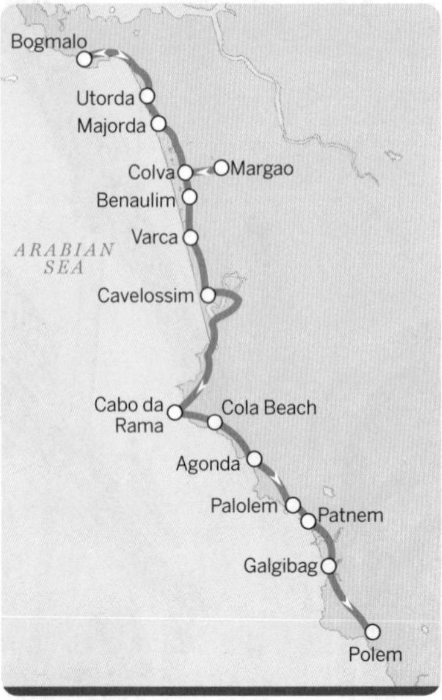

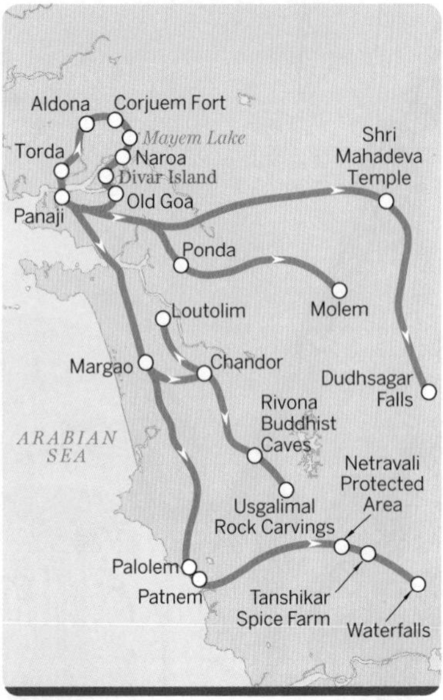

2 WEEKS Southern Sun

South Goa is as much about lazing on the beaches as the north, but there are some interesting inland adventures here and much less of a party vibe.

Start in busy **Margao**, where you can browse the market and grab a bite to eat at Longhuino's. The beach at **Colva** is just 6km west of Margao and stretches up and down the coast. If you're into scuba diving, head north to **Bogmalo**, via pretty **Majorda** and **Utorda** beaches, or make your way south to **Benaulim** (visit Goa Chitra museum here) through five-star territory at **Varca** and **Cavelossim** to the lovely spit of land at Mobor where the coast meets the Sal River.

Follow the coastal road through bucolic Betul to lovely **Agonda**, calling in at **Cabo da Rama** and secluded **Cola Beach**. The final coastal stretch leads to Goa's little paradise beach at **Palolem**, great for swimming, yoga, cooking courses and beach huts. **Patnem** is a little more peaceful. Intrepid travellers should hire a bike and explore further south to **Galgibag** and Talpona, or all the way to **Polem** beach.

5 DAYS Inland Adventures

Take a few days to explore inland Goa off the beaten track.

From **Panaji**, start out early to Colem for **Dudhsagar Falls**. On the way back stop at Tambdi Surla for **Shri Mahadeva Temple** or visit one of the spice farms around **Molem** or **Ponda**. Another excellent self-drive day trip from Panaji is to take a picturesque circuit from **Old Goa**, to serene **Divar Island** (via a ferry), catch another ferry to **Naroa**, where you can take in **Mayem Lake**, **Corjuem Fort** and **Aldona**. Return to Panaji via **Torda**, visiting the Houses of Goa Museum.

Head south to **Margao**, from where you can explore the villages of **Chandor**, with one of Goa's grandest Portuguese mansions, **Loutolim** and the ancient **Rivona Buddhist caves** and prehistoric **Usgalimal rock carvings**.

Return to Margao and then continue on to **Palolem** or **Patnem**, from where you can head inland through forest and farmland to the **Netravali Protected Area** to discover the mysterious bubble lake, the **Tanshikar Spice Farm** and jungle treks to remote **waterfalls**.

Plan Your Trip

Beach Planner

With more than 100km of sand-fringed coastline shelving into the Arabian Sea, Goa's beaches can exude the feel of a tropical island and at times it's easy to forget you're in India. Whether laying out your sarong or just lazing about in the shade of a palm-thatch beach shack while nursing a cold beer, the question is: which beach?

Which Beach?

When deciding which Goan beach to visit, the decision doesn't rest on just the aesthetics of sand and sea: it's about choosing the beach community that suits your style of travel and sense of place. The villages and resorts vary in character, depending on the types of tourists and travellers who congregate there, the standards of accommodation, restaurants, nightlife and activities on offer.

Locating the perfect beach is the secret to making the most of your stay. It could be backpacker-filled beach huts; book-friendly, people-free sands; yoga *shalas* (school) or the party crowd. Goa is small enough that you can easily jump on a scooter or in a taxi and explore. And you can watch the sunset from *all* of Goa beaches!

Swimming & Water Sports

Most of Goa's main beaches offer water sports in season – tandem parasailing, jet skis, speedboat rides, kayaks and the like. Swimming is safest at patrolled beaches.

Palolem (p184) Calm waters offer the safest ocean swimming in Goa. Also the best place for kayaking and stand-up paddleboarding.

Best Beaches for...

Partying

- Calangute and Baga (p129)
- Anjuna and Vagator (p136)
- Candolim (p123)
- Palolem (p184)
- Morjim (p151)

Families

- Palolem (p184)
- Patnem (p190)
- Mandrem (p155)
- Asvem (p153)
- Arambol (p157)

Peace

- Agonda (p181)
- Galgibag and Talpona (p192)
- Mandrem (p155)
- Polem (p194)
- Querim (Keri; p161)
- Benaulim (p176)

Water Sports

- Candolim and Sinquerim (p123)
- Calangute and Baga (p129)
- Colva (p171)
- Benaulim (p176)
- Arambol (p157)
- Asvem (p153)

Calangute (p129) & **Candolim** (p123) Several water-sports operators offer a full range of activities on Goa's busiest beach strip. Also has scuba-diving outfits.

Arambol (p157) Another relatively gentle beach for swimming, with a surf club and cliff-top paragliding.

Colva (p171) & **Benaulim** (p176) Not as busy as Calangute but all of the adrenalin sports are on offer at respective beach entrances; Colva is popular with domestic tourists.

Asvem (p153) A good choice mainly for its excellent surfing and kite-surfing school and kayaking on the river.

Family Fun

Palolem (p184) One of the best all-round beaches for families with plenty of activities, safe swimming and beach-facing huts.

Patnem (p190) Similar to Palolem but smaller and quieter, Patnem is very family-friendly with a large expat community, and schools and kindergartens nearby.

Arambol (p157) A popular beach with long-staying families, Arambol has a relaxed backpacker vibe, good budget accommodation and relatively safe waters.

Calangute and Baga (p129) Snow Park, wax museum, night markets and lots of beach fun.

SAFE SWIMMING

One of the most deceptive dangers in Goa is to be found right in front of you. The Arabian Sea, with its strong currents, often steeply shelving sands and dangerous rips (undertows), claims lives each year. Goa's main beaches are patrolled by lifeguards during 'swimming season' (November to March). Be vigilant with children, avoid swimming after drinking alcohol and don't even consider swimming during the monsoon.

If you do get caught in a rip, stay calm and raise one arm to signal distress if there are lifeguards on the beach. To escape the rip, swim parallel to the beach, not against the current.

Partying & Drinking

Goa loves to party and there's a liberal attitude to drinking, but it's not quite Ibiza on the subcontinent.

Anjuna (p136) Late-night parties are legendary at Anjuna's southern beach shacks, especially popular Curlies.

Baga (p135) Tito's Lane is the place of choice for many young Indians on a weekend away from their IT jobs, and package tourists staying in the area.

Vagator (p145) Some traces of Goa trance and hippie heyday remain in Vagator and Chapora.

Candolim (p123) Two of Goa's most upmarket nightclubs are found here, along with busy bar-restaurants along Fort Aguada Rd.

Morjim (p151) Fast taking over the beachfront nightclub scene with Euro raves and Goa trance.

Relaxing with a Good Book

Mandrem (p155) Along with Asvem and Morjim, this broad, hassle-free beach is ideal for lounging, with just a scattering of beach shacks.

Patnem (p190) Not crowded like its popular neighbour, peaceful Patnem will re-energise your soul.

Benaulim (p176) With just a few beach shacks and most accommodation back in the village, you'll find plenty of quiet spots on Benaulim and Sernabatim beaches.

Polem (p194) Goa's southernmost beach has just one basic place to stay so don't come looking for action.

Querim (Keri) (p161) Near the Terekhol River, this empty northern beach feels remote but is just around the headland from Arambol.

Backpackers & Budget Travellers

Arambol (p157) Huts and rooms along the clifftop path remain some of the cheapest in Goa, making this area popular with backpackers.

Anjuna (p136) A wide range of accommodation, mushrooming backpacker hostels, good cafes and plenty of bikes to rent.

BEACH SHACKS

One of the distinguishing features of Goa's beaches are the seasonal restaurant shacks that line the sands on just about every beach. Of the 360-plus shacks erected each year (2017), some 200 are along the mega-busy Candolim–Calangute–Baga beach strip. Other beaches, especially in the south, might have just one or two shacks every few hundred metres.

Depending on the granting of licences, the lateness of the monsoon or availability of materials, shacks start to go up in early October (some are not built until November) and are dismantled again in late April. Goan tourism department licencing regulations are quite strict on size, location and ownership (foreigners are technically not permitted to own or work in the shacks). They're usually constructed from timber and bamboo with palm-thatch roofing and sand floors but some are rather more sophisticated and all are required to have electricity, refrigeration, effective sewerage and waste systems and CCTV. Most also offer free wi-fi to customers.

As for food and drink, fresh fish and seafood is usually bought from local markets or fishing boats each day, but there's also a lengthy menu of Indian, Goan and Western dishes, including breakfast, usually printed in English and Russian Cyrillic. Most shacks have a full bar, with chairs and candle-topped tables spilling out onto the sand and music playing from competing sound systems.

Vagator & Chapora (p145) Picturesque beach, cool fort, cheap rooms; these laid-back villages attract budget travellers who like to chill *and* party.

Palolem (p184) & **Patnem** (p190) There's a hut to suit all tastes and budgets here, along with a genuine traveller vibe.

Yoga & Spirituality

Anjuna (p136) This is the closest beach to the retreats at Assagao and there are frequent drop-in classes and courses in Anjuna itself.

Mandrem (p155) & **Asvem** (p153) A number of reputable yoga schools and spiritual retreats call Mandrem home in season and there's a good ayurvedic massage centre.

Palolem (p184) & **Patnem** (p190) Patnem in particular has become a popular place for beachfront yoga retreats and there are lots of drop-in classes at these perennially popular beaches.

Arambol (p157) Popular Iyengar yoga school and numerous drop-in classes and retreats.

Five-star Treatment

Goa has more five-star resorts and boutique hotels per square kilometre than anywhere else in India. Even if you're not staying, you can almost always book a table at a fancy in-house restaurant, an afternoon at a spa or even pay to use the pool.

Cavelossim & Mobor (p178) South Goa's five-star strip includes the Leela, Holiday Inn and Radisson Blu.

Candolim & Sinquerim (p123) Two sprawling Taj Vivanta resorts plus some fine boutique hotels such as Aashyana Lakhanpal.

Rajbag (p192) Dominated by the five-star Lalit Golf & Spa Resort, complete with championship nine-hole golf course.

Betalbatim, Majorda & Utorda (p173) Resorts such as ITC Grand, Kenilworth and boutique Vivenda Dos Palhacos make this an upmarket strip with mostly quiet beaches.

Nature

Talpona & Galgibag (p192) The beach strip between the Talpona and Galgibag rivers is wonderfully deserted, backed by pines and with protected olive ridley turtle–nesting sites.

Cola (p180) With its lagoon and pair of swimming beaches, this is one of the coast's prettiest spots and you'll often see langur monkeys in the trees.

Morjim (p151) Popular with long-staying Russian visitors, this is also a protected turtle-nesting site where the Chapora River meets the sea.

Agonda (p181) Good walks around the forested headlands, turtle-nesting sites and dolphin-spotting.

Plan Your Trip
Activities

Even away from the beaches and nightlife, Goa has plenty to keep you active, from impromptu cricket and beach volleyball matches to hilltop paragliding or cooking classes. You'll find plenty of seasonal eco-slanted activities on offer: yoga and meditation, nature walks and day trips, river cruises, birdwatching and guided hikes through the state's national parks. As with most Goan activities, outfits change regularly and it's best to check online or noticeboards in hotels, restaurants and cafes for up-to-the-minute offerings.

Which Yoga Class?

Ashtanga

Often referred to as 'power yoga', active and physically demanding, good for some serious toning.

Bikram

Also known as 'hot yoga', with a focus on correct alignment, Bikram's 26 poses are performed at 41°C (105°F) and 40% humidity – not hard to achieve on a Goan April day.

Hatha

Covers a whole gamut of styles, but generally refers to yoga focused on breath work (pranayama), and slow, gentle stretching, making it good for beginners.

Iyengar

Slow and steady, often using 'props', in the form of blocks, balls and straps.

Kundalini

Aims to free the base of the spine, to unleash energy hidden there, and usually involves lots of core, spine and sitting work.

Vinyasa

An active, fluid series of changing poses characterises Vinyasa, sometimes called 'flow yoga'.

Yoga

India is widely regarded as the birthplace of yoga and Goa is the place that many teachers and practitioners set up for the winter season. From your open-air beachfront or jungle yoga *shala* (school), there are few better places to downward dog or salute to the sun.

Yoga Season

The best time to visit is mid-November to early April, when all outfits or retreats are open and courses are in full swing. A handful of smaller classes operate year-round, so it's still possible to get your yoga fix, even during the monsoon.

Palolem, Agonda and Patnem in the south of the state, and Arambol, Mandrem, Anjuna and Assagao in the north are particularly great places to take classes or longer courses. At most beach centres you'll find no shortage of morning and afternoon drop-in classes.

Teachers and practitioners are largely an ever-changing parade of foreigners or Indian teachers who set up shop in Goa as soon as the monsoon subsides. Peruse hotel, restaurant or cafe noticeboards for current and upcoming courses.

Yoga Centres

Scattered across Goa are a number of respected options for yoga classes, courses, retreats and teacher certification. Many hotels, guesthouses and resorts also offer yoga classes.

Anand Yoga Village (p185), Palolem

Ashiyana Retreat Centre (p156), Mandrem

Bamboo Yoga Retreat (p191), Patnem

Bhakti Kutir (p187), Palolem

Brahmani Yoga (p137), Anjuna

Himalaya Yoga Valley (p155), Mandrem

Himalayan Iyengar Yoga Centre (p157), Arambol

Kranti Yoga (p191), Patnem

Mandala (p156), Mandrem

Oceanic Yoga (p155), Mandrem

Purple Valley Yoga Retreat (p137), Assagao

Space Goa (p189), Palolem

Swan Yoga Retreat (p137), Assagao

Yoga Land (p187), Colomb Bay

Yoga Magic (p139), Anjuna

ALTERNATIVE ACTIVITIES

Not into yoga? No time for volunteering? Try these activities in Goa instead.

Baga Snow Park (p131) Snowball fights, ice sculptures and a toboggan ride.

Mandovi River Cruises (p88) Music, dancing and river cruising at Panaji.

Dolphin-spotting boat trips From Palolem to Arambol, fishermen will take you out to spot dolphins and possibly crocodiles.

Make it Happen (p89) Heritage walks in Panaji.

Goa Jungle Adventure (p185) Remote canyoning adventures start in Palolem.

Ayurveda

Goa offers plenty of opportunities to explore ayurvedic treatments. Briefly defined as an ancient science of plant-based medicine, ayurveda's Sanskrit name comes from a combination of *ayu* (life) and *veda* (knowledge); ancient ayurveda resources described 2000 species of plants, of which at least 550 are still in use today. Illness, in the doctrine of ayurveda, comes from a loss of internal balance, which can be restored through a regime of massage and *panchakarma* ('five therapies' internal purification).

The first part of this regime (and without doubt the most popular) comprises an hour-long massage with warm medicated oils, followed by a cleansing steam bath. Other treatments include aromatherapy and *shirodhara* (pouring of warm oil on the forehead).

The second part of the full regime, the internal purification, takes longer and most people opt for a fortnight's course of treatment and strict diet in order to feel its full advantages.

Ayurvedic therapy treatments can be found at most beach villages, but ask around for personal recommendations and ensure that a massage is conducted by a female if you're a woman and a male if you're a man. Another option is to head to one of the swanky spas at Goa's five-star hotels. It won't be cheap but you can be certain of well-trained staff and superluxurious treatments.

Meditation

Vipassana, roughly meaning 'to see things for what they really are', is a meditation technique most often taught in Goa as a 10-day residential retreat, concentrating on 'self-transformation through self-observation'. In practice it's an extremely strict regime that translates as 10 days of meditation, clear thought and near silence, abstaining from killing, stealing, lying, sexual activity and intoxicants, and concentrating at length on one's own breathing. Consult www.dhamma.org for more detailed information on the art of silence and courses in Goa.

Most yoga retreats also offer some form of meditation classes.

Outdoor Activities

Diving

Although Goa is not internationally renowned as a diving destination, its waters are regarded as the third-best spot for diving in India (after the Andaman and Lakshadweep Islands).

The shallow waters off the coast are ideal for less-experienced divers; typical dives are at depths of 10m to 12m, with abundant marine life to be seen. The main problem is that visibility is unpredictable and is adversely affected by the Mandovi and Zuari rivers; on some days it's 30m, on others it's closer to 2m, so it's best to check daily before deciding to go out. A Discover Scuba course costs around ₹5000 and a four-day PADI open-water course starts from ₹20,000. For certified divers, one dive costs ₹3000, two dives cost ₹5000. The dive season runs from late October to April.

The highlights of diving in Goa are the wreck dives – there are hundreds of wrecks along Goa's coastline, including Portuguese and Spanish galleons and more recent wrecks of merchant and naval ships. It's said that vast quantities of treasure still lie on its ocean beds, remnants from the wrecks carrying wealthy Portuguese traders.

Popular dive sites include Grande Island and St George's Island. PADI-accredited operations in Goa include the following:

Barracuda Diving (p131)

Dive Goa (p126)

Goa Aquatics (p131)

Goa Diving (p175)

GOA'S BIRD & SNAKE MAN

Wildlife guide, photographer, snake-handler, twitcher, naturalist and author – there are few people in Goa better equipped to lead you into the wilds than **Rahul Alvares** (☎9881961071; www.rahulalvares.com; tours for 2 people ₹4200-7200). The speciality is custom birdwatching tours, but he also offers butterfly tours (to the conservatory near Ponda), night tours, reptile and amphibian-watching tours and photography workshops.

Water Sports

Most water-sports outfits are run on a seasonal, itinerant basis, and it's enough to turn up at a beach and look around for a shack offering your activity of choice. Calangute and Colva are the busiest beaches for water sports. Activities include jet skiing (tandem), parasailing (tandem), wake-boarding, kayaking, surfing and kitesurfing. Paragliding is popular from the cliffs at Arambol. The best places for kayaking are Palolem's calm bay or the state's numerous rivers and estuaries.

Surfing

Although Goa doesn't have big surf, its gentle 'green' waves are ideal for beginners and there are a number of surf schools and board-hire shops to get you started.

Vaayu Waterman's Village (p154), Asvem

Surf Wala (p157), Arambol.

Banana Surf School (p152), Morjim

Aloha Surf India (p181), Agonda

Wildlife Watching

Goa's hinterland is great for spotting wildlife, from the blazing kingfishers that fleck the coastal strip's luminescent paddy fields, to the water buffalo that wander home come sunset after a hard day's wallowing.

Goa's wildlife sanctuaries host hard-to-spot wonders such as gaurs (Indian bison), porcupines, wild boar and the occasional pangolin (scaly anteater) or leopard. A loud rustle in the leaves overhead often signals the arrival of a troop of mischievous langur monkeys.

Taking a riverine trip inland, you might be rewarded with sightings of crocodiles, otters and yet more birdlife: just try spotting a Ceylon frogmouth or a fairy bluebird without at least the hint of a satisfied smile.

Day Trips & Tours

A great way to see more of Goa, especially if time is tight, is to sign up for a day trip or two. Travel agents and taxi drivers at

Paragliding, Utorda (p173)

any beach resort can organise tours, offering visits to otherwise hard-to-reach sights, including river cruises and Keralan-style houseboat stays.

Goa Tourism (p231)

KOKOindia (p191)

Betty's Place Boat Trips (p179)

Canopy Ecotours (p163)

John's Boat Tours (p126)

Make It Happen (p89)

Goa Jungle Adventure (p185)

Cooking Classes

Cooking classes are gaining popularity in Goa. Some of the best include:

Mukti Kitchen (p147), Vagator

Rahul's Cooking Class (p185), Palolem

Masala Kitchen (p185), Palolem

Spicy Mama's (p142), Assagao

Cozy Corner Cooking School (p151), Siolim

Volunteering

Many travellers to Goa are keen to give something back to this beautiful, but sometimes vulnerable, state. One great way to do this is to spend part of your stay volunteering: whether it's a few hours, days or weeks working with stray animals or disadvantaged people, there are some rewarding opportunities.

Lonely Planet does not endorse any organisation that we do not work with directly. Travellers should investigate any volunteering option thoroughly before committing to a project.

Planning

Most of Goa's volunteering options require a little advance planning, and it pays to be in touch with nonprofit organisations well before you depart home. Check any organisations out thoroughly before you offer your time – the website www.ethicalvolunteering.org has some useful tips. To legally work with a registered charity in India, even as a volunteer, you must technically have an employment visa.

MUMBAI ACTIVITIES

Mumbai has an eclectic range of city-based activities, guided tours, cooking courses and harbour tours.

Bollywood Tours (p75) See stars' homes and a film or TV studio.

Khaki Tours (p55) Immersive city tours led by locals include walks, food tours, sailing and 'urban safaris'.

Flavour Diaries (p55) Modern, interactive cooking studio with master classes.

Reality Tours & Travel (p55) Thought-provoking tours of Mumbai's Dharavi slum.

Yoga Institute (p55) Daily yoga classes as well as weekend and residential courses.

Bombay Heritage Walks (p56) Heritage tours led by architects and historians.

Moreover, working with children requires criminal record background checks, so it takes a few months to organise. Minimum placements are usually one month but can be as long as one year.

A number of charity organisations offer volunteer placements, often with accommodation and meals included for a fee, and they can usually organise the necessary paperwork for visas.

Some local animal-related organisations are happy to receive casual visitors to play with the animals or help with walking, cleaning and feeding, but you may need evidence of a recent rabies vaccination – drop in or call ahead.

Getting Involved

El Shaddai (p142) This British-founded charity aids impoverished and homeless children throughout Goa, running a number of day and night shelters, an open school and children's homes throughout the state. Skilled volunteers for a minimum four-week placement can apply through the website subject to police checks and visas. Help with fund-raising activities or donations is also welcomed. For more information, El Shaddai operates an information stall at the Anjuna flea market.

Mango Tree Goa (p144) This UK-registered organisation helps Goa's disadvantaged children by providing daycare centres, medical, educational, nutritional and other essential aid. Volunteers can fill a variety of roles, as teachers, childcare assistants and outreach workers, while there are also positions available for qualified doctors and nurses.

Goa Animal Welfare Trust (p184) Based in South Goa, this trust operates an animal shelter at Curchorem helping sick, stray and injured dogs, cats and even a calf or two. Volunteers are welcome, if only for a few spare hours to walk or play with the dogs. GAWT also operates a shop and information centre in Colva.

International Animal Rescue (p142) An internationally active charity operating Animal Tracks rescue facility in Assagao. Visitors and volunteers (both short and long term) are always welcome, though rabies vaccination is expected.

Animal Rescue Centre (p185) About 3km from Palolem this centre takes in sick, injured or stray animals.

Bethesda Life Centre (☎0832-2459962; www.blcgoa.org; Bambolim Complex, Alto Santa Cruz, Tiswadi) This Goan charity supports shelters for disadvantaged women and children, including HIV sufferers. Volunteer placement is available; see the website for details.

Plan Your Trip

Travel with Children

Goa is the most family-friendly state in India. What could be better than taking the kids to the beach every day? Goa excels as a holiday destination on many fronts: its short travel distances, wide range of foods, reliable climate and range of activities for kids...even away from the beach.

Goa for Kids

Though India's sensory overload may at first prove overwhelming for younger kids, the colours, scents, sights and sounds of Goa more than compensate by setting young imaginations ablaze. With a little planning and an open mind, travelling with children will open up a whole new world for you too.

Goa's beaches are excellent for playing in the sand with a bucket and spade, and for paddling and water sports, though strong currents make swimming at most beaches risky, even for adults. Beaches are patrolled but children may feel safer swimming at a hotel pool or water park.

At the busiest beaches you'll be surprised by how many kids and families are around – mostly Indian families holidaying from outside Goa. Foreign children, especially fair-haired ones, can be quite a novel attraction. Don't be surprised if groups of people ask to pose for photographs with your child. Generally it's good-natured attention but if it gets too much, offer a polite 'no'.

Away from the beach kids should enjoy boat trips on calm local rivers, trips to spice farms and wildlife sanctuaries, shopping at markets or a day at the movies.

Best Regions for Kids

Goa's beaches are all a little different in character and some are more family-friendly than others.

Palolem

The calm, shallow waters in this crescent bay (p184) are the safest for swimming in all of Goa, and the beach is clean. You can also hire kayaks, boogie boards and stand-up paddleboards, or go on a sunset boat trip.

Patnem

Good paddling on calm days, Patnem (p190) has fewer people than Palolem and a more relaxed vibe, as well as Goa's best drop-in kindergartens and a school.

Baga & Calangute

Goa's busiest beach strip (p129) has lots of bucket-and-spade vendors, water sports and plenty of other children to make friends with.

Arambol

There are shallow seas popular with long-stayers, safe swimming in Sweetwater Lake and paragliding from the hilltop (p157).

Mandrem & Asvem

Lovely white-sand beaches (p155) with few hawkers, sophisticated hut accommodation and a surf shop.

Mumbai for Kids

Kidzania (p74) is an educational activity centre where kids can learn all about flying, fire-fighting and policing, and get stuck into lots of arts and crafts. It's on the outskirts of the city, 10km northeast of the Bandra Kurla Complex.

Little tykes with energy to burn will love the Gorai Island amusement parks, Esselworld (p74) and **Water Kingdom** (www.waterkingdom.in; Global Pagoda Rd, Borivali West; adult/child ₹1050/696, with Esselworld ₹1390/950; ⏲10am-7pm). Both have lots of rides, slides and shade.

The free **Hanging Gardens**, in Malabar Hill, have animal topiaries, swings in the shade and coconut-wallahs. **Kamala Nehru Park**, across the street, has a two-storey 'boot house'.

Bombay Natural History Society (p55) conducts nature trips for kids.

SNEHAL JEEVAN PAILKAR/SHUTTERSTOCK ©

Old Woman's Shoe by Soli Arceivala, Kamala Nehru Park

Beach-free Highlights

Splashdown Water Park (p136) Water slides, pools, fountains and waterfalls to entertain everyone from toddlers to adults.

Spice Farms (p110) Central Goa's commercial spice farms are a surprisingly entertaining family day out: there's a hint of jungle adventure on the spice plantation tours, and a thali lunch is included.

Dolphin-spotting Trips (p126) Charter an outrigger fishing boat and spot dolphins on a trip from Candolim (or from Coco, Baga or Palolem).

Goa Science Centre & Planetarium (p87) Most kids will enjoy the planetarium and simple science exhibits on a rainy day.

INOX Cinema (p94) Panaji's modern cinema shows mainstream Hollywood (as well as Bollywood) films. Check the website.

Caculo Mall (p94) Timezone arcade, 7D cinema, play centre, bowling alley, fast food and boutique fashion stores.

Cooking classes (p37) Get the kids involved in a spicy cooking class.

SCHOOL & KINDER

With lots of long-staying foreigners, Goa has a number of seasonal child-care centres – look for notices locally. The Palolem region, with a large expat community, has recommended schools, as does Anjuna.

Planning

- Ask your local doctor or travel clinic about immunisations and antimalarials.
- Pack loose-fitting, lightweight clothing (with long sleeves and pants) for evening mosquito protection.
- Most hotels and guesthouses are child-friendly and will supply a spare mattress or have a family room. Kids will love staying in beach shacks.
- If you've got fussy eaters, don't fret. Beach shacks and restaurants can prepare nonspicy pizzas, pancakes, toast, eggs or tasty rice and dhal. Supermarkets in Candolim, Panaji and Anjuna stock all sorts of Western foods.
- There are loads of taxis for day trips around Goa (none have child seats) but families should consider using the women's taxi service (p236).

Regions at a Glance

Though Goa is a relatively small state, the differences in character between the regions, villages and beach enclaves are surprisingly pronounced.

Central Goa is home to the capital, Panaji, an unmissable example of Goa's Portuguese heritage, as well as the state's biggest historical attraction in nearby Old Goa.

North Goa's buzzing resorts offer plenty of nightlife, shopping, yoga retreats and fine dining, with just a few patches of quiet sands but plenty of action. Goa's busiest beach strip is between Candolim and Baga.

South Goa is more serene, with a largely laid-back tourist vibe, Goa's biggest five-star resorts and its most picturesque beach community at busy little Palolem. Don't miss some inland exploration here, from traditional villages to wildlife sanctuaries.

Mumbai

Architecture
Food
Nightlife

Colonial Edifices

Indian stonemasons and the British share honours for Mumbai's glorious colonial-era architecture, merging grandiose Gothic flourishes with local motifs and adornments. Chhatrapati Shvaji Maharaj train terminus is the pinnacle of the form.

Street Food to Haute Cuisine

Mumbai has some of India's most spectacular dining options, from humble street carts to five-star sophistication. Sample hot and sour *dhansak* (curried lentil stew) in Parsi canteens, munch *bhelpuri* (crisp noodle salad) on Chowpatty Beach, or go all out in the city's top dining rooms.

Bollywood & Partying

The glitz and glamour of the world's most prolific film industry spills over into real life: Mumbaikars are enthusiastic party people, and you may spot the odd Bollywood celeb among the beautiful people in Mumbai's sleek bars and neon-filled nightclubs.

p44

Panaji & Central Goa

History
Wildlife
Temples

Colonial History

Picturesque Portuguese-era homes and historic riverside buildings are a highlight in the relaxed state capital of Panaji. Not far away, Old Goa's glorious cathedrals once earned it the title 'Rome of the East'.

Birds Galore

Dr Salim Ali Bird Sanctuary, on lovely Chorao Island, makes for a leisurely spot of birdwatching beside the river. Further afield are Bondla and Bhagwan Mahavir Wildlife Sanctuaries, and Backwoods Camp is another ornithologist's dream.

Hindu Heritage

Temples abound around Ponda, where the Shri Manguesh and Shri Laxmi Narasimha temples are especially worth a visit. Further east, Tambdi Surla is home to an interesting little 12th-century temple, which has survived centuries of conquerors and temple demolitions.

p82

North Goa

Nightlife
Yoga
Beaches

Party Time

North Goa is the place to party. Calangute, Baga and Candolim are popular for clubs and live music, while Anjuna, Vagator and Morjim pull out the stops with late-night rave parties.

Luxury Spirituality

Yoga and spirituality are big business with dozens of retreats, courses and drop-in classes setting up for the winter, especially in Anjuna, Assagao, Mandrem and Arambol.

Beach Bonanza

From the boisterous beaches of Baga to the relatively empty white sand at Mandrem, there's a beach to fit every inclination in North Goa. Arambol, Vagator and Anjuna's beaches are popular with backpackers; Calangute, Candolim and Sinquerim are the places to head for water sports, while Arambol is best for paragliding.

p121

South Goa

Beaches
Luxury
Heritage

Chilling Out

South Goa has some of India's finest beaches and with its chilled-out vibe this is the place to find a patch of peaceful paradise. An almost uninterrupted strip of sand stretches from Velsao to Mobor via Colva and Benaulim, but in the far south Palolem, Patnem, Agonda and tiny Cola show off Goa's coastline at its best.

Five-star Pampering

The south has a string of five-star, beachfront resorts, from the Leela in Mobor to the Lalit in Rajbag, with golf courses, spas and all-round pampering.

Exploring the Past

Getting off the beaten track is easy in South Goa, where tiny coastal villages invite exploration by scooter, motorbike or rental car and inland villages shine a light on Goa's colonial past. Trips to Usgalimal, Netravali and Cotigao are adventurous. The ride down the coast from the Sal River to Agonda is one of the prettiest in the state.

p162

On the Road

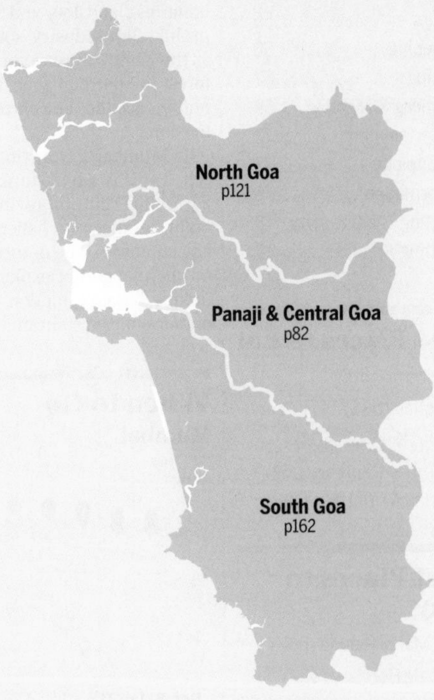
North Goa
p121
Panaji & Central Goa
p82
South Goa
p162

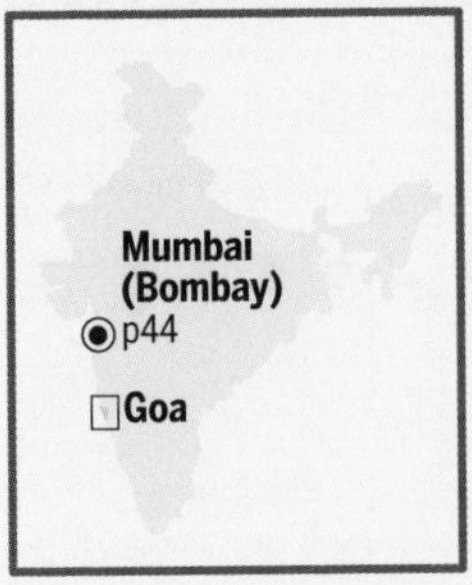
Mumbai
(Bombay)
p44
Goa

Mumbai (Bombay)

☎022 / POPULATION 21.1 MILLION

Includes ➡

Best Places to Eat

- Peshawri (p68)
- Bastian (p68)
- Bohri Kitchen (p63)
- Bombay Canteen (p69)
- Pancham Puriwala (p65)

Best Places to Stay

- Taj Mahal Palace (p57)
- Abode Bombay (p57)
- Residency Hotel (p58)
- Sea Shore Hotel (p57)
- Juhu Residency (p58)

Why Go?

Mumbai, formerly Bombay, is big. It's full of dreamers and hard-labourers, starlets and gangsters, stray dogs and exotic birds, artists and servants, fisherfolk and *crorepatis* (millionaires), and lots and lots of people. It has India's most prolific film industry, some of Asia's biggest slums (as well as the world's most expensive home) and the largest tropical forest in an urban zone. Mumbai is India's financial powerhouse, fashion epicentre and a pulse point of religious tension.

If Mumbai is your introduction to India, prepare yourself. The city isn't a threatening place but its furious energy, limited (but improving) public transport and punishing pollution make it challenging for visitors. The heart of the city contains some of the grandest colonial-era architecture on the planet, but explore a little more and you'll uncover unique bazaars, hidden temples, hipster enclaves and India's premier restaurants and nightlife.

When to Go

Mumbai

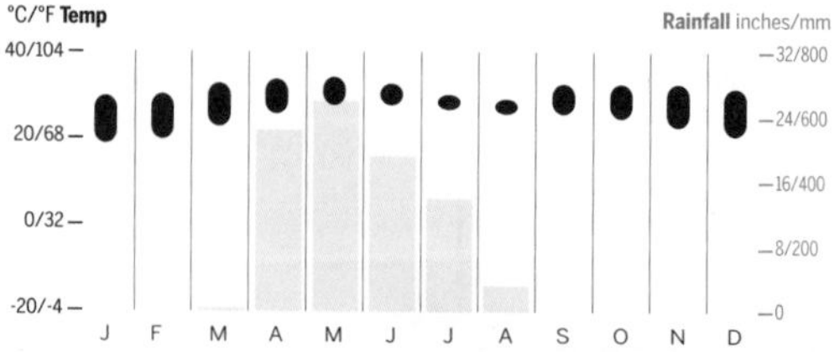

Dec & Jan The very best, least-sticky weather.

Aug & Sep Mumbai goes Ganesh-crazy during its most exciting festival, Ganesh Chaturthi.

Oct–Apr There's very little rain, postmonsoon; the best time of year for festivals.

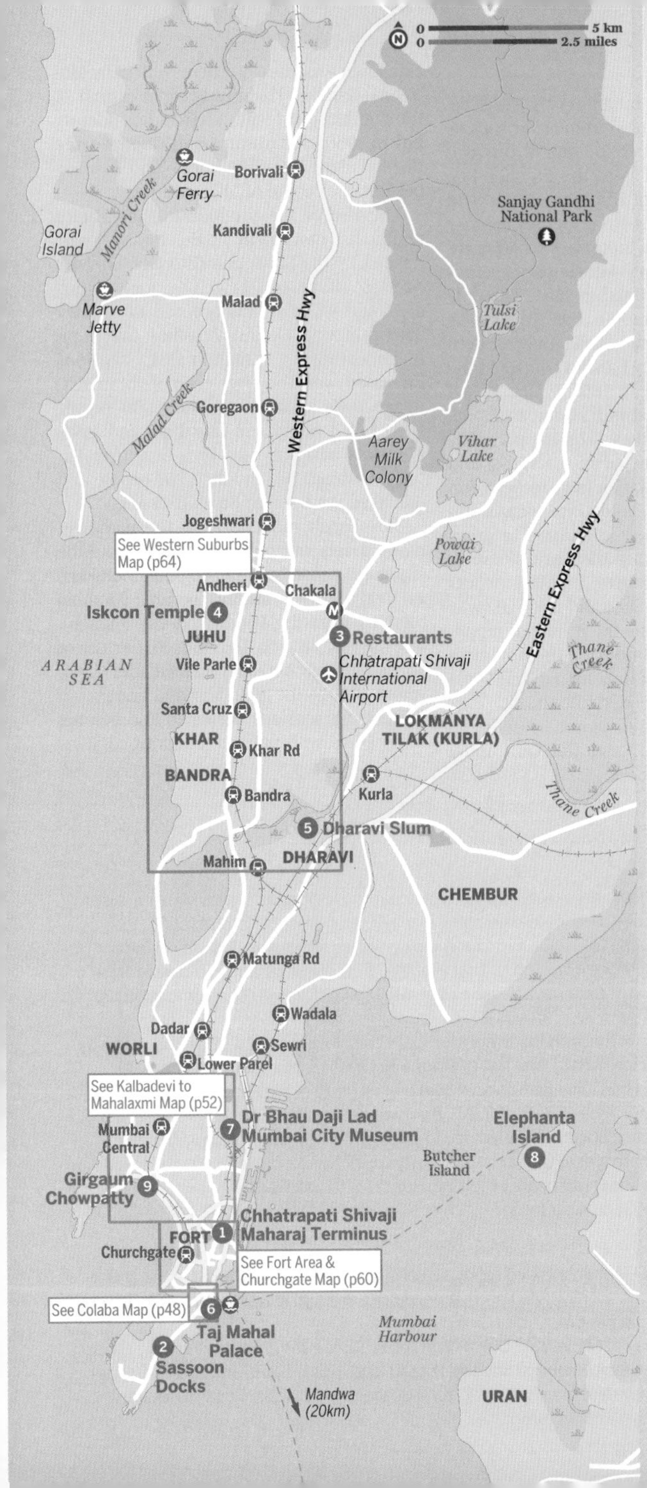

Mumbai Highlights

1 **Chhatrapati Shivaji Maharaj Terminus** (p49) Marvelling at the magnificent Unesco-listed colonial-era architecture, including this monumental train station.

2 **Sassoon Docks** (p49) Waging war on your senses at Mumbai's cinematic fishing docks.

3 **Restaurants** (p68) Dining like a maharaja at one of India's best restaurants, such as Peshawri.

4 **Iskcon Temple** (p51) Feeling the love with the Krishna crowd at this unique temple.

5 **Dharavi Slum** (p56) Touring through the self-sufficient world of Asia's largest shanty town.

6 **Taj Mahal Palace** (p47) Staying at one of the world's most iconic hotels, or dropping in for a drink at its bar, Mumbai's first.

7 **Dr Bhau Daji Lad Mumbai City Museum** (p50) Ogling this museum's gorgeous Renaissance-revival interiors.

8 **Elephanta Island** (p54) Beholding the commanding triple-headed Shiva on this Mumbai Harbour island.

9 **Girgaum Chowpatty** (p51) Snacking on *bhelpuri* (puffed rice and spices) among playing kids, big balloons and a hot-pink sunset.

History

Koli fisherfolk have inhabited the seven islands that form Mumbai from as far back as the 2nd century BC. Remnants of this culture remain huddled along the city shoreline today. A succession of Hindu dynasties held sway over the islands from the 6th century AD until the Muslim Sultans of Gujarat annexed the area in the 14th century, eventually ceding it to Portugal in 1534. The only memorable contribution the Portuguese made to the area was christening it Bom Baia (Good Bay). They handed control to the English government in 1665, which leased the islands to the East India Company.

Bombay flourished as a trading port. The city's fort was completed in the 1720s, and a century later ambitious land-reclamation projects joined the islands into today's single landmass. The city continued to grow, and in the 19th century the fort walls were dismantled and massive building works transformed the city in grand colonial style. When Bombay became the principal supplier of cotton to Britain during the American Civil War, the population soared and trade boomed as money flooded into the city.

Bombay was a major player in the independence movement, and the Quit India campaign was launched here in 1942 by Mahatma Gandhi. The city became capital of the Bombay presidency after Independence, but in 1960 Maharashtra and Gujarat were divided along linguistic lines – and Bombay became the capital of Maharashtra.

The rise of the pro-Marathi, pro-Hindu regionalist movement in the 1980s, spearheaded by the Shiv Sena (literally 'Shivaji's Army'), shattered the city's multicultural mould when it was accused of actively discriminating against Muslims and non-Maharashtrians. Communalist tensions increased, and the city's cosmopolitan self-image took a battering when 900 people were killed in riots in late 1992 and 1993. The riots were followed by a dozen retaliatory bombings which killed 257 people and damaged the Bombay Stock Exchange.

Shiv Sena's influence saw the names of many streets and public buildings – and the city itself – changed from colonial monikers. In 1996 the city officially became Mumbai (derived from the Hindu goddess Mumba). The airport, Victoria Terminus and Prince of Wales Museum were all renamed after Chhatrapati Shivaji, the great Maratha leader.

Religious tensions deepened and became intertwined with national religious conflicts

MUMBAI IN...

Two Days

Begin at one of Mumbai's architectural masterpieces, the Chhatrapati Shivaji Maharaj Vastu Sangrahalaya museum (p49), before grabbing lunch Gujarati-style at Samrat (p66).

In the afternoon head to Colaba and tour the city's iconic sights, the Gateway of India (p48) and Taj Mahal Palace hotel (p57). That evening, drink cocktails and fine-dine at Miss T (p65) or chow down at Bademiya Seekh Kebab Stall (p62), followed by a nightcap at hip Colaba Social (p71).

The next day, take in the granddaddy of Mumbai's colonial-era giants, Chhatrapati Shivaji Terminus (p49), and **Crawford Market** (Mahatma Jyotiba Phule Mandai; Map p52; cnr DN & Lokmanya Tilak Rds, Fort; ⏲10am-8pm, to noon Sun) and its maze of bazaars, hidden temples and unique street life. Lunch at Revival (p68), then wander the tiny lanes of Khotachiwadi (p51), followed by beach *bhelpuri* (puffed rice tossed with fried rounds of dough, lentils, onions, herbs and chutneys) at Girgaum Chowpatty (p51). Need a drink? Hip nightlife hub Lower Parel beckons with craft beers at Toit Tap Room (p70) followed by dinner at sceney Bombay Canteen (p69) or Koko (p69).

Four Days

Sail to Unesco-listed Elephanta Island (p54), returning for lunch in artsy Kala Ghoda at Burma Burma (p67). In the evening head north for exquisite seafood at Bastian (p68), followed by serious bar action in Bandra.

Spend your last day at Mahalaxmi Dhobi Ghat (p51), **Shree Mahalaxmi Temple** (Map p52; www.mahalakshmi-temple.com; off Bhulabhai Desai Marg; ⏲6am-10pm) and Haji Ali Dargah (p50); or Sanjay Gandhi National Park (p77) for a peaceful forest walk. End with modern Indian fare at Bombay Canteen (p69).

TOP FESTIVALS

Mumbai Sanskruti (www.asiaticsociety.org.in; ⏲Jan) This free, two-day celebration of Hindustani classical music is held on the steps of the gorgeous Asiatic Society Library.

Kala Ghoda Arts Festival (www.kalaghodaassociation.com; ⏲Feb) Getting bigger and more sophisticated each year, this two-week-long art fest held in Kala Ghoda and the Fort area sees tons of performances and exhibitions.

Elephanta Festival (www.maharashtratourism.gov.in; Elephanta Island; ⏲Feb) Unesco-listed Elephanta Island comes to life with dancers, musicians and dramatists over the two-day classical-music and dance festival, usually in February.

Nariyal Poornima (⏲Aug) This Koli celebration in Colaba marks the start of the fishing season and the retreat of monsoon winds.

Ganesh Chaturthi (www.ganeshchaturthi.com; ⏲Aug/Sep) Mumbai gets totally swept up by this 10- to 12-day celebration of the elephant-headed Hindu god Ganesh. On the festival's first, third, fifth, seventh and 11th days, families and communities take their Ganesh statues to the seashore at Chowpatty and Juhu beaches and auspiciously submerge them.

Jio Mami Mumbai Film Festival (MFF; www.mumbaifilmfestival.com; ⏲Oct/Nov) New films from the subcontinent and beyond are screened at the weeklong MFF at various cinemas.

and India's relations with Pakistan. A series of bomb attacks on trains killed over 200 in July 2006. Then, in November 2008, a coordinated series of devastating attacks (by Pakistani gunmen) targeted landmark buildings across the city, as the Taj Mahal Palace hotel burned, passengers were gunned down inside the Chhatrapati Shivaji railway station and 10 people were killed inside the Leopold Cafe backpacker haunt.

In late 2012, when the Sena's charismatic founder Bal Thackeray died (500,000 attended his funeral), the Shiv Sena mission begin to falter, and in the 2014 assembly elections, President Modi's Bharatiya Janata Party (BJP) became the largest party in Mumbai.

Mumbaikars are a resilient bunch. Increased security is very much part of everyday life today and the city's status as the engine room of the Indian economy remains unchallenged. However, Mumbai politicians certainly have their work cut out, with the megacity's feeble public transport, gridlocked streets, pollution and housing crisis all in desperate need of attention.

Sights

Mumbai is an island – originally seven before land reclaiming sewed them together – connected by bridges to the mainland. The city's commercial and cultural centre is at the southern, claw-shaped end of the island known as South Mumbai. The southernmost peninsula is Colaba, traditionally the travellers' nerve centre, with many of the major attractions.

North of Colaba is the busy commercial area known as Fort, where the British fort once stood. This part of the city is bordered on the west by a series of interconnected grassy areas known as maidans (may-*dahns*).

Continuing north you enter 'the suburbs', which contain the airport and many of Mumbai's best restaurants, shops and nightspots. The upmarket districts of Bandra, Juhu and Lower Parel are key areas (the bohemians and hippies that used to claim Bandra have now moved further north to Andheri West and Vesova).

Colaba

Along the city's southernmost peninsula, Colaba is a bustling district packed with elegant art deco and colonial-era mansions, budget-to-midrange lodgings, bars and restaurants, street stalls and a fisherfolk quarter. Colaba Causeway (Shahid Bhagat Singh Marg) dissects the district. If you're here in August, look out for the Koli festival Nariyal Poornima.

★**Taj Mahal Palace, Mumbai** LANDMARK
(Map p48; https://taj.tajhotels.com; Apollo Bunder) Mumbai's most famous landmark, this stunning hotel is a fairy-tale blend of Islamic and Renaissance styles, and India's second-most-photographed monument. It was built in 1903 by the Parsi industrialist JN Tata, supposedly after he was refused entry to nearby European hotels on account of being 'a native'. Dozens were killed inside the

Colaba

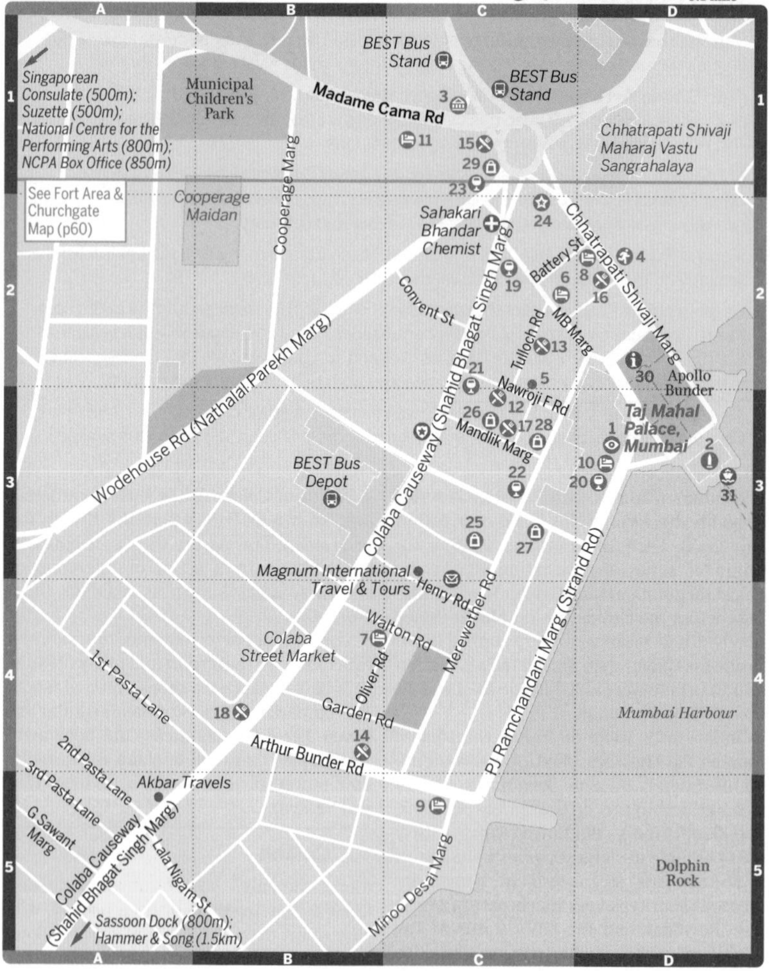

hotel when it was targeted during the 2008 terrorist attacks, and images of its burning facade were beamed worldwide. The fully restored hotel reopened on Independence Day 2010.

Much more than an iconic building, the Taj's history is intrinsically linked with the nation: it was the first hotel in India to employ women, the first to have electricity (and fans), and it also housed freedom fighters (for no charge) during the struggle for independence.

Today the Taj fronts the harbour and Gateway of India, but it was originally designed to face the city (the entrance has been changed).

Gateway of India MONUMENT

(Map p48; Apollo Bunder) This bold basalt arch of colonial triumph faces out to Mumbai Harbour from the tip of Apollo Bunder. Incorporating Islamic styles of 16th-century Gujarat, it was built to commemorate the 1911 royal visit of King George V, but wasn't completed until 1924. Ironically, the British builders of the gateway used it just 24 years later to parade the last British regiment as India marched towards independence.

Colaba

Top Sights
1 Taj Mahal Palace, Mumbai D3

Sights
2 Gateway of India D3
3 National Gallery of Modern Art C1

Activities, Courses & Tours
4 Palms Spa D2
5 Reality Tours & Travel C2

Sleeping
6 Abode Bombay C2
7 Backpacker Panda B4
8 Hotel Suba Palace D2
9 Sea Shore Hotel C5
10 Taj Mahal Palace, Mumbai D3
11 YWCA C1

Eating
12 Bademiya Restaurant C3
13 Bademiya Seekh Kebab Stall C2
14 Basilico B4
15 Bombay Vintage C1
16 Indigo Delicatessen D2
17 Miss T C3
Table ..... (see 8)
18 Theobroma B4

Drinking & Nightlife
19 Cafe Mondegar C2
20 Harbour Bar D3
21 Leopold Café C2
22 Social C3
23 Woodside Inn C1

Entertainment
24 Regal Cinema C2

Shopping
25 Clove C3
26 Cottonworld C3
27 Good Earth C3
28 Nappa Dori C3
29 Phillips C1

Information
30 MTDC Booth D2

Transport
Launches to Elephanta Island ..... (see 31)
31 Launches to Mandwa D3
Maldar Catamarans ..... (see 30)
PNP ..... (see 30)

★**Sassoon Docks** WATERFRONT
(Sassoon Dock Rd; 24hr) No sense is left unaffected at Mumbai's incredibly atmospheric fishing docks, dating to 1875, the oldest and largest wholesale fish market in Mumbai. A scene of intense and pungent activity begins around 5am, when colourfully clad Koli fisherfolk sort the catch unloaded from fishing trawlers at the quay, and carries on throughout the morning.

Fort Area & Churchgate

Lined up in a row and vying for your attention with aristocratic pomp, many of Mumbai's majestic Victorian buildings pose on the edge of Oval Maidan. This land, and the Cross and Azad Maidans immediately to the north, were all on the oceanfront in those days, and this series of grandiose structures faced west directly to the Arabian Sea.

Kala Ghoda (Black Horse) is a hip, atmospheric subneighbourhood of Fort just north of Colaba (see the neighbourhood's new Spirit of Kala Ghoda monument, erected in 2017, which might strike some as notable for being a riderless horse). It contains many of Mumbai's museums, galleries and design boutiques alongside a wealth of colonial-era buildings and some of the city's best restaurants and cafes.

★**Chhatrapati Shivaji Maharaj Terminus** HISTORIC BUILDING
(Victoria Terminus (VT); Map p60; Chhatrapati Shivaji Terminus Area, Fort) Imposing, exuberant and overflowing with people, this monumental train station is the city's most extravagant Gothic building and an aphorism of colonial-era India. It's a meringue of Victorian, Hindu and Islamic styles whipped into an imposing Dalí-esque structure of buttresses, domes, turrets, spires and stained glass. It's also known as CSMT.

★**Chhatrapati Shivaji Maharaj Vastu Sangrahalaya** MUSEUM
(Prince of Wales Museum; Map p60; www.csmvs.in; 159-161 MG Rd, Fort; Indian/foreigner ₹83/500, mobile/camera ₹50/100; 10.15am-6pm) Mumbai's biggest and best museum displays a mix of India-wide exhibits. The domed behemoth, an intriguing hodgepodge of Islamic, Hindu and British architecture, is a flamboyant Indo-Saracenic design by George Wittet (who also designed the Gateway of India). Its vast collection includes impressive Hindu and Buddhist sculpture, terracotta figurines from the Indus Valley, Indian miniature paintings and some particularly vicious-looking weaponry.

Keneseth Eliyahoo Synagogue SYNAGOGUE

(Map p60; Dr VB Gandhi Marg, Kala Ghoda; 11am-6pm Sun-Thu) Built in 1884, and tenderly maintained by the city's dwindling Jewish community, this white and indigo-trimmed synagogue emerged from under years of scaffolding in 2019, restored to its original 19th-century color scheme. It now dazzles inside with neoclassical splendour, awash in Burmese teak furnishings and Victorian stained glass. Staff are friendly, but it's protected by very heavy security – bring a copy of your passport to gain entry.

Marine Dr WATERFRONT

(Map p60; Netaji Subhashchandra Bose Rd; 24hr) Built on reclaimed land in 1920 and a part of Mumbai's recently crowned Victorian Gothic and Art Deco Ensembles Unesco World Heritage Site, Marine Dr arcs along the shore of the Arabian Sea from Nariman Point past Girgaum Chowpatty and continues to the foot of Malabar Hill. Lined with flaking art deco apartments, it's one of Mumbai's most popular promenades and sunset-watching spots. Its twinkling night-time lights have earned it the nickname 'the Queen's Necklace'.

University of Mumbai HISTORIC BUILDING

(Bombay University; Map p60; www.mu.ac.in; Bhaurao Patil Marg) Looking like a 15th-century French-Gothic mansion plopped incongruously among Mumbai's palm trees, this structure was designed by Gilbert Scott of London's St Pancras station fame. There's an exquisite University Library and Convocation Hall, as well as the 84m-high Rajabai Clock Tower, decorated with detailed carvings. Since the 2008 terror attacks there has been no public access to the grounds, though pressure is beginning to be put on the vice chancellor to open the campus (check ahead).

Jehangir Art Gallery GALLERY

(Map p60; www.jehangirartgallery.com; 161B MG Rd, Kala Ghoda; 11am-7pm) FREE Renovated in recent years, this excellent gallery hosts exhibitions across several galleries of all types of visual arts by Mumbaikar, national and international artists.

National Gallery of Modern Art MUSEUM

(NGMA; Map p48; www.ngmaindia.gov.in; MG Rd; Indian/foreigner ₹20/500; 11am-6pm Tue-Sun) Well-curated shows of Indian and international artists in a bright and spacious five-floor exhibition space.

DAG GALLERY

(Delhi Art Gallery; Map p60; www.discoverdag.com; 58 Dr VB Gandhi Marg, Kala Ghoda; 10.30am-7pm Mon-Sat) FREE This top gallery is spread over three floors of a beautifully restored cream-coloured colonial-era structure. Its quarterly-changing exhibitions are curated from the largest collection of 20th-century modern Indian art in the world and its wares are showcased in museums throughout India as well as additional galleries in New Delhi and New York.

St Thomas' Cathedral CHURCH

(Map p60; 3 Veer Nariman Rd, Churchgate; 7am-6pm) This charming cathedral, begun in 1672 and finished in 1718, is the oldest British-era building standing in Mumbai and the city's first Anglican church: it was once the eastern gateway of the East India Company's fort (the 'Churchgate' itself). The cathedral is a marriage of Byzantine and colonial-era architecture, and its airy interior is full of grandiose colonial memorials.

Kalbadevi to Mahalaxmi

★Dr Bhau Daji Lad Mumbai City Museum MUSEUM

(Map p52; www.bdlmuseum.org; Dr Babasaheb Ambedkar Rd; Indian/foreigner ₹10/100, audio guides ₹30/50; 10am-6pm Thu-Tue) This gorgeous museum, built in Renaissance revival style in 1872 as the Victoria & Albert Museum, contains 3500-plus objects centring on Mumbai's history – photography, maps, textiles, books, manuscripts, *bidriware* (Bidar's metalwork), lacquerware, weaponry and exquisite pottery. The landmark building was renovated in 2008, with its Minton-tile floors, gilded ceiling mouldings, ornate columns, chandeliers and staircases all gloriously restored.

Haji Ali Dargah MOSQUE

(Map p52; www.hajialidargah.in; off V Desai Chowk; 5.30am-10pm) FREE Floating like a sacred mirage off the coast, this Indo-Islamic shrine located on an offshore inlet is a striking sight. Built in the 19th century, it contains the tomb of the Muslim saint Pir Haji Ali Shah Bukhari. Legend has it that Haji Ali died while on a pilgrimage to Mecca and his casket miraculously floated back to this spot.

It's only possible to visit the shrine at low tide, via a long causeway (check tide times locally). Thousands of pilgrims, especially on Thursday and Friday (when there may be *qawwali;* devotional singing), cross it daily, many donating to beggars who line the

WORTH A TRIP

KHOTACHIWADI

This storied *wadi* (hamlet), **Khotachiwadi** (Map p52) is a heritage village nearly 180 years old, is clinging onto Mumbai life as it was before high-rises. A Christian enclave of elegant two-storey Portuguese-style wooden mansions (of which only 23 out of 65 have survived), it's 500m northeast of Girgaum Chowpatty, lying amid Mumbai's predominantly Hindu and Muslim neighbourhoods. The winding lanes allow a wonderful glimpse into a quiet(ish) life away from noisier Mumbai.

It's not large, but you can spend a while wandering the alleyways and admiring the old homes and, around Christmas, their decorations. You can also plan an East Indian feast in advance or sleep at the home of celebrated fashion designer, Khotachiwadi activist and amateur chef James Ferreira (www.jamesferreira.co.in – find his rooms on Airbnb).

To find Khotachiwadi, head for **St Teresa's Church** (Map p52; cnr Jagannath Shankarsheth (JSS) Marg & Rajarammohan Roy (RR) Marg), on the corner of Jagannath Shankarsheth Marg (JSS Marg) and Rajarammohan Roy Marg (RR Rd/Charni Rd), then head directly opposite the church on JSS Marg and duck down the third lane on your left (look for the faded Khotachiwadi wall stencil map that says 'Khotachiwadi Imaginaries').

way. Sadly, parts of the shrine are in a poor state, damaged by storms and the saline air, though a renovation plan exists. It's visited by people of all faiths.

Mahalaxmi Dhobi Ghat GHAT
(Map p52; Bapurao Jagtap Marg, Mahalaxmi; ⏲4.30am-dusk) This 140-year-old dhobi ghat (place where clothes are washed) is Mumbai's biggest human-powered washing machine: every day hundreds of people beat the dirt out of thousands of kilograms of soiled Mumbai clothes and linen in 1026 open-air troughs. The best view is from the bridge across the railway tracks near Mahalaxmi train station.

Girgaum Chowpatty BEACH
(Map p52) This city beach is a favourite evening spot for courting couples, families, political rallies and anyone out to enjoy what passes for fresh air. Evening *bhelpuri* (puffed rice tossed with fried rounds of dough, lentils, onions, herbs and chutneys) at the throng of stalls at the beach's southern end is an essential part of the Mumbai experience. Forget about taking a dip: the water's toxic. On the 10th day of the Ganesh Chaturthi festival (p47) millions flock here to submerge huge Ganesh statues: it's joyful mayhem.

Western Suburbs

★**Iskcon Temple** HINDU TEMPLE
(Map p64; www.iskconmumbai.com; Hare Krishna Land, Sri Mukteshwar Devalaya Rd, Juhu; ⏲4.30am-1pm & 4-9pm) Iskcon Juhu plays a key part in the Hare Krishna story, as founder AC Bhaktivedanta Swami Prabhupada spent extended periods here (you can visit his modest living quarters-cum-museum in the adjacent building; 10.30am to 12.30pm and 5.30pm to 8.30pm). The temple compound comes alive during prayer time as the faithful whip themselves into a devotional frenzy of joy, with *kirtan* dancing accompanied by crashing hand symbols and drumbeats.

Juhu Beach BEACH
(Map p64; Juhu Tara Rd, Juhu) This sprawling suburban beach draws legions of Indian families and courting couples frolicking in the Arabian Sea for 6km all the way to Versova. As far as beaches go, it's no sun-toasted Caribbean dream, but it's a fun place to have a drink or try some Mumbai street food from the nearby stalls. It's particularly vibrant during Ganesh Chaturthi (p47).

Gilbert Hill MOUNTAIN
(Map p64; Sagar City, Andheri West; ⏲24hr) Smack dab among the residential apartment blocks of Andheri West sits this 61m-tall black basalt mountain that resembles a chocolate molten cake (unsurprisingly, as it was formed as result of Mesozoic era molten lava squeeze – it's 66 million years old. Climb the steep rock-carved staircase for panoramic views and the two Hindu temples set around a garden.

Gorai Island

Global Vipassana Pagoda BUDDHIST TEMPLE
(☎022-62427500; www.globalpagoda.org; Global Pagoda Rd, Borivali West; ⏲9am-7pm, meditation classes 9.30am-6.30pm) Rising up like a

Kalbadevi to Mahalaxmi

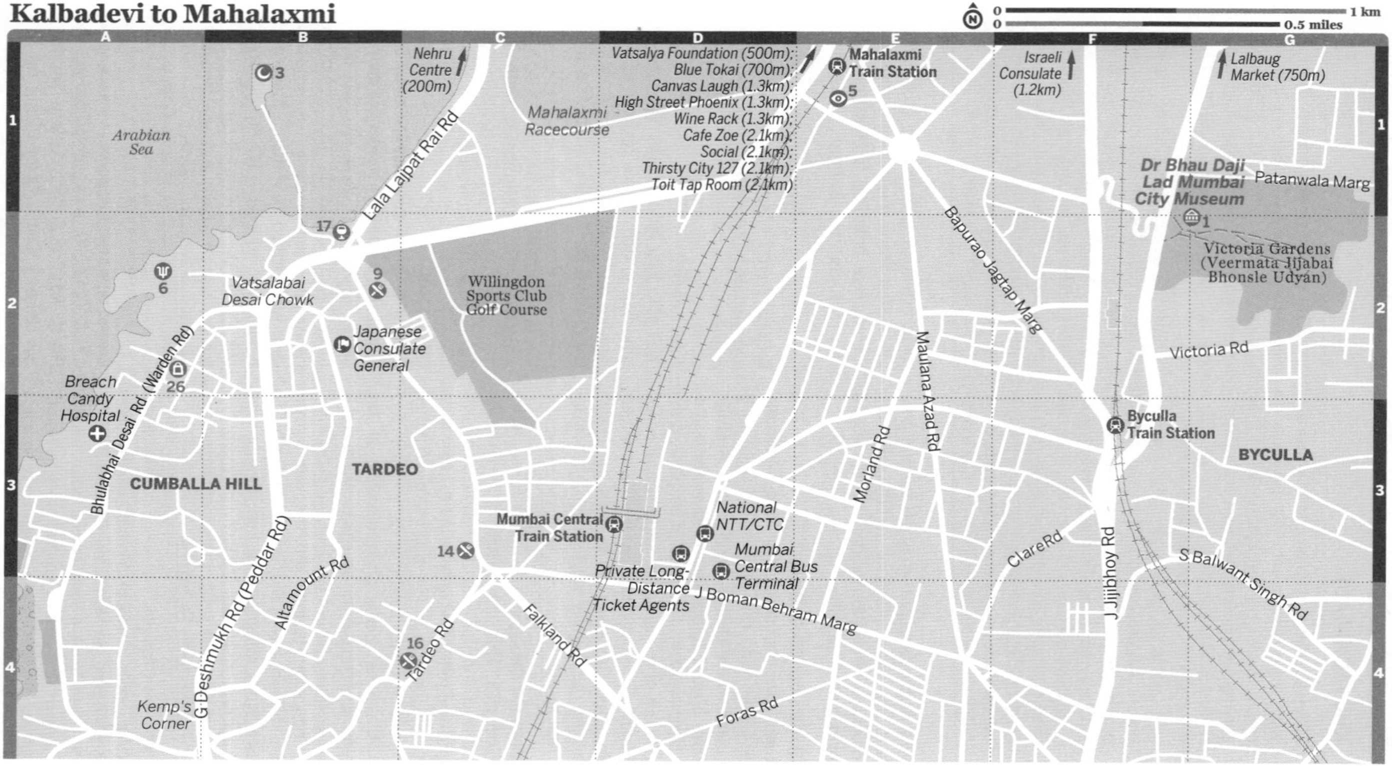
0 — 1 km
0 — 0.5 miles
A B C D E F G
1 2 3 4
Nehru Centre (200m)
Vatsalya Foundation (500m); Blue Tokai (700m); Canvas Laugh (1.3km); High Street Phoenix (1.3km); Wine Rack (1.3km); Cafe Zoe (2.1km); Social (2.1km); Thirsty City 127 (2.1km); Toit Tap Room (2.1km)
Mahalaxmi Train Station
Israeli Consulate (1.2km)
Lalbaug Market (750m)
Arabian Sea
Mahalaxmi Racecourse
Lala Lajpat Rai Rd
Dr Bhau Daji Lad Mumbai City Museum
Patanwala Marg
Victoria Gardens (Veermata Jijabai Bhonsle Udyan)
Bapurao Jagtap Marg
Willingdon Sports Club Golf Course
Vatsalabai Desai Chowk
Japanese Consulate General
Maulana Azad Rd
Victoria Rd
Breach Candy Hospital
Bhulabhai Desai Rd (Warden Rd)
Byculla Train Station
BYCULLA
CUMBALLA HILL
TARDEO
Morland Rd
Mumbai Central Train Station
National NTT/CTC
Mumbai Central Bus Terminal
Private Long-Distance Ticket Agents
G Deshmukh Rd (Peddar Rd)
Altamount Rd
Clare Rd
J Jijibhoy Rd
S Balwant Singh Rd
J Boman Behram Marg
Falkland Rd
Tardeo Rd
Foras Rd
Kemp's Corner
1 3 5 6 9 14 16 17 26

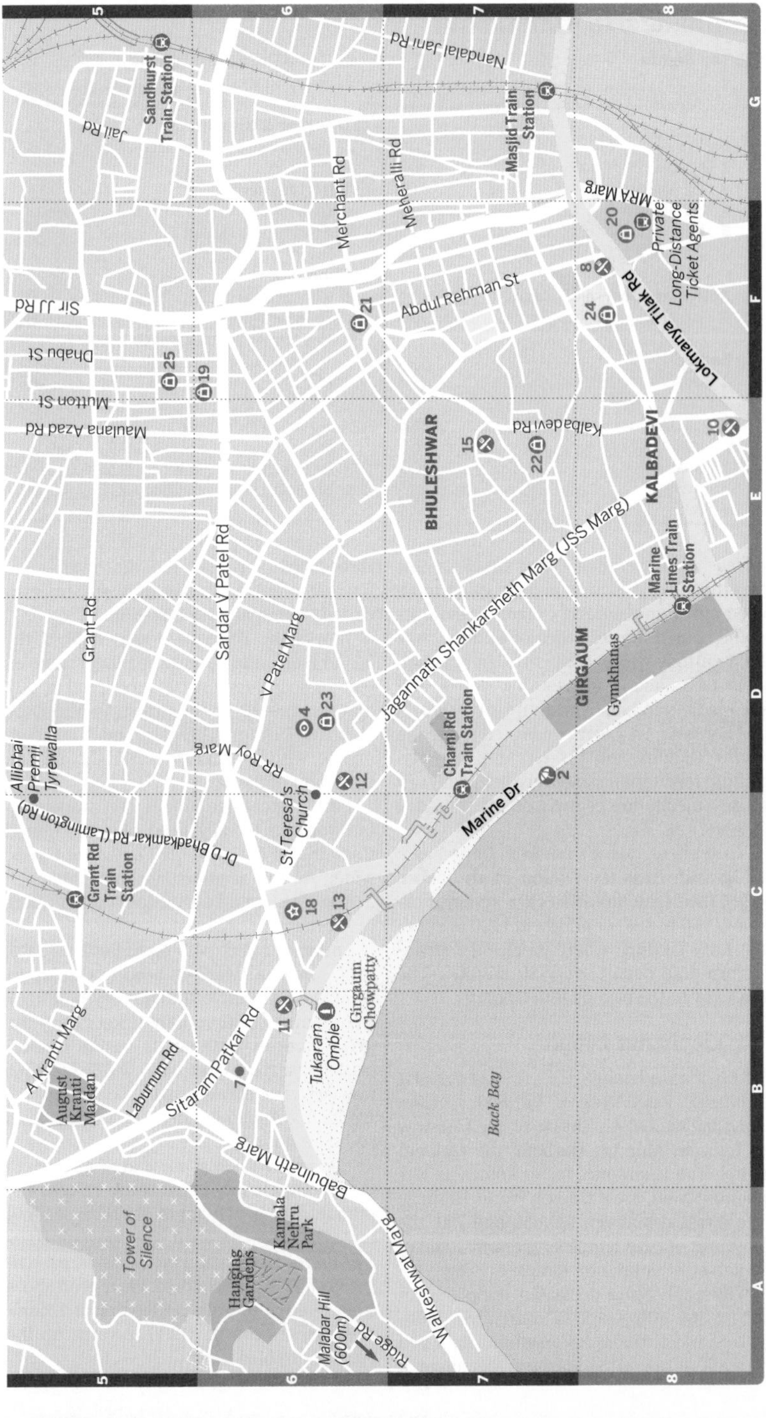
Sandhurst Train Station
Jail Rd
Nandalal Jani Rd
Masjid Train Station
Merchant Rd
Meheralli Rd
MRA Marg
Private Long-Distance Ticket Agents
Abdul Rehman St
Sir JJ Rd
Dhabu St
Mutton St
Maulana Azad Rd
Kalbadevi Rd
BHULESHWAR
KALBADEVI
Lokmanya Tilak Rd
Jagannath Shankarsheth Marg (JSS Marg)
Marine Lines Train Station
Sardar V Patel Rd
Grant Rd
V Patel Marg
GIRGAUM
Gymkhanas
Charni Rd Train Station
Marine Dr
RR Roy Marg
Allibhai Premji Tyrewalla
Dr D Bhadkamkar Rd (Lamington Rd)
St Teresa's Church
Grant Rd Train Station
Girgaum Chowpatty
Tukaram Omble
A Kranti Marg
August Kranti Maidan
Laburnum Rd
Sitaram Patkar Rd
Back Bay
Babulnath Marg
Tower of Silence
Kamala Nehru Park
Hanging Gardens
Walkeshwar Marg
Malabar Hill (600m)
Ridge Rd
25
19
21
24
8
20
15
22
10
4
23
12
2
18
13
11
7
A
B
C
D
E
F
G
5
6
7
8

Kalbadevi to Mahalaxmi

Top Sights
1 Dr Bhau Daji Lad Mumbai City Museum....G2

Sights
2 Girgaum Chowpatty....D7
3 Haji Ali Dargah....B1
4 Khotachiwadi....D6
5 Mahalaxmi Dhobi Ghat....E1
6 Shree Mahalaxmi Temple....A2

Activities, Courses & Tours
7 Bharatiya Vidya Bhavan....B6

Eating
8 Badshah Cold Drinks....F8
9 Cafe Noorani....B2
10 Kyani & Co....E8
11 New Kulfi Centre....B6
12 Panshikar....D6
13 Revival....C6
14 Sardar....C3
15 Shree Thakkar Bhojanalay....E7
16 Swati Snacks....C4

Drinking & Nightlife
17 Haji Ali Juice Centre....B2

Entertainment
Quarter....(see 18)
18 Royal Opera House....C6

Shopping
19 Chor Bazaar....F6
20 Crawford Market....F8
21 Haji Mohammad Bashir Oil Shop....F6
22 M/S KN Ajani....E7
23 No Borders....D6
24 No-Mad Fabric Shop....F8
Play Clan....(see 18)
25 Poster Stuff....F5
26 Shrujan....A2

mirage from polluted Gorai Creek is this breathtaking, golden 96m-high stupa modelled on Myanmar's Shwedagon Pagoda. Its dome, which houses relics of Buddha, was built entirely without supports using an ancient technique of interlocking stones, and the meditation hall beneath it seats 8000.

There's an art gallery dedicated to the life of the Buddha and his teaching. Twenty-minute meditation classes are held daily; an on-site meditation centre also offers 10-day courses.

To get here, take a train from Churchgate to Borivali (exit the station at the 'West' side), then take bus 294 (₹10), an autorickshaw (₹60 to ₹65) or an Uber (₹420 or so) to the ferry landing, where Esselworld ferries (return ₹50) depart every 30 minutes. The last ferry to the pagoda is at 5.30pm.

Elephanta Island

★Elephanta Island HINDU TEMPLE
(Gharapuri; Indian/foreigner ₹40/600; caves 9am-5pm Tue-Sun) Northeast of the Gateway of India in Mumbai Harbour, the rock-cut temples on Gharapuri, better known as Elephanta Island, are a Unesco World Heritage Site. Created between AD 450 and 750, the labyrinth of cave temples represent some of India's most impressive temple carving.

The main Shiva-dedicated temple is an intriguing latticework of courtyards, halls, pillars and shrines; its magnum opus is a 6m-tall statue of Sadhashiva, depicting a three-faced Shiva as the destroyer, creator and preserver of the universe, his eyes closed in eternal contemplation.

It was the Portuguese who dubbed the island Elephanta because of a large stone elephant near the shore (this collapsed in 1814 and was moved by the British to Mumbai's Jijamata Udyan). There's a small museum on-site, with informative pictorial panels on the origin of the caves.

Pushy, expensive guides are available – but you don't really need one as Pramod Chandra's *A Guide to the Elephanta Caves*, widely for sale, is more than sufficient.

The Elephanta Festival (p47) is held here in February.

Launches (Map p48; Apollo Bunder, Colaba; economy/deluxe ₹145/200) head to Gharapuri from the Gateway of India every half hour from 9am to 3.30pm. Buy tickets from the **MTDC booth** (Maharashtra Tourism Development Corporation; Map p48; 022-22841877; www.maharashtratourism.gov.in; 9am-3pm Tue-Sun) at Apollo Bunder. The voyage takes about an hour.

The ferries dock at the end of a concrete pier, from where you can walk or take the miniature train (₹10) to the stairway leading up to the caves (it's lined with souvenir stalls and patrolled by pesky monkeys). A passenger tax (₹5) is also charged. Wear good shoes (those opting to walk are looking at 1.2km). *Doli*-carriers charge ₹1200 to carry up the aged or disabled.

Activities

Mumbai has surprisingly good butterfly- and birdwatching opportunities. Sanjay Gandhi National Park (p77) is popular for woodland birds, while the mangroves of Godrej (13km east of Bandra) are rich in waders. The **Bombay Natural History Society** (BNHS; Map p60; ☎022-22821811; www.bnhs.org; Hornbill House, Colaba Causeway, Fort; ⏰9.30am-5.30pm Mon-Fri) runs excellent trips every weekend.

Outbound Adventure OUTDOORS
(☎9820195115; www.outboundadventure.com) Runs one-day rafting trips on the Ulhas River from July to early September (₹2300 per person). After a good rain, rapids can get up to Grade III+, though usually the rafting is calmer. Also organises guided nature walks, birdwatching, camping (from ₹2000 per person per day) and canoeing trips in the Western Ghats.

Antara Day Spa SPA
(☎022-66117777; https://theclubmumbai.com/room/antara-spa; 197 DN Nagar, Andheri West; 1hr massage from ₹2500; ⏰10am-7.30pm) Midrange day spa on private club grounds with skilled therapists offering a range of therapies and treatments, including Swedish, Thai and hot-stone massages. Nonguests must pay a ₹100/120 (week/weekend) entry fee.

Weekdays between 10.30am and 4pm nets a 30% discount on massages.

Palms Spa SPA
(Map p48; ☎022-66349898; www.thepalmsspaindia.com; ground fl, Dhanraj Mahal, Chhatrapati Shivaji Marg, Colaba; 1hr massage from ₹3400; ⏰10am-10pm) Indulge in a rub, scrub or tub at this long-standing Colaba spa. The exfoliating lemongrass and green-tea scrub is ₹2500.

Vatsalya Foundation VOLUNTEERING
(☎022-24962115; www.thevatsalyafoundation.org; Anand Niketan, King George V Memorial, off Dr E Moses Rd, Mahalaxmi) Works with Mumbai's street children; there are long- and short-term opportunities in teaching English, computer skills and sports.

Lok Seva Sangam VOLUNTEERING
(☎022-24070718; http://loksevasangam.org; D/1 Everard Nagar Eastern Express Hwy, Sion) Lok Seva Sangam has been working to improve lives in the city's slums since 1976. Medical staff who can speak Hindi/Marathi or those with fundraising skills are needed.

Yogacara YOGA
(Map p64; ☎022-26511464; www.yogacara.in; 1st fl, SBI Bldg, 18A New Kant Wadi Rd, Bandra West; ⏰yoga per class ₹700, massage 1hr from ₹1850, unlimited per week/month ₹1900/5600) Classic hatha and Iyengar yoga institute, with excellent massages and treatments; the Abhyangam rejuvenating massage is recommended. Ayurvedic cooking, meditation and chakra-healing classes are also offered sporadically.

Courses

★ **Flavour Diaries** FOOD & DRINK
(Map p64; ☎9820143404; www.flavourdiaries.com; 3rd fl, Rohan Plaza, 5th Rd, Khar West; session from ₹4000; ⏰11am-6pm) If you fancy some good food and a chance to make friends with local Mumbaikars, head to Flavour Diaries in Khar. This interactive cooking studio is spearheaded by renowned UK-born international chef Anjali Pathak, and courses cover everything from Asian and Indian cuisine to American, European and Mediterranean specialities.

★ **Yoga Institute** YOGA
(Map p64; ☎022-26122185; www.theyogainstitute.org; Shri Yogendra Marg, Prabhat Colony, Santa Cruz East; courses per 1st/2nd month from ₹700/500) At its peaceful leafy campus near Santa Cruz, the respected Yoga Institute has daily classes as well as weekend and week-long programs, and longer residential courses including teacher training (with the seven-day course a prerequisite).

Tours

★ **Khaki Tours** OUTDOORS
(Map p60; ☎8828100111; www.khakitours.com; 3rd fl, Hari Chambers, 58/64 Shadid Bhagat Singh Marg, Fort; walks from ₹4000, jeep rides from ₹10,000; ⏰9am-5pm) The best way to get under the skin of Mumbai is to meet and strike up a conversation with a true Mumbaikar. The tours developed by Bharat Gothoskar (and led by city ambassadors with regular day jobs) – city walks, food tours, sailing outings, 'urban safaris' by private jeep – showcase an unseen side of Mumbai in the name of awesomely coined 'heritage evangelism'.

★ **Reality Tours & Travel** TOURS
(Map p48; ☎9820822253; www.realitytoursandtravel.com; 1/26 Unique Business Service Centre, Akber House, Nowroji Fardonji Rd, Colaba; most tours ₹750-1700; ⏰8am-9pm) 🌿 Compelling

DHARAVI SLUM

Mumbaikars were ambivalent about the stereotypes in 2008's *Slumdog Millionaire*, but slums are very much a part of – some would say the foundation of – Mumbai city life. An astonishing 60% of Mumbai's population lives in slums, and one of the city's largest slums is Dharavi, originally inhabited by fisherfolk when the area was still creeks, swamps and islands. It became attractive to migrant workers from South Mumbai and beyond when the swamp began to fill in due to natural and artificial causes. It now incorporates 2.2 sq km of land sandwiched between Mumbai's two major railway lines, and is home to perhaps as many as a million people.

While it may look a bit shambolic from the outside, the maze of dusty alleys and sewer-lined streets of this city-within-a-city is actually a collection of abutting settlements. Some parts of Dharavi have mixed populations, but in other parts inhabitants from different regions of India, and with different trades, have set up homes and tiny factories. Potters from Saurashtra (Gujarat) live in one area, Muslim tanners in another; embroidery workers from Uttar Pradesh work alongside metalsmiths; while other workers recycle plastics as women dry pappadams in the searing sun. Some of these thriving industries, as many as 20,000 in all, export their wares, and the annual turnover of business from Dharavi is thought to exceed US$700 million.

Up close, life in the slums is fascinating to witness. Residents pay rent, most houses have kitchens and electricity, and building materials range from flimsy corrugated-iron shacks to permanent multistorey concrete structures. Perhaps the biggest issue facing Dharavi residents is sanitation, as water supply is irregular – every household has a 200L drum for water storage. Very few dwellings have a private toilet or bathroom, so some neighbourhoods have constructed their own (to which every resident must contribute financially) while other residents are forced to use run-down public facilities.

Many families have been here for generations, and education achievements are higher than in many rural areas: around 15% of children complete higher education and find white-collar jobs. Many choose to stay, though, in the neighbourhood they grew up in.

Slum tourism is a polarising subject, so you'll have to decide for yourself. If you opt to visit, the award-winning Reality Tours & Travel (p55) has an illuminating tour (from ₹900), and puts 80% of profits back into Dharavi social programs. They can also now arrange a meal with a local family for further insight. Photography is strictly forbidden.

Some tourists opt to visit on their own, which is OK as well – just don't take photos. Take the train from Churchgate station to Mahim, exit on the west side and cross the bridge into Dharavi.

To learn more about Mumbai's slums, check out Katherine Boo's 2012 book *Behind the Beautiful Forevers*, about life in Annawadi, a slum near the airport, and *Rediscovering Dharavi* (2000), Kalpana Sharma's sensitive and engrossing history of Dharavi's people, culture and industry.

tours of the Dharavi slum, with 80% of post-tax profits going to the agency's own NGO, Reality Gives (www.realitygives.org). Street-food, pottery, market, bicycle and sightseeing tours are also excellent.

Bombay Heritage Walks WALKING
(☎9821887321; www.bombayheritagewalks.com; per 2hr tour (up to 5 people) from ₹3750) Started by two enthusiastic architects and operating with a slew of architects, journalists and art historians, BHW has terrific tours of heritage neighbourhoods.

Mumbai Magic Tours TOURS
(☎9867707414; www.mumbaimagic.com; 2hr tour per 2/4 people from ₹1750/1500; ⏰10am-5pm Mon-Fri, to 2pm Sat) Designed by the authors of the fabulous blog Mumbai Magic (www.mumbai-magic.blogspot.com), these city tours focus on Mumbai's quirks, culture, community, food, bazaars, festivals, Jewish heritage and more.

Sleeping

Mumbai has the most expensive accommodation in India and you'll never quite feel like you're getting your money's worth.

Colaba is compact, has the liveliest tourist scene and many budget and midrange options, but hassles are greater there (hash dealers, beggars). The neighbouring Fort area is convenient for the main train stations and hip dining and shopping epicentre. Most top-end places are along Marine Dr and in the western suburbs.

🛏 Colaba

Backpacker Panda HOSTEL **$**
(Map p48; ☑ 9607900991; www.backpacker panda.com; 15 Walton Rd; dm ₹800-1200, d with AC ₹2600-4200; ❄ @ 🛜) Mumbai's best hostel fills four floors of a crusty, can't-miss-it grey-and-pastel-rosé residential building in Colaba, with tiled stairwells and other heritage accents. Four-, six- and eight-bed dorm configurations are spacious and boast air-con and lockers; private rooms are disappointingly simple, but all have fantastic modern bathrooms, a trend seen in the common bathrooms as well.

There's a rooftop lounge and game room as well as a smoking area, plus filtered water on every floor. No breakfast is served. The huge Garage Inc. Public House is in the same building. Also in **Andheri** (Map p64; ☑ 022-28367141; Shaheed Bhagat Singh Society; dm with AC ₹650-750; ❄ 🛜).

Sea Shore Hotel GUESTHOUSE **$**
(Map p48; ☑ 022-22874237; 4th fl, 1/49 Kamal Mansion, Arthur Bunder Rd; s/d without bathroom ₹700/1230; 🛜) This place is really making an effort, with small but immaculately clean and inviting rooms, all with flat-screen TVs, set off a railway-carriage-style corridor. Half the rooms even have harbour views (the others don't have a window). The modish communal bathrooms are well scrubbed and have a little gleam and sparkle. Wi-fi in the reception and *some* rooms.

★ YWCA GUESTHOUSE **$$**
(Map p48; ☑ 022-22025053; www.ywcaic.info; 18 Madame Cama Rd; s/d/tr with AC incl breakfast & dinner ₹2678/4457/6478; ❄ 🛜) Efficiently managed, and within walking distance of all the sights in Colaba and Fort, the YWCA is a good deal and justifiably popular. The spacious, well-maintained rooms boast desks, wardrobes and multichannel TVs. Tariffs include a buffet breakfast, dinner, a daily newspaper and bed tea. In addition to the room rates there's a one-time ₹59 membership fee.

★ Abode Bombay BOUTIQUE HOTEL **$$$**
(Map p48; ☑ 8080234066; www.abodeboutique hotels.com; 1st fl, Lansdowne House, MB Marg; d with AC incl breakfast ₹5310-14,975; ❄ 🛜) A terrific 20-room boutique hotel, stylishly designed with colonial-style and art deco furniture, reclaimed teak flooring and original artwork; the luxury rooms have glorious free-standing bathtubs. Staff are very switched on to travellers' needs, and breakfast is excellent, with fresh juice and delicious local and international choices. A little tricky to find, it's located behind the Regal Cinema.

★ Taj Mahal Palace, Mumbai HERITAGE HOTEL **$$$**
(Map p48; ☑ 022-66653366; https://taj.taj hotels.com; Apollo Bunder; s/d tower from ₹13,000/15,000, palace from ₹25,000/27,000; ❄ @ 🛜 ≋) The grande dame of Mumbai is one of the world's most iconic hotels and has hosted a roster of presidents and royalty. Sweeping arches, staircases and domes, and a glorious garden and pool ensure an unforgettable stay. Rooms in the adjacent tower lack the period details of the palace itself, but many have spectacular, full-frontal Gateway of India views. With a myriad of excellent in-house eating and drinking options, plus spa and leisure facilities, it can be a wrench to leave the hotel premises. There's even a small but discernibly curated art gallery. Heritage walks at 3.30pm daily (for guests) provide illuminating context about the hotel's role in the city's history.

Hotel Suba Palace HOTEL **$$$**
(Map p48; ☑ 022-22020636; www.subahotels. com/hotel/suba-palace; Battery St; s/d with AC incl breakfast from ₹5900/7320; ❄ 🛜) 'Palace' is pushing it slightly, but this modern, brilliantly located little place is certainly a comfortable choice with its contemporary decor: neutral tones from a 2015 upgrade keep the tasteful rooms teetering on modern. There's a good in-house restaurant, and foodie destination the Table (p63) shares the same location.

SLEEPING PRICE RANGES

The following price ranges refer to a double room and are inclusive of tax.

$ less than ₹3000

$$ ₹3000–7000

$$$ more than ₹7000

Fort Area & Churchgate

Traveller's Inn HOTEL $

(Map p60; 022-22644685; www.hoteltravellersinn.co; 26 Adi Marzban Path, Fort; dm with/without AC ₹700/600, d with/without AC ₹2300/1800;) On a quiet, tree-lined street, this small hotel is a very sound choice. It has clean, if tiny, rooms with cable TV and king-sized beds that represent good value. The two dorms are cramped (the non-AC one Hades-hot in summer; the AC one requires a minimum of three people) but are a steal for Mumbai. A new mosaic-floored hang-out space catches a nice breeze.

The location's excellent and staff are helpful. Breakfast is ₹100.

★ **Residency Hotel** HOTEL $$

(Map p60; 022-22625525; www.residencyhotel.com; 26 Rustom Sidhwa Marg, Fort; s/d with AC incl breakfast from ₹5080/5550;) The Residency is the kind of dependable place where you can breathe a sigh of relief after a long journey and be certain you'll be looked after well. It's fine value, too, with contemporary rooms, some boasting mood lighting, minibars, flat-screen TVs and hip en suite bathrooms. Best of all, staff are friendly, polite and understand the nuance of unforced hospitality. Its Fort location is also excellent, though noise is will be an issue through 2022 due to metro-station construction right outside its door. The best-run midranger in Mumbai.

Western & Northern Suburbs

Cohostel HOSTEL $

(Map p64; 9856564545; bandra@cohostels.com; 43 Chapel Rd, Bandra West; dm incl breakfast ₹800-1000;) Village-like Ranwar along Chapel Rd leads to Bandra's first noteworthy hostel, which occupies the top floor of a pre-Partition bungalow. Six six-bed dorms feature Australian-pine dorm beds, lockers, air-con and private baths, one of which is female-only. But it's the airy, spacious rooftop and kitchen (induction stovetops!) where you'll want to hang out. Coffee and tea are made to order.

★ **Juhu Residency** BOUTIQUE HOTEL $$

(Map p64; 022-67834949; www.facebook.com/JuhuResidency; 148B Juhu Tara Rd, Juhu; d with AC incl breakfast from ₹5900;) The aroma of sweet lemongrass greets you in the lobby at this excellent 18-room boutique hotel with an inviting atmosphere – and a fine location, five minutes' walk from Juhu beach. The chocolate-and-coffee colour scheme in the modish rooms works well, each room boasting marble floors, dark woods, artful bedspreads and flat-screen TVs. To top it all off, free airport pickups are included.

Iskcon GUESTHOUSE $$

(Map p64; 022-26206860; www.iskconmumbai.com/guest-house; Hare Krishna Land, Sri Mukteshwar Devalaya Rd, Juhu; s/d with AC ₹3550/4050, without AC ₹3150/3450;) An intriguing place to stay inside Juhu's lively Iskcon complex. Though the hotel building is a slightly soulless concrete block, some rooms enjoy vistas over the Hare Krishna temple compound. Spartan decor is offset by the odd decorative flourish such as Gujarati *sankheda* (lacquered country wood) furniture, and staff are very welcoming.

Anand Hotel HOTEL $$

(Map p64; 022-26203372; anandpremises@gmail.com; Gandhigram Rd, Juhu; s/d with AC from ₹2464/4130;) Yes, the decor's in 50 shades of beige but the Anand's rooms are comfortable, spacious and represent decent value, considering the prime location on a quiet street next to Juhu beach. The excellent in-house Dakshinayan restaurant (p68) scores highly for authentic, inexpensive meals, too. It's a particularly good deal for solo travellers.

★ **ITC Maratha** HOTEL $$$

(Map p64; 022-28303030; www.itchotels.in; Sahar Rd, Andheri East; s/d incl breakfast from ₹15,360/17,900;) This five-star, Leadership in Energy and Environmental Design (LEED) Platinum-certified hotel channels the most luxurious local character. The details are extraordinary: Muhammed Ali Rd–inspired *jharokas* (lattice windows) around the atrium, Maratha-influenced Resident's Bar (a guest-only level overlooking public areas), Warli painting–inspired tower rooms with fiery orange marble. The rooms, awash in lush colour schemes, exude Indian opulence. Peshawri (p68), Mumbai's most memorable Northwest Frontier restaurant, is located here.

★ **Taj Santacruz** BOUTIQUE HOTEL $$$

(Map p64; 022-62115211; https://taj.tajhotels.com/en-in/taj-santacruz-mumbai; Chhatrapati Shivaji International Airport (T1), Airport Rd, Santa Cruz East; s/d from ₹12,000/14,000;) Forget the 3500 hand-blown chandelier bulbs or the 75-species aquarium in the lobby of this newer hotel connected to the domestic airport

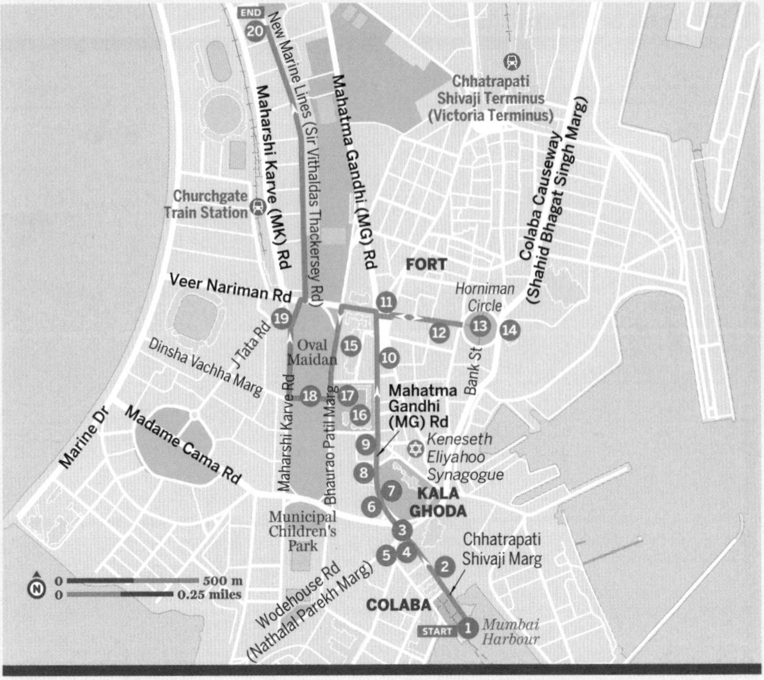

City Walk
Architectural Mumbai

START GATEWAY OF INDIA
END LIBERTY CINEMA
LENGTH 3.5KM; 1¾ HOURS

Mumbai's defining feature is its mix of colonial-era and art deco architecture. Starting from the ❶ **Gateway of India** (p48), walk up Chhatrapati Shivaji Marg past the art deco residential-commercial complex ❷ **Dhunraj Mahal**, towards ❸ **Regal Circle**. Walk the circle for views of the surrounding buildings, including the art deco ❹ **Regal Cinema** and ❺ **Majestic Hotel**, now the Sahakari Bhandar cooperative store. Continue up Mahatma Gandhi (MG) Rd, past the beautifully restored facade of the ❻ **National Gallery of Modern Art** (p50). Opposite is landmark ❼ **Chhatrapati Shivaji Maharaj Vastu Sangrahalaya** (p49), built in glorious Indo-Saracenic style. Back across the road is the 'Romanesque Transitional' ❽ **Elphinstone College** and the ❾ **David Sassoon Library & Reading Room** where members escape the afternoon heat lazing on planters' chairs on the upper balcony. Continue north to admire the vertical deco stylings of the ❿ **New India Assurance Company Building**. On an island ahead lies ⓫ **Flora Fountain**, depicting the Roman goddess of flowers. Turn east down Veer Nariman Rd, walking towards ⓬ **St Thomas' Cathedral** (p50). Ahead lies the stately ⓭ **Horniman Circle**, an arcaded ring of buildings laid out in the 1860s around a beautifully kept botanical garden. It's overlooked by the neoclassical ⓮ **Town Hall**, home to the Asiatic Society library. Backtrack to Flora Fountain, continuing west and turning south onto Bhaurao Patil Marg to see the august ⓯ **High Court** (Map p60; www.bombayhighcourt.nic.in; Eldon Rd; ⏲10.30am-5.30pm) and ornate ⓰ **University of Mumbai** (p50). The university's 84m-high ⓱ **Rajabai Clock Tower** (p50) is off limits for visitors, but is best observed from within the ⓲ **Oval Maidan**. Turn around to compare the colonial edifices with the row of art deco beauties lining Maharshi Karve (MK) Rd – notably the wedding-cake tower of the ⓳ **Eros cinema** (Map p60; www.eroscinema.co.in; Maharshi Karve Rd, Churchgate). Divert east to New Marine Lines and head 1km north to the ⓴ **Liberty Cinema**, a dazzling, 1200-capacity single-screen art deco gem opened in 1949.

Fort Area & Churchgate

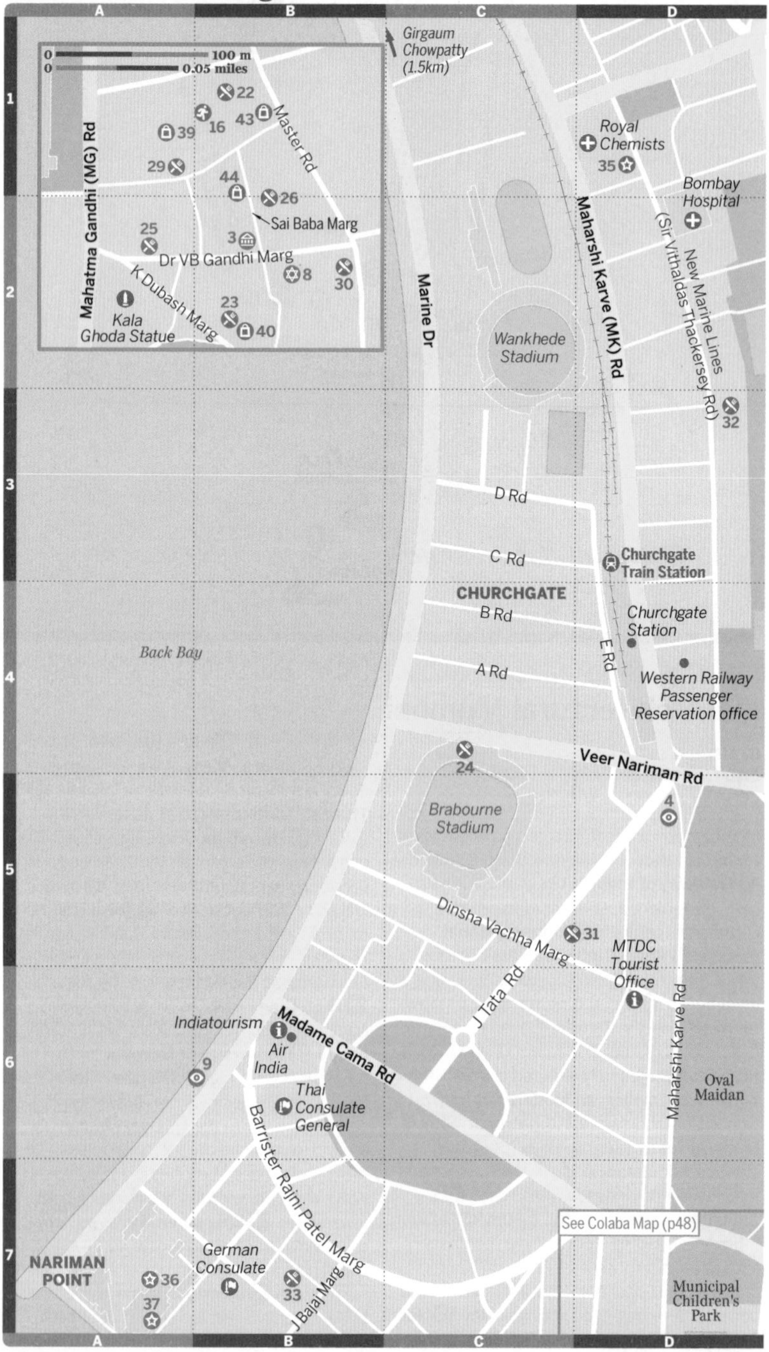

0 100 m
0 0.05 miles
Mahatma Gandhi (MG) Rd
Master Rd
Sai Baba Marg
Dr VB Gandhi Marg
K Dubash Marg
Kala Ghoda Statue
Girgaum Chowpatty (1.5km)
Royal Chemists
Bombay Hospital
Maharshi Karve (MK) Rd
New Marine Lines (Sir Vithaldas Thackersey Rd)
Marine Dr
Wankhede Stadium
D Rd
C Rd
B Rd
A Rd
E Rd
CHURCHGATE
Churchgate Train Station
Churchgate Station
Western Railway Passenger Reservation office
Back Bay
Veer Nariman Rd
Brabourne Stadium
Dinsha Vachha Marg
J Tata Rd
MTDC Tourist Office
Indiatourism
Air India
Madame Cama Rd
Thai Consulate General
Maharshi Karve Rd
Oval Maidan
Barrister Rajni Patel Marg
J Bajaj Marg
German Consulate
NARIMAN POINT
See Colaba Map (p48)
Municipal Children's Park

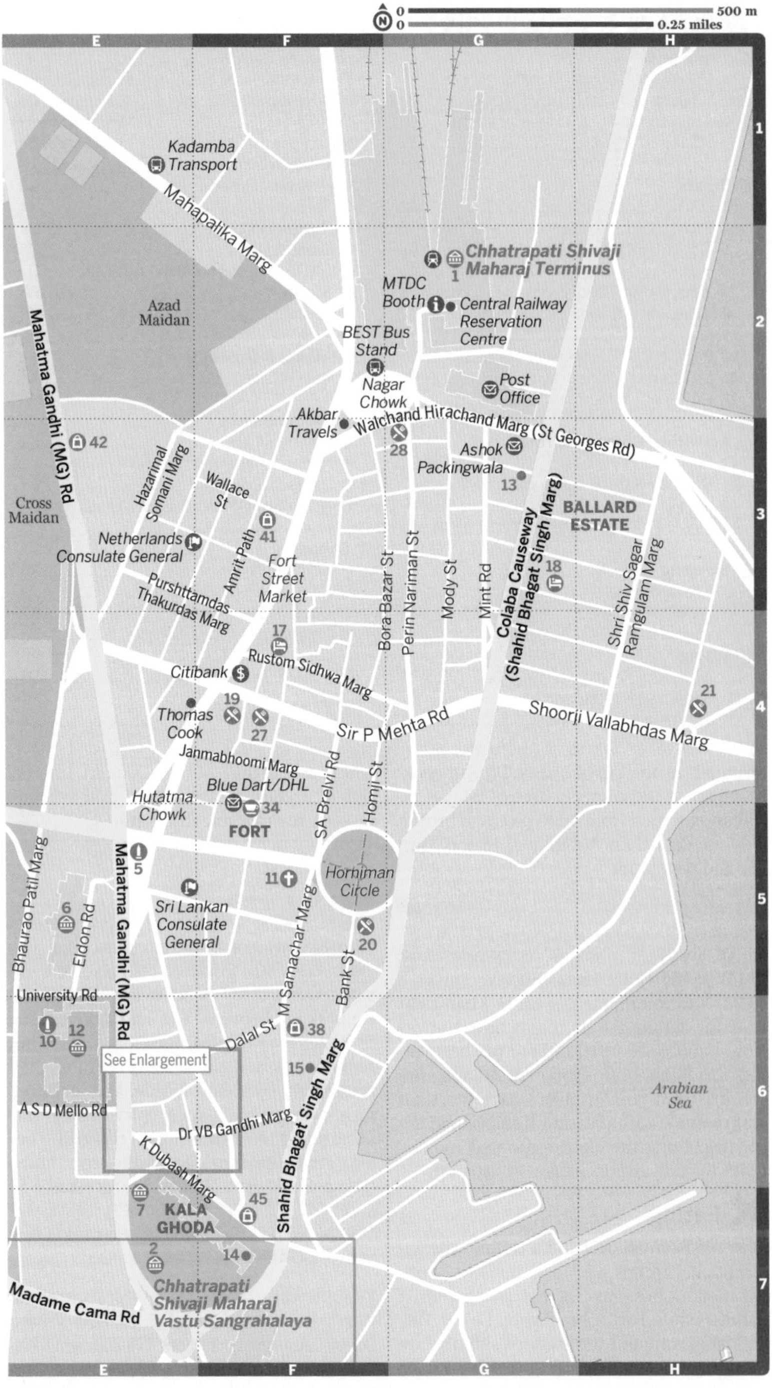
0 500 m
0 0.25 miles
N
E
F
G
H
1
2
3
4
5
6
7
Kadamba Transport
Mahapalika Marg
Chhatrapati Shivaji Maharaj Terminus
1
MTDC Booth
Central Railway Reservation Centre
Azad Maidan
BEST Bus Stand
Nagar Chowk
Post Office
Akbar Travels
Walchand Hirachand Marg (St Georges Rd)
28
Ashok Packingwala
13
Mahatma Gandhi (MG) Rd
42
Hazarimal Somani Marg
Wallace St
BALLARD ESTATE
Cross Maidan
41
Netherlands Consulate General
Amrit Path
Fort Street Market
Bora Bazar St
Perin Nariman St
Mody St
Mint Rd
Colaba Causeway (Shahid Bhagat Singh Marg)
18
Shri Shiv Sagar Ramgulam Marg
Purshttamdas Thakurdas Marg
17
Rustom Sidhwa Marg
Citibank
21
19
Thomas Cook
27
Sir P Mehta Rd
Shoorji Vallabhdas Marg
Janmabhoomi Marg
SA Brelvi Rd
Homji St
Blue Dart/DHL
34
Hutatma Chowk
FORT
Bhaurao Patil Marg
5
Mahatma Gandhi (MG) Rd
11
Horniman Circle
Sri Lankan Consulate General
6
Eldon Rd
M Samachar Marg
20
Bank St
University Rd
10
12
Dalal St
38
See Enlargement
15
Arabian Sea
A S D Mello Rd
Shahid Bhagat Singh Marg
Dr VB Gandhi Marg
K Dubash Marg
7
KALA GHODA
45
2
14
Chhatrapati Shivaji Maharaj Vastu Sangrahalaya
Madame Cama Rd

Fort Area & Churchgate

Top Sights
1 Chhatrapati Shivaji Maharaj Terminus G2
2 Chhatrapati Shivaji Maharaj Vastu Sangrahalaya E7

Sights
3 DAG B2
4 Eros D5
5 Flora Fountain E5
6 High Court E5
7 Jehangir Art Gallery E7
8 Keneseth Eliyahoo Synagogue B2
9 Marine Dr B6
10 Rajabai Clock Tower E6
11 St Thomas' Cathedral F5
12 University of Mumbai E6

Activities, Courses & Tours
13 Bollywood Tours G3
14 Bombay Natural History Society F7
15 Khaki Tours F6
16 Welfare of Stray Dogs B1

Sleeping
17 Residency Hotel F4
18 Traveller's Inn G3

Eating
19 A Taste of Kerala F4
20 Bademiya Restaurant F5
21 Britannia & Co. H4
22 Burma Burma B1
23 Chetana B2
24 K Rustom C4
25 Khyber A2
26 La Folie du Chocolate B2
27 Mahesh Lunch Home F4
28 Pancham Puriwala G3
29 Pantry A1
30 Rue du Liban B2
31 Samrat C5
32 SNDT to Cross Maiden Khao Gali D3
33 Suzette B7
Trishna .... (see 26)

Drinking & Nightlife
34 Raju Ki Chai F5

Entertainment
35 Liberty Cinema D1
36 National Centre for the Performing Arts A7
37 NCPA Box Office A7

Shopping
38 Bombay Paperie F6
39 Bombay Shirt Company A1
40 Chetana Book Centre B2
41 Chimanlals F3
42 Fashion Street E3
43 Kulture Shop B1
44 Nicobar B1
45 Sabyasachi F7

terminal. At the lap-of-luxury Taj Santacruz it's all about the gorgeous Tree of Life art installation forged from 4000 pieces of broken glass (a Rajasthani technique) in the Tiqri bar and restaurant.

Hotel Regal Enclave HOTEL $$$
(Map p64; 022-67261111; www.regalenclave.com; 4th Rd, Khar West; d with AC incl breakfast from ₹7670;) Hotel Regal Enclave enjoys a stellar location in a leafy part of Khar, right near the station (some rooms have railway views) and close to all of Bandra's best eating, drinking and shopping. Rooms are spacious and comfortable – save the tight bathrooms – with pleasant if unoriginal decor (excluding the eight renovated rooms). Rates include airport pickup or drop-off.

Eating

Flavours from all over India collide with international trends and taste buds in Mumbai. Colaba has most of the cheap tourist haunts, while Fort, Churchgate, Lower Parel, Mahalaxmi and the western suburbs are more upscale and trendy; it's these hoods where you'll find Mumbai's most international, expensive restaurants and see-and-be-seen gastronomic destinations.

Colaba

Bademiya Seekh Kebab Stall MUGHLAI, FAST FOOD $
(Map p48; www.bademiya.com; Tulloch Rd; light meals ₹130-250; 5pm-4am) These side-by-side, outrageously popular late-night street stalls (split between veg and nonveg) are in Bademiya's original location, where they remain a key Colaba hang-out for their trademark buzz and bustle and delicious meat-heavy menu. Expect spicy, fresh-grilled kebabs and tikka rolls hot off the grill. They also have sit-down restaurants in **Colaba** (Map p48; 19A Ram Mention, Nawroji Furdunji St; meals ₹80-370; 1pm-2am) and **Fort** (Map p60; 022-22655657; Botawala Bldg, Horniman Circle; mains ₹180-410; noon-1am).

Theobroma CAFE $$
(Map p48; www.theobroma.in; 24 Cusrow Baug, Colaba Causeway; confections ₹70-250, light meals ₹125-240; 9am-midnight;) Perfectly ex-

ecuted cakes, tarts and brownies go well with the coffee at this staple Mumbai patisserie. The pastries change regularly; if you're lucky, you'll find popular decadence like the chocolate-opium pastry, but it's all great. For brunch have the *akoori* (Parsi-style scrambled eggs) with green mango. The **Bandra branch** (Map p64; 33rd Rd, near Linking Rd; confections ₹70-250; ⌚8am-midnight; 📶) is big and airy, though with a smaller menu.

Bombay Vintage INDIAN **$$**
(Map p48; ☎022-22880017; www.facebook.com/bombayvintage; Regal Circle, Oriental Mansion Bldg, Madame Cama Rd; mains ₹350-970; ⌚noon-midnight; 📶) Brought to you by the same hospitality team as Woodside Inn (p70), **Pantry** (Map p60; www.thepantry.in; ground fl, Yashwanth Chambers, Military Square Ln, B Bharucha Marg, Kala Ghoda; breakfast ₹1275-345, mains ₹320-600; ⌚8.30am-11pm; 📶) and Miss T (p65), this cool throwback restaurant resurrects Bombay recipes of yore, often elevated versions of back-alley street food and dive-bar grub. Either way, you don't see a lot of options on this menu that pop up elsewhere, which is a refreshing change of pace for Colaba.

★**Bohri Kitchen** BOHRI **$$$**
(☎9819447438; www.thebohrikitchen.com; ₹1500; ⌚12.30pm Fri & Sat) Served up in a family home, this weekend-only pop-up dining experience was cooked up by former Google employee Munaf Kapadia. It showcases both the spectacular home cooking of his mother, Nafisa, and the unique cuisine of the Bohra Muslim community, which draws on influences from as far afield as Yemen and Gujarat. The concept was so successful that the Maharashtra Government even lifted the idea for an initiative to empower local communities and increase tourism through visitors' bellies! Predictably, the seven-course, home-dining experience is easily one of Mumbai's most magical. Nafisa's smoked mutton *kheema* samosas and 48-hour *raan* are always included in the weekly-changing menu, which is announced on Facebook.

You must book ahead and pay a deposit – this is not a traditional restaurant! – and the address is revealed 24 hours in advance. Then settle in for a special afternoon with the Kapadia family.

Indigo Delicatessen CAFE **$$$**
(Map p48; www.indigodeli.com; Pheroze Bldg, Chhatrapati Shivaji Marg; mains ₹665-710; ⌚8.30am-12.30am; 📶) A bustling and fashionable cafe-restaurant with cool tunes and wooden tables. The menu includes all-day breakfasts (₹300 to ₹710) and straightforward international classics like pork ribs, thin-crust pizza and inventive sandwiches. It's always busy, so service can get stretched.

Table FUSION **$$$**
(Map p48; ☎022-22825000; www.thetable.in; Kalapesi Trust Bldg, Apollo Bunder Marg; small plates ₹575-1200, mains ₹700-1375; ⌚noon-4pm & 11.30pm-1am, tea 4.30-6.30pm Mon-Sat, noon-4pm Sun; 📶) The market-fresh, globally inspired fusion menu, most of which was designed by former San Francisco chef Alex Sanchez, changes daily and does everything

THE PARSIS

Mumbai is home to the world's largest surviving community of Parsis, people of the ancient Zoroastrian faith, who fled Iran in the 10th century to escape religious persecution by the new Muslim rulers of Persia. 'Parsi' literally means Persian. Zoroastrians believe in a single deity, Ahura Mazda, who is worshipped at *agiari* (fire temples) across Mumbai, which non-Parsis are forbidden to enter. Parsi funeral rites are unique: the dead are laid out on open-air platforms to be picked over by vultures. The most renowned of these, the Tower of Silence, is located below the Hanging Gardens in Malabar Hill, yet screened by trees and hidden from public view.

The Mumbai Parsi community is extremely influential and successful, with a 98.6% literacy rate (the highest in the city). Famous Parsis include the Tata family (India's foremost industrialists), author Rohinton Mistry and Freddie Mercury. The best way for travellers to dig into the culture is by visiting one of the city's Parsi cafes. These atmospheric time capsules of a bygone era are a dying breed, but several sail on, including the excellent Britannia & Co. restaurant (p66), **Kyani and Co** (Map p52; 657 JSS Marg, Jer Mahal Estate, Marine Lines; snacks ₹10-180; ⌚7am-8.30pm Mon-Sat, to 6pm Sun) and tourist hotbed Cafe Mondegar (p70).

Western Suburbs

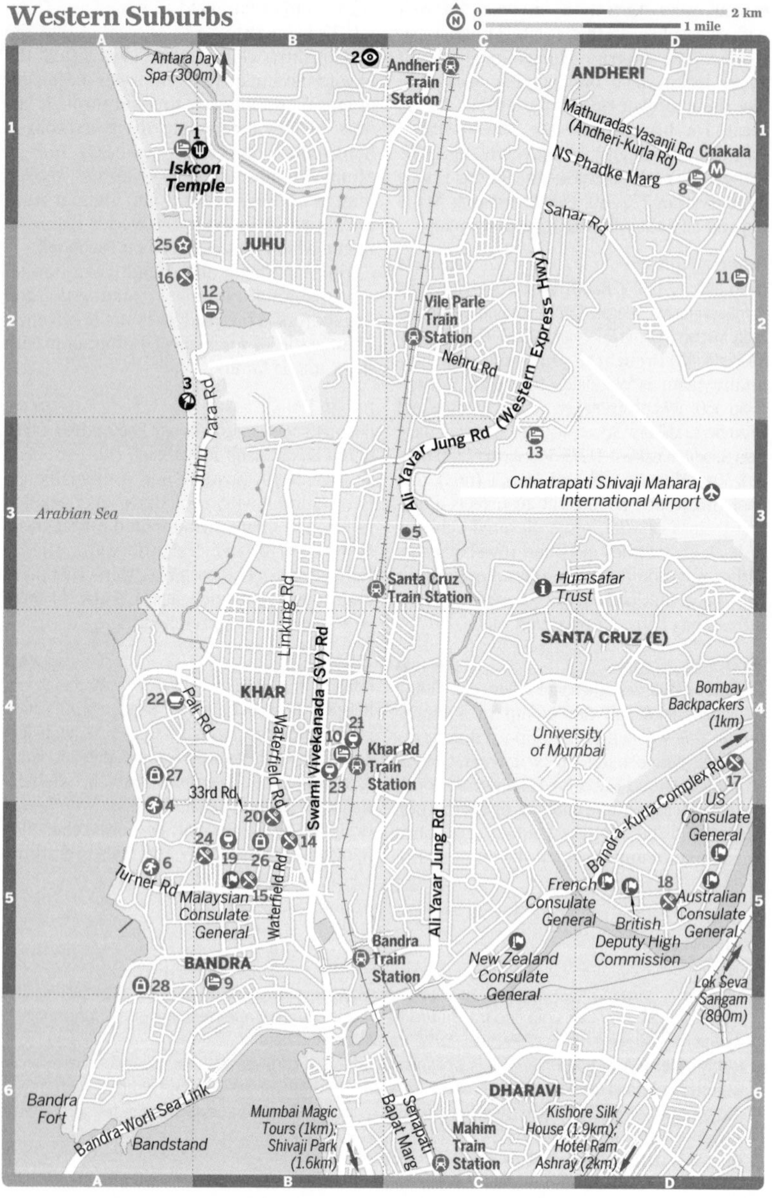

in its power to satisfy your cravings for a curry-free evening out. There's a lot to love: a crunchy kale salad with Iranian dates and toasted pistachios, zucchini spaghetti with almonds and Parmesan, and house-made black-truffle *taglierini*.

Basilico MEDITERRANEAN $$$
(Map p48; www.cafebasilico.com; Sentinel House, Arthur Bunder Rd; mains ₹320-680; ⌚9am-12.30am; 📶) Euro-style Basilico does decadent sweets and especially creative fare when it comes to vegans and vegetarians. There are exquisite salads (from ₹330) like quinoa, organic

Western Suburbs

avocado and papaya, and numerous other interesting options like veg Moroccan tagine. It draws a top-end Indian crowd. If you can walk past that hazelnut chocolate crunch cake without biting, you're better than us.

Miss T SOUTHEAST ASIAN $$$

(Map p48; 022-22801144; www.miss-t.in; 4 Mandalik Marg, Apollo Bunder; mains for 2 ₹700-2500; noon-3pm & 7.30pm-1am, bar from 6pm;) The Colaba Cartel, an impressive team of Mumbai foodies with a proven culinary track record including Pantry (p63), Woodside Inn (p70) and Table (p63), is the mind and manner behind Mumbai's coolest new restaurant. In a historic Mandalik Rd bungalow, Miss T's kitchen magicians include an executive chef from Hoi An (Vietnam) who draws menu inspiration equally from his neighbours (Thailand, Myanmar, Laos).

Fort Area & Churchgate

K Rustom SWEETS $

(Map p60; 87 Stadium House, Veer Nariman Rd, Churchgate; desserts ₹40-70; 9.30am-11pm Mon-Sat, 3-7pm Sun) K Rustom has nothing but a few metal freezers, but the ice-cream sandwiches here have been pleasing Mumbaikar palates since 1953. Pick from 50 flavours; roasted almond crunch is the bestseller.

Pancham Puriwala NORTH INDIAN $

(Map p60; 8/10 Perin Nariman St, Ballard Estate; mains ₹40-150; 8.30am-midnight) Located just outside CSMT, this budget eatery is a heritage icon, serving *puri bhaji* (puffed-up bread with a potato-and-pea curry) for over a century. The interiors are not fancy – there's no AC and diners sit on plain stainless benches – but the fun lies in listening to the stories of its owners, who set up this restaurant before the first train services started in India.

SNDT to Cross Maiden Khao Gali STREET FOOD $

(Map p60; Vitthaldas Thackersey Marg, Marine Lines; mains from ₹20-120; 11am-11pm) A heaven for food lovers, Mumbai's famous *khau galis* (literally 'eat lanes') pack in some tantalising street treats, serving up a potpourri of cuisines and historic influences. Students and office workers are lured to the *khau galli* running from SNDT to Cross Maidan by the popular Bombay Sandwich (a toastie made with cheese, chutney and masala spices) and Frankie (a roti rolled with vegetables).

★ **Shree Thakkar Bhojanalay** INDIAN $$

(Map p52; 022-22011232; www.facebook.com/shreethaker1945; 31 Dadisheth Agyari Ln, Marine Lines; thali week/weekend ₹500/600; 11.30am-3pm & 7-10.30pm Mon-Sat, 11.30am-3.30pm Sun) With a cult following and festive lavender

STREET EATS

Mumbai's street cuisine is vaster than many Western culinary traditions. Stalls tend to get started in late afternoon, when chai complements much of the fried deliciousness; items are ₹10 to ₹80.

Most street food is vegetarian. Chowpatty Beach is a great place to try Mumbai's famous *bhelpuri* (puffed rice tossed with fried rounds of dough, lentils, onions, herbs and chutneys). Stalls offering samosas, *pav bhaji* (spiced vegetables and bread), *vada pav* (deep-fried spiced lentil-ball sandwich), *bhurji pav* (scrambled eggs and bread) and *dabeli* (a mixture of potatoes, spices, peanuts and pomegranate, also on bread) are spread through the city.

For a meaty meal, Mohammed Ali and Merchant Rds in Kalbadevi are famous for kebabs. In Colaba, Bademiya Seekh Kebab Stall (p62) is a late-night Mumbai rite of passage, renowned for its chicken tikka rolls.

The office workers' district on the north side of Kala Ghoda is another good hunting ground for street snacks.

tables to boot, this thali mainstay – one of the oldest in the city – puts on the full-court flavour with its never-ending Gujarati/Rajasthani set meals, full of *farsans* (bite-size snacks) and scrumptious veg curries. The air-con environs are a welcome retreat from the busy congestion below. It has been open since 1945.

La Folie du Chocolate CAFE **$$**
(Map p60; www.lafolie.in; 16 Commerce House, Rope Walk Ln, Kala Ghoda; cakes ₹240-300; ⏲9am-11.30pm) Chocoholics and cake fetishists look no further – this minuscule Kala Ghoda place will seduce and hook you. Owner Sanjana Patel spent seven years in France studying the art of pastry- and chocolate-making, which was obviously time well spent. Try the Intense Caramel with Haitian chocolate mousse, burnt caramel crème brûlée and butterscotch praline. Koinonia coffee is served – even in keto-butter style.

Samrat GUJARATI **$$**
(Map p60; www.prashantcaterers.com/samrat; Prem Court bldg, J Tata Rd, Churchgate; thali lunch/dinner ₹345/450; ⏲noon-11pm) Samrat has an à la carte menu but most rightly opt for the famous Gujarati thali – a cavalcade of taste and texture, sweetness and spice that includes numerous curries and chutneys, curd, rotis and other bits and pieces. Samrat is air-conditioned and beer is available.

A Taste of Kerala KERALAN **$$**
(Map p60; Prospect Chambers Annex, Pitha St, Fort; mains ₹105-455, thali from ₹120-160; ⏲9am-midnight) An inexpensive Keralan eatery with lots of coconut and southern goodness on the menu. Try one of the epic thalis, served on a banana leaf and priced higher at ₹250 on Sundays. There are also seafood specials like prawn-pepper masala. Don't skip the *payasam* (rice pudding with jaggery and coconut milk) for dessert.

Britannia & Co. PARSI **$$**
(Map p60; Wakefield House, 11 Sport Rd, Ballard Estate; mains ₹200-950; ⏲noon-4pm Mon-Fri, to 10pm Sat) This Parsi institution is the domain of 97-year-old Boman Kohinoor, who will warm your heart with his stories (and he still takes the orders!). The signature dishes are the *dhansak* (meat with curried lentils and rice) and the berry *pulao* – spiced and boneless mutton or chicken, veg or egg, buried in basmati rice and tart barberries imported from Iran. Cash only.

Rue du Liban LEBANESE **$$**
(Map p60; ☎022-30151205; 43, Sasoon Bldg, VB Gandhi Marg, Kala Ghoda; small plates ₹550-800, mains ₹850-950; ⏲noon-4pm & 7pm-midnight) Moodily lit, art deco–era Beirut-inspired interiors complement the hyperauthentic dishes of the Levant in this sexy Kala Ghoda newcomer. The hummus? Texture-perfect, a precedent followed with lovely *moutabel* (charred eggplant puree with pomegranate, spring onion and sumac), the crunchy, Middle Eastern–authentic falafel, and a long list of excellent hot and cold meze.

Suzette FRENCH **$$**
(Map p60; www.facebook.com/suzette.cafe; Atlanta Bldg, Vinayak K Shah Marg, Nariman Point; meals ₹390-700; ⏲9am-10.30pm Mon-Sat, 11am-5.30pm Sun; 📶) 🍃 Relaxed Parisian-style place steeped where possible in organically sourced ingredients. Delectable crêpes, croques, salads, juices and soothing lounge music attract flocks of foreigners in need of a curry recess. On the crêpe front, sweet tooths should try the organic jaggery (₹120); for a savoury flavour, order a croque feta with tomato, mozzarella, creamed spinach and feta (₹490).

The **Bandra West branch** (Map p64; www.facebook.com/suzette.cafe; St John St, Pali Naka; mains 120-760; ⏲9am-10.30pm) has outdoor seating and is open daily.

★Khyber MUGHLAI, INDIAN $$$
(Map p60; ☎022-40396666; www.khyberrestaurant.com; 145 MG Rd; mains ₹590-1110; ⏲12.30-4pm & 7.30-11.30pm) The much-acclaimed Khyber has a Northwest Frontier–themed design that incorporates murals depicting turbaned Mughal royalty, lots of exposed brickwork and oil lanterns – just the sort of place an Afghan warlord might feel at home. The meat-centric menu features gloriously tender kebabs, rich curries and lots of tandoori favourites roasted in the Khyber's famous red-masala sauce.

★Trishna SEAFOOD $$$
(Map p60; ☎022-22703214; Ropewalk Ln, Kala Ghoda; mains ₹460-1830; ⏲noon-3.30pm & 6.30pm-midnight) Behind a modest entrance on a quiet Kala Ghoda lane is this often-lauded, intimate South Indian seafood restaurant. It's not a trendy place – the decor is old school, the seating a little cramped and the menu perhaps too long – but the cooking is superb. Witness the Hyderabadi fish tikka, jumbo prawns with green-pepper sauce, and the outstanding king crab and lobster dishes.

Burma Burma BURMESE $$$
(Map p60; ☎022-40036600; www.burmaburma.in; Oak Ln, off MG Rd, Kala Ghoda; meals ₹360-490; ⏲noon-2.45pm & 7-11pm; 📶) A sleek, stylish restaurant that marries contemporary design with a few traditional artefacts (prayer wheels line one wall), providing a beautiful setting for the cuisine of Myanmar (Burma). The menu is well priced, intricate and ambitious, with inventive salads (the pickled tea leaf is extraordinary), curries and soups: *Oh no khow suey* is a glorious coconut-enriched noodle broth. No alcohol.

Mahesh Lunch Home SEAFOOD $$$
(Map p60; ☎022-22023965; www.maheshlunchhome.com; 8B Cowasji Patel Rd, Fort; mains ₹200-750; ⏲11.30am-4pm & 6-11pm) A great place to try Mangalorean or Chinese-style seafood in Mumbai. It's renowned for its ladyfish, pomfret, lobster, crab (try it with butter garlic pepper sauce) and anything else out of the sea.

There's also a bigger **Juhu branch** (Map p64; ☎022-66955554; Juhu Tara Rd; mains ₹275-1475; ⏲12-3.30pm & 7pm-12.30am; 📶) with an extended menu.

Kalbadevi to Mahalaxmi

Badshah Cold Drinks INDIAN $
(Map p52; www.badshahcolddrinks.com; 52/156 Umrigar Bldg, Lokmanya Tilak Marg, Lohar Chawl; snacks & drinks ₹38-240; ⏲7am-12.30am) Opposite Crawford Market, Badshah has been serving snacks, fruit juices and its famous *falooda* (rose-flavoured drink of milk, cream, nuts and vermicelli), *kulfi falooda* (with ice cream) and *kesar pista falooda* (with saffron and pistachios) to hungry bargain hunters since 1905. A must.

New Kulfi Centre ICE CREAM $
(Map p52; 556 Marina Mansion, Sukh Sagar, Sardar V Patel Rd, Girgaon; kulfi per 100g ₹50-100; ⏲9.30am-1am) Serves 36 flavours of the best *kulfi* (Indian firm-textured ice cream) you'll have anywhere. Killer flavours include pistachio, *malai* (cream) and mango.

Swati Snacks FAST FOOD $
(Map p52; www.swatisnacks.com; 248, Karai Estate, Tardeo Rd, Tardeo; snacks ₹20-310, mains ₹135-315; ⏲noon-10.45pm) Get in line for the upscale street food at this Mumbaikar classic, dishing up mostly Gujarati specialities since 1963. Amid minimalist, industrial aluminium diner-like tables offset by wooden banquettes, tasty treats like *panki chatni* (banana leaf–steamed savoury-rice pancakes), *mung dal chilla* (mung-dal pancakes) and *sabudana khichdi* (soaked sago cooked with coconut, green chilli and spices) are worth the wait.

Sardar STREET FOOD $
(Map p52; 166A Tardeo Rd Junction, Tulsiwadi; pav bhaji from ₹140; ⏲noon-2am) If you're spooked about Indian street food, try one of the city's most beloved street staples, *pav bhaji,* at this Mumbai institution. The curried-veg mix is cooked to death on a series of scalding *tawas* (hotplates) and served with a butter floater the size of a Bollywood ego. Get in line; the entire restaurant turns over at once.

Panshikar INDIAN $
(Map p52; www.panshikarfoods.com; Mohan Bldg, Jagannath Shankar Sheth Rd, Girgaon; snacks ₹40-80; ⏲9am-9pm-Sat) This clean and wonderful cheapie near Khotachiwadi is an excellent spot for snacks any time of day, but it all goes down especially well at breakfast. *Subudani wadi* (fried pearl-tapioca balls), *misal pav* (spicy bean sprouts and pulses), *potato wada* (mashed-potato patty), *kothimbir vadi* (crispy gram flour, coriander leaves and spices) – it's all excellent.

Wash it down with a masala chai or *kokum sharbat* (kokum juice).

★ Revival INDIAN $$

(Map p52; 39B Chowpatty Seaface, Chowpatty; thali ₹450; noon-3.30pm & 7-11.30pm;) Waiters at this thali mecca saunter around Chowpatty sea-view digs in silken dhotis, filling your plates with dozens of delectable (veg-only) curries, sides, chutneys, rotis and rice dishes in an all-you-can-eat gastronomic onslaught. The dishes change daily and, all said and done, is probably Mumbai's best thali.

Cafe Noorani MUGHLAI $$

(Map p52; www.cafenoorani.com; Tardeo Rd, Haji Ali Circle; mains ₹80-575; 8am-midnight) Inexpensive, old-school eatery that's a requisite stop before or after visiting Haji Ali Dargah (p50). Mughlai and Punjabi staples dominate, with kebabs chargrilled to perfection and great biryani; try the chicken tikka biryani (₹330).

Western Suburbs

★ Hotel Ram Ashraya SOUTH INDIAN $

(Bhandarkar Rd, King's Circle, Matunga East; light meals ₹40-90; 5am-9.30pm) In the Tamil enclave of King's Circle, 80-year-old Ram Ashraya is beloved by southern families for its spectacular dosas, *idli* (spongy, round, fermented rice cake) and *uttapa* (pancake with toppings). Filter coffee is strong and flavoursome. The menu changes daily. It's just outside Matunga Rd train station's east exit and draws Mumbaikars of all persuasions.

Hoppumm SRI LANKAN $

(Map p64; 8, Rafi Mansion, 28th Rd, Bandra West; mains ₹180-300; 11.30-3.30pm & 7.30-11.30pm) Mumbai's best new budget eats are served up in this tiny – four tables and a counter – hipsterised Sri Lankan joint. It does absolutely delicious prawn *moilee* (seafood curry) and Ceylon roasted-chicken curries, served in hoppers (bowl-shaped, *appam* pancakes made from fermented rice flour and coconut milk) served alongside Keralan chutney-and-onion sambal. Portions aren't huge, so don't be afraid to order two items.

★ Dakshinayan SOUTH INDIAN $$

(Map p64; Anand Hotel, Gandhi Gram Rd, Juhu; mains ₹100-280; 11am-11pm Mon-Fri, from 8am Sat & Sun) With *rangoli* (elaborate designs) on the walls, servers in lungis, and sari-clad women lunching (*chappals* – sandals – off under the table), Dakshinayan channels Tamil Nadu. There are delicately textured dosas, *idli* and *uttapam,* village-fresh chutneys and perhaps the best *rasam* (tomato soup with spices and tamarind) in Mumbai. Finish off with a South Indian filter coffee, served in a stainless-steel set.

Chilli-heads should order *molagapudi idli,* a dozen *idli* coated in 'gunpowder' (potent spices).

★ Kitchen Garden by Suzette CAFE $$

(Map p64; www.facebook.com/KitchenGardenbySuzette; 9 Gasper Enclave, St John's St, Bandra West; light meals ₹360-770; 9am-11pm;) From the same French trio that brought us Suzette (p66) comes this superb organic cafe, a haven of health and homesick-remedying salads, sandwiches, cold-press juices and coffee sourced from local cooperatives and organic farms around Maharashtra and worldwide. The burrata, made by an American Indian Hare Krishna in Gujarat, is outstanding, but then again, so is everything.

O Pedro GOAN $$$

(Map p64; 022-26534700; www.opedromumbai.com; BKC Bldg, No 2, Bandra Kurla Complex, Bandra East; mains ₹295-1400;) The first restaurant that makes it worth venturing into the Bandra Kurla Complex just to eat. The elevated Goan dishes are fantastic: spicy chorizo *bhakri* tacos, creamy seabass ceviche with tamarind, stir-fried prawn *sukhhe* with fresh coconut, Goa chillies and tamarind, fried *rawas* stuffed with green chilli-coconut chutney – it's all an explosion of flavour and spice and everything nice.

★ Peshawri NORTH INDIAN $$$

(Map p64; 022-28303030; www.itchotels.in; ITC Maratha, Sahar Rd, Andheri East; mains ₹1600-3225; 12.45-2.45pm & 7-11.45pm) Make this Northwest Frontier restaurant, outside the international airport, your first or last stop in Mumbai. It's a carbon copy of Delhi's famous **Bukhara** (011-26112233; ITC Maurya, Sardar Patel Marg; mains ₹1500-3000; 12.30-2.45pm & 7-11.30pm; M Durgabai Deshmukh South Campus), with the same menu and decor. Folks flock here for the buttery dhal *bukhara,* a 24-hour simmered black dhal (₹945), but don't miss kebabs. Try the Murgh Malai (marinated tandoor-grilled chicken) and *raan* (impossibly succulent slow-roasted lamb hock).

★ Bastian SEAFOOD $$$

(Map p64; www.facebook.com/bastianmumbai; B/1, New Kamal Bldg, Linking Rd, Bandra West;

DABBA-WALLAHS

A small miracle of logistics, Mumbai's 5000 *dabba-wallahs* (literally 'food-container person'; also called tiffin wallahs) work tirelessly to deliver hot lunches to office workers throughout the city (and to the poor later on in the evenings, a 2015 initiative).

Lunch boxes are picked up each day from restaurants and homes and carried on heads, bicycles and trains to a centralised sorting station. A sophisticated system of numbers and colours (many wallahs don't read) identifies the destination of each lunch. More than 200,000 meals are delivered – always on time, come (monsoon) rain or (searing) shine.

This system has been used for over a century and there's only about one mistake per six million deliveries. (In a 2002 analysis, *Forbes Magazine* found that the *dabba-wallahs* had a six-sigma, or 99.999999%, reliability rating.) The system was also the subject of a Harvard Business School study in 2010 and a hit feature film in 2013 (*The Lunchbox*).

Look for these master messengers midmorning at Churchgate and Chhatrapati Shivaji Maharaj Terminus (CSMT) stations.

mains for 2 ₹1100-3200; noon-3pm & 7pm-midnight;) All the praise bestowed upon this trendy seafooder is indisputably warranted. Chinese-Canadian chef Boo Kwang Kim and his culinary sidekick, American-Korean Kelvin Cheung, have forged an East-meets-West gastronomic dream. Go with the market-fresh side menu: choose your catch (prawns, fish, mud crab or lobster) then pick from an insanely difficult list of impossibly tasty pan-Asian sauces.

★Bombay Canteen INDIAN **$$$**
(022-49666666; www.thebombaycanteen.com; Process House, Kamala Mills, SB Marg, Lower Parel; small plates ₹225-650, mains ₹450-975; noon-1am;) Bombay Canteen is one of Mumbai's hottest restaurants, courtesy of former New York chef and *Top Chef Masters* winner Floyd Cardoz, and executive chef Thomas Zacharias, who spent time at New York's three-Michelin-star Le Bernardin. India-wide regional dishes and traditional flavours dominate – Kejriwal toast, Goan pulled-pork-vindaloo tacos, mustard chicken curry – each dish an explosion of texture and flavour.

Koko SUSHI **$$$**
(8451011124; www.facebook.com/KOKOAsianGastropub; C2, Trade World, ground fl, Kamala Mills, SB Rd, Lower Parel; sushi rolls ₹900-1350, mains ₹590-3100; 12.30-4.30pm & 7pm-12.30am Mon-Thu, to 1am Fri & Sat;) Creative cocktails at this hot Asian gastrobar include the Tom Yum Cup (basically a tom yam soup laced with vodka), mixed by genuinely talented and friendly bartenders at the lengthy Burmese teak bar. Fantastic sushi – try the wild Japanese salmon truffle roll – and pan-Asian dishes come from Eric Sifu, a Chinese chef from Malaysia with Michelin on his resume. Reservations essential; style recommended.

Masala Library MODERN INDIAN **$$$**
(Map p64; 022-66424142; www.masalalibrary.co.in; ground fl, First International Financial Centre, G Block, BKC Rd, Bandra East; mains ₹575-1250, tasting menu ₹2500-2700, with wine ₹4250-4450; noon-2.15pm & 7-11pm) Daring and imaginative Masala Library dangles the contemporary Indian carrot to foodies and gastronauts, challenging them to rethink their notions of subcontinent cuisine. The tasting menus are an exotic culinary journey – think wild-dehydrated-mushroom chai with truffle-oil crumbs; langoustine *moilee* (seafood curry) with gunpowder mash; and a betel-leaf fairy floss to finish. Reservations essential.

Drinking & Nightlife

Colaba is rich in unpretentious pub-like joints (but also has some very classy places), while Bandra, Juhu and Andheri are home turf for the film and model set. Lower Parel has become a gourmet-dining hub, while the best craft-beer places are now way the hell up in Andheri. Wednesday and Thursday are big nights at some clubs, as well as the traditional Friday and Saturday; there's usually a cover charge. Dress codes apply, so don't rock up in shorts and sandals. Many places deny entry to men on their own. The trend in Mumbai is towards resto-lounges as opposed to full-on nightclubs. You're also technically supposed to have a licence to drink in Maharashtra; some bars require you to buy a temporary one, for a nominal fee, though we've never been asked.

CRAFT BREW MUMBAI

Few visitors to India would argue that an ice-cold Kingfisher in a dingy, smoke-filled bar isn't a quintessential Indian experience, but craft-beer connoisseurs might also add that India's ubiquitous native lager gets old pretty quick. And then there's those distinctly disgusting YouTube videos of oily, urine-coloured *something* being drained from beer bottles before drinking (it's usually glycerine, widely used in Indian beers as a preservative). Cheers? Not really.

While certainly late to the craft-brew boozefest, Mumbai has finally embraced hop-heavy IPAs, roasty, chocolatey porters and refreshing saisons, thanks to the city's very own craft-beer wallah, American expat Greg Kroitzsh. Kroitzsh opened Mumbai's first microbrewery, the now-shuttered Barking Deer, in 2013, and the taps began flowing in Mumbai as they already had been for some time in craftier Indian cities like Pune, Bangalore and Gurgaon.

Fancy a pint? Hoptimists now head north. In Andheri West, Independence Brewing Company (p71) and **Brewbot** (www.brewbot.in; Morya Landmark 1, off New Link Rd; pint ₹295; ⏲4pm-1am Mon-Fri, noon-1am Sat; 🛜), and the 16-tap **Woodside Inn** (Map p48; www.facebook.com/WoodsideInn; Indian Mercantile Mansion, Wodehouse Rd; ⏲11am-1.30am; 🛜) in Colaba, are within pub-crawl range of each other and are worth the journey, as is the good-time Doolally Taproom (p71) in Khar (also in Andheri and Kemps Corner) and the **Gateway Taproom** (Map p64; www.gatewaybrewery.com; BKC Bldg, No 3, G Block Bandra Kurla Complex; ⏲noon-1.30am; 🛜) in Bandra East. In Lower Parel, **Toit Tap Room** (www.toit.in; Zeba Centre, Mathuradas Mill Compound, Senapati Bapat Marg; ⏲noon-1.30am; 🛜) – a Bangalore transplant – is one of Mumbai's liveliest beer destinations; and Thirsty City 127 (p71) does tasty work next door in a more upscale ambience with the ex-Barking Deer brewer and a Sheffielder master brewer.

It's only a matter of time before taps start flowing in Fort and Colaba as well. The best of the production-only craft beer includes Pune's Great State Ale Works (www.facebook.com/greatstate.aleworks), which often holds tap takeovers in Mumbai (its salted kokum ale is one of India's best craft brews). White Owl (www.whiteowl.in), which has closed its excellent taproom to concentrate on bottling, is also worth seeking out.

The city's signature brew has quickly become Belgian Wit – citrusy and refreshing, it's a perfect accompaniment for hot and humid Mumbai.

Colaba

Cafe Mondegar PUB

(Map p48; www.facebook.com/cafemondegar; Metro House, 5A Colaba Causeway; ⏲7.30am-11.30pm) Iranian-founded 'Mondy's' has been drawing a heady mix of foreigners and locals since 1871. It's first and foremost a rowdy bar serving ice-cold mugs of Kingfisher (₹220), but don't discount its wide range of American, English and Parsi breakfast choices (₹130 to ₹350).

Harbour Bar BAR

(Map p48; www.tajhotels.com/en-in/taj/taj-mahal-palace-mumbai/restaurants; Taj Mahal Palace, Apollo Bunder; ⏲11am-11.45pm) With unmatched views of the Gateway of India and harbour, this timeless bar inside the Taj Mahal Palace is an essential visit. Drinks aren't uberexpensive (from ₹500/700/750 for a beer/wine/cocktail) given the surrounds and the fact that they come with very generous portions of nibbles, including jumbo cashews.

Leopold Café BAR

(Map p48; www.leopoldcafe.com; cnr Colaba Causeway & Nawroji F Rd; ⏲7.30am-1am) Love it or hate it, most tourists end up at this clichéd Mumbai travellers' institution at one time or another. Around since 1871, Leopold's has wobbly ceiling fans, a rambunctious atmosphere conducive to swapping tales with strangers, and an upstairs DJ most nights from 8pm.

Hammer & Song COCKTAIL BAR

(www.flamboyante.in; Shop 10, The Arcade, World Trade Centre, Cuffe Parade; ⏲noon-1.30am; 🛜) Off the tourist trail and full of Mumbai's beautiful set, this new bar tucked away inside Cuffe Parade's World Trade Centre is a fun night out, with an emphasis on craft beer and craft cocktails (barrel-aged old-fashioneds, for example) set to a DJ/live saxophonist tag team most nights. The crowd skews upscale and the seats are notably comfy – settle in.

Mixologist Ayush Arora trained at the European Bartender School in Australia.

★**Social** BAR
(Map p48; www.socialoffline.in; ground fl, Glen Rose Bldg, BK Boman Behram Marg, Apollo Bunder; 9am-1.30am;) Colaba is the best of the locations of the hip Social chain, which combines a restaurant/bar with a collaborative work space. The happening bar nails the cocktails (from ₹295) – the Acharroska is the perfect marriage of Indian pungency and Brazilian sweetness.

The food (mains ₹190 to ₹490) spans everything from Bollywoodised fish and chips and *poutine* (French fries and cheese curds topped with gravy) to Thai thalis and great Parsi dishes for breakfast. There are also Social locations at **Todi Mill** (www.socialoffline.in; 242 Mathuradas Mill Compound, 9am-1am;) in Lower Parel and **Khar** (Map p64; www.socialoffline.in; Rohan Plaza, 5th Rd, Ram Krishna Nagar; cocktails from ₹295; 9am-1am;).

Fort Area & Churchgate

Raju Ki Chai TEAHOUSE
(Map p60; www.facebook.com/rajukichai; Shop 4, Kamar Bldg, Cowasji Patel Rd, Kala Ghoda; 9am-midnight Mon-Sat, from 2pm Sun) It's nearly impossible to saunter past this tiny brick-and-mortar chai joint – its colourful facade and vibrant interiors lure you in like an industrial-strength magnetic kaleidoscope. Taking street chai to a welcoming new level without disregarding tradition, the concoctions here (₹35 to ₹50) are served in customary clay cups, but not discarded on the pavement as at street stalls.

Kalbadevi to Mahalaxmi

★**Haji Ali Juice Centre** JUICE BAR
(Map p52; www.hajialijuicecentre.in; Lala Lajpat Rai Rd, Haji Ali Circle; 5am-1.30am) Serves fresh juices and milkshakes (₹50 to ₹400), mighty fine *falooda* and fruit salads. Strategically placed at the entrance to Haji Ali mosque, it's a great place to cool off after a visit. Try the Triveni, a gorgeous trifecta of mango, strawberry and kiwi (₹270).

Blue Tokai COFFEE
(www.bluetokaicoffee.com; Unit 20-22, Laxmi Woollen Mill, Dr E Moses Marg, Mahalaxmi; 9am-9pm;) Coffee's Third Wave has finally arrived in India. This speciality coffeehouse, one of four Mumbai locations, roasts its 100% Indian, traceable single-estate Arabica beans from farms like Vethilaikodaikanal (Tamil Nadu) and Thogarihunkal (Karnataka). It then brews them into espresso (from ₹100), cortados and flat whites (on the hot side) and pourovers and nitro (on the cold side). Coffee connoisseurs unite!

Western Suburbs

★**Independence Brewing Company** CRAFT BEER
(www.independencebrewco.com; Boolani Estate Owners Premises Co-Op, New Link Rd, Andheri West; pints ₹400; 1pm-1am Mon-Sat, noon-1am Sun;) A California-trained Indian master brewer oversees the craft at this trendy new Andheri West taproom from Pune-based Independence Brewing Company. Nine of the 10 taps are devoted to IBC brews, like four-grain saison, juicy Indian Pale Ales (IPAs), occasional sours and one of India's only double IPAs. There's Bollywoodised bar food to go along with it (grilled pickled paneer sandwiches, hot paprika wings).

★**Doolally Taproom** CRAFT BEER
(Map p64; www.doolally.in; Rajkutir 10A, E854, 3rd Rd, Khar West; pints ₹300; 7am-1am;) This Pune transplant, the vision of German brewmaster Oliver Schauf, was India's craft-beer pioneer. The fresh IPA, tangy Belgian Wit and apple cider are staples among the weekly changing 11 taps; and there are gourmet burgers and fat, hand-cut fries. It's steps from Khar station.

Wine Rack WINE BAR
(www.facebook.com/TheWineRackMumbai; ground fl, High Street Phoenix,Tulsi Pipe Rd, Lower Parel; noon-1am;) Sorely needed and refreshingly well done, Mumbai's first take on a serious wine bar should please connoisseurs. Part shop (over 300 bottles), part bar (48 wines by the glass, 21 of which are Indian; ₹325 to ₹995), it draws a sophisticated crowd, though not quite as sexy as the backdrop bar mural would suggest. Impressively stocked bar as well.

★**Thirsty City 127** BAR
(www.facebook.com/pg/thirstycity127; Todi Mills, Mathuradas Mill Compound, Tulsi Pipe Rd, Lower Parel; 6pm-1.30am Tue-Sun;) The former space of Mumbai's first microbrewery has been revamped into a slick craft beer and cocktail destination under the direction of Indian beer maven/visual artist Vir Kotak.

The striking space catches attention with copper-plated fermentation tanks, velvet and turquoise banquettes, but the swill reigns: eight taps (solid Neipa, Kölsch, Hefeweizen, etc served in Teku glassware) and cocktails (₹800) themed by beer ingredients.

★Cafe Zoe BAR

(www.cafezoe.in; Mathurdas Mills Compound, NM Joshi Marg, Lower Parel; ⌚7.30am-1.30am; 📶) Exposed brick and railing dominate the bi-level hipster hideaway inside a redeveloped cotton mill at Mathurdas Mills Compound. Forty wines by the glass, along with strong, well-mixed cocktails (₹700 to ₹1200) – like black grape caipiroskas and sage and lime martinis – ensure a lively crowd, who mingle alongside the old B&W photos of the space's former life dotting the walls.

Live jazz on Wednesdays at 9pm.

★Toto's Garage BAR

(Map p64; ☎022-26005494; 30th Rd, Bandra West; ⌚6pm-1am) A highly sociable, down-to-earth local dive done up in a car-mechanic theme, where you can go in your dirty clothes, drink draught beer (₹200 a glass) and listen to classic rock. Check out the up-ended VW Beetle above the bar. It's always busy and caters to all kinds.

★Bonobo BAR

(Map p64; www.facebook.com/Bonobo Bandra; Kenilworth Mall, 33rd Rd, off Linking Rd, Bandra West; ⌚6pm-1am) This bar champions underground and alternative music. DJs spin drum and bass and electronica, big beats and funky tech-house, and musicians play folk and blues. There's a great rooftop terrace and better-than-average craft beer on tap (Gateway and Brewbot). It's always a fun night out with a wildly eclectic crowd.

★Koinonia Coffee Roasters COFFEE

(Map p64; www.koinoniacoffeeroasters.com; 66 Chuim Village Rd, Chuim Village, Khar West; ⌚7am-10pm; 📶) Mumbai's best speciality coffee is served in this tiny Third Wave coffeehouse in atmospheric Chium Village. Single-origin Indian estate coffee is roasted in-house with a top-end Probat roaster. It comes cold-brewed, via Clever and Aeropress methods, as exquisite espresso (₹140), or with a dollop of ice cream from the affogato bar. Selections include salted caramel, Pondicherry vanilla or dark chocolate Italian truffle oil.

☆ Entertainment

Mumbai has an exciting live-music scene, some terrific theatres, an emerging network of comedy clubs and, of course, cinemas and sporting action.

Consult Time Out Mumbai (www.timeout.com/mumbai) and Insider (https://insider.in/mumbai) for events and/or live-music listings. Unfortunately, Hindi films aren't shown with English subtitles. You can book movies, theatre and sporting events online with Book My Show (https://in.bookmyshow.com).

★Royal Opera House OPERA

(Map p52; ☎022-23668888; www.royalopera house.in; Mama Parmanand Marg, Girgaon; ⌚10am-6pm) India's only surviving opera house reopened to suitably dramatic fanfare with a 2016 performance by Mumbai-born British soprano Patricia Rozario, after a meticulous six-year restoration project that saw the regal address returned to full British-rule glory. Architect Abha Narain Lambah combed through old photographs of gilded ceilings, stained-glass windows and a baroque Indo-European foyer to restore the three-level auditorium.

Quarter LIVE MUSIC

(Map p52; ☎8329110638; www.thequarter.in; Mathew Rd, Royal Opera House, Girgaon; ⌚10pm-1am) The Royal Opera House's signature entertainment venue (besides the Opera House itself, that is), the Quarter counts unique spaces like an airy, glass-fronted cafe and mozzarella bar, a Creole-cuisine-inspired restaurant and, most interestingly, a live-music venue evocative of a 1950s art deco jazz bar.

Canvas Laugh COMEDY

(www.canvaslaughclub.com; 3rd fl, Palladium Mall, High Street Phoenix, Lower Parel; tickets ₹200-750) A popular comedy club that hosts around 50 shows per month, with twice-nightly programs on weekends (most comedians use English). It's 900m west of Lower Parel train station inside the High Street Phoenix shopping complex. Book tickets online.

National Centre for the Performing Arts THEATRE, LIVE MUSIC

(NCPA; Map p60; www.ncpamumbai.com; NCPA Marg, Nariman Point) This vast cultural centre is the hub of Mumbai's highbrow music, theatre and dance scene. In any given week, it might host experimental plays, poetry readings, photography exhibitions, a jazz band

QUEER MUMBAI

Although homosexuality was decriminalised by India's highest court in 2018, Mumbai's LGBTIQ scene is still quite underground, especially for women, but it's gaining momentum. No dedicated LGBTIQ bars/clubs have opened yet, but gay-friendly 'safe house' venues often host private gay parties (announced on Gay Bombay, www.gaybombay.org).

Gay Bombay is a great place to start, with event listings including meetups in Bandra, GB-hosted bar and film nights (including somewhat-regular gay Saturday nights at Liquid Lounge in Girgaum Chowpatty), plus hiking trips, picnics and other queer-community info. Following are some other useful resources.

Gaylaxy (www.gaylaxymag.com) India's best gay e-zine; well worth consulting and has lots of Mumbai content.

Gaysi (www.gaysifamily.com) Mumbai-based lifestyle e-zine.

Humsafar Trust (Map p64; ☎022-26673800; www.humsafar.org; 3rd fl, Manthan Plaza Nehru Rd, Vakola Santa Cruz East; ⏰10am-6.30pm Mon-Fri) Mumbai's most well-known LGBTIQ community organisation. It's also closely connected to the erratically published but pioneering magazine Bombay Dost (www.bombaydost.co.in).

Kashish Mumbai International Queer Film Festival (☎022-28618239; www.mumbaiqueerfest.com; ⏰May) Excellent annual event with a mix of Indian and foreign films; in 2018, 140 films from 45 countries were featured, including 33 LGBTIQ films from India.

LABIA (Lesbian & Bisexuals in Action; www.sites.google.com/site/labiacollective/home) Lesbian and bi support group based in Mumbai; provides a counselling service for women.

Queer Azaadi Mumbai (www.facebook.com/qam.mumbaipride) Organises Mumbai's Pride Parade (www.mumbaipride.in), which is usually held in early February.

Queer Ink (www.queer-ink.com) Online publisher with excellent books, DVDs and merchandise. Also hosts a monthly arts event with speakers, workshops, poetry, comedy, music and a marketplace.

RAGE-by D'kloset Gay parties and events organised via Instagram (www.instagram.com/ragebydkloset).

Salvation Star Community on Facebook (www.facebook.com/SalvationStar) and Twitter (@SalvationStar) that organises and promotes queer events and parties.

from Chicago or Indian classical music. Many performances are free. The **box office** (Map p60; ☎022-66223724; ⏰9am-7pm) is at the end of NCPA Marg.

Prithvi Theatre THEATRE

(Map p64; ☎022-26149546; www.prithvitheatre.org; Juhu Church Rd, Juhu) A Juhu institution that's a great place to see both Hindi- and English-language theatre or an art-house film, with the **Prithvi Cafe** (light meals ₹40-180; ⏰10am-10.30pm) for drinks. Its excellent theatre festival in November showcases contemporary Indian theatre and includes international productions.

Regal Cinema CINEMA

(Map p48; ☎022-22021017; www.regalcinema.in; Colaba Causeway, Regal Circle, Apollo Bunder, Colaba; tickets ₹80-250) A faded art deco masterpiece – Mumbai's oldest – that's good for Hollywood and Indian blockbusters. Dating to 1933, it was the first centrally air-conditioned theatre in Asia.

Liberty Cinema CINEMA

(Map p60; ☎022-22084521; www.facebook.com/TheLibertyCinema; 41/42 New Marine Lines, Fort; ⏰tickets ₹100-200) The stunning art deco Liberty was once the queen of Hindi film – think red-carpet openings with Dev Anand. It fell on hard times in recent years, but is on the rebound and is now hosting films again. It's near Bombay Hospital.

Shopping

Mumbai is India's great marketplace, with some of the country's best shopping. Spend a day at the markets north of CSMT for the classic Mumbai shopping experience. Booksellers set up daily on the footpaths along the main thoroughfare between Colaba and Fort. Snap up a bargain backpacking wardrobe at **Fashion Street** (Map p60; MG Rd, Marine Lines;

hours vary). Kemp's Corner and Kala Ghoda have good shops for designer threads.

Colaba

Cottonworld CLOTHING
(Map p48; www.cottonworld.net; Mandlik Marg; 10.30am-8pm) A great shop for stylish Indian-Western-hybrid goods made from cotton, linen and natural materials. Think Indian Gap, but cooler.

Phillips ANTIQUES
(Map p48; www.phillipsantiques.com; Wodehouse Rd; 10am-7pm Mon-Sat) Art deco and colonial-era furniture, wooden ceremonial masks, silver, Victorian glass, plus high-quality reproductions of old photos, maps and paintings.

Clove CONCEPT STORE
(Map p48; www.clovethestore.com; Churchill Chambers, JA Allana Marg; 11am-8pm) Under the discerning eye of gourmet entrepreneur Samyukta Nair, this Colaba concept store occupies a late-19th-century art deco building chock-full of homegrown designer homewares (gorgeous coffee mugs, copper and clay dishware), jewellery, small-batch body scrubs and top-end designer *chappals* (sandals), *anarkali* (umbrella-flared dresses) and tunics for women, plus sleepwear for both sexes and children.

Nappa Dori DESIGN
(Map p48; www.nappadori.com; Shop 2, Sunny House, Merewether Rd; 10.30am-9pm) This very hip designer-leather shop from Delhi features a near-all-India lineup of carefully curated wallets, passport holders, truck-style travel cases, notebooks and other stylish writing and travel essentials (only the Novesta shoes aren't Indian, they hail from Slovakia). Discerning travellers and writers – take a look.

Fort Area & Churchgate

★**Sabyasachi** CLOTHING
(Map p60; www.sabyasachi.com; Ador House, 6 K Dubash Marg, Fort; 11am-7pm Mon-Sat) It's worth popping in to this high-end traditional garment shop to see the space itself, a gorgeous, cavernous, rose-oil-scented stunner chock-full of owner and designer Sabyasachi Mukherjee's collection of chandeliers, antiques, ceramics, paintings and carpets. As far as retail goes, it's unlike anything you have ever seen.

★**Kulture Shop** DESIGN
(Map p60; www.kultureshop.in; 9 Examiner Press, 115 Nagindas Master Rd, Kala Ghoda; 11am-8pm) Mumbai's coolest design shop has thankfully arrived in South Mumbai! Fittingly, the Pop Art cool kid from **Bandra** (Map p64; 241 Hill Rd, Bandra West; 11am-8pm) has set up shop in Kala Ghoda, where its thought-provoking and conceptually daring art prints, notebooks, coffee mugs, stationery, T-shirts and other immensely desirable objets d'art from a cutting-edge collective of Indian artists will leave your head spinning.

Chimanlals ARTS & CRAFTS
(Map p60; www.chimanlals.com; A2 Taj Bldg, Wallace St, Fort; 9.30am-6pm Mon-Fri, to 5.30pm Sat) The beautiful traditional printed papers here will make you start writing letters.

Nicobar HOMEWARES, CLOTHING
(Map p60; www.nicobar.com; 10 Ropewalk Ln, Kala Ghoda; 11am-8pm) This new and excellent high-end boutique from the same folks who brought us **Good Earth** (Map p48; www.goodearth.in; 2 Reay House, Colaba; 11am-8pm) is a great spot to pick up carefully curated homewares, travel totes and select Indian hipsterware.

MUMBAI FOR CHILDREN

Kidzania (www.kidzania.in; 3rd fl, R City, LBS Marg, Ghatkopar West; child/adult from ₹1000/500; 10am-8pm Tue-Fri, 10am-3pm & 4-9pm Sat & Sun) Kidzania is predictably one of Mumbai's kid-tastic attractions, an educational activity centre where kids can learn all about piloting a plane, fighting fires, policing and get stuck into lots of art- and craft-making. It's on the outskirts on the city, 10km northeast of the Bandra Kurla Complex.

Esselworld (022-61589888; www.esselworld.in; Global Pagoda Rd, Borivali West; adult/child from ₹1050/750, with Water Kingdom ₹1390/950; 11am-6pm Mon-Thu, to 7pm Fri & Sat) This Gorai Island amusement park is well maintained and has lots of rides, slides and shade. Ferries leave every 15 minutes (₹50) from Borivali jetty at Gorai Creek, best reached by bus 294 from Borivali Station.

Bombay Shirt Company CLOTHING
(Map p60; ☎022-40043455; www.bombayshirts.com; ground fl, 3 Sassoon Bldg, Fabindia Ln, Kala Ghoda; shirts from ₹2000; ⏲10.30am-9pm) A trendy, bespoke shirt tailor for men and women. You can customise everything – collars, buttons, cuffs and twill tapes. The results are stunning and the prices a fraction of those back home (unless home is Vietnam). Shirts take two weeks, and the business will deliver or ship internationally. It's also in **Bandra** (Map p64; ☎022-26056125; www.bombayshirts.com; ground fl, Kamal Vishrantee Kutir, 24th Rd;; shirts from ₹2000; ⏲10.30am-9pm).

Bombay Paperie ARTS & CRAFTS
(Map p60; ☎022-66358171; www.bombaypaperie.com; 63 Bombay Samachar Marg, Fort; ⏲10.30am-6pm Mon-Sat) Championing a dying art, this fascinating shop sells handmade, cotton-based paper crafted into charming cards, sculptures and lampshades.

Chetana Book Centre BOOKS
(Map p60; www.chetana.com; 34 K Dubash Marg, Kala Ghoda; ⏲10.30am-7.30pm Mon-Sat, 11.30-7pm Sun) This great spirituality bookshop has lots of books on Hinduism, yoga and philosophy, and the attached **restaurant** (thalis ₹500-635; ⏲12.30-3pm, 4-7pm & 7.30 to 11pm) does excellent Gujarati and Rajasthani thalis (₹499 to ₹635).

Kalbadevi to Mahalaxmi

★**Chor Bazaar** ANTIQUES
(Map p52; Mutton St, Kumbharwada; ⏲10am-9pm) Chor Bazaar is known for antiques, though be wary of reproductions. The main area of activity is Mutton St, where shops specialise in these 'antiques' and miscellaneous junk. Dhabu St, to the east, is lined with fine leather goods. It's an atmospheric spot for an afternoon browse, especially if you are looking for household trinkets and other nontouristy bric-a-brac.

★**Haji Mohammad Bashir Oil Shop** HEALTH & WELLNESS
(Map p52; 426A Hamidiya Masjid, Bapu Khote Rd, Bhuleshwar; ⏲10am-10.30pm Mon-Sat, 9am-9pm Sun) Worth a visit as much for the spectacle if not to buy, this near-century-old traditional oil shop still hand-presses its medicinal, cooking and massage oils (often to order) with a sesame wood and metal press. The menu reaches long and wide (turmeric, avocado, sandalwood, neem, tulsi, almond, jojoba, cardamom – the list goes on and on, priced per kilo from ₹400 to ₹25,000). It's attached to the lovely Hamidiyah Masjid (mosque).

BOLLYWOOD DREAMS

Mumbai is the glittering epicentre of India's gargantuan Hindi-language film industry. The Lumière brothers screened the first film ever shown in India at the Watson Hotel in Mumbai in 1896, and beginning with the 1913 silent epic *Raja Harishchandra* (with an all-male cast, some in drag) and the first talkie, *Alam Ara* (1931), Bollywood now churns out more than 1000 films a year – doubling Hollywood's output, and not surprising considering it has a captive audience of one-sixth of the world's population.

Every part of India has its regional film industry, but Bollywood continues to entrance the nation with its escapist formula in which all-singing, all-dancing lovers fight and conquer the forces keeping them apart. These days, Hollywood-inspired thrillers and action extravaganzas vie for moviegoers' attention alongside the more family-oriented saccharine formulas.

Bollywood stars can attain near-god-like status in India and star-spotting is a favourite pastime in Mumbai's posher establishments. You can also see the stars' homes as well as a film/TV studio with **Bollywood Tours** (Map p60; ☎9820255202; www.bollywoodtours.in; 8 Lucky House, Goa St, Fort; per person half-/full-day tour ₹8140/12,580; ⏲9am-6pm Mon-Fri, to 5pm Sat), but you're not guaranteed to see a dance number and you may spend much of the tour in traffic.

★**Play Clan** GIFTS & SOUVENIRS
(Map p52; www.theplayclan.com; Shop 1 & 2, Royal Opera House, Parmanand Marg, Girguam; ⏲11am-7pm) Kitschy, design-y goods such as stylish embroidered T-shirts, funky coffee mugs and coasters, and superhip graphic art, including beaded embroidered art and illustrative wood prints that are pricey but unique.

M/S KN Ajani HOMEWARES
(Map p52; Shop 102, Krishna Galli, Swadeshi Market, Kalbadevi Rd, Kalbadevi; ⏲noon-7pm Mon-Sat) One of Mumbai's oldest shops and born of a dying breed, this family-run retailer kicked off in 1918. Today, friendly grandson Paresh still hawks the family jewels: brass,

carbon-steel and aluminium scissors, nutcrackers, locks and knives inside the otherwise textile-driven Swadeshi Market. It's certainly not a conventional souvenir, but it's immensely satisfying to not buy your scissors at an office-supply shop.

No-Mad Fabric Shop HOMEWARES
(Map p52; 022-22091787; www.no-mad.in; 3C-209, 1st fl, Mangaldas Market bldg, Kitchen Garden Ln; 11am-7pm Mon-Sat) One of Mumbai's hottest new brands, this small showroom, overseen by Nandi the Holy Cow in logo, art and design, is an interior-design oasis in Mangaldas Market. Pick up colourful, India-inspired cocktail napkins, handbags, pillow covers, throws, candles, incense, and copper and brass serving trays, among other stylish items.

No Borders CLOTHING
(Map p52; www.facebook.com/nobordersshop; 47G, 1st fl, Khotachi Wadi Ln, Kotachiwadi; 11am-7pm Tue-Sun) This top-end shop occupies the former studio of fashion designer James Ferreira, located inside his 200-year-old Kotachiwadi bungalow. It curates designer threads from ethnic South Asian tastemakers as well as contemporary Indian, Norwegian and Israeli fashion designers, among others.

Lalbaug Market SPICES
(Putibal Chawl, Dr Baba Saheb Ambedkar Rd, Lalbaug; 11am-4.30pm Mon, 9am-7pm Tue-Sun) You could buy your packaged-for-tourists spices at hassle-y Crawford Market; or, go where Mumbaikars go, which is this fragrant market in Dadar that's considered top-rate for fresh, unadulterated hand-ground powdered goodness, fresh chillies and other chef essentials.

Shrujan ARTS & CRAFTS
(Map p52; 022-23521693; www.shrujan.org; Krishnabad Bldg, 43 Bhulabhai Desai Marg, Breach Candy; 10am-7.30pm Mon-Sat) Selling the intricate embroidery work of women in villages across Kutch, Gujarat, the nonprofit Shrujan aims to help women earn a livelihood while preserving the spectacular embroidery of the area. The sophisticated clothing, wall hangings and purses make great gifts.

Poster Stuff ART
(Map p52; 8976605743; 113 Mutton St, Kumbharwada; 11am-9pm) Haji Abu's small Chor Bazaar shop offers a cornucopia of vintage Bollywood posters, lobby cards and show cards dating to the 1930s (originals and reprints), some 500,000 in total curated from his grandfather's much larger collection. Prices start at ₹400 on up to ₹400,000. For Bollywood art buffs, this is your Holy Grail.

Western Suburbs

★Indian Hippy ART
(Map p64; 8080822022; www.hippy.in; 17C Sherly Rajan Rd, off Carter Rd, Bandra West; portraits ₹7500-15,000; by appointment) Indian Hippy will put your name in lights, with custom-designed Bollywood posters hand-painted on canvas by the original studio artists (a dying breed since the advent of digital illustrating). Bring or email a photo and your imagination (or let staff guide you). Also sells vinyl LP record clocks, vintage posters and all manner of frankly bizarre Bollywood-themed products. Ships worldwide.

Kishore Silk House CLOTHING, HANDICRAFTS
(Dedhia Estate, 5/353 Bhandarkar Rd, Matunga East; 10am-8.30pm Tue-Sun) Handwoven saris (from ₹300) and dhotis (from ₹250) from Tamil Nadu and Kerala.

High Street Phoenix MALL
(www.highstreetphoenix.com; 462 Senapati Bapat Marg, Lower Parel; 11am-10pm) High Street Phoenix, one of India's first and largest shopping malls, and its mall-within-a-mall, luxury-oriented Palladium, is an indoor/outdoor retail orgy that hosts top shops, great restaurants, fun bars and clubs, a 20-lane bowling alley and an IMAX cineplex. It's also where you go when you want a few horn-free hours.

Information

DANGERS & ANNOYANCES

For a city of its size, Mumbai affords few serious dangers and annoyances. However, it's worth being mindful of the following points:

- The city has a well-documented history of terrorism. Be vigilant – if you notice something off, or tell-tale signs like unattended bags, tell the police as soon as possible.
- Be alert for pickpocketing in crowded areas like Crawford Market, Mahalaxmi Temple, the Gateway of India and on crowded trains.

INTERNET ACCESS

While cybercafes are increasingly scarce, all but the simplest hotels, restaurants, cafes and bars now have wi-fi. Commercial establishments generally require a connection via social-media accounts or via a mobile-phone number, to which a unique one-time password (OPT) is sent.

The Maharashtra government also supports a wide network of over 500 public hot spots known as Aaple Sarkar Mumbai Wi-Fi. Check out www.

WORTH A TRIP

SANJAY GANDHI NATIONAL PARK

It's hard to believe that within 1½ hours of the teeming metropolis you can be surrounded by this 104-sq-km protected tropical **forest** (022-28868686; https://sgnp.maharashtra.gov.in; Borivali; adult/child ₹53/28, vehicle ₹177-266; 7.30am-6pm Tue-Sun, last entry 4pm). Here, bright flora, birds, butterflies and elusive wild leopards replace pollution and concrete, all surrounded by forested hills on the city's northern edge. Urban development has muscled in on the fringes of the park, but its heart is very peaceful.

The park's most intriguing option, the **Kanheri Caves** (https://sgnp.maharashtra.gov.in; Borivali; Indian/foreigner ₹25/300; 9am-5pm Tue-Sun) is a set of 109 dwellings and monastic structures for Buddhist monks 6km inside the park. The caves, not all of which are accessible, were developed over 1000 years, beginning in the 1st century BC, as part of a sprawling monastic university complex. Avoid the zoo-like lion and tiger 'safari' as the animals are in cages and enclosures.

Inside the park's main northern entrance is an information centre with a small exhibition on the park's wildlife. The best time to see birds is October to April and butterflies from August to November. Activities can now also be booked online.

The nearest station is Borivali, served by trains on the Western Railway line from Churchgate station (₹15 to ₹165, 30 minutes, frequent).

aaplesarkar.maharashtra.gov.in/file/Mumbai-Wifi-hotspots.pdf to locate the one nearest you. **RailWire** (www.railwire.co.in) also offers a signal at select train stations, part of an over 700-station initiative throughout India.

MEDICAL SERVICES

Bombay Hospital (Map p60; 022-22067676; www.bombayhospital.com; 12 New Marine Lines, Marine Lines; 24hr) A private hospital with the latest medical technology and equipment.

Breach Candy Hospital (Map p52; 022-23672888, emergency 022-23667809; www.breachcandyhospital.org; 60A, Bhulabhai Desai Marg, Breach Candy) The best hospital in Mumbai, if not India. It's 2km northwest of Girgaum Chowpatty.

Royal Chemists (Map p60; www.royalchemists.com; 89A Queen's Chambers, Maharshi Karve Rd, Marine Lines; 8.30am-8.30pm Mon-Sat) Has delivery services.

Sahakari Bhandar Chemist (Map p48; Colaba Chamber, ground fl, Colaba Causeway, Colaba; 10am-8.30pm)

MONEY

ATMs are everywhere, and foreign-exchange offices are also plentiful. There are numerous Citibank branches, including a handy **Fort branch** (Map p60; Bombay Mutual Bldg, 293 Dr Dadabhai Naoroji Rd, Fort), which is handy for its larger, ₹20,000 withdrawal limits. Thomas Cook (p78) has a branch in the Fort area with foreign exchange.

POST

Blue Dart/DHL (Map p60; 022-22049333; www.bluedart.com; ground fl, Shri Mahavir Chamber, Cawasji Patel St, Fort; 9am-9pm Mon-Sat) International courier services.

Post office (GPO; Map p60; www.indiapost.gov.in; Walchand Hirachand Marg, Fort; 9am-8pm Mon-Sat, to 4pm Sun) The main post office is an imposing building beside CSMT. Opposite gate 4 of the post office in front of Marine Supply is **Ashok Packingwala** (Map p60; 9323693870; opp GPO, Gate 4, Walchand Hirachand Marg, Fort) – parcel-wallahs who will stitch up your parcel (for between ₹60 and ₹300). There's also a convenient branch in **Colaba** (Map p48; www.indiapost.gov.in; Henry Rd; 10am-5pm Mon-Fri, to 1pm Sat).

TOURIST INFORMATION

Indiatourism (Government of India Tourist Office; Map p60; 022-22074333; www.incredibleindia.com; ground fl, Air India Bldg, Vidhan Bhavan Marg, Narimen Point; 8.30am-6pm Mon-Fri, to 2pm Sat) Provides information for the entire country, as well as contacts for Mumbai guides and homestays.

MTDC Tourist Office (Maharashtra Tourism Development Corporation; Map p60; 022-22845678; www.maharashtratourism.gov.in; 4th fl, Apeejay House, 3 Dinsha Vachha Marg, Churchgate; 9am-5.30pm Mon-Sat, closed 2nd & 4th Sat of month) The MTDC's head office has helpful staff and lots of pamphlets and information on Maharashtra, as well as bookings for MTDC hotels. It's also the only MTDC office of note that accepts credit cards. There are additional booths at Apollo Bunder (p54) and **Chhatrapati Shivaji Maharaj Terminus** (Maharashtra Tourism Development Corporation; Map p60; 022-22622859; www.maharashtratourism.gov.in; Chhatrapati Shivaji Maharaj Terminus, Fort; 10am-5.30pm Mon-Sat, closed 2nd & 4th Sat of month).

TRAVEL AGENCIES

Akbar Travels (Map p48; ☎022-22823434; www.akbartravels.com; 30 Alipur Trust Bldg, Colaba Causeway, Colaba; ⏲10am-10pm) Extremely helpful and can long-distance book car/drivers and buses. There's another branch in **Fort** (Map p60; ☎022-22633434; 167/169 Dr Dadabhai Naoroji Rd, Fort; ⏲10am-7pm Mon-Sat).

Magnum International Travel & Tours (Map p48; ☎022-61559700; www.magnuminternational.com; 10 Henry Rd, Colaba; ⏲10am-6pm Mon-Fri, to 1pm Sat) Handy Colaba travel agency.

Thomas Cook (Map p60; ☎022-48795009; www.thomascook.in; 324 Dr Dadabhai Naoroji Rd, Fort; ⏲9.30am-6pm Mon-Sat) Flight and hotel bookings, plus foreign exchange.

ℹ Getting There & Away

AIR

Mumbai's carbon-neutral **Chhatrapati Shivaji Maharaj International Airport** (Map p64; ☎022-66851010; www.csia.in; Santa Cruz East), about 30km from the city centre, was recently modernised to the tune of US$2 billion. Now handling all international arrivals is the impressive, remodelled international Terminal 2 (T2), which includes India's largest public-art program (a skylighted, 3.2km multistorey Art Wall along moving walkways, boasting over 5000 pieces of art from every corner of India). The international terminal has its own app (Android/iPhone; Mumbai T2 App).

Domestic flights operate out of both the new T2 and the older Terminal 1 (T1), also known locally as Santa Cruz Airport, 5km away. An interterminal fixed-rate taxi service (non-AC/AC ₹230/260 from T1 to T2, ₹230/250 from T2 to T1) operates between the terminals. Both terminals have ATMs and foreign-exchange counters, and T2 also houses the luxurious **Niranta Transit Hotel** (☎022-67296729; www.nirantahotels.com; s/d 4 hrs ₹5510/5900, 7 hrs ₹7080/7670, 24 hrs 11,529/13,800; @ 📶). There's left luggage near the hotel.

Air India (Map p60; ☎1800-1801407, 022-22023031; www.airindia.com; Air India Bldg, cnr Marine Dr & Madame Cama Rd, Nariman Point; ⏲9.15am-6.30pm Mon-Thu, 9.15am-6.15pm Fri, 9.15am-1pm & 1.45-5pm Sat), Jet Airways (www.jetairways.com) and Vistara (www.airvistara.com) operate out of T2, while GoAir (www.goair.in), IndiGo (www.goindigo.in) and SpiceJet (www.spicejet.com), among others, operate out of T1 – be sure to check ahead for any changes on the ground. Travel agencies and the airlines' websites are usually best for booking flights.

BUS

Numerous private operators and state governments run long-distance buses to and from Mumbai.

Long-distance government-run buses depart from the **Mumbai Central bus terminal** (Map p52; ☎1800-221250, enquiries 022-23024076; Jehangir Boman Behram Marg, RBI Staff Colony) right by Mumbai Central train station. They're cheaper and more frequent than private services, but standards are usually lower with the exception of semiluxury ShivShahi and luxury Shivneri services (always look for those first). The website of the **Maharashtra State Road Transport Corporation** (MSRTC; ☎022-23023900; www.msrtc.gov.in) has online schedules and booking at https://public.msrtcors.com/ticket_booking/index.php, though you'll need a resident to book for you if you don't have an Indian credit card.

Private buses are usually more comfortable and simpler to book (if a bit more costly). Many normally depart from Dr Anadrao Nair Rd near Mumbai Central train station, but that has stopped due to metro construction without any timeline for ever returning. If you are in that area, **National NTT/CTC** (Map p52; ☎022-23015652; Dr Anadrao Nair Rd, RBI Staff Colony; ⏲6am-11pm)

MAJOR LONG-DISTANCE BUS ROUTES

DESTINATION	PRIVATE NON-AC/AC SLEEPER (₹)	GOVERNMENT NON-AC (₹)	DURATION (HR)
Ahmedabad	500-2000/670-2500	N/A	7-12
Aurangabad	650-1100/550-2500	from 560 (four daily)	9-11
Hyderabad	1200-2000/1310-3000	N/A	16
Mahabaleshwar	1550/450-1349	from 300 (four daily)	7-8
Murud	2500 (seats only)	from 210 (eight daily)	8-10
Nashik	350-1500/400-2510	from 240 (12 per day, 6am-10.45pm)	13-16
Panaji (Panjim)	475-1500/1430-2500	N/A	14-16
Pune	600-2000/350-3000	from 210 (half-hourly, 6.35am-12.30am)	3-5
Udaipur	600-1400/1210-1810	N/A	14-17

remains open behind the metro construction and is a reliable ticketing agent.

The most centralised place to catch private buses these days is around Dadar TT Circle (Dadar East) under the flyover of the same name (free transport is usually provided to both by ticketing agents), but with the exception of the **MSRTC Shivneri buses to Pune** (www.msrtc.org.in; Dadar TT Flyover, Dadar East), you are going to need help to find your bus. The flyover is lined on both sides with private ticketing agents – make sure you arrive early and get specific indications from them where to find your bus. **Neeta Tours & Travels** (☎022-24162565; www.neetabus.in; Shop 9, opp Dadar Post Office, Dr Ambedkar Rd, Dadar East) is a good place to start.

Internet ticketing resources such as redBus (www.redbus.in) are in play, though some sites still require Indian mobile numbers and/or domestic payment options – most foreigners will still need to visit the ticketing agents (or have an Indian friend buy your ticket). Be sure to check your departure point (often called 'pickup point') as the reality is that private bus companies depart from numerous points around the city.

In addition to **Dr Anadrao Nair Road** (Map p52; RBI Staff Colony) near Mumbai Central bus station and along both sides of Dr Baba Saheb Ambedkar Rd near the **Dadar TT Flyover** (Dr Baba Saheb Ambedkar Rd) in Dadar East, you'll also find private long-distance ticket agents near **Paltan Road** (Map p52; Sitaram Bldg, F-Block, opp Paltan Rd) in Fort.

Private buses to Goa are more convenient; these vary in price from as little as ₹760 (a bad choice) to ₹3000. Many leave from way out in the suburbs, but government-run **Kadamba Transport** (Map p60; ☎9969561146; www.goakadamba.com; 5 Mahapalika Marg, Fort; ⏲7.30am-5.30pm Mon-Sat) is convenient for the centre, leaving from in front of Azad Maidan. The trip takes 14 hours.

Fares to popular destinations (like Goa) are up to 75% higher during holiday periods.

TRAIN

Three train systems operate out of Mumbai, but the most important services for travellers are Central Railway and Western Railway. Tickets for either system can be bought from any station that has computerised ticketing.

MAJOR TRAINS FROM MUMBAI

DESTINATION	TRAIN NO & NAME	SAMPLE FARE (₹)	DURATION (HR)	DEPARTURE
Agra	12137 Punjab Mail	585/1555/2250/3855 (A)	22	7.35pm CSMT
Ahmedabad	12901 Gujarat Mail	315/815/1150/1940 (A)	8½	10.05pm BCT
	12009 Shatabdi Exp	1030/1885 East	6½	6.25am BCT
Aurangabad	11401 Nandigram Exp	235/630/900/1510 (A)	7	4.35pm CSMT
	17617 Tapovan Exp	140/505 (C)	7	6.15am CSMT
Bengaluru	11301 Udyan Exp	500/1355/1975/3370 (A)	24	8.10am CSMT
Chennai	12163 Chennai Exp	570/1505/2175/3720 (A)	23½	8.30pm CSMT
Delhi	12951 Mumbai Rajdhani	2725/4075/4730 (D)	15¾	5pm BCT
Hyderabad	12701 Hussainsagar Exp	425/1075/1555/2625 (A)	14½	9.50pm CSMT
Indore	12961 Avantika Exp	440/1165/1660/2815 (A)	14	7.10pm BCT
Jaipur	12955 Mumbai Central Jaipur Superfast Exp (MMCT JP SF)	535/1420/2050/3495 (A)	18	6.50pm BCT
Kochi	16345 Netravati Exp	615/1655/2430 (B)	27	11.40am LTT
Madgaon (Goa)	10103 Mandovi Exp	390/1070/1540/2610 (A)	13	7.10am CSMT
	12133 Mangalore Exp	420/1150/1590 (B)	10¾	10.02pm CSMT
	11085 Mao Doubledecker	840 (F)	12	5.33am Wed, Fri & Sun LTT
Pune	11301 Udyan Exp	140/495/700/1165 (A)	3½	8.10am CSMT

Station abbreviations: CSMT (Chhatrapati Shivaji Maharaj Terminus); BCT (Mumbai Central); LTT (Lokmanya Tilak)

Fares: (A) sleeper/3AC/2AC/1AC; (B) sleeper/3AC/2AC; (C) second class/CC; (D) 3AC/2AC/1AC; East CC/Exec CC; (F) CC

Central Railway (www.cr.indianrailways.gov.in) – handling services to the east, south, plus a few trains to the north – operates from CSMT (also known as 'VT'). Foreign-tourist-quota tickets and Indrail passes can be bought at Counter 4 of the **reservation centre** (Map p60; ☎139; www.cr.indianrailways.gov.in; Chhatrapati Shivaji Maharaj Terminus Area, Fort; ⌚8am-8pm Mon-Sat, to 2pm Sun). There is a prepaid taxi scheme near the MTDC tourist information booth (p77). It's ₹160 to Colaba, ₹360 to Bandra, ₹430 to the domestic terminal and ₹500 to the international terminal.

Some Central Railway trains depart from Dadar (D), a few stations north of CSMT, or Lokmanya Tilak (LTT), 16km north of CSMT.

Western Railway (www.wr.indianrailways.gov.in) has services to the north from Mumbai Central train station, usually called Bombay Central (BCT). The **passenger reservation office** (Map p60; ☎139; www.wr.indianrailways.gov.in; Station Bldg, Vithaldas Thackersey Marg, Churchgate; ⌚8am-8pm Mon-Sat, to 2pm Sun), opposite Churchgate station, has foreign-tourist-quota tickets.

Mumbai's local rail infrastructure has come under fire in recent years. The collapse of Andheri's Gokhale overbridge connecting Andheri West and East stations in 2018 killed two, a stampede killed 23 at Prabhadevi station in 2017, and there was a skywalk cave-in at Charni Road, also in 2017. A system-wide structural audit was underway at the time of writing – and for good reason, as 18,847 people have died riding the rails since 2013!

Getting Around

M-Indicator (http://m-indicator.soft112.com) is an invaluable app for Mumbai public transit – from train schedules to rickshaw fares it covers the whole shebang.

TO/FROM THE AIRPORT

Terminal 1

Autorickshaw If it's not rush hour (7am to 11am and 4pm to 8pm), catch an autorickshaw (between ₹25 and ₹48) to Vile Parle station, where you can get a train to Churchgate (from ₹10, 45 minutes).

Ride-share An off-peak UberGo from the airport runs ₹220 to Bandra Kurla Complex or Bandra West, ₹400 to Fort and ₹425 to Colaba. The Uber and Ola pickup point is a straight shot out the arrivals door to sections Z1–7 in the parking lot (Uber can hot-spot those without a connection from their information booth).

Taxi There's a prepaid taxi counter in the arrivals hall. A non-AC/AC taxi with one bag costs ₹570/695 to Colaba or Fort and ₹295/350 to Bandra (a bit more at night).

Terminal 2

Autorickshaw Although available, they only go as far south as Bandra; walk out of the terminal and follow the signs. Prices are ₹50 to ₹60 to Vila Parle, ₹50 to ₹70 to Andheri (a traffic warden *should* keep them honest).

Prepaid taxi Set-fare taxis cost ₹670/810 (non-AC/AC; including one piece of luggage) to Colaba and Fort and ₹400/480 to Bandra. The journey to Colaba takes about an hour at night (via the Sea Link) and 1½ to two hours during the day.

Ride-share Uber and Ola have specific pickup points at the P7 West and East levels respectively; and information booths can hot-spot those without a connection on arrival in order to get you on the road. An off-peak UberGo from the airport runs ₹250 to Bandra Kurla Complex, ₹260 to Bandra West, ₹460 to Fort and ₹560 to Colaba. A ₹105 pickup fee is automatically embedded into the fare.

Train If you arrive during the day (but not during rush hour, and are not weighed down with luggage), consider the train: take an autorickshaw to Andheri train station and then the Churchgate or CSMT train (from ₹10, 45 minutes).

Taxi The trip from South Mumbai to the international airport in an AC taxi should cost from ₹700 to ₹750, plus the ₹70 toll if you take the time-saving Sea Link Bridge. Allow two hours for the trip if you travel between 4pm and 8pm; 45 minutes to 1½ hours otherwise.

BOAT

PNP (Map p48; ☎022-22885220; Apollo Bunder, Colaba) and **Maldar Catamarans** (Map p48; ☎022-23734841; Apollo Bunder, Colaba) run regular ferries to Mandwa (one way ₹135 to ₹185), useful for access to Murud-Janjira and other parts of the Konkan Coast, avoiding the long bus trip out of Mumbai. Buy tickets at their Taj Gateway Plaza offices.

Launches to Elephanta Island (p54) head to Gharapuri from the Gateway of India every 30 minutes from 9am to 3.30pm (one hour). Buy tickets from the MTDC booth (p54) at the Taj Gateway Plaza. Launches also run to **Mandwa** (Map p48; Apollo Bunder, Colaba). Buy tickets with PNP and Maldar Catamarans.

An overnight luxury cruise liner – the country's first such domestic operation – set sail in late 2018. **Angriya Cruises** (☎8314810440; www.angriyacruises.com; Victoria Docks 15, Purple Gate, off Ferry Wharf, Mazagão; d with/without window from ₹6800/5300), connecting Mumbai with Goa, departs Monday, Wednesday and Friday at 4pm from Victoria Docks just north of Fort, arriving by 10am the following day in Mormugao, 30km south of Panaji.

BUS

M-Indicator has a useful 'search bus routes' facility for hardcore shoestringers and masochists – you'll also need to read the buses' Devanagari numerals on older buses and beware of pickpockets. Fares start at ₹8. Check routes and timetables at http://routenetwork.bestundertaking.com.

BEST (www.bestundertaking.com) bus stands are numerous but include the **east** (Map p48; MG Rd, Colaba) and **west** (Map p48; MG Rd, Colaba) sides of Mahatma Gandhi (MG) Rd and at **CSMT** (Map p60; Chhatrapati Shivaji Maharaj Terminus Area, Fort); as well as **Colaba depot** (Map p48; Colaba Causeway).

METRO

Line 1 of the Mumbai Metro (www.reliancemumbaimetro.com) opened in 2014, the first of a long-phase project expected to finish by 2025. It connects 12 stations in the far northern suburbs to Ghatkopar Station in the east, mostly well away from anywhere of interest to visitors save the growing nightlife hubs of Andheri West and Versova, accessed by DN Nagar and Versova stations respectively. However, Line 1 of the monorail should have been extended south as far as Jacob Circle (5km north of CSMT) by the time you read this (after missing years of deadlines), bringing it past nightlife hub Lower Parel.

Single fares are based on distance and cost between ₹10 and ₹40, with monthly Trip Passes (₹750 to ₹1350) also available. Access to stations is by escalator, carriages are air-conditioned, and there are seats reserved for women and the disabled.

Line 3 (aka Colaba–Bandra-SEEPZ) will be a 33.5km, 27-station underground line connecting Cuffe Parade south of Colaba, Fort, all the main railway terminals, Dadar, Bandra Kurla Complex, Bandra, both airport terminals and on to Andheri. It will be of most interest to tourists but won't open until at least 2021. Station construction is currently wreaking havoc on main thoroughfares around all of these areas, causing major traffic issues and other navigation problems.

TAXI & AUTORICKSHAW

Mumbai's black-and-yellow taxis are very inexpensive and the most convenient way to get around southern Mumbai; drivers *almost* always use the meter without prompting. The minimum fare is ₹22 (for up to 1.5km); a 5km trip costs about ₹80. Meru Cabs (www.meru.in) is a reliable taxi service in Mumbai. Book online or via app, including outstation (long-distance) trips.

Ride-share apps in play include Uber (www.uber.com) and Ola (www.olacabs.com); the latter is good for booking autorickshaws as well – no more rickshaw-wallah price gouging (bear in mind with Ola, you will need to give the driver a one-time password – OTP – set when booking in order to commence the ride).

Autorickshaws are the name of the game north of Bandra. The minimum fare is ₹18, up to 1.5km; a 3km trip is about ₹36 during daylight hours.

Taxis and autorickshaws tack 50% onto the fare between midnight and 5am; and a possible ₹2 fare hike for both was being bandied about at the time of research. Tip: Mumbaikars tend to navigate by landmarks, not street names (especially new names), so have some details before heading out.

TRAIN

Mumbai's suburban train network is one of the world's busiest; forget travelling during rush hours (7am to 11am and 4pm to 8pm). Trains run from 4.15am to 1am and there are two main lines of most interest to travellers: Western Line and Central Line.

Western Line The most useful; operates out of Churchgate north to Charni Rd (for Girgaum Chowpatty), Mumbai Central, Mahalaxmi (for the Dhobi Ghat), Bandra, Vile Parle (for the domestic airport), Andheri (for the international airport) and Borivali (for Sanjay Gandhi National Park), among others. Make sure you don't catch an express train when you need a slow train – the screens dictate this by an 'S' (Slow) or 'F' (Fast) under 'Mode'.

Mumbai's first AC local train was also introduced on this line in late 2017, running at least five times per day Monday through Friday (8.54am, 11.50am, 2.55pm & 7.49pm to Virar plus an additional 5.49pm departure as far as Borivali).

Central Line Runs from CSMT to Byculla (for Veermata Jijabai Bhonsle Udyan, formerly Victoria Gardens), Dadar and as far as Neral (for Matheran).

From Churchgate 2nd-/1st-class fares are ₹5/50 to Mumbai Central, ₹10/105 to Vile Parle and ₹15/140 to Borivali. 'Tourist tickets' permit unlimited travel in 2nd/1st class for one (₹75/275), two (₹115/445) or five (₹135/510) days. AC fares from Churchgate are ₹60 to Mumbai Central, ₹85 to Bandra, ₹125 to Andheri and ₹165 to Borivali.

To avoid the queues, buy a rechargeable **Smart-Card** (₹100, ₹50 of which is retained in credit, ₹50 of which is a refundable deposit), good for use on either train line, then print out your tickets at the numerous automatic ticket vending machines (ATVMs) before boarding. (Place your card on the reader, touch the zone of your station, pick the specific station, choose the amount of tickets, choose 'Buy Ticket' and then 'Print'.) Mobile ticketing is also available via the UTS app (Android; www.utsonmobile.indianrail.gov.in) but set-up is more trouble than its worth for nonresidents.

Watch your valuables, and women, stick to the ladies-only carriages except late at night, when it's more important to avoid empty cars.

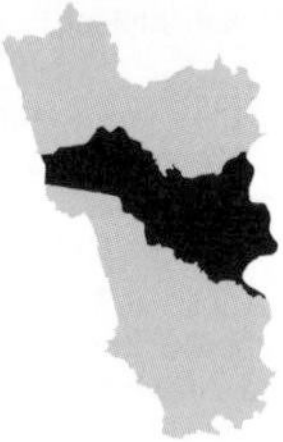

Panaji & Central Goa

Includes ➡

Best Places to Eat

- ➡ Black Sheep Bistro (p93)
- ➡ Cafe Bodega (p92)
- ➡ Hotel Venite (p93)
- ➡ Viva Panjim (p92)
- ➡ Fisherman's Wharf (p92)

Best Places to Stay

- ➡ Panjim Inn (p90)
- ➡ Goa Marriott Resort (p91)
- ➡ Old Quarter Hostel (p90)
- ➡ Afonso Guesthouse (p90)
- ➡ Dudhsagar Spa Resort (p113)

Why Go?

Some travellers see Goa as one big beach resort, but the central region – with few beaches of note – is the state's historic and cultural heart and soul. Wedged between Goa's two biggest rivers, the Mandovi and the Zuari, this region is home to the state capital, Panaji, the glorious churches of Old Goa, inland islands, bird sanctuaries, spice plantations and the wilds of the Western Ghats.

No visit to Goa is complete without a day or two spent cruising on the Mandovi River and exploring the old Latin Quarter in laid-back Panaji. Less than 10km away, Old Goa is the state's major cultural attraction, where the grand 17th-century churches and cathedrals are humbling in their scale and beauty, while further east are the Hindu temples and spice plantations around Ponda.

You could spend a week here without making it to a single beach. Don't miss it.

When to Go

Panaji

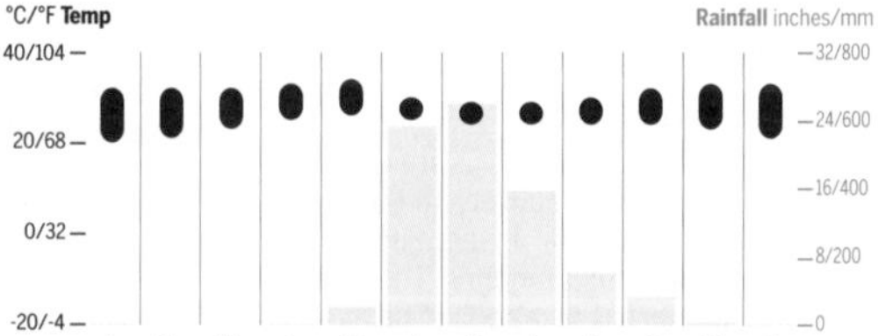

Nov–Mar High season is the best time to visit Central Goa's bird sanctuaries and national parks.

Christmas, Easter & Carnival Goa's festivals are at their best around Panaji.

Aug–Oct Monsoon season offers a different and very green side of Central Goa.

Panaji & Central Goa Highlights

1 **Panaji** (p84) Exploring the historic Latin Quarter, shopping and eating in India's most laid-back state capital.

2 **Old Goa** (p99) Standing in silence in the extraordinary churches and cathedrals of Old Goa.

3 **Dudhsagar Falls** (p111) Trekking out to India's second-highest waterfall and taking a dip in the natural pool.

4 **Ponda spice farms** (p110) Visiting an aromatic organic spice farm near Ponda.

5 **Dr Salim Ali Bird Sanctuary** (p98) Floating in a dugout canoe through the mangrove swamps of Chorao Island.

6 **Mandovi River Cruises** (p88) Taking a sunset cruise on the Mandovi or trying your luck on one of Panaji's floating casinos.

7 **Shri Mahadeva Temple** (p112) Seeing the last of the Kadambas at this ancient temple at Tambdi Surla.

Panaji

☎0832 / POP 241,000

One of India's most relaxed state capitals, Panaji (Panjim) crowds around the peninsula overlooking the broad Mandovi River, where cruise boats and floating casinos ply the waters, and advertising signs cast neon reflections in the night.

A glorious whitewashed church lords over the animated city centre, a broad leafy boulevard skirts around the river, and grand colonial-era buildings rub shoulders with arty boutiques, old-school bookshops, state-of-the-art malls and backstreet bars.

But it's the tangle of narrow streets in the old Latin Quarter of Fontainhas that really steal the show. Nowhere is the Portuguese influence felt more openly than here, where the late afternoon sun lights up yellow houses with purple doors, and around each corner you'll find restored ochre-coloured mansions with terracotta-tiled roofs, wrought-iron balconies and arched oyster-shell windows.

A day or two in Panaji really is an essential part of the Goan experience.

Sights

★Church of Our Lady of the Immaculate Conception CHURCH

(cnr Emilio Gracia & Jose Falcao Rds; 9am-12.30pm & 3-7.30pm Mon-Sat, 11am-12.30pm & 3.30-5pm Sun, English Mass 8am daily) Panaji's spiritual, as well as geographical, centre is this elevated, pearly white church, built in 1619 over an older, smaller 1540 chapel, and stacked like a fancy white wedding cake. When Panaji was little more than a sleepy fishing village, this church was the first port of call for sailors from Lisbon, who would give thanks for a safe crossing, before continuing to Ela (Old Goa) further east up the river. The church is beautifully illuminated at night.

By the 1850s the land in front of the church was being reclaimed and the distinctive crisscrossing staircases were added in the late 19th century. Today the entrance to its gloriously technicolor interior is along the left-hand side wall. A tangle of ropes leads up to the enormous shiny church bell in the belfry, saved from the ruins of the Augustinian monastery at Old Goa and installed here in 1871. The church is the focus for celebrations during the Feast of Our Lady of the Immaculate Conception, on 8 December.

Goa State Museum & Secretariat Building MUSEUM

(☎0832-2438006; www.goamuseum.gov.in; Avenida Dom Joao Castro; 9.30am-5.30pm Mon-Fri) FREE Currently housed in the Secretariat, the oldest colonial building in Goa, the state museum features an eclectic, if not extensive, collection of items tracing aspects of Goan history. As well as some beautiful Hindu and Jain sculptures and bronzes, there are nice examples of Portuguese-era furniture, coins, an intricately carved chariot and a pair of quirky antique rotary lottery machines.

The most interesting exhibit is in the furniture room: an elaborately carved table and high-backed chairs used by the notoriously brutal Portuguese Inquisition in Goa during its reign of terror. The table's legs feature carved lions and an eagle on one side, and four human figures on the other.

The Secretariat building stands on the site of the grand summer palace of Goa's 15th-century sultan Yusuf Adil Shah, which was originally fortified and surrounded by a saltwater moat. After falling to the Portuguese in 1510, the palace was further reinforced and used as a customs post, also serving as temporary accommodation for incoming and outgoing Portuguese viceroys. It later housed Goa's State Assembly.

Altinho Hill AREA

On the hillside above Panaji is the well-to-do residential district of Altinho. Apart from good views over the city and river, the main attraction here is the Bishop's Palace, an imposing building completed in 1893.

The archbishop of Goa came to reside in Panaji early in the 20th century, laying claim to the palatial residence at Cabo Raj Bhavan. But it was not to be: when the Portuguese governor-general realised that it was the best property in Goa, the archbishop was forced to change his plans and settle instead for this palace. The pope stayed at the Bishop's Palace during his visit to Goa in 1999. These days it's used for government offices.

Goa State Central Library LIBRARY

(Sanskruti Bhavan, Patto; 9am-7.30pm Mon-Fri, 9.30am-5.45pm Sat & Sun) FREE Panaji's modern state library has six floors of reading material, a bookshop and gallery. The 2nd floor features a children's book section and internet browsing (free, but technically only for academic research). The 4th floor has Goan

DON'T MISS

LATIN QUARTER – FONTAINHAS & SAO TOMÉ

When the capital moved from plague-ridden Old Goa around 1843, Panjim was centred around its church square and the banks of the Mandovi River. But the settlement soon began to spread out and today the most atmospheric, Portuguese-flavoured districts of Panaji are east of the centre, squeezed between the hillside of Altinho and the banks of Ourem Creek. Fontainhas, Sao Tomé and, further south, Mala – collectively known as the Latin Quarter or Old Quarter – are unquestionably the most seductive and intriguing parts of the city, perfect for a late afternoon stroll.

Fontainhas, said to take its name from local springs, is the larger of the districts, comprising pastel-shaded houses towards Altinho Hill. The land here was originally reclaimed in the late 18th century by a returning self-made Goan, known as 'the Mosmikar', so-called for the riches he had amassed during a stay in Mozambique.

Fontainhas' main thoroughfare is 31st January Rd and it's between here, Ourem Rd, Rue de Natal and further south to Altinho that you'll find many of the colourful mansions, Portuguese homes and bougainvillea blooms that make this district so photogenic.

Fontainhas is notable for being home to the pretty **Chapel of St Sebastian** (St Sebastian Rd; ⌚mass 6.45am daily), built in 1818. This small whitewashed church at the end of a lovely lane contains one of only a few relics remaining as testament to the Goan Inquisition: a striking crucifix, which originally stood in the Palace of the Inquisition in Old Goa. Christ's unusual open eyes are said to have been conceived especially to strike fear into the hearts of 'heretical' suspects brought before the Inquisitors, and awaiting their usually grisly fate. In mid-November a street fair sets up outside the chapel to celebrate the Feast of Our Lady of Livrament.

To the north of Fontainhas, the tiny area around the main post office is known as Sao Tomé. The post office was once the tobacco-trading house for Panaji, and the building to the right of it was the state mint. The square that these buildings face once housed the town pillory, where justice turned into spectacle when executions took place. It was here that several conspirators involved in the Pinto Revolt were put to death for plotting to overthrow Portuguese rule in 1787.

history books and the 6th a large collection of Portuguese books.

Mario Gallery GALLERY
(☎0832-2421776; www.mariodemiranda.com; Duarte Pacheco Rd; ⌚10am-5.30pm Mon-Fri, to 1pm Sat) FREE This gallery and shop showcases work by India's favourite cartoonist, Loutolim local Mario de Miranda, who died in 2011 at the age of 85. Along with prints, books and drawings, there are printed T-shirts, mugs and bags. His works are so popular that there are similar galleries in Calangute, Margao and Porvorim.

Gitanjali Gallery GALLERY
(☎0832-2423331; www.gallerygitanjali.com; 31st January Rd; ⌚9am-7pm) FREE Worth a look while walking around the district of Fontainhas, this spacious gallery in the beautiful Panjim Peoples displays works by local and international artists. It also functions as an art studio, gallery and hosts special exhibitions, workshops and art classes throughout the year.

Miramar BEACH
Miramar, 3km southwest of the city, is Panaji's nearest beach. The couple of kilometres of exposed sand facing Aguada Bay are hardly inspiring compared to other Goan beaches but it is a popular local place to watch the sun sink into the Arabian Sea. It's not a great place for swimming and bikinis are likely to attract unwanted attention. Local buses run frequently between Panaji's Kadamba bus stand and Miramar beach (₹4, 10 minutes).

Statue of Abbé Faria MONUMENT
(Avenida Dom Joao Castro) Beside the Secretariat Building, look out for the sublime, starkly black statue of a caped man, arms, hands and fingers outstretched, towering over an apparently frightened woman. This is the statue of Abbé Faria, considered the 'father of modern hypnotism', a contemporary of Franz Mesmer (from where the term 'mesmerise' derives) and a native of Goa.

Born the son of a monk and a nun in a Candolim mansion in 1756, Abbé Faria is one of history's fabulously enigmatic

Panaji (Panjim)

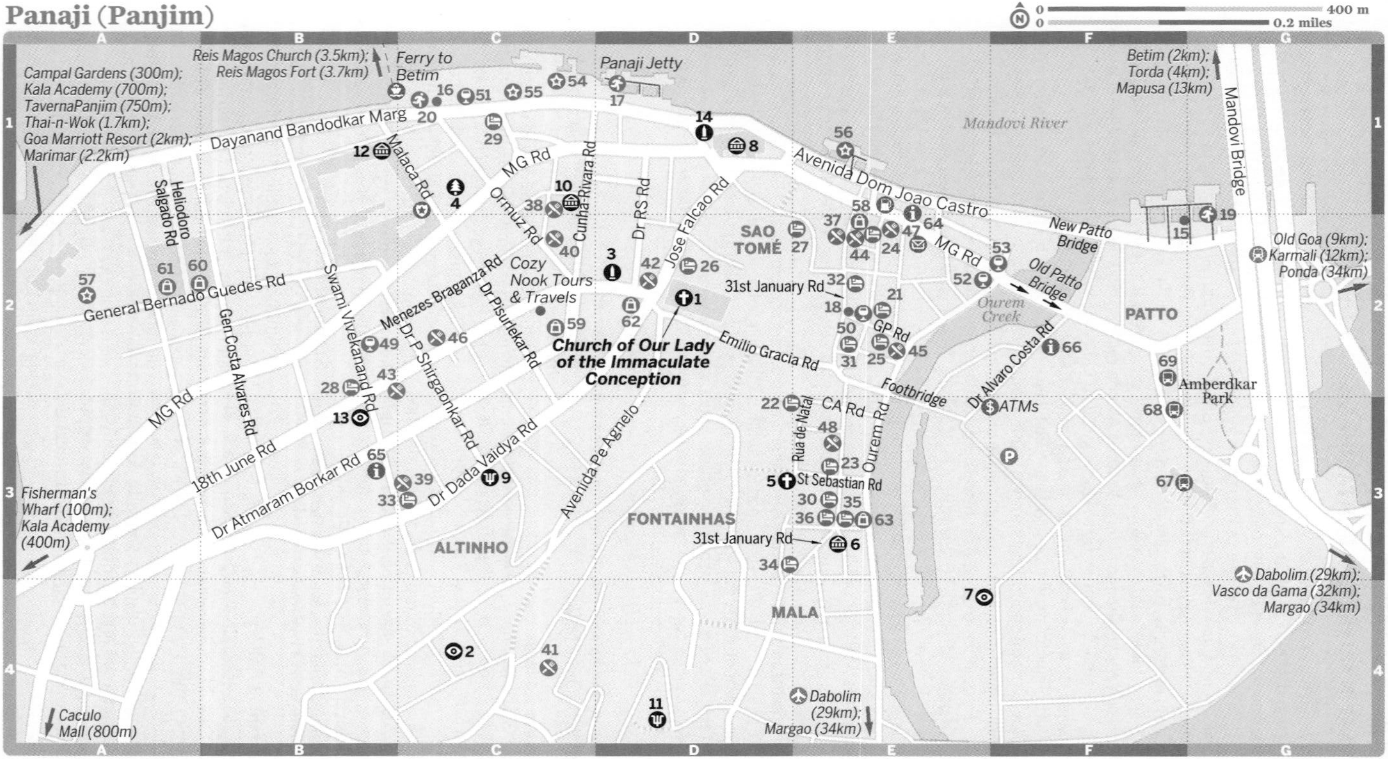

Panaji (Panjim)

Top Sights
1 Church of Our Lady of the Immaculate Conception ... D2

Sights
2 Altinho Hill ... C4
3 Ashokan Pillar ... D2
4 Azad Maidan ... C1
5 Chapel of St Sebastian ... D3
6 Gitanjali Gallery ... E3
7 Goa State Central Library ... E4
8 Goa State Museum & Secretariat Building ... D1
9 Mahalaxmi Temple ... C3
10 Mario Gallery ... C1
11 Maruti Temple ... D4
12 Menezes Braganza Institute ... B1
13 Public Observatory ... B3
14 Statue of Abbé Faria ... D1

Activities, Courses & Tours
15 GTDC River Cruise ... F2
16 Joey's Cruises ... C1
17 Kapitol Cruises ... D1
18 Make It Happen ... E2
19 Paradise Cruises ... G2
20 Paulo Cruise ... C1

Sleeping
21 A Pousada Guest House ... E2
22 Abrigo de Botelho ... D3
23 Afonso Guesthouse ... E3
24 Caravela Homestay ... E2
25 Casa Nova ... E2
26 Casa Paradiso ... D2
27 Crown Goa ... E2
28 Hotel Fidalgo ... B2
29 Hotel Mandovi ... C1
30 La Maison ... E3
31 Marquito's Guesthouse ... E2
32 Mateus ... E2
33 Mayfair Hotel ... C3
34 Old Quarter Hostel ... D3
35 Panjim Inn ... E3
Panjim Peoples ... (see 6)
36 Panjim Pousada ... E3

Eating
37 Anandashram ... E2
38 Bhonsle's Seetalaya ... C1
39 Black Sheep Bistro ... C3
40 Cafe Bhonsle ... C2
41 Cafe Bodega ... C4
42 George Bar & Restaurant ... D2
43 Gujarat Sweet Mart ... B2
44 Hotel Venite ... E2
45 Route 66 ... E2
46 Sher-E-Punjab ... C2
Verandah ... (see 35)
47 Vihar Restaurant ... E2
48 Viva Panjim ... E3

Drinking & Nightlife
49 Cafe Mojo ... B2
50 Joseph Bar ... E2
51 Quarterdeck ... C1
52 Riverfront & Down the Road ... E2
53 Soho ... F2

Entertainment
54 Casino Pride ... C1
55 Deltin JAQK ... C1
56 Deltin Royale ... E1
57 INOX Cinema ... A2

Shopping
58 Barefoot ... E2
59 Khadi India ... C2
Marcou Artifacts ... (see 48)
60 Municipal Market ... A2
61 New Municipal Market ... A2
62 Singbal's Book House ... D2
Sosa's ... (see 45)
63 Velha Goa Galeria ... E3

Information
64 Disability Rights Association of Goa ... E2
65 Forest Department ... B3
66 Goa Tourism ... F2
Government of India Tourist Office ... (see 66)

Transport
67 Kadamba Bus Stand ... F3
Konkan Railway Reservation Office ... (see 67)
68 Paulo Travels ... F3
69 Private Bus Agents ... F2

figures, having hovered handsomely on the sidelines of the greatest events of the 18th century and flirted with its main players (the Portuguese royal family, Robespierre, Marie Antoinette and Napoleon among them), somehow ingratiating himself with every successive regime while remaining an elusive outsider, caught in a world of black magic and esoteric pursuits. He was considered to be at the forefront of modern hypnotism for his explanations, and belief in, the power of suggestion – uncharted territory at the time.

Goa Science Centre & Planetarium MUSEUM
(Marine Hwy, Miramar; ₹20, planetarium ₹25, 3D cinema ₹20; ⏲10am-6pm) Kids and families will enjoy the Goa Science Centre &

Planetarium in Miramar, with an outdoor park, hands-on interactive displays, 3D movies and a planetarium.

Ashokan Pillar MONUMENT

This pillar at the centre of the Municipal Gardens was once topped by a bust of Vasco da Gama, the first Portuguese voyager to set foot in Goa in 1498, but he was replaced, upon independence in 1961, by the seal of present-day India: four lions sitting back to back, atop an abacus, with the inscription 'Truth Alone Triumphs'.

Maruti Temple HINDU TEMPLE

(Mala) Dedicated to the monkey god Hanuman, this large orange temple built up the Altinho hillside is resplendently lit at night, and affords pleasant views over the city's Old Quarter from its verandah by day. It forms the epicentre of a roughly 10-day festival celebrated in February, when enormous and colourful statues of Hanuman are placed in the street, and festive street stalls are set up throughout the surrounding Hindu quarter of Mala.

Menezes Braganza Institute HISTORIC BUILDING

(Malaca Rd) The yellow-and-white Menezes Braganza Institute occupies part of the old buildings that were once the Portuguese army headquarters. It's worth poking your head in at the building's northeast entrance to examine the grand and dramatic *azulejos* (glazed coloured tiles) adorning the wall, which depict scenes from *Os Lusíadas,* a famously epic Portuguese poem by Luís Vaz de Camões (p104) that tells the tale of Portugal's 15th- and 16th-century voyages of discovery.

Azad Maidan PARK

(Freedom Park) To the west of the Municipal Gardens, the grassy Azad Maidan won't win any prizes at a flower show. Its centrepiece is a small pavilion (whose Corinthian pillars were reclaimed from the rubble in Old Goa), which houses a modern sculpture dedicated to freedom fighter and 'Father of Goan Nationalism' Dr Tristao de Braganza Cunha (1891–1958).

Campal Gardens PARK

The road to Miramar from Panaji runs through the Campal district. Just before you reach the Kala Academy are the strollable riverside Campal Gardens, also known as the Children's Park. The gardens offer a nice view over to Reis Magos Fort and the boats that cruise along the Mandovi River each evening.

Public Observatory OBSERVATORY

(www.afagoa.org; 7th fl, Junta House, Swami Vivekanand Rd; ⌚7-9pm mid-Nov–May) FREE If you're interested in gazing at the clear winter night skies over Goa, the local branch of the Association of Friends of Astronomy has a public observatory with giant telescopes on the terrace of the Junta building. The local volunteer enthusiasts are only too happy to welcome visitors and explain what you're looking at. The view over Panaji by night is lovely too.

Mahalaxmi Temple HINDU TEMPLE

(off Dr Dada Vaidya Rd) This modern, technicolor temple is not particularly imposing, but it's worth a look inside as it was the first Hindu shrine established in the city during Portuguese rule. It amply demonstrates that among Panaji's ubiquitous whitewashed churches there is a large and thriving Hindu community. The temple was built in 1818 and is devoted to the goddess Mahalaxmi, goddess of wealth and beauty and the Hindu deity of Panaji.

Activities

The nearest beach for swimming is at Miramar (p85), about 4km southwest of the centre, but it's really more of a sunset people-watching place than a bathing beach. Nonguests can swim in the small but nice pool (₹500) at the hilltop Crown Goa (p91).

One-hour evening boat cruises run by Goa Tourism and private operators leave from the Tourism Jetty near Mandovi Bridge and are a popular way to see the river – depending on the crowd they tend to turn into booze cruises with DJ entertainment, traditional dancing and an on-board bar. Similar cruises and dolphin-spotting trips depart from Panaji Jetty near the casino boat offices closer to the city centre.

GTDC River Cruise CRUISE

(Avenida Dom Joao Castro, Tourism Jetty; sunset cruise ₹300; ⌚6pm) Goa Tourism operates an entertaining hour-long cruise along the Mandovi River aboard the *Santa Monica,* with a live band and/or performances of Goan folk songs and dances. There are also twice-weekly, two-hour dinner cruises. Departs from the Santa Monica Jetty next to the Mandovi Bridge.

DON'T MISS

CARNIVAL CRAZINESS

Panaji's annual **carnival** (⌚Mar) has been hitting the city centre for three chaotic days, sometime in late February or early March, since the 18th century, when it was introduced by the Catholic Portuguese as one last opportunity for excess before the strictures of Lent.

The origins of Carnival are far older, however, dating back as far as the Bacchanalias of ancient Rome, and later enlivened by African slaves in the Portuguese colonies. Once introduced into Goa, of course, an entirely local twist was added to the fun-filled goings on, with the inclusion of *tiatrs*, the satirical folk plays that are still performed throughout Carnival today.

Carnival begins – as it has done for centuries – with the arrival in Panaji of a character called King Momo on Sabado Gordo (Fat Saturday), and his instruction to the people of the city to, in essence, 'don't worry, be happy'. Dancing, drinking, processions of floats through the streets, cross-dressing and *assaltos* (amiable battles) – with sticky mixtures of flour, coloured tikka powder and water – ensue.

Though various criticisms of Carnival have emerged over the years – ranging from its post-Independence shunning due to its links to colonialism, to its recent commercialisation and excuse for the over-consumption of alcohol – Panaji's three days of mayhem are still celebrated by many thousands each year, seeing hotels booked solid, streets filled with revellers, and bars doing a brisk trade. Don't come dressed in your best, and prepare to be soaked to the skin.

Paulo Cruise CRUISE
(Dayanand Bandodkar Marg, Panaji Jetty; ₹400; ⌚5.30pm, 7pm & 8.30pm) This 75-minute Mandovi river cruise proudly announces it is the only one offering karaoke in the air-conditioned upper deck. It's slightly more upmarket than other cruises and departs from Panaji Jetty in the city centre.

Joey's Cruises CRUISE
(☎0832-2228989; Dayanand Bandodkar Marg, Panaji Jetty; adult/child ₹300/free; ⌚from 6am) Dolphin-spotting cruises on smaller boats depart from next to the Betim Ferry and from Miramar beach throughout the day.

Kapitol Cruises CRUISE
(☎0832-2904223; www.kapitolcruises.com; Dayanand Bandodkar Marg, Panaji Jetty; ₹350) With a more modern boat, the range of cruises here is aimed at families and couples but still with Bollywood music and sunset drinks. Call ahead for times or tour details.

Paradise Cruises CRUISE
(☎0832-2437239; www.paradisecruises.in; Avenida Dom Joao Castro, Tourism Jetty; per person ₹300; ⌚cruises 5.45pm, 6.45pm & 7.45pm) This private operator runs three evening 'party' cruises on the Mandovi River aboard its triple-decker boat. There's a bar on board and usually a DJ and cultural or dance show on the upper deck. Very popular with Indian tourists.

Tours

Make It Happen WALKING
(www.makeithappen.co.in; 1/143 Dr Cunha Gonsalves Rd; walking tours from ₹700) For a local insight into Goan history and culture, this Panaji-based outfit of local tour guides leads a number of walks and tours, including Fontainhas and Old Goa heritage walks and tours of Divar Island, Chandor and Saligao. The Fontainhas walk includes access to heritage homes and a performance of fado (a melancholic form of Portuguese singing). Book online.

Festivals & Events

Feast of Our Lady of the Immaculate Conception RELIGIOUS
(Margao, Panaji; ⌚8 Dec) Fairs and concerts are held, as is a beautiful church service at Panaji's Church of Our Lady of the Immaculate Conception.

Sabado Gordo CARNIVAL
(Panaji; ⌚Feb/Mar) A procession of floats and street parties on the Saturday before Lent.

International Film Festival of India FILM
(www.iffigoa.org; Panaji; ⌚Nov) Film screenings and Bollywood glitterati everywhere.

Sleeping

Panaji has its fair share of accommodation for all budgets but it's not saturated like the beach resorts. In the middle range are some of Goa's better boutique heritage hotels and guesthouses, mostly in the Fontainhas area.

Fontainhas also has budget guesthouses and a hostel, while business hotels are generally on the west side of town.

★Old Quarter Hostel HOSTEL **$**
(☎7410069108; www.thehostelcrowd.com; 5/146 31st January Rd; dm ₹600-650, s/d with AC from ₹1100/1700;) In an old Portuguese house in historic Fontainhas, this flamboyant hostel is a beacon for budget travellers to Panaji. Slick four-bed dorms with lockers as well as private doubles in a separate building, along with the excellent Bombay Roasters Cafe, arty murals, good wi-fi and bikes for hire. Noon checkout.

A Pousada Guest House GUESTHOUSE **$**
(☎0832-2422618, 9850998213; sabrinateles@yahoo.com; Luis de Menezes Rd; s/d from ₹950/1200, d with AC ₹1800;) The five rooms in this bright-yellow place are simple but clean and come with comfy spring-mattress beds and TV. Owner Sabrina is friendly and no-nonsense, and it's one of the better budget guesthouses in Fountainhas.

★Panjim Inn HERITAGE HOTEL **$$**
(☎0832-2226523, 9823025748; www.panjiminn.com; 31st January Rd; s/d from ₹5900/6500, superior ₹8200/8700;) One of the original heritage hotels in Fontainhas, the Panjim Inn has been a long-standing favourite for its character and charm. Run by the lovely Sukhija family and overseen by helpful staff, this beautiful 19th-century mansion has 12 charismatic rooms in the original house, along with newer rooms with modern touches to complement four-poster beds, colonial-era furniture and artworks.

Head up to the small rooftop for views over Fontainhas and a dip in the jacuzzi. Buffet breakfast is included, and the Verandah restaurant (p92) is a popular spot serving excellent Goan food and cold beer. Panjim Inn is the original of a trio of heritage hotels, including Panjim Peoples and Panjim Pousada.

If you're interested in a farmstay retreat, ask here about Cajueiro Homestead (p113) in the east of the state.

Afonso Guesthouse GUESTHOUSE **$$**
(☎0832-2222359, 9764300165; www.afonsoguesthouse.com; St Sebastian Rd; d ₹2500-3250;) Run by the friendly Jeanette, this pretty Portuguese townhouse offers eight spacious, well-kept rooms with timber ceilings. The little rooftop terrace makes for sunny breakfasting (not included) with Fontainhas views. It's a simple, serene stay in the heart of the most atmospheric part of town. Checkout is 9am and bookings are accepted online but not by phone.

Panjim Pousada GUESTHOUSE **$$**
(☎0832-2226523; www.panjiminn.com; 31st January Rd; s/d from ₹5900/6500, superior ₹8200/8700;) In an old Hindu mansion, the nine divine, colonial fantasy rooms at Panjim Pousada are set off by a stunning central courtyard, with antique furnishings and lovely art on the walls. Various doorways and spiral staircases lead to the rooms; those on the upper level are the best but all have bags of character with modern conveniences.

Mateus BOUTIQUE HOTEL **$$**
(☎7447488889; www.mateusgoa.com; 432 31st January Rd; d incl breakfast ₹4500-5000;) The nine boutique rooms are compact but delightful in this renovated 1879 Portuguese mansion. The whole place, with a striking canary-yellow facade, has been beautifully refurbished with a lounge and breakfast area, colonial-era furnishings and rear garden with a tiny pool. It's in the heart of the Old Quarter.

Caravela Homestay BOUTIQUE HOTEL **$$**
(☎0832-2237448; 27 31st January Rd; d/ste incl breakfast from ₹2500/4000;) In a beautiful Sao Tomé heritage building, Caravela has 10 minimalist but comfortable rooms with extra touches such as minibar and toiletries. Across the lane is the cafe where breakfast is served.

La Maison BOUTIQUE HOTEL **$$**
(☎0832-2235555; www.lamaisongoa.com; 31st January Rd; r incl breakfast ₹4700-5300;) One of the growing range of boutique heritage hotels in Fontainhas, La Maison is historic on the outside but thoroughly modern and swanky within, with a Euro-meets-Orient vibe. The eight rooms are deceptively simple and homey but five-star comfortable with soft beds, cloud-like pillows, writing desks and flat-screen TVs. Breakfast is included and attached is the French fusion Desbue restaurant.

Abrigo de Botelho BOUTIQUE HOTEL **$$**
(☎9527778884; www.hadbgoa.com; Rue de Natal; r incl breakfast ₹3250-5250;) At the end

of a quiet lane in the Old Quarter, the six rooms in this lovely sky-blue heritage house are spacious, neatly furnished and enhanced with antiques, but still offer cable TV, AC and wi-fi.

Hotel Fidalgo   HOTEL $$

(☑0832-6658000; www.fidalgogroup.com; 18th June Rd; d ₹7000-8500, ste from ₹14,000; ✳⚶⛱) The city centre's long-running business hotel is slightly stuffy and old-fashioned but Fidalgo works with snappy service and a good range of cuisines courtesy of its 'food enclave', including a good vegetarian Indian restaurant. Cheaper deals online.

Marquito's Guesthouse   GUESTHOUSE $$

(☑9325122039; Dr Cunha Consalves Rd; s/d/tr incl breakfast ₹3000/3250/4100; ✳⚶) This attractive olive-green Portuguese house down a lane off 31st January Rd in Sao Tomé is equipped with compact, clean and plain-white rooms, but there's certainly a cosiness here. The rooms are all air-conditioned with TV and hardwood floors, some with balcony.

Casa Paradiso   HOTEL $$

(☑0832-3290180; www.casaparadisogoa.com; Jose Falcao Rd; d/tr with AC ₹2000/2800; ✳⚶) Location is the key to this place, just around the corner from the main church in the heart of the city. Up a small flight of stairs, the simple but clean rooms come with TV, hot water and noon checkout.

Mayfair Hotel   HOTEL $$

(☑0832-2223317; manishafernz@yahoo.com; Dr Dada Vaidya Rd; s/d from ₹3100/3500; ✳⚶) The oyster-shell windows and mosaic tiling in the lobby of this popular corner hotel are promising and the refurbished rooms are mostly in good shape. Ask to see a few as there are new and old wings with rooms of varying quality, some overlooking a potentially nice back garden. Noon checkout.

Hotel Mandovi   HOTEL $$

(☑0832-2426270; www.hotelmandovigoa.com; Dayanand Bandodkar Marg; standard s/d ₹4200/4800, executive s/d ₹4800/5500, ste ₹9000; ✳⚶) A Panaji institution for more than 50 years, the Mandovi offers dated rooms, many looking out onto the wide Mandovi River. For ambience, style and facilities, it's outdone by other top-end hotels in town, but it's well-priced in the mid-range bracket. There are a couple of good restaurants.

★Panjim Peoples   HOTEL $$$

(☑0832-2435628, 0832-2226523; www.panjiminn.com; 31st January Rd; d ₹8900; ✳⚶) The Panjim Peoples is an atmospheric and beautifully restored heritage hotel with just four enormous upstairs rooms in what was formerly the Peoples High School. There are mosaic-covered bathrooms, deep bath tubs, antique furnishings and nautical ship lights.

Goa Marriott Resort   HOTEL $$$

(☑0832-2463333; www.marriott.com; Miramar Beach; d incl breakfast ₹17,800-23,500; ✳⚶⛱) Miramar's plush Goa Marriott Resort is the best in Panaji, with a price tag to match. It's expertly choreographed, with the five-star treatment beginning in the lobby and extending right up to the rooms-with-a-view, fitness centre and extravagant buffet breakfast. The 24-hour Waterfront Terrace & Bar is a great place for a sundowner overlooking the exclusive riverside pool.

Crown Goa   HOTEL $$$

(☑0832-240 0000; www.thecrowngoa.com; Bairo Alto Dos Pilotos, Jose Falcao Rd; d incl breakfast ₹11,200-14,000, ste from ₹15,500; ✳⚶⛱) Perched on a small hill above the Sao Tomé district, with fine views over the Mandovi, this spa-hotel-casino is a good option for a little bit of old-school luxury in the midst of the city. A lift takes you up to a lovely terrace with swimming pool (nonguests ₹500) and bar. Spacious rooms are airy and tastefully done in mustards and whites, some with balconies and views. Along with the casino, there's a day spa and well-equipped gym.

Casa Nova   GUESTHOUSE $$$

(☑9423889181; www.casa-nova-homestay.goa-india-hotels-resorts.com; Gomes Pereira Rd; apt ₹7800; ✳⚶) In a gorgeous Portuguese-style house (c 1831) in Fontainhas, Casa Nova comprises just one stylish, exceptionally comfy double-bed apartment, accessed via a little alley and complete with arched windows, wood-beam ceilings, and mod-cons including a kitchenette and wi-fi. Book well ahead.

✗ Eating

You'll never go hungry in Panaji, where food is enjoyed fully and frequently. A stroll down 18th June or 31st January Rds will turn up a number of cheap but tasty canteen-style options, as will a quick circuit of the Municipal Gardens.

The Latin Quarter has a developing foodie scene, where you can dine on traditional Goan specialities.

Anandashram GOAN $
(31st January Rd; thalis ₹90-140, mains ₹100-350; ⏲noon-3.30pm & 7.30-10.30pm Mon-Sat, noon-3pm Sun) This little place is renowned locally for seafood, serving up simple but tasty fish curries, as well as veg and nonveg thalis for lunch and dinner.

Bhonsle's Seetalaya GOAN $
(☎9822089176; thalis ₹110-170; ⏲11.30am-3pm & 7-11pm) For some of the best-value fish curry rice (fish thali) in town, this 1st-floor local eatery specialises in Goan seafood dishes. Simple and tasty. Also has cheap beer.

Cafe Bhonsle CAFE $
(Ormuz Rd; veg thalis ₹100, mains ₹100-250; ⏲9am-10pm) Well known for its delicious lunchtime thalis and *bhaji puri* (deep-fried bread with curry), Cafe Bhonsle has expanded upstairs into a multicuisine place serving fish thalis and other seafood dishes. Thalis are served between noon and 2.30pm.

Vihar Restaurant SOUTH INDIAN $
(☎0832-2225744; MG Rd; veg thalis ₹110-160; ⏲7-10.30pm) A vast menu of 'pure veg' food, great big thalis, South Indian dosas and a plethora of fresh juices make this clean, simple canteen a popular place for locals and visitors. One of the few places in this area that's still busy late into the evening. Beer bar upstairs.

Gujarat Sweet Mart SWEETS $
(Gujarat Lodge, 18th June Rd; drinks & snacks ₹30-60; ⏲9am-9pm) For Indian sweets, snacks and lassis, this hole-in-the-wall counter is a good place to indulge, though times have changed and the traditional lassi tin cups have been replaced by throwaway paper cups.

★ **Viva Panjim** GOAN $$
(☎0832-2422405; 31st January Rd; mains ₹160-300; ⏲11.30am-3.30pm & 7-11pm Mon-Sat, 7-11pm Sun) Well-known to tourists, this little side-street eatery, in an old Portuguese house and with a few tables out on the laneway, delivers tasty Goan classics at reasonable prices. There's a whole page devoted to pork dishes, along with tasty *xacuti* (a spicy chicken or meat dish cooked in red coconut sauce) and *cafreal* (a marinated chicken dish) meals.

Other specialities include seafood such as kingfish curry and crab *xec xec* (vindaloo), steaks and desserts such as *bebinca* (Goan 16-layer cake).

★ **Cafe Bodega** CAFE $$
(☎0832-2421315; www.cafebodegagoa.in; Altinho; mains ₹170-340; ⏲10am-7pm Mon-Sat, to 4pm Sun; 📶) It's well worth a trip up to Altinho Hill to visit this serene inner courtyard cafe-gallery in an azure-and-white Portuguese mansion in the grounds of Sunaparanta Centre for the Arts. Enjoy good coffee, juices and freshly baked cakes around the inner courtyard or lunch on super pizzas and sandwiches.

Thai-n-Wok ASIAN $$
(☎0832-2461980; www.thainwokgoa.com; Miramar; mains ₹220-680; ⏲11am-3pm & 7-11pm Wed-Tue; ❄) As the name suggests, this tranquil place has both Thai and Chinese menus, with all the classic Thai curries and soups, along with dishes like Beijing chicken or sweet-and-sour pork. The food is authentic but if you like your Thai food spicy, request it when ordering.

Fisherman's Wharf SEAFOOD $$
(☎8888493333; www.thefishermanswharf.in; Dr Braganza Pereira Rd; mains ₹320-550; ⏲noon-11pm) The successful formula from its long-running restaurant down in Mobor has been transplanted in the capital with fresh seafood, North Indian tandoor, kebabs and Goan specialities. The atmosphere in the open-side restaurant is relaxed but upmarket.

Verandah GOAN $$
(☎0832-2226523; 31st January Rd; mains ₹180-420; ⏲11am-11pm) The breezy 1st-floor restaurant at Panjim Inn is indeed on the balcony, with just a handful of finely carved tables, Fontainhas street views and snappy service. Goan cuisine is the speciality, but there's also a range of Indian and continental dishes and local wines.

Sher-E-Punjab NORTH INDIAN $$
(☎0832-2227975; 18th June Rd; mains ₹200-380; ⏲11am-11.30pm) Sher-E-Punjab is widely regarded as one of the best North Indian places in Panaji, catering to well-dressed locals and business visitors with its generous, carefully spiced Punjabi dishes, including tandoori classics and rich butter chicken. Also does a few Goan dishes. The pleasant garden terrace out back is refreshing.

George Bar & Restaurant GOAN $$
(18th June Rd; mains ₹160-350; ⏲11.30am-3.30pm & 6-10.30pm Mon-Sat) There's something very rustic and local about this cramped restaurant in the shadow of Panaji's main church. Seafood and Goan classics are done well though, and beef steaks are on the menu, though prices have risen to reflect the location. The upstairs section has air-con.

★**Hotel Venite** GOAN $$$
(31st January Rd; mains ₹320-440; ⏲9am-10.30pm) With its cute rickety balcony tables overhanging the cobbled street, Venite has long been among the most atmospheric of Panaji's Goan restaurants. The menu is traditional, with spicy sausages, fish curry rice, pepper steak and *bebinca*, but Venite is popular with tourists and prices are consequently inflated. Drop in for a beer or shot of feni (Goan liquor) before deciding.

★**Black Sheep Bistro** EUROPEAN $$$
(☎0832-2222901; www.blacksheepbistro.in; Swami Vivekanand Rd; tapas ₹250-400, mains ₹350-600; ⏲noon-4pm & 7pm-midnight) Among the best of Panaji's burgeoning boutique restaurants, Black Sheep's impressive pale-yellow facade gives way to a sexy dark-wood bar and loungy dining room. The tapas dishes are light, fresh and expertly prepared in keeping with their farm-to-table philosophy. Salads, pasta, seafood and dishes like lamb osso buco grace the menu, while an internationally trained sommelier matches food to wine.

The Black Sheep is serious about food and it shows. It's also a sophisticated bar with Goan craft beers, feni cocktails and Indian and imported wines.

Route 66 DINER $$$
(☎9623922796; Ourem Rd; mains ₹200-850; ⏲noon-11.30pm; ❄📶) Styled on an American diner, this roomy restaurant across from Ourem Creek specialises in burgers such as the SOB or Wolverine, but also excels at hot dogs, cheese chilli fries, hickory barbecue ribs and New York–style pizzas. For comfort fast food it's hard to beat and there's live music on Thursday, Friday and Saturday nights.

Drinking & Nightlife

Panaji's local drinking scene has traditionally been in the city's tiny, tucked-away male-oriented bars, but times are changing and more contemporary bars and pubs are flourishing. You can still find a spot to pull up a stool and drink a shot of feni with a local though.

★**Cafe Mojo** BAR
(☎0832-2431973; www.cafemojo.in; Menezes Braganza Rd; ⏲10am-5am Mon-Thu, to 6am Fri-Sun) The decor is a dark cosy English pub, the clientele young and up for a late party, and the novelty is the e-beer system. Each table has its own beer tap and LCD screen: you buy a card (₹500), swipe it at your table and start pouring – it automatically deducts what you drink (use the card for spirits, cocktails and food, too).

Soho BAR
(☎7702897753; MG Rd; ⏲7pm-1am, to 3am Fri-Sun) Take the side entrance (behind the music shop) and climb the stairs to the top floor for this sophisticated little bar and music venue where, let's face it, the beautiful people hang out. With its icy air-con, backlit bar, balcony overlooking the Ourem River and party nights, it's part of the new wave of Panaji bars.

Joseph Bar BAR
(Gomes Pereira Rd, Sao Tomé; ⏲6-11.30pm) This hole-in-the-wall bar is a place where locals and tourists gather streetside to chat and drink at tiny tables or perched on scooters. It's a warm and welcoming place with Goan craft beer available.

Taverna Panjim PUB
(☎9049630982; Dayanand Bandodkhar Marg; ⏲noon-3pm & 7pm-2am; 📶) It's as much about the Goan food as the drinking at this bright two-level pub in the Campal district but we like the fun atmosphere, live music and weekend DJs. Wednesday is karaoke night.

Riverfront & Down the Road BAR
(cnr MG & Ourem Rds; ⏲11am-1am) The balcony of this restaurant-bar overlooking the creek and Old Patto Bridge makes for a cosy beer or cocktail spot with carved barrels for furniture. The ground-floor bar (from 6pm) is an old-school nightspot with occasional live music.

Quarterdeck BAR
(Dayanand Bandodkar Marg; ⏲11am-11pm) The riverside location on the banks of the Mandovi is the main redeeming feature of this open-air garden restaurant and bar near the Betim Ferry dock. Drinks (and food) are overpriced, but it's a nice place to enjoy a sundowner and watch the casino boats light up.

Entertainment

Panaji's most visible form of entertainment are the casino boats anchored out in the Mandovi River, but the city is also home to India's biggest international film festival (p89) and the cultural offerings of the excellent Kala Academy.

Kala Academy PERFORMING ARTS
(☎0832-2420452; www.kalaacademygoa.co.in; Dayanand Bandodkar Marg) On the west side of the city, in Campal, is Goa's premier cultural centre, which features a program of dance, theatre, music and art exhibitions throughout the year. Many shows are in Konkani, but there are occasional English-language productions. The website usually has an up-to-date calendar of events.

INOX Cinema CINEMA
(☎0832-2420900; www.inoxmovies.com; Old GMC Heritage Precinct; tickets ₹210-240) This comfortable, plush multiplex cinema shows Hollywood and Bollywood blockbusters. Book online to choose your seats in advance.

Shopping

Panaji is a decent place for a boutique-style shopping stop, with international brand-name stores dotting Mahatma Gandhi (MG) Rd (at around a third of European prices), Goa's largest shopping mall, and a slew of 'lifestyle stores' selling high-end faux antiques, well-made textiles and richly illustrated coffee-table tomes. For local grit and grime head to the municipal markets.

Municipal Market MARKET
(Heliogordo Salgado Rd; ⌚from 7.30am) This atmospheric place, where narrow streets have been converted into covered markets, makes for a nice wander, offering fresh produce, clothing stalls and some tiny, enticing eateries. The fish market is a particularly interesting strip of activity.

Caculo Mall MALL
(☎0832-2222068; www.caculomall.in; 16 Shanta, St Inez; ⌚10am-9pm) Goa's biggest mall is four levels of air-conditioned family shopping heaven with brand-name stores, food court, kids' toys, bowling alley and arcade games.

PANAJI'S FLOATING CASINO'S

Live gaming is illegal in most of India but back in 2001 the powers that be in Goa decided that if the gambling was offshore, it could circumvent this law. The results are the controversial floating casinos moored on the Mandovi River. Over the past decade there have been political rumblings about moving the boats out of the river or closing down the industry altogether, but money talks and as of 2018 there were at least six casino boats on the Mandovi.

Still, the latest news is that the government intends to ban local Goans from using the casinos (bona fide tourists only) and the idea of moving the boats out of the river – where they are very visible to the public – and into a designated 'gaming zone' is still being mooted.

The casinos vary a little in size and shape, but are quite luxurious cruise-style ships. All offer gaming tables with croupiers, including blackjack, poker, roulette, baccarat, Indian flush and slot machines. Buffet meals, free drinks and entertainment are part of the deal in the evenings and some or all of your admission cost is redeemable in gaming chips. Dress codes apply.

Deltin JAQK (☎9819698196; www.deltingroup.com/deltin-jaqk; Fisheries Jetty, Dayanand Bandodkar Marg; ₹2000; ⌚24hr, entertainment 9pm-1am) Has three floors with 50 tables, a lavish buffet and floorshow entertainment from 9pm.

Deltin Royale (☎9819698196; www.deltingroup.com/deltin-royale; Noah's Ark, RND Jetty, Dayanand Bandodkar Marg; weekday/weekend ₹2500/3500; ⌚24hr, entertainment 9pm-1am) Goa's biggest and best luxury floating casino, Deltin Royal has 123 tables, the Vegas Restaurant, a Whisky Bar and a crèche.

Casino Pride I & II (☎0832-6516666; www.bestgoacasino.com; Dayanand Bandodkar Marg, Captain of Ports Jetty; ₹1500, Fri-Sun ₹2000; ⌚24hr, entertainment 9-11pm) These two casino boats are loosely modelled on Mississippi-style paddle boats.

Khadi India ARTS & CRAFTS
(Dr Atmaram Borkar Rd; 9am-1pm & 3-7pm) Goa's only outpost of the government's Khadi & Village Industries Commission has a fine range of hand-woven cottons, oils, soaps, spices and other handmade products that come straight from (and directly benefit) regional villages.

Singbal's Book House BOOKS
(0832-2425747; Church Sq; 9.30am-1pm & 3.30-7.30pm Mon-Sat) On the corner opposite Panaji's main church, Singbal's is a local landmark with an excellent selection of international magazines and newspapers, and lots of books on Goa and travel.

New Municipal Market MARKET
(Heliogordo Salgado Rd; from 7.30am) This light-filled redeveloped building comprises mostly stacks of fresh fruit and vegetables downstairs and a few drab electronics shops and tailors upstairs. Less atmosphere than the nearby Municipal Market.

Marcou Artifacts ARTS & CRAFTS
(0832-2220204; www.marcouartifacts.com; 31st January Rd; 9am-8pm Mon-Sat) This cute little Fontainhas shop showcases one-off painted tiles, fish figurines and hand-crafted Portuguese and Goan ceramics at reasonable prices. Also has showrooms at Hotel Delmon and Margao's market.

Velha Goa Galeria ARTS & CRAFTS
(Ourem Rd; 10am-1pm & 3-7pm Mon-Sat) One of several places in town specialising in *azueljos* (glazed coloured tiles), this gallery and shop is next door to Panjim Inn and offers tiles, vases and other ceramic objects reproduced in the old style by Portuguese artist, Anabela Cardosa. Pricey but great gifts or souvenirs.

Barefoot ARTS & CRAFTS
(31st January Rd; 10am-8pm Mon-Sat) Part of Panaji's new wave of high-end shops, specialising in design. Though pricey, it has some nice gifts ranging from traditional Christmas paintings on wood to jewellery and beaded coasters.

Sosa's CLOTHING
(0832-2228063; E245 Ourem Rd; 10.30am-7pm Mon-Sat) A boutique carrying local labels such as Horn Ok Please, Hidden Harmony and Free Falling, Sosa's is among the best places in Panaji to source upscale Indian women's fashion.

Information

MONEY
International 24-hour ATMs are widespread in Panaji; look out for HDFC, State Bank of India, ICICI and Axis.

POST
Hidden in the lanes around the main post office, there are privately run parcel-wrapping services that charge reasonable prices for their essential services.

Main Post Office (MG Rd; 9.30am-5.30pm Mon-Sat) Offers swift parcel services and Western Union money transfers.

TRAVEL AGENCIES
There are several travel agencies where you can book and confirm flights; many are along 18th June Rd.

Cozy Nook Tours & Travels (18th June Rd; 9am-8.30pm)

TOURIST INFORMATION
Goa Tourism (p231) The GTDC office is in the large Paryatan Bhavan building across the Ourem Creek and near the bus stand. However, it's more marketing office than tourist office and is of little use to casual visitors, unless you want to book one of GTDC's host of tours.

Government of India Tourist Office (0832-2438812; www.incredibleindia.com; Paryatan Bhavan, Dr Alvaro Costa Rd; 9.30am-1.30pm & 2.30-6pm Mon-Fri, 10am-1pm Sat) In the same building, staff at this tourist office can be helpful, especially for information outside Goa.

Getting There & Away

AIR
Dabolim Airport (p232) is around 30km south of Panaji. A new airport bus (www.goakadamba.com) between Dabolim and Calangute stops at Panaji on request. Some higher-end hotels offer a minibus service, often included in the room tariff.

A taxi from Panaji to the airport should cost ₹900 and takes about 45 minutes, but allow an hour for traffic. From the airport, the prepaid taxi fare is ₹870 (₹920 for AC). Alternatively, if you don't have much luggage, you can catch a bus from the main road to Vasco da Gama, then a bus direct from Vasco to Panaji (₹30, 45 minutes).

BOAT
Taking the rusty but free passenger/vehicle ferry across the Mandovi River to the fishing village of Betim makes a fun shortcut en route to the northern beaches. It departs the jetty on Dayanand Bandodkar Marg. From Betim there are regular buses onwards to Calangute and Candolim.

BUS

All local buses depart from Panaji's **Kadamba bus stand** (☎ interstate 0832-2438035, local 0832-2438034; www.goakadamba.com; Patto Centre; ⏱ reservations 8am-8pm), with frequent local services (running to no apparent timetable) heading out every few minutes; major destinations are Mapusa (₹30, 30 minutes) in the north, Margao (₹40, one hour) to the south and Ponda (₹25, one hour) to the east. Most bus services run from 6am to 10pm. Ask at the bus stand to be directed to the right bus for you, or check the signs on the bus windscreens.

To get to the beaches in South Goa, take an express bus to Margao and change there; to get to beaches north of Baga, it's best to head to Mapusa and change there. There are direct buses to Candolim (₹20, 35 minutes), Calangute (₹25, 25 minutes) and Baga (₹30, 30 minutes).

State-run long distance services also depart from the Kadamba bus stand, but prices offered by private operators are similar and they offer greater choice in type of bus and departure times. Many private operators have **booths** (Patto Place) outside the entrance to the bus stand (go there to compare prices and times). At the time of writing all interstate buses were operating from the Kadamba stand but there are plans to move them to a new stand on the Ponda bypass road.

Private bus fares are seasonal and can change depending on the type of bus, time of year and even day of the week. December to February, festivals/holidays and weekends are highest.

The Kadamba bus stand has an internet cafe, ATM and lots of cheap snack joints.

Paulo Travels (☎ 0832-2438531; www.paulobus.com; G1, Kardozo Bldg) Operates a number of services with varying levels of comfort to many long-distance destinations. You can book tickets online.

TRAIN

The closest train station to Panaji is Karmali (Old Goa), 12km to the east near Old Goa. A number of long-distance services stop here, including services to and from Mumbai, and many trains coming from Margao also stop here – but check in advance. Panaji's **Konkan Railway Reservation Office** (www.konkanrailway.com; Patto Place; ⏱ 8am-8pm Mon-Sat) is on the 1st floor of the Kadamba bus stand – not at the train station. You can check times, prices and routes online at www.konkanrailway.com and www.indianrail.gov.in.

Getting Around

It's easy enough to get around central Panaji and Fontainhas on foot, which is just as well because taxis and autorickshaws charge extortionately for short trips (minimum ₹100). A return taxi to Old Goa costs around ₹500, and an autorickshaw should agree to take you there for ₹350.

Lots of taxis hang around at the Municipal Gardens, making it a good place to haggle for the best price. Autorickshaws and motorcycle taxis can also be found in front of the post office, on 18th June Rd, and just south of the church.

Locals buses run to Miramar (₹5, 10 minutes), Dona Paula (₹8, 15 minutes) and to Old Goa (₹10, 20 minutes).

Goa Tourism's **Hop on Hop off bus** (☎ 7447473495; www.hohogoa.com; 1/2 route pass ₹400/700) plies a recurring route along the riverfront taking in the state museum, Kala Academy, Miramar Beach and Dona Paula, then returning and heading out to Old Goa and back.

Around Panaji

Dona Paula

Situated on the headland that divides the Zuari and Mandovi Rivers, 9km southwest of Panaji, Dona Paula allegedly takes its name from Dona Paula de Menenez, a Portuguese viceroy's daughter who threw herself into the sea from the clifftop after being prevented from marrying a local fisherman. Her tombstone still stands in the chapel at nearby Cabo Raj Bhavan. Though the views over Mormugao Bay are nice enough, the village is drab, the small beaches raggedy and the hawkers persistent. The popular jetty promenade was closed in 2018 for urgent structural repairs.

For the last 40 years, Baroness Yrsa von Leistner's (1917–2008) whitewashed *Images of India* statue has graced a mock acropolis on an outcrop of rock at the end of the Dona Paula road. It portrays a couple looking off in different directions, the man towards the past and the woman towards India's future.

Sights

Cabo Raj Bhavan FORT
(Cabo Raj Niwas; www.rajbhavan.goa.gov.in; ⏱ chapel Sun Mass 9.30-10.30am, Christmas, Easter & feast days) On the westernmost point of the peninsula stands an old fortress, Cabo Raj Bhavan, nowadays the official residence of the governor of Goa. Plans to build a fortress here, to guard the entrance to the Mandovi and Zuari Rivers, were first proposed in 1540, and although the 16th century had become the 17th before work on the fortress began, a chapel was raised on the spot almost immediately.

The fortress was subsequently completed and the chapel extended to include a

PORTUGUESE LEGACY

The Portuguese departed Goa in 1961 after more than 400 years of colonial rule but they left behind a rich legacy of culture, architecture, churches, schools and medical colleges.

Religion & Festivals

Around one quarter of the Goan population is Christian (largely Roman Catholic), mostly as a result of religious conversion during Portuguese rule. Today this legacy is most obvious in the many whitewashed parish churches across the state but also in the Christian festivals such as Christmas, Easter, Carnival and the Feast of St Francis Xavier.

Food

Goan cuisine is distinct from its South Indian neighbours with its liberal use of pork and uniquely spiced sauces such as *xacuti, cafreal* and *recheado. Vindaloo* is a Goan derivative of Portuguese port stew steeped in wine vinegar and garlic. Seafood is still king though and fish curry rice was a staple here long before colonisation. The Portuguese also introduced cashews to Goa, providing the basis for the national alcoholic drink, feni.

Architecture

You don't have to look far to see the fine architecture left behind by the Portuguese in residential mansions and palacios. Your first stop should be Panaji's Latin Quarter of Fontainhas and Sao Thome, where many Portuguese homes have been converted into boutique heritage hotels. In the countryside, South Goan villages such as Chandor, Loutolim and Quepem are awash with grand mansions, but if you look past the tourist tat you'll see many well-preserved examples of Portuguese architecture in the backstreets of beach resorts such as Candolim and Calangute.

Susegad

This one is a little less tangible but you'll find it in everyday life during your time in Goa. Derived from the Portuguese *sossegado* (quiet), *susegad* is a uniquely Goan term that describes a laid-back attitude and contentment with life. Life might not look very relaxed during peak season in downtown Calangute but the concept of *susegad* lives on in the people of Goa.

Franciscan friary. The fort itself, though equipped with several cannons, was never used in defence of Goa, and from the 1650s was instead requisitioned as a grand and temporary residence for Goa's lucky archbishop.

From 1799 to 1813 the site (along with Fort Aguada and Reis Magos Fort, to the north) was occupied by the British who, during the Napoleonic Wars, deemed it necessary in order to deter the French from invading Goa. Now all that remains of the British presence is a forlorn little **British cemetery**, with gravestones spanning just over a century. It's tucked away behind the Institute of Oceanography – look for the hand-painted sign to the cemetery and the clam-shaped Oceanography Institute roof off the main roundabout. Cabo Raj Bhavan's 500-year-old chapel also draws thousands of locals to its **Feast of the Chapel** for prayers and festivities each 15 August.

After the departure of the British, the buildings were once again inhabited by the archbishop of Goa, but it didn't remain long in his possession: in 1866 the Portuguese viceroy took a shine to the buildings, and had them refurbished and converted into the governor's palace, packing the poor old archbishop off to the hilltop Bishop's Palace in Altinho (p84).

Sleeping

O Pescador HOTEL **$$**
(☎0832-2453863; www.opescador.com; d ₹5600-7200, ste ₹7850; ❄️📶🏊) Part of the Indy resort chain, O Pescador's waterfront site has been utilised to create well-decorated mock-Portuguese villas with a nice view of the 'private' beach. It's a firm favourite among the UK package-holiday crowd, with comfy rooms and a nice little pool deck.

Cidade de Goa HOTEL **$$$**
(☎0832-2454545; www.cidadedegoa.com; d ₹16,700-20,000; ❄️📶🏊) Indulgence is the order of the day at this swanky village-style place, designed by renowned local architect

Charles Correa, located 1km down the coast from Dona Paula at Vanguinim Beach. All the usual opulence is on offer, including pool, spa and casino, and eight restaurants.

Getting There & Away

Frequent buses to Dona Paula depart the Kadamba bus stand in Panaji (₹8, 15 minutes), running along riverfront Dayanand Bandodkar Marg, and passing through Miramar.

Chorao Island

Lazy Chorao Island, accessible by the free vehicle ferry from Ribandar or Divar Island, is mainly known for its beautiful bird sanctuary. If you arrive here with your own transport it's worth a ride through the countryside to little Chorao village, with its handful of whitewashed village churches and picturesque Portuguese homes. You can also ride or drive to the Divar ferry crossing, explore that island and ferry back to the mainland at Old Goa.

Sights

Dr Salim Ali Bird Sanctuary BIRD SANCTUARY
(admission ₹20, forest department boat ₹750-900; 6am-6pm) Named after the late Dr Salim Moizzudin Abdul Ali, India's best-known ornithologist, this serene sanctuary on Chorao Island was created by Goa's Forestry Department in 1988 to protect the birdlife that thrives here and the mangroves that have grown up in and around the reclaimed marshland. Apart from the ubiquitous white egrets and purple herons, you can expect to see colourful kingfishers, eagles, cormorants, kites, woodpeckers, sandpipers, curlews, drongos and mynahs, to name just a few.

Marsh crocodiles, foxes, jackals and otters have also been spotted by some visitors, along with the bulbous-headed mudskipper fish that skim across the water's surface at low tide. There's a birdwatching tower in the sanctuary that can be reached by boat when the river level, dependent on the tide, is not too low.

Even for those not especially interested in the birds themselves, a leisurely drift in a dugout canoe through the sanctuary's mangrove swamps offers a fascinating insight into life on this fragile terrain.

The best time to visit is either in the early morning (around 8am) or in the evening (a couple of hours before sunset), but since the Mandovi is a tidal river, boat trips depend somewhat on tide times. You'll find boatmen, in possession of dugout canoes to take you paddling about the sanctuary, waiting around at the ferry landing on Chorao Island; the going rate is around ₹800 for a 1½-hour trip. The forest department also operates two boats, which can hold up to 10 or 12 people, for ₹750 or ₹900 respectively. Don't forget to bring binoculars and a field guide to all things feathered if you're a keen birdwatcher.

To get to Chorao Island by bus, board a bus from Panaji bound for Old Goa and ask to be let off at the Ribandar ferry crossing.

Sleeping

Chorao is virtually undeveloped tourism-wise with just a couple of low-key guesthouses.

Island Pool Villa GUESTHOUSE $$$
(971505583613; opposite St Batholomew's Church; villa incl breakfast from ₹11,700;) This beautiful four-bedroom Portuguese villa on Chorao Island sleeps up to 12 people, so is a good deal for a family or group looking to get away from the beach and enjoy village life. Rooms are filled with antiques and four-poster beds but are air-conditioned and the shady garden with swimming pool is serene. Meals available.

Getting There & Away

The main route to Chorao is on the regular free vehicle ferry from the village of Ribandar, about 5km east of Panaji via the scenic Ponte de Linhares Causeway. There's another ferry linking Chorao with Divar Island.

Divar Island

Stepping off the ferry from Old Goa or San Pedro onto beautiful little riverine Divar Island, you have the distinct feeling of entering the land that time forgot. Surrounded by marshy waters and crisscrossed with sleepy single-lane roads, the island makes for lovely, languid exploration, and though there's not much particularly to see, it's a serene and seldom-visited place to take in the atmosphere of old-time rural Goa.

The largest settlement on the island is sleepy but picturesque **Piedade**. But Divar, whose name stems from the Konkani *dev* and *vaddi* (translated as 'place of the Gods'), has an important Hindu history that belies its modern day tranquillity.

Sights

Before the coming of the Portuguese, Divar was the site of two particularly important temples – the Saptakoteshwara Temple (moved across the river to Bicholim when the Portuguese began to persecute the Hindus), as well as a Ganesh temple that stood on the solitary hill in Piedade. The former contained a powerful Shivalingam (phallic symbol representing the god Shiva), which was smuggled during the Inquisition to Naroa on the opposite side of the river, just before more than 1500 Divar residents were forcibly converted to Christianity. It's likely that the Ganesh temple, meanwhile, was destroyed by Muslim troops near the end of the 15th century, since the first church on this site was built in around 1515.

The church that occupies the hill today, the **Church of Our Lady of Compassion**, combines an impressive facade with an engagingly simple interior. The ceiling is picked out in plain white stucco designs, and the windows are set well back into the walls, allowing only a dim light to penetrate into the church; the views alone, however, make Piedade and its church worth the trip.

Beside the church, a small cemetery offers one of only a few fragments of the once grand Kadamba dynasty. The small chapel in its grounds was converted from an older Hindu shrine, and the carving, painted plaster ceiling and faint stone tracery at the window all date from before the death of the Kadamba dynasty in 1352. Look around for the priest, who'll unlock the chapel for you to take a look.

Sleeping

Divar has just a handful of guesthouses and family homes with rooms to rent.

Island House B&B $$
(8322280605; www.islandhousegoa.com; No 45 Piedade; r incl breakfast ₹5600;) Island House is a divine family-run homestay in a beautiful old Portuguese mansion. The villa and heritage rooms come with bathroom and colonial furnishings while outside is a pretty garden and pool, part of the rambling grounds. Home-cooked meals can be enjoyed inside or by the pool. It's just west of the main village but there's no sign – call ahead.

Getting There & Away

Divar Island can only be reached by one of three free vehicle ferry services. A boat from Old Goa (near the Viceroy's Arch) runs to the south side of the island, while the east end of the island is connected by ferry to Naroa in the Bicholim taluk (district). Another ferry operates to Ribandar from the southwest of the island. Ferries run frequently from around 7am to 8pm.

Old Goa

From the 16th to the 18th centuries, when Old Goa's population exceeded that of Lisbon or London, Goa's former capital was considered the 'Rome of the East'. You can still sense that grandeur as you wander what's left of the city, with its towering churches and cathedrals and majestic convents. Its rise under the Portuguese, from 1510, was meteoric, but cholera and malaria outbreaks forced the abandonment of the city in the 17th century. In 1843 the capital was officially shifted to Panaji. Some of the most imposing churches and cathedrals are still in use and are remarkably well preserved, while other historical buildings have become museums or simply ruins. It's a fascinating day trip, but it can get crowded: consider visiting on a weekday morning.

History

The first records of a settlement on the site of Old Goa date back to the 12th century and a Brahmin colony known as Ela. Though continuously occupied, it wasn't until the 15th century that Ela rose to prominence, with the Muslim Bahmani rulers choosing it as the site for a new Goan capital, in place of the ransacked and silted-up port capital of Govepuri (today Goa Velha).

Within a short time the new capital was a thriving city. Contemporary accounts tell of the magnificence of the city and of the grandeur of its royal palace, the city enlarged and strengthened with ramparts and a moat. It became a major trading centre and departure point for pilgrims to Mecca, and also gained prominence for its shipbuilding.

With the arrival of the Portuguese in the 16th century, Ela became the new Portuguese capital and a base for the shipment of spices back to the Old World. Soon came missionaries (including the young Francis Xavier), intent on converting the natives, followed in 1560 by the Inquisition, who came to put paid to the legendary licentious

Old Goa

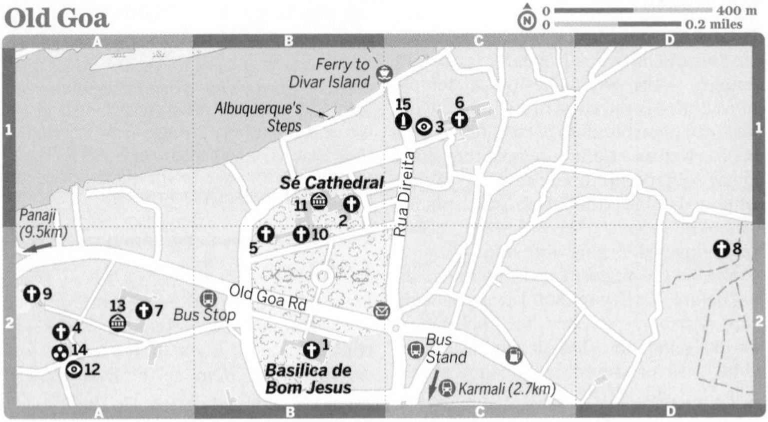

Old Goa

Top Sights
1 Basilica de Bom Jesus B2
2 Sé Cathedral B1

Sights
3 Adil Shah Palace Gateway C1
Archaeological Museum .... (see 5)
4 Chapel of St Anthony A2
5 Chapel of St Catherine B2
6 Church & Convent of St Cajetan C1
7 Church & Convent of St Monica A2
8 Church of Our Lady of the Mount D2
9 Church of Our Lady of the Rosary A2
10 Church of St Francis of Assisi B2
11 Kristu Kala Mandir Art Gallery B1
12 Monastery of St Augustine A2
13 Museum of Christian Art A2
14 Ruins of the Church of St Augustine A2
15 Viceroy's Arch C1

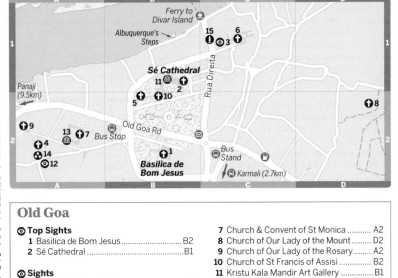

behaviour of both locals and colonials. Though their methods were gruesome, the behaviour they were targeting was widespread: despite the proliferation of churches and cathedrals, Old Goa was a city of drunkenness and debauchery; even the clerics themselves sometimes kept harems of slave girls, and death from syphilis was rife.

Syphilis, however, wasn't to be Old Goa's most widespread disease. The city had been built on swamps, a breeding ground for mosquitoes and malaria, while water sources tainted with sewage caused cholera to sweep its streets. Moreover, by the end of the 16th century the Mandovi River was silting up and Portuguese supremacy on the seas had been usurped by the British, Dutch and French. The city's decline was accelerated by another devastating cholera epidemic in 1635. Finally, by 1759, the Portuguese had had enough, and the Viceroy moved his official residence to Panjim.

In 1843 Panjim was officially declared the new capital, and by 1846 only Old Goa's convent of Santa Monica was in regular use, though that was also eventually abandoned, leaving the shadow of a grand and desolate city behind.

From the late 19th century until the mid-20th century, Old Goa remained a city of ghosts, empty but for one or two buildings used as military barracks. When archaeological interest started to increase, work was done to clear the area, and some buildings were returned to their former uses. But for many of the once-glorious buildings, plundered for building materials or simply fallen victim to the elements, the reprieve came too late; the starkest reminder of this is the skeletal tower of the Church of St Augustine, which can be seen for miles around.

Sights

★ Sé Cathedral CATHEDRAL

(8am-6pm, Mass 7am & 6pm Mon-Sat, 7.15am, 10am & 4pm Sun) At over 76m long and 55m wide, the cavernous Sé Cathedral is the largest church in Asia. Building commenced in 1562, on the orders of King Dom Sebastiao of Portugal, and the finishing touches were finally made some 90 years later. The exterior is notable for its plain style, in the Tuscan tradition. Also of note is its rather lopsided look resulting from the loss of one of its bell towers, which collapsed in 1776 after being struck by lightning.

The remaining tower houses the famous Sino de Ouro (Golden Bell), the largest in Asia and renowned for its rich tone, which once tolled to accompany the Inquisition's notoriously cruel *autos-da-fé* (trials of faith), held out the front of the cathedral on what was then the market square.

The huge interior of the cathedral is surprisingly plain. To the right as you enter is a small, locked area that contains a font made in 1532, said to have been used by St Francis Xavier. Two small statuettes, inset into the main pillars, depict St Francis Xavier and St Ignatius Loyola. There are four chapels on either side of the nave, two of which have screens across the entrance. Of these, the **Chapel of the Blessed Sacrament** is outstanding, with every inch of wall and ceiling gorgeously gilded and decorated – a complete contrast to the austerity of the cathedral interior.

Opposite, to the right of the nave, is the other screened chapel, the **Chapel of the Cross of Miracles**. The story goes that in 1619 a simple cross (known as the Cruz dos Milagres), made by local shepherds, was erected on a hillside near Old Goa. The cross grew bigger and several witnesses saw an apparition of Christ hanging on it. A church was planned on the spot where the vision had appeared and while this was being built the cross was stored nearby. When it came time to move the cross into the new church it was found that it had grown again and that the doors of the church had to be widened to accommodate it. The cross was moved to the cathedral in 1845, where it soon became, and remains, a popular place of petition for the sick.

Towering above the main altar is the huge gilded reredos (ornamental screen), its six main panels carved with scenes from the life of St Catherine, to whom the cathedral is dedicated. She was beheaded in Alexandria, and among the images here are those showing her awaiting execution and being carried to Mt Sinai by angels.

★**Basilica de Bom Jesus** CHURCH

(⏲7.30am-6.30pm) Famous throughout the Roman Catholic world, the imposing Basilica de Bom Jesus contains the tomb and mortal remains of St Francis Xavier, the so-called Apostle of the Indies. St Francis Xavier's missionary voyages throughout the East became legendary. His 'incorrupt' body is in the mausoleum to the right, in a glass-sided coffin amid a shower of gilt stars. Freelance guides at the entrance will show you around for ₹100.

Construction on the basilica began in 1594 and was completed in 1605, to create an elaborate late-Renaissance structure, fronted by a facade combining elements of Doric, Ionic and Corinthian design. Prominent in the design of the facade is the intricately carved central rectangular pediment, embellished with the Jesuit emblem 'IHS', an abbreviation of the Latin 'Iesus Hominum Salvator' (Jesus, Saviour of Men).

This is the only church in Old Goa not plastered on the outside, the lime plaster having been stripped off by a zealous Portuguese conservationist in 1950. Apparently his notion was that exposed to the elements, the laterite stone of which the basilica is built would become more durable and thus the building would be strengthened. Despite proof to the contrary, no one has got around to putting the plaster back yet; hence, some of the intricate carving is eroding with the dousing of each successive monsoon.

Inside, the basilica's layout is simple but grand, contained beneath a simple wooden ceiling. The huge and ornate gilded reredos, stretching from floor to ceiling behind the altar, takes pride of place, its baroque ornament contrasting strongly with the classical, plain layout of the cathedral itself. It shows a rather portly St Ignatius Loyola, protecting a tiny figure of the infant Jesus. His eyes are raised to a huge gilded sun above his head,

VISITING OLD GOA

As Goa's top historical attraction and a focal point for pilgrims and domestic bus tours, Old Goa can get very crowded on weekends and feast days. The best time to visit is on a weekday morning, when you can take in Mass at Sé Cathedral or the Basilica de Bom Jesus and explore the rest of the site before the afternoon heat sets in. Remember to cover your shoulders and legs when entering the churches and cathedral, and observe the various signs – for instance, still photography is allowed in the churches, but not photos of people posing in the church. So no selfies.

OLD GOA'S ARCHITECTURE

In order to make the most of what you encounter in Old Goa, it's worth a brief brush-up on its architectural heritage.

Most churches are made of laterite, a local red and highly porous stone, which was traditionally coated in white lime wash, mixed with crushed clam shells, in an effort to prevent erosion. Some were embellished with harder-wearing basalt, much of it quarried from Bassein, near Mumbai, though some is thought to have been brought as ballast by ships from Portugal.

Built in an era of colonialism, much of what's on display today is staunchly European, inspired by the building fashions of late-Renaissance Rome. The pinnacle of building here (in the early 17th century) coincided with the rise in Europe of the baroque movement, characterised by its love of dripping gilt, scrollwork and ornamentation. This pomp and splendour served an important purpose for its priests and missionaries, as it kept the locals awed into submission, feeling dwarfed and vulnerable when confronted with an immense gold altarpiece.

The second style evident at Old Goa is more wholly Portuguese, known as Manueline, after its main patron King Manuel I. This vernacular approach saw the embellishment of buildings with symbols reflecting Portuguese might; anchors, ropes and other maritime motifs represent Portugal's ascendancy on the high seas. Though not too much Manueline architecture has survived the test of time, the Church of Our Lady of the Rosary (p104) remains a well-preserved example.

on which 'IHS' is again emblazoned, above which is a representation of the Trinity.

To the right of the altar is the slightly grisly highlight for the vast majority of visitors: the body of St Francis Xavier himself. The body was moved into the church in 1622, and installed in its current mausoleum in 1698 courtesy of the last of the Medicis, Cosimo III, Grand Duke of Tuscany, in exchange for the pillow on which St Francis' head had been resting. Cosimo engaged the Florentine sculptor Giovanni Batista Foggini to work on the three-tiered structure, constructed of jasper and marble, flanked with stars, and adorned with bronze plaques that depict scenes from the saint's life. Topping it all off, and holding the shrivelled saint himself, is the casket, designed by Italian Jesuit Marcelo Mastrili and constructed by local silversmiths in 1659, whose sides were originally encrusted with precious stones which, over the centuries, have been picked off.

Crowds are busiest at the basilica during the **Feast of St Francis Xavier**, held annually on 3 December and preceded by a nine-day devotional novena, with lots of lighthearted festivity alongside the more solemn open-air Masses. Once every 10 years, the saint is given an exposition, and his body hauled around Old Goa before scores of pilgrims. The next one is in 2024.

Passing from the chapel towards the sacristy there are a couple of items relating to St Francis' remains and, slightly further on, the stairs to a gallery of modern art.

Next to the basilica is the **Professed House of the Jesuits**, a two-storey laterite building covered with lime plaster. It actually predates the basilica, having been completed in 1585. It was from here that Jesuit missions to the east were organised. Part of the building burned down in 1633 and was partially rebuilt in 1783.

Mass is held in the basilica in Konkani at 7am and 8am Monday to Saturday, at 8am and 9.15am on Sunday, and in English at 10.15am on Sunday. Confession is held daily in the sacristy from 5pm to 6pm.

Church & Convent of St Cajetan CHURCH
(⌚8am-6pm) Modelled on the original design of St Peter's in Rome, this impressive church was built by Italian friars of the Order of Theatines, sent here by Pope Urban VIII to preach Christianity in the kingdom of Golconda (near Hyderabad). The friars, however, were refused entry to Golconda, so settled instead at Old Goa in 1640. The construction of the church began in 1655, and although it's perhaps less interesting than the other churches, it's still a beautiful building and the only domed church remaining in Goa.

Though the altar is dedicated to Our Lady of Divine Providence, the church is named after the founder of the Theatine order, St Cajetan (1480–1547), a contemporary of

St Francis Xavier. Born in Vicenza, St Cajetan spent his whole life in Italy, establishing the Order of Theatines in Rome in 1524. He was known for his work in hospitals and with 'incurables', and for his high moral stance in an increasingly corrupt Roman Catholic church. He was canonised in 1671.

The facade of the church is classical in design and the four niches on the front contain statues of apostles. Inside, clever use of internal buttresses and four huge pillars have given the interior a cruciform construction, above the centre of which is the towering dome. The inscription around the inside of the base of the dome is a verse from the Gospel of St Matthew. The largest of the altars on the right-hand side of the church is dedicated to St Cajetan himself. On the left side are paintings illustrating episodes in the life of St Cajetan; in one it appears, quite peculiarly, that he is being breastfed at some distance by an angel whose aim is remarkably accurate. Traditionally, the last mortal remains of deceased Portuguese governors were kept in the church's crypt, beneath the reredos, in lead coffins until their shipment home to their final resting place. The last few, forgotten for more than three decades, were finally sent back to Lisbon in 1992.

Adjoining the church, the Convent of St Cajetan is nowadays a college for recently ordained priests.

Church of St Francis of Assisi CHURCH

(⏲9am-5pm) West of the Sé Cathedral, the Church of St Francis of Assisi is no longer in use for worship, and consequently exudes a more mournful air than its neighbours.

The church started life as a small chapel, built on this site by eight Franciscan friars on their arrival in 1517. In 1521 it was replaced by a church consecrated to the Holy Ghost, which was then subsequently rebuilt in 1661, with only the doorway of the old building incorporated into the new structure. This original doorway, in ornate Manueline style, contrasts strongly with the rest of the facade, the plainness of which had become the fashion by the 17th century.

Maritime themes – unsurprising given Old Goa's important port status – can be seen here and there, including navigators' globes and coats of arms, which once adorned ships' sails.

The interior of the church, though now rather ragged and faded, is nevertheless beautiful, in a particularly 'folk art' style. The walls and ceiling are heavily gilded and decorated with carved wood panels, with large paintings depicting the works of St Francis adorning the walls of the chancel. Look out for the huge arch that supports the choir, painted vividly with floral designs, and the intricately carved pulpit. The reredos dominates the gilded show, although this one is different to others in Old Goa, with a deep recess for the tabernacle. The four statues in its lower portion represent apostles, and above the reredos hangs Christ on the cross. The symbolism of this scene is unmistakable: Jesus has his right arm free to embrace St Francis, who is standing atop the three vows of the Franciscan order – Poverty, Humility and Obedience.

Museum of Christian Art MUSEUM

(☎0832-2285299; www.museumofchristianart.com; ₹50, camera ₹100; ⏲9.30am-5pm Mon-Sat) This museum, housed in part of the 1627 Convent of St Monica, contains a collection of statues, paintings and sculptures. Interestingly, many of the works of Goan Christian art made during the Portuguese era, including some of those on display here, were produced by local Hindu artists. Unfortunately the museum is closed for refurbishment but will reopen in 2020.

Archaeological Museum MUSEUM

(adult/child ₹10/free; ⏲9am-5pm) The archaeological museum houses some lovely fragments of sculpture from Hindu temple sites in Goa, and some *sati* stones, which once marked the spot where a Hindu widow committed suicide by flinging herself onto her husband's funeral pyre.

You'll also find two large bronze statues here: one of the Portuguese poet Luís Vaz de Camões (p104), which once stood more prominently in the central grassy area of Old Goa, and one of Afonso de Albuquerque, the Portuguese conqueror and first governor of Goa, which stood in the Azad Maidan in Panaji, before being moved here after Independence.

Upstairs, a gallery contains portraits of some 60 of Goa's Portuguese viceroys, spanning more than 400 years of Portuguese rule. Not particularly exciting in terms of portraiture, they're an interesting insight into Portugal's changing fashions, each as unsuitable for the tropical heat as the last.

Church & Convent of St Monica CHURCH

(⏲8am-5pm) Work on this three-storey laterite church and convent commenced in 1606 and was completed in 1627, only to burn

LUÍS VAZ DE CAMÕES

Luís Vaz de Camões (1524–80), regarded as Portugal's greatest poet, was banished to Goa in 1553 at the age of 29, after being accused of fighting with, and wounding, a magistrate in Lisbon. He was obviously no soft touch, for he enlisted in the army and fought with some distinction before attracting further official disapproval for publicly criticising Goa's Portuguese administration.

His reward this time was to be exiled to the Moluccas, and he returned to Goa only in 1562 to write his most famous work, *Os Lusíadas*, an epic poem glorifying the adventures of Vasco da Gama, which, classical in style and imperialist in sentiment, has since become an icon of Portuguese nationalism.

A statue of Camões, erected in 1960, stood at the centre of Old Goa until 1983, when many Goans decided that it was an unacceptable relic of colonialism. An attempt by radicals to blow it up met with failure, but the authorities took the hint and removed the statue. It now stands, along with Afonso de Albuquerque and various other disgraced Portuguese colonials, in the Archaeological Museum (p103) in Old Goa.

down nine years later. Reconstruction began the following year and it's from this time that the current buildings date. Once known as the 'Royal Monastery' because of the royal patronage that it enjoyed, the building comprised the first nunnery in the East and was finally abandoned when the last sister died in 1885.

During the 1950s and '60s the buildings housed first Portuguese and then Indian troops, before being returned to the church in 1968. The building is now used by nuns of the Mater Dei Institute. The high point of a visit is a peek at the 'miraculous' cross behind the high altar, said to have opened its eyes in 1636, when blood began to drip from its crown of thorns.

Church of Our Lady of the Rosary CHURCH

(⌚8am-5pm) Passing beneath the buttresses of the Convent of St Monica, about 250m further along the road is the Church of Our Lady of the Rosary, which stands on the top of a high bluff. It's one of the earliest churches in Goa; legend has it that Afonso de Albuquerque surveyed the action during his troops' attack on the Muslim city from this bluff and vowed to build a church there in thanks for his victory.

It's also thought to be here that St Francis Xavier gave his first sermon upon his arrival in Old Goa. The church, which has been beautifully restored, is Manueline in style and refreshingly simple in design. There are excellent views of the Mandovi River and Divar Island from the church's dramatic position, but unfortunately the building is frequently locked.

The only ornaments on the outside of the church are simple rope-twist devices, which bear testimony to Portugal's reliance on the sea. Inside the same is true; the reredos is wonderfully plain after all the gold decorating in the churches down in the centre of Old Goa, and the roof consists simply of a layer of tiles. Set into the floor in front of the altar is the tombstone of one of Goa's early governors, Garcia de Sá, and set into the northern wall of the chancel is that of his wife, Caterina a Piró.

Chapel of St Catherine CHURCH

About 100m to the west of the Church of St Francis of Assisi stands the small Chapel of St Catherine. An earlier chapel was erected on this site by Portuguese conqueror Afonso de Albuquerque in 1510 to commemorate his triumphant entry into the city on St Catherine's Day. In 1534 the chapel was granted cathedral status by Pope Paul III and was subsequently rebuilt; the inscribed stone added during rebuilding states that Afonso de Albuquerque actually entered the city at this spot, and thus it's believed that the chapel stands on what used to be the main gate of the Muslim city, then known as Ela.

Chapel of St Anthony CHURCH

The Chapel of St Anthony, dedicated to the saint of the Portuguese army and navy, was one of the earliest to be built in Goa, again on the directions of Afonso de Albuquerque in order to celebrate the assault on the city. Like the other institutions around it, St Anthony's was abandoned in 1835 but was brought back into use at the end of the 19th century and is now partly in use as a convent.

Monastery of St Augustine HISTORIC SITE
The melancholy, evocative ruins of this once vast and impressive Augustinian monastery are all that remain of a huge structure founded in 1572 and abandoned in 1835. The building's facade came tumbling down in 1942; all that remains, amid piles of rubble, is the towering skeletal belfry, though the bell itself was rescued and now hangs in Panaji's Church of Our Lady of the Immaculate Conception.

Kristu Kala Mandir Art Gallery GALLERY
(₹10; ⏲9.30am-5.30pm Tue-Sun) This gallery, sandwiched between the Church of St Francis of Assisi and Sé Cathedral, is located in what used to be the archbishop's house, and contains a hodgepodge collection of contemporary Christian art and religious objects.

Church of Our Lady of the Mount CHURCH
This church is often overlooked due to its location on a wooded hilltop, some 2km east of the central area. A sealed road leads to an overgrown flight of steps (don't walk it solo) and the hill on which the church stands commands an excellent view of Old Goa, with the church spires seemingly rising out of a sea of palms.

The church was built by Afonso de Albuquerque, completed in 1519, and has been rebuilt twice since; it now makes the perfect, suitably sorrowful place to watch the sunset over the ruins of once-mighty Old Goa. Usually locked, you can gain entry during the Feast of St Francis Xavier in December, and the Monte Music Festival in February, when concerts are held here.

Ruins of the Church of St Augustine RUINS
Standing on Holy Hill (Monte Santo) is perhaps the most mournful memorial to Old Goa's fallen might. All that's left today of the Church of St Augustine is the 46m-high tower, which served as a belfry and formed part of the church's facade. The church was constructed in 1602 by Augustinian friars who had arrived in Old Goa in 1587 and was abandoned in 1835.

As Old Goa emptied due to a continual series of deadly epidemics, the church fell into neglect and the vault collapsed in 1842. In 1931 the facade and half the tower fell down, followed by more sections in 1938. The tower's huge bell was moved in 1871 to the Church of Our Lady of the Immaculate Conception (p84) in Panaji, where it can be seen (and heard) today.

Viceroy's Arch MONUMENT
(Rua Direita) Perhaps the best way to arrive in Old Goa is the same way that visitors did in the city's heyday. Approaching along the wide Mandovi River, new arrivals would have first glimpsed the city's busy wharf just in front of the symbolic arched entrance to the city.

This archway, known as the Viceroy's Arch, was erected by Vasco da Gama's grandson, Francisco da Gama, who became viceroy in 1597. On the side facing the river, the arch (which was restored in 1954 following a collapse) is ornamented with the deer emblem on Vasco da Gama's coat of arms. Above it in the centre of the archway is a statue of da Gama himself.

Adil Shah Palace Gateway HISTORIC SITE
Next to the Convent of St Cajetan, this freestanding basalt doorway, atop five steps, is the only remains of the grand palace of Goa's 16th-century Muslim ruler Adil Shah. It was later converted into the notorious Palace of the Inquisition, in whose dungeons countless 'heretics' languished, awaiting their dreadful fate. The palace was torn down in the 18th century and its materials repurposed for building in Panaji.

Festivals & Events

Feast of St Francis Xavier RELIGIOUS
(Old Goa; ⏲3 Dec) A celebration of Goa's patron saint; a nine-day novena precedes the feast day, when Old Goa's churches are packed. Once every 10 years, the saint's body is paraded through Old Goa past the visiting pilgrims. Next is 2024.

Procession of All Saints RELIGIOUS
(⏲Mar/Apr) On the fifth Monday in Lent, this is the only procession of its sort outside Rome, whereby 30 statues of saints are paraded around Old Goa and neighbouring villages.

Information

Old Goa has no tourist office, but willing tour guides linger outside the main churches and charge around ₹100 for a tour. You can enquire at the Archaeological Museum (p103), which stocks books on Old Goa, including S Rajagopalan's excellent booklet *Old Goa*, published by the Archaeological Survey of India. One of the most comprehensive is *Old Goa: the Complete Guide* by Oscar de Noronha (2004).

Getting There & Away

There are frequent buses to Old Goa (₹10, 20 minutes) from the Kadamba bus stand in Panaji to Old Goa's **bus stand** (Old Goa Rd) by the main roundabout. Buses to Panaji or Ponda from Old Goa leave when full (around every 10 minutes) from either the main roundabout bus stand or the bus stop/ATM at the western end of Old Goa Rd.

From the waterfront near the Viceroy's Arch, a free **ferry** runs to Divar Island. There's a petrol station near the main roundabout.

Goa Velha

Though it's hard to envisage it today, the little village of Goa Velha – nowadays just a blur of roadside buildings on a trip south towards Margao along the national highway NH66 – was once home to Govepuri, a grand international port and capital city, attracting Arab traders who settled the surrounding area, rich from the spoils of the spice trade.

History

Before the establishment of Old Goa (then known as Ela) as Goa's Muslim capital around 1472, Govepuri, clinging to the banks of the Zuari River, flourished under the Hindu Kadamba dynasty. It was only centuries later, long after grand Govepuri had fallen, that the place was renamed Goa Velha by the Portuguese, to distinguish it from their new capital, Old Goa, known to them simply as Goa.

The city, which in its heyday was southwest India's wealthiest, was established by the Kadambas around 1054, but in 1312 was almost totally destroyed by Muslim invaders from the north, and over the following years was repeatedly plagued by Muslim invasions. It wasn't until Goa came under the control of the Hampi-based Vijayanagar Empire in 1378 that trade revived, but by this time the fortunes of the old capital had declined beyond repair, due to both its crushing destruction and the gradual silting-up of its once lucrative port. In 1472 the Muslim Bahmani sultanate took Goa, destroyed what remained of Govepuri, and moved the capital to Old Goa.

Sights

Just off the main road at the northern extent of Goa Velha is the **Church of St Andrew**, which hosts an annual Saints Procession festival. On the Monday a fortnight before Easter, 30 statues of saints are taken from their storage place in Old Goa and paraded around the roads of the village. The festivities include a small fair, and the crowds that attend this festival are so vast that police have to restrict movement on the highway that runs through the village.

Church of St Anne CHURCH

(Talaulim) About 5km north of Goa Velha, in the small village of Talaulim, the massive Church of St Anne (known to the local people simply as Santana) is an imposing

PILAR SEMINARY

A few kilometres north of Goa Velha, and 12km southeast of Panaji, set on a hill high above the surrounding countryside, is **Pilar Seminary**, one of four theological colleges built by the Portuguese. Only two of these seminaries still survive, the other being Rachol Seminary (p169) near Margao. The hill upon which the seminary stands was once the site of a large and ancient Hindu temple, dedicated to Shiva; it's thought that this was the Goveshwar Mandir, from whose name Goa is thought to have derived. The college was established here in 1613 by Capuchin monks, naming it Our Lady of Pilar, after the statue they brought with them from Spain.

Abandoned in 1835 when the Portuguese expelled the religious orders, the seminary was rescued by the Carmelites in 1858 and became the headquarters of the Missionary Society of St Francis Xavier in 1890. The movement gradually petered out and in 1936 the buildings were handed over to the Xaverian League. Today the seminary is still in use, as a training centre for missionaries, and is also the site of local pilgrimages by those who come to give thanks for the life of Father Agnelo de Souza, a director of the seminary in the early 20th century who was beatified after his death.

Aside from the beautiful views afforded from its roof terrace, the seminary is home to a small **museum** (8am-1pm & 3-6pm Mon-Sat) FREE, which holds some of the Hindu relics discovered on-site, as well as some lovely religious paintings, carvings and artefacts. The 1st floor of the building houses a small, but brilliantly lit, chapel.

OFF THE BEATEN TRACK

CAVES OF KHANDEPAR

In the village of Khandepar, 5km northeast of Ponda, and set back in the dense forest behind the Mandovi River, are four small (well-hidden) rock-cut caves believed to have been carved into the laterite stone around the 12th century, though some archaeologists date their origin back as early as the 9th century. These are among Goa's oldest remaining historical treasures, but were only rediscovered in 1970.

Ask around locally for the exact whereabouts of the caves – someone will eventually point you in the right direction.

Thought to have been used by a community of Buddhist monks, each of the four caves consists of two simple cells, with tiered roofs added in the 10th or 11th centuries by the Kadamba dynasty who, it's thought, appropriated the caves and turned them into Hindu temples. The fourth cave supports the Buddhist theory, containing a pedestal used for prayer and meditation. There are also niches in the walls for oil lamps, and pegs carved for hanging clothes. The first cave, meanwhile, has a lotus medallion carved into its ceiling, typical of the later Kadambas.

17th-century structure which, after years of monsoon rain and neglect, had begun to crumble. Restoration work in the early 2000s brought the stunning facade largely back to its former glory as one of the greatest churches of its type – baroque, with Indian influences – in existence. Its massive five-storey facade is covered in intricate carving, and the interior – largely dating from the 18th and 19th centuries – is still intact. If you find the chapel locked, tug on the church bell to summon the key-holder.

Church of St Lawrence CHURCH

About 3km south of Goa Velha, at the south end of the small village of Agassim, is the Church of St Lawrence, a plain and battered-looking building that houses one of the most flamboyantly decorated reredos in Goa. The heavily gilded construction behind the altar is unique not only for its wealth of detail but also for its peculiar design, which has multitudes of candlesticks projecting from the reredos itself. The panelled blue-and-white ceiling of the chancel sets the scene.

Ponda Region

POP 22,664

Ponda is more Indian in appearance and character than any other Goan town and has no attractions – or much in the way of hotels or worthwhile restaurants – in the city itself. The main reason to visit Ponda is to explore Goa's oldest and best-preserved Hindu temple complexes scattered in the countryside outside town. This region is also home to several spice plantations, which offer farm tours and lunch.

Sights

For nearly 250 years after the arrival of the Portuguese in 1510, Ponda taluk (district) remained under the control of Muslim or Hindu rulers, and many of its temples came into existence when Hindus were forced to escape Portuguese persecution by fleeing across its district border, bringing their sacred temple deities with them as centuries-old edifices were destroyed by the new colonial regime.

Here the temples remained, safe from the destruction that occurred in the Velhas Conquistas (Old Conquests), and by the time that Ponda itself came under Portuguese control, increased religious tolerance meant that the temples remained unharmed.

But despite the temples' intrepid history, true temple junkies may be disappointed with the area's architectural collection. Most were built during the 17th and 18th centuries, making them modern compared to those elsewhere in India. Nevertheless, what they lack in ancient architecture they make up for with their highly holy ancient deities, salvaged on devout Hindus' flights from probable death at the hands of the Inquisition.

The temples are clustered in two main areas: the first in the countryside 5km west of Ponda, and the second north along the route of the NH4A highway. If you're not a true temple-traipser, the two with most appeal are the Shri Mahalsa (p108) and Shri Manguesh (p109) temples, both near the villages of Priol and Mardol.

Ponda

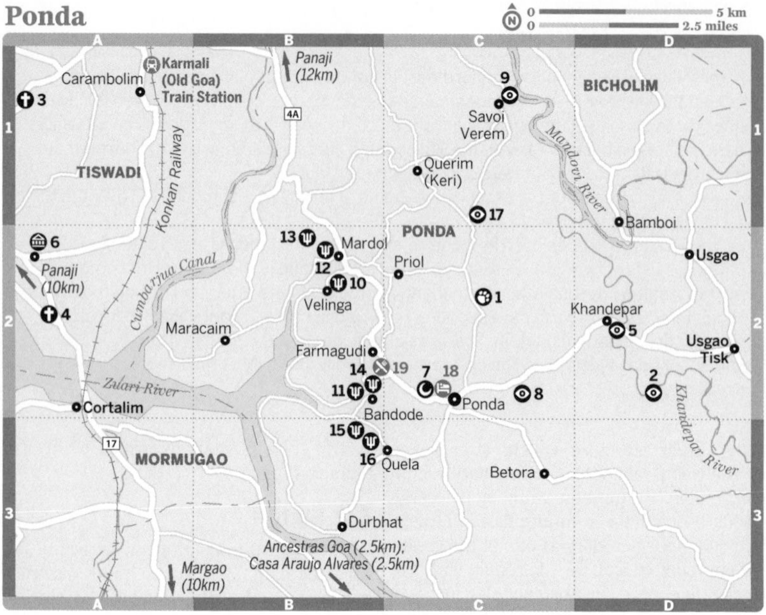

Ponda

Sights

1 Butterfly Conservatory of Goa C2
2 Caves of Khandepar D2
3 Church of St Anne A1
4 Church of St Lawrence A2
5 Pascoal Spice Farm D2
6 Pilar Museum A2
7 Safa Shahouri Masjid C2
8 Sahakari Spice Farm C2
9 Savoi Plantation C1
10 Shri Laxmi Narasimha Temple B2
11 Shri Mahalaxmi Temple B2
12 Shri Mahalsa Temple B2
13 Shri Manguesh Temple B2
14 Shri Naguesh Temple B2
15 Shri Ramnath Temple B3
16 Shri Shantadurga Temple B3
17 Tropical Spice Plantation C1

Sleeping

18 Hotel Sun Inn C2

Eating

19 Sandeep Cold Drinks B2

Shri Mahalsa Temple HINDU TEMPLE

(Mardol) The Mahalsa Temple, 1km down the road from the Shri Manguesh Temple, is in the tiny village of Mardol. This temple's deity originally resided in an ancient shrine in the village of Verna in Salcete taluk (district). The buildings were reputedly so beautiful that even the Portuguese priest whose job it was to oversee their destruction requested that they should be preserved and converted into a church.

Permission was refused, but before the work began in 1543 the deity was smuggled to safety. Mahalsa is a uniquely Goan deity, this time an incarnation of Vishnu in female form. Various legends suggest how Mahalsa came into being. In one, Vishnu, who was in a particularly tight corner during a struggle with the forces of evil, disguised himself as Mohini, the most beautiful woman ever seen, in order to distract his enemies. The trick worked and Mohini, with her name corrupted to Mahalsa, was born. To complicate matters, Mahalsa also fits into the pantheon as an incarnation of Shiva, the destroyer. In general, however, she is regarded by her devotees as a representative of peace; for this, and for her multifaceted identity, she has many devotees.

Once you pass through the entrance gate off the busy side street, the temple is pleasantly peaceful. The inner area is impressive, with huge wooden pillars and slatted windows and, like most of the other temples in this area, an ornamented silver frame surrounds the doorway to the sanctum. Walk around to the back of the main building and peer through the archway to the water tank; the combination of the ancient stonework, palm trees and paddy fields beyond is quite a sight.

In front of the temple stands a large *deepastambha* (lamp tower) and a 12.5m-high brass oil lamp that is lit during festivals; it's thought to be the largest such lamp in the world.

In addition to the annual chariot procession held in February for the **Zatra festival**, the temple is also famous for two other festivals. Jasmine flowers are offered in tribute to the god Mahalsa during the **Zaiyanchi Puja festival**, which falls in August or September. The full-moon festival of **Kojagiri Purnima** is also celebrated here; on this particular night (usually in September) the goddess Lakshmi (Laxmi) descends to earth to bestow wealth and prosperity on those who stay awake to observe the night-time vigil.

Shri Manguesh Temple HINDU TEMPLE

Around 9km north of Ponda, this temple is one of the most visited of Goa's Hindu temples, admirably combining two key features of Goan Hinduism: first, it's dedicated to a solely Goan deity (in this case the local god Manguesh), and second, it exhibits the mixture of architectural styles that typifies the region's temples.

The temple's original location was on the south side of the Zuari River, near the present-day village of Cortalim. When the Portuguese took control, its ancient Shivalingam stone was brought to Priol and installed in a new temple (enlarged later in the mid-18th century), an effort that saw Hindus from Portuguese-held districts risking death, arriving in the dead of night to worship here. Today the temple has grown to encompass a substantial complex that includes accommodation for pilgrims and administrative offices.

Architecturally, Shri Manguesh shows the influences of both Christian and Muslim styles. There's evidence of Christian influence in the octagonal tower above the sanctum, the pillared facade of the impressive seven-storey *deepastambha* (lamp tower), the largest in Goa, and the balustrade design around the roof, while the domed roofs indicate a Muslim influence. The tank (reservoir) in front of the temple is the oldest part of the complex. If you walk down to the right-hand side of the temple you can also see the giant *raths* (chariots) that are used to parade the deities during the temple's festival, which takes place in the last week of January or the first week of February.

Manguesh, the temple's god, is said in Goan Hindu mythology to be an incarnation of Shiva. The story goes that Shiva, having lost everything to his wife Parvati in a game of dice, came to Goa in a self-imposed exile. When Parvati eventually came looking for him, he decided to frighten her and disguised himself as a tiger. In horror, Parvati cried out *'Trahi mam girisha!'* (Oh lord of mountains, save me!), whereupon Shiva resumed his normal form. The words *'mam girisha'* became associated with the tale, and Shiva's tiger incarnation, with time, became known as Manguesh. The Shivalingam left to mark the spot where all this happened was eventually discovered by a shepherd, and a temple was built to house it at the temple's original location near Cortalim.

Shri Shantadurga Temple HINDU TEMPLE

Surrounded by forest and paddy fields, the Shri Shantadurga Temple is one of the most famous shrines in Goa and is consequently packed with those who come to worship, as well as day trippers brought in by the busload. Hustle past the rows of roadside hawkers to get a look at this heavily European-inspired creation, built in 1738, 200 years after its deity had been smuggled in from Quelossim, not far from present-day southern Colva.

The goddess Shantadurga is another form taken by Parvati, Shiva's consort. As the most powerful of the goddesses, Parvati could either adopt a violent form, Durga, or she could help to bring peace, as Shanta. The legend goes that during a particularly savage quarrel between Shiva and Vishnu she appeared in her Durga form and helped to make peace between the two gods – thus embodying the contradiction that the name Shantadurga implies. In Goa she has come to be worshipped as the goddess of peace and has traditionally had a large following.

Shri Laxmi Narasimha Temple HINDU TEMPLE

(Velinga) Almost immediately after leaving the village of Mardol on the main road, a side road to the right takes you up a hill towards the little village of Velinga and the Laxmi Narasimha Temple, one of the most

WORTH A TRIP

SPICE UP YOUR LIFE

The Ponda region is the centre of commercial spice farms in Goa and several have opened their doors as tourist operations, offering a guided tour of the plantation, buffet thali-style lunch and in some cases a cultural show.

These farms typically produce spices such as vanilla, pepper, cardamom, nutmeg, chilli and tumeric, along with crops such as cashew, betel nut, coconut, pineapple and papaya.

Savoi Plantation (☎9423888899, 0832-2340272; www.savoiplantations.com; adult/child ₹700/350; ⏰9am-4.30pm) This 200-year-old plantation, 12km north of Ponda, is the least touristy in the region. Knowledgeable guides will walk you through the 40-hectare plantation. Local crafts are also for sale and there are a couple of cottages for overnight stays.

Sahakari Spice Farm (☎0832-2312394; www.sahakarifarms.com; admission incl lunch ₹400; ⏰8am-4.30pm) This well-touristed farm is just 2km from Ponda near the village of Curti.

Pascoal Spice Village (☎0832-2344268; farm tour & lunch ₹400; ⏰9am-4.30pm) About 7km east of Ponda, Pascoal offers bamboo river-rafting and cultural shows, along with farm tours and lunch.

Tropical Spice Plantation (☎0832-2340329; www.tropicalspiceplantation.com; Keri; tour incl lunch ₹400; ⏰9am-4pm) Around 5km north of Ponda, this is one of the most popular farms with tour groups, so is often busy and probably best avoided by independent travellers on weekends.

attractive and secluded temples around Ponda. It's dedicated to Narasimha, or Narayan, a half-lion half-human incarnation of Vishnu, which he created to defeat a formidable adversary.

The deity was moved here from the district of Salcete in 1567, and the most picturesque part of the temple is the old water tank, to the left of the compound as you enter, spring-fed and entered via a ceremonial gateway. Although the temple has a sign by the door announcing that entry is for the 'devoted and believers only', respectful nonbelievers will probably be allowed to have a look.

Shri Naguesh Temple HINDU TEMPLE

In the village of Bandode is the small and peaceful Naguesh Temple. The most striking part of the temple is the ancient water tank, with its overhanging palms, fishy depths and weathered stones, together making an attractive scene. Also of note are colourful images in relief around the base of the *deepastambha* (lamp tower), and the frieze of Ramayana scenes running inside along the tops of the pillars.

Unlike its neighbours, this temple was in existence well before Albuquerque ever set foot in Goa, but the buildings you see today are newish and rather uninteresting. The temple is dedicated to Shiva, known in this incarnation as Naguesh, and is particularly rich in animal representation.

Shri Ramnath Temple HINDU TEMPLE

Though undoubtedly one of Ponda's less-attractive temples, Shri Ramnath is notable for the impressive and extravagant silver screen on the door to the sanctum. Other temples have similar finery but the work here is exceptional, in particular the two unusual scenes depicted at the top of the lintel.

Shri Mahalaxmi Temple HINDU TEMPLE

Only 4km outside Ponda, and a stone's throw from Naguesh Temple, is the relatively uninspiring Mahalaxmi Temple. The goddess Mahalaxmi, looked upon as the mother of the world, was particularly worshipped by the Shilahara rulers and by the Kadambas, and thus has featured prominently in the Hindu pantheon in southern India. Here she wears a lingam (phallic symbol of Shiva) on her head, symbolising her connection with Shiva.

Safa Shahouri Masjid MOSQUE

(Safa Masjid) The Safa Shahouri Masjid, Goa's oldest remaining mosque, is on Ponda's northern outskirts. Built by Bijapuri ruler Ali Adil Shah in 1560, it was originally surrounded by gardens, fountains and a palace, and is said to have matched the mosques at Bijapur in size and quality. Today little remains of the mosque's former grandeur, despite attempts at restoration by the Archaeological Survey of India.

Bondla Wildlife Sanctuary WILDLIFE RESERVE
(adult/child ₹50/10, camera/video camera ₹30/150; ⏲9am-5pm Tue-Sun) At only 8 sq km, Bondla Wildlife Sanctuary is Goa's smallest protected wildlife sanctuary. Though not particularly remote, it's really only accessible if you have your own transport or a car and driver. You're unlikely to see animals just by wandering around the sanctuary, though the park's jungly reaches are home to wild boar, gaurs (Indian bison), monkeys, jackals, leopard and deer, but if you're committed, it's a butterfly-spotter and birdwatcher's paradise. The sanctuary is about 10km from Usgao village. A return taxi here from Panaji should cost around ₹2000, or ₹1000 from Ponda.

Bondla has Goa's only zoo, a very small moated offering, which is a bit sad considering it's within a wildlife sanctuary; still, it gives you a look at a leopard, crocodiles, porcupines and snakes. There's also a nature interpretation centre and botanical gardens (neither of which are worth the trip out here in themselves).

There are some Forest Department cottages here if you want to spend the night.

Butterfly Conservatory of Goa SANCTUARY
(☎0832-2985174; Priol; ₹100; ⏲9am-4.30pm) This small butterfly sanctuary, 5km north of Ponda, is home to more than 100 species of free-flying butterflies (it's not enclosed) in a small patch of jungle. It's a labour of love for the owners and worth a look if you're visiting nearby spice plantations.

Sleeping & Eating

There's little reason to stay overnight in Ponda but it has a scattering of unremarkable hotels ranged along the main road, with budget rooms priced from ₹1200, plus a few decent midrangers.

Hotel Sun Inn HOTEL $$
(☎0832-2318180; www.hotelsuninn.com; s/d incl breakfast from ₹2900/4000; ❄📶) Sun Inn is a comfortable multistorey business hotel a few kilometres from central Ponda on the highway to Panaji, making it handy for temple visits. Expect clean, orderly rooms with TV and air-con. The upper-floor rooms have good views over the countryside.

Sandeep Cold Drinks FAST FOOD $
(Nageshi Temple Rd; snacks from ₹25) This little stall is a local institution, specialising in *vada pau* (deep-fried spicy potato served with a fluffy fresh bun). Filling and cheap. It's just off the highway at Farmagudi, north of Ponda.

Getting There & Away

There are regular buses from Ponda to Panaji (₹25, one hour) and Margao (₹20, one hour).

To reach Shri Mahalsa and Shri Manguesh temples, both near the villages of Priol and Mardol, any bus between Panaji and Ponda can drop you off near the temples. To get to other temples of the region, or to the spice farms, it's easiest to hire a scooter or motorbike, or negotiate a day rate with a taxi from Panaji, Ponda or Margao. Alternatively, take one of the GTDC's lightning day trips.

Molem Region

If you're keen to visit Goa's largest protected wildlife area, the state's oldest temple, or the second-highest waterfall in India, then make tracks for Molem, a dusty village on the main road heading east into Karnataka state.

About 7km south of Molem, the small village of Colem (Kulem) is a train stop on the South Central Railway and the jumping off point for Dudhasaghar Falls.

Sights & Activities

Dudhsagar Falls WATERFALL
(admission/camera ₹50/300) Situated in the far southeastern corner of the Bhagwan Mahavir Wildlife Sanctuary, Goa's most impressive waterfall splashes down just west of the border with Karnataka state. At 603m this is the second highest in India, after Jog Falls. The falls are best visited as soon after monsoon as possible (October is perfect), when the water levels are highest and the cascades earn their misty nomenclature, Dudhsagar, meaning 'Sea of Milk' in Konkani.

Getting to the falls starts with a trip to the village of Colem (Kulem), around 7km south of Molem, either by car or by the scenic 8.15am local train from Margao or the 7.50am VSG Horawh Express – the South Central Railway line actually crosses over the falls, offering excellent views. Check

GOA'S TEMPLE ARCHITECTURE

Though Goa's temples often exhibit a strange and colourful blend of traditional Hindu, Christian and Muslim architectural elements, several of their key components remain constant.

On entering a temple, you'll first reach the *prakara* (courtyard), which surrounds the whole complex, often encompassing a *tirtha* (water tank), in which worshippers bathe before continuing into the temple. Next you'll pass one or two pillared *mandapas* (assembly halls), used for music, dancing and congregational prayer.

Through these, you'll arrive at the *antaralya* (main shrine), surrounded by a *pradakshena* (passage) for circumambulation, and flanked by two shrines of the temple's lesser deities. Within the main shrine is the *garbhagriha* (shrine room), which houses the *devta* (sacred deity) – in elaborate statue or simple stone form – and forms the most sacred part of the temple. Only high-caste Brahmin priests are admitted to the shrine room, where they perform regular ritual purifications. Topping off the shrine room is the *shikhara* (sanctuary tower), which symbolises the Divine Mountain, the source of the sacred River Ganges.

Sanctuary towers tend to have been influenced by Portuguese church trends, often resulting in octagonal towers topped by a copper dome. *Mandapa* roofs are often terracotta-tiled, decorated with oriental images imported from Macau, another Portuguese colony, and embellished with Muslim motifs. The most distinct of all, however, are the Maratha-conceived *deepastambhas* or *deepmals* (lamp towers) – multistoreyed pagodas usually standing beside the temple's main entrance, whose multiple cubby holes hold dozens of oil lamps stunningly illuminated on special occasions and during the weekly ceremonial airing of the *devta*.

return train times in advance, as they vary seasonally. From Colem, pick up a shared jeep (₹500 per person for seven people) for the bumpy 45-minute journey, then it's a 10-minute clamber up over the rocks to reach the falls themselves.

Dudhsagar is an extremely popular day trip with a limit of 300 jeeps allowed in per day and there can often be long waits and queuing for tickets. To alleviate this you can now book a jeep or time-slot online through Ticket Papa (www.tiketpapa.com). It requires a registration process, valid mobile phone number and credit card.

The jeep takes you into the sanctuary, through a rough but scenic jungle track (there are three streams to be forded). En route, you'll pass **Devil's Canyon**, a beautiful gorge with a river running between the steep-sided rocks.

Swimming is possible at the falls themselves (compulsory life jackets are provided for ₹40), but don't picture yourself taking a romantic swim on your own – there will be plenty of other bathers joining in. You can also walk the distance to the head of the falls (though it's unwise without a local to guide you), a real uphill slog, but resulting in beautiful views.

Goa Tourism runs one of its trademark whirlwind day trips, the 'Dudhsagar Special' (₹2300) to the waterfall, with stops at Old Goa, Ponda and lunch at Molem and Shri Mahadeva Temple at Tambdi Surla. Tours depart at 6.30am from Calangute or Panaji. Private travel agents also offer tours.

It's no longer possible to trek to the falls or take your own transport.

Shri Mahadeva Temple HINDU TEMPLE

(Tambdi Surla) FREE If you're a history or temple buff, don't miss the atmospheric remains of the unusual little Hindu Shri Mahadeva Temple at Tambdi Surla, 12km north of Molem. Built around the 12th century by the Kadamba dynasty, it's the only temple of dozens of its type to have survived both the years and the various conquerings and demolishings by Muslim and Portuguese forces, probably due to its remote jungle setting.

No one quite knows why this spot was chosen, since historically there was no trade route passing by here and no evidence of there having been any major settlement nearby.

The temple itself is very small, facing eastward so that the rays of dawn light up its deity. At the eastern end, the open-sided *mandapa* (assembly hall) is reached through doorways on three sides. The entrance to the east faces a set of steps down to the river, where ritual cleansing was carried out before worship. Inside the *mandapa* the plain slab ceiling is supported by four huge carved pillars. The clarity of the designs on the stone is testimony not only to the skill of the artisans, but also to the quality of the rock that was imported for the construction; look out for the image on one of the bases of an elephant crushing a horse, thought to symbolise Kadambas' own military power at the time of the temple's inauguration.

The best examples of the carvers' skills, however, are the superb lotus-flower relief panel set in the centre of the ceiling, and the finely carved pierced-stone screen that separates the outer hall from the *antaralya* (main shrine), flanked by an image of Ganesh and several other deities. Finally, beyond the inner hall is the *garbhagriha* (shrine room), where the lingam resides.

The exterior of the temple is plain, with a squat appearance caused by the partial collapse of its *shikhara* (sanctuary tower). On the remains of the tower are three relief carvings depicting the three most important deities in the Hindu pantheon: on the north side is Vishnu, to the west is Shiva and to the south is Brahma.

Bhagwan Mahavir Wildlife Sanctuary WILDLIFE RESERVE

(adult/child ₹20/10, camera/video camera ₹30/150; ⏲8.30am-5.30pm) The entrance to Bhagwan Mahavir Wildlife Sanctuary is easily accessible from Molem and, with an area of 240 sq km, this is the largest of Goa's four protected wildlife areas; it also encompasses the 107-sq-km **Molem National Park**. In theory, tickets are available at the Forest Interpretation Centre, 2km before the park entrance, close to Molem town.

The best way to explore the park is to organise a tour through a travel agent or hire a jeep for the day in Molem or Colem. Most tours will also visit Dudhsagar Falls and the Devil's Canyon. At Dudhsagar Spa Resort, staff can arrange trips into the park's interior.

Shy and hard-to-spot wildlife include jungle cats, Malayan giant squirrels, gaurs, sambars, leopards, chitals (spotted deer), slender loris, Malayan pythons and cobras. There's an observation platform a few kilometres into the park; as with most parks, the best time to see wildlife is in the early morning or late evening.

Dudhsagar Plantation FARM

(☎9765364456; www.dudhsagarplantation.com; guided tour incl lunch ₹600) A less-touristy alternative to the Ponda region spice plantations, this relatively remote farm is about 30km from Margao on the road to Colem. As well as a spice tour and lunch, you can take a dip in the river or arrange transport to the falls. Tours require minimum five people. There's also farm-stay accommodation available (double room from ₹3300).

Sleeping

Dudhsagar Spa Resort RESORT $$

(☎9766337696, 0832-2877766; www.dudhsagarsparesort.com; Molem; d/tents incl breakfast ₹3100/3500; ❄📶🏊) Molem's main accommodation option, Dudhsagar Spa Resort is quite a bargain with air-con bungalows and luxury tents, set up around a garden. The tents are great, with huge beds, sleek modern furnishings and gorgeous deep baths, set on the quiet side of the site amid tall trees filled with monkeys. Online rates are often cheaper.

Cajueiro Homestead FARMSTAY $$

(☎0832-2221122; www.cajueirohomestead.com; Advoi Village; d incl meals ₹7200) This remote-feeling farm retreat, 26km northwest of Molem and 23km northeast of Ponda, is the kind of place you book to get away from the beach, the traffic and the outside world. On a sprawling cashew and coconut plantation, the six rooms are comfortable and thoughtfully furnished, the restaurant provides meals and there's even a natural swimming pool.

Walks around the farm and quiet introspection are the main attraction here. It's

THE DHANGARS

Goa's green eastern reaches are home to the Dhangars, one of the state's nomadic tribes who have lived, for centuries, on buffalo herding. Their lifestyle, like that of many other nomadic tribes, is today threatened (in their case by deforestation and high levels of alcoholism), and many have been forced to move to cities in search of work, or attempt settled forms of agriculture. You might, however, still see them in far-flung stretches of the park, tending their lowing, leathery livestock as they have for centuries.

hard to find (Valpoi is the nearest town) but transfers can be arranged from Panaji.

Getting There & Away

Molem is on the main Panaji–Belgaum highway (NH748), so frequent buses run here from Panaji (₹60, 2½ hours) or Margao (₹50, two hours).

For Dudhsagar Falls, catch the 8.15am passenger train from Margao to Kulem station (₹10, one hour).

Beyond Goa

East of Goa, the most popular excursion – an overnight trip or longer – is to the magical ruins and traveller centre of Hampi in Karnataka state.

Hampi

08394 / POP 3600

The magnificent ruins of Hampi dot an unearthly landscape that has captivated travellers for centuries. Heaps of giant boulders perch precariously over kilometres of undulating terrain, their rusty hues offset by jade-green palm groves, banana plantations and paddy fields. While it's possible to see this World Heritage Site in a day or two, plan on lingering for a while.

The main travellers' ghetto has traditionally been Hampi Bazaar, a village crammed with budget lodges, shops and restaurants, and towered over by the majestic Virupaksha Temple. Tranquil Virupapur Gaddi, across the river, has become a popular hang-out.

History

Hampi and its neighbouring areas are mentioned in the Hindu epic Ramayana as Kishkinda, the realm of the monkey gods. In 1336 Telugu prince Harihararaya chose Hampi as the site for his new capital Vijayanagar, which – over the next couple of centuries – grew into one of the largest Hindu empires in Indian history. By the 16th century it was a thriving metropolis of about 500,000 people, its busy bazaars dabbling in international commerce and brimming with precious stones and merchants from faraway lands. All this, however, ended with a stroke in 1565, when a confederacy of Deccan sultanates razed Vijayanagar to the ground, striking it a blow from which it never recovered.

Sights

Set over 36 sq km, the Hampi area has some 3700 monuments to explore – it would take months if you were to do it all justice. The ruins are divided into two main areas: the **Sacred Centre** around Hampi Bazaar with its temples, and the **Royal Centre** towards Kamalapuram, where the Vijayanagara royalty lived and governed.

Your ticket for Vittala Temple entitles you to same-day admission to most of the paid sites across the ruins (including around the Royal Centre and the Archaeological Museum), so don't lose it.

Sacred Centre

★ **Virupaksha Temple** HINDU TEMPLE

(Map p115; ₹2, camera/video ₹50/500; dawn-dusk) The focal point of Hampi Bazaar is this temple, one of the city's oldest structures, and Hampi's only remaining working temple. The main *gopuram* (gateway), almost 50m high, was built in 1442; a smaller one was added in 1510. The main shrine is dedicated to Virupaksha, an incarnation of Shiva.

An elephant called Lakshmi blesses devotees as they enter, in exchange for dona-

HAMPI BAZAAR DEMOLITIONS

While in 1865 it was the Deccan sultanates who levelled Vijayanagar, today a different battle rages in Hampi, between conservationists bent on protecting Hampi's architectural heritage and the locals who have settled there.

In 1999 Unesco placed Hampi on its list of World Heritage Sites in danger because of 'haphazard informal urbanisation' around the temples, particularly the ancient bazaar area near Virupaksha Temple. The government consequently produced a master plan that aimed to classify all of Hampi's ruins as protected monuments. In 2011 and again in 2016 this resulted in the dramatic and heavy-handed demolition of shops, hotels and homes in the ancient bazaar and later in the old village of Virupapur Gaddi.

By late 2018 things seemed to have stabilised: Hampi Bazaar still exists as an enclave of guesthouses and restaurants north of Virupaksha Temple and businesses were also open over the river in Virupapur Gaddi. But the future for both areas remains uncertain.

Hampi Bazaar

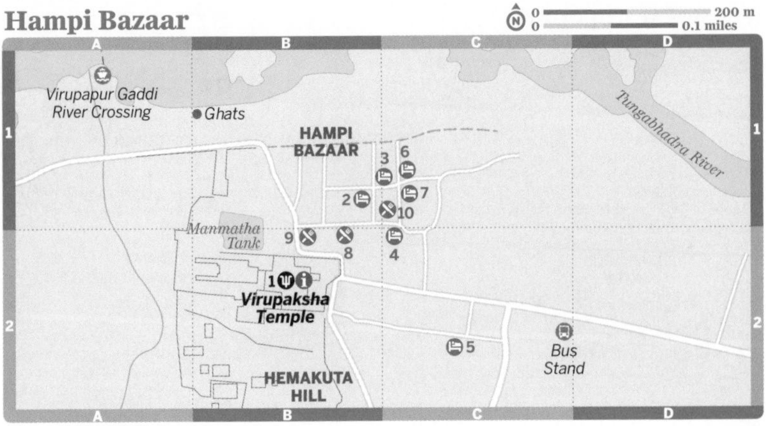

Hampi Bazaar

Top Sights
1 Virupaksha Temple B2

Sleeping
2 Ganesh Guesthouse B1
3 Gopi Guest House C1
4 Manash Guesthouse C2
5 Padma Guest House C2
6 Pushpa Guest House C1
7 Thilak Homestay C1

Eating
8 Mango Tree B2
9 Moonlight B2
10 Ravi's Rose C1

tions; she gets time off for a morning bath down by the river **ghats**.

★Vittala Temple HINDU TEMPLE
(Map p116; Indian/foreigner/child under 15yr ₹40/500/free; ⏲8.30am-5.30pm) Hampi's most exquisite structure, the 16th-century Vittala Temple stands amid boulders 2.5km from Hampi Bazaar. Work possibly started on the temple during the reign of Krishnadevaraya (r 1509–29). The structure was never finished or consecrated, yet its incredible sculptural work remains the pinnacle of Vijayanagar art.

The courtyard's ornate **stone chariot** (illustrated on the ₹50 note) is the temple's showpiece and represents Vishnu's vehicle with an image of Garuda within. Its wheels were once capable of turning.

★Achyutaraya Temple HINDU TEMPLE
(Map p116; Tiruvengalanatha Temple) At the southern end of Sule Bazaar is the beautiful Achyutaraya Temple, dating from 1534, one of the last great monuments constructed before the fall of Hampi. You approach the temple via two partly ruined *gopuram* (gateways). The central hall boasts elaborately carved pillars and sculptures, including Krishna dancing with a snake. Its isolated location at the foot of Matanga Hill makes it quietly atmospheric – doubly so since it's rarely visited.

Sule Bazaar HISTORIC SITE
Halfway along the path from Hampi Bazaar to Vittala Temple, a track to the right leads over the rocks to deserted Sule Bazaar, one of ancient Hampi's principal centres of commerce and reputedly its red-light district. A near-kilometre-long stone colonnade flanking its eastern side is very well preserved. At the southern end of this area is the beautiful 16th-century Achyutaraya Temple. Admission included with Vittala admission.

Lakshimi Narasmiha HINDU TEMPLE
An interesting stop along the road to Virupaksha Temple is the 6.7m monolithic statue of the bulging-eyed Lakshimi Narasmiha in a cross-legged lotus position and topped by a hood of seven snakes.

Krishna Temple HINDU TEMPLE
Built in 1513, Krishna Temple is fronted by an *apsara* (celestial nymph) and 10 incarnations of Vishnu. It's on the road to Virupaksha Temple near Lakshimi Narasmiha.

Hampi & Anegundi

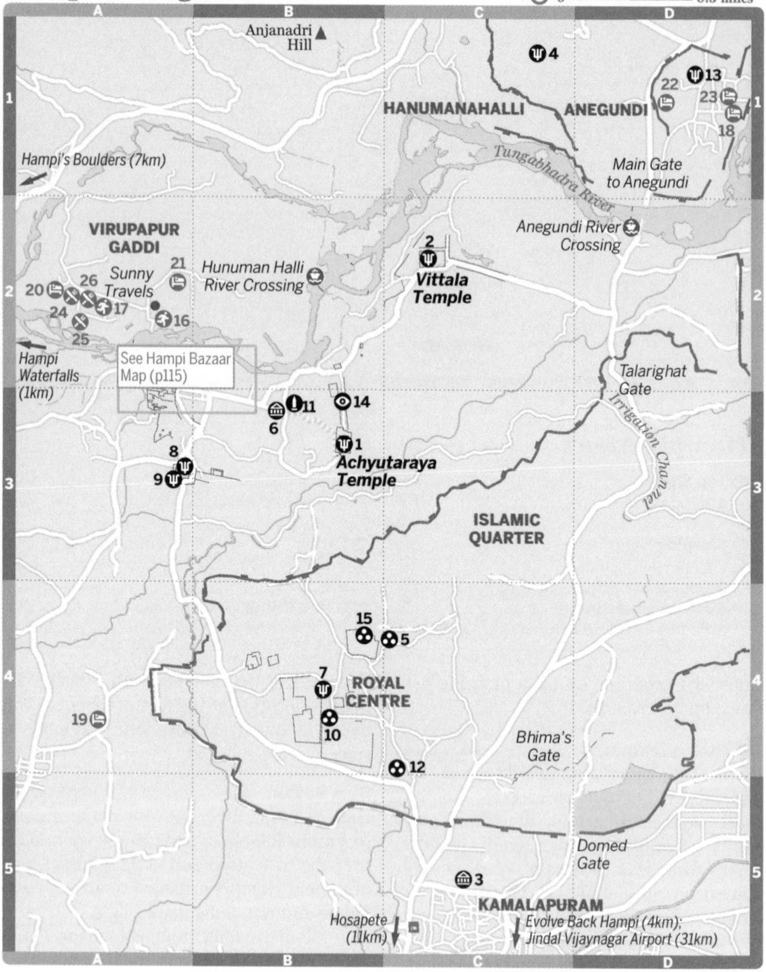

Nandi Statue STATUE
(Map p116) At the eastern end of Hampi Bazaar is a Nandi statue, around which stand some of the colonnaded blocks of the ancient marketplace. This is the main location for Vijaya Utsav (p118), the Hampi arts festival.

Hampi Heritage Gallery GALLERY
(Map p116; ⏲10am-1pm & 3-6pm Tue-Sun) FREE A photo exhibition on Hampi's history and architecture.

Royal Centre

While it can be accessed by a 2km foot trail from the Achyutaraya Temple, the Royal Centre is best reached via the Hampi–Kamalapuram road. A number of Hampi's major sites stand here.

Queen's Bath RUINS
(⏲8.30am-5.30pm) South of the Royal Centre you'll find various temples and elaborate waterworks, including the Queen's Bath, deceptively plain on the outside but amazing within, featuring Indo-Islamic architecture.

Hampi & Anegundi

Top Sights

1	Achyutaraya Temple	B3
2	Vittala Temple	C2

Sights

3	Archaeological Museum	C5
4	Durga Temple	C1
5	Elephant Stables	C4
6	Hampi Heritage Gallery	B3
7	Hazarama Temple	B4
8	Krishna Temple	A3
9	Lakshimi Narasmiha	A3
	Lotus Mahal	(see 15)
10	Mahanavami-diiba	B4
11	Nandi Statue	B3
12	Queen's Bath	C4
13	Ranganatha Temple	D1
14	Sule Bazaar	B3
15	Zenana Enclosure	B4

Activities, Courses & Tours

16	Thimmaclimb	A2
17	Tom & Jerry	A2

Sleeping

18	Peshegaar Guest House	D1
19	Shankar Homestay	A4
20	Shanthi	A2
21	Sunny Guesthouse	A2
22	Uramma Cottage	D1
23	Uramma House	D1

Eating

24	Gouthami	A2
25	Laughing Buddha	A2
26	Nargila	A2

Admission included with Vittala Temple (p115) admission.

Zenana Enclosure RUINS
(Map p116; Indian/foreigner ₹40/500; 8.30am-5.30pm) Northeast of the Royal Centre, within the walled ladies' quarters, is the Zenana Enclosure. Its peaceful grounds and manicured lawns feel like an oasis in the arid surrounds. The **Lotus Mahal** and Elephant Stables are found here.

Elephant Stables ARCHAEOLOGICAL SITE
(Map p116; 8.30am-5.30pm) This grand building with 11 domed chambers is where the state elephants once resided – each chamber has a small opening where mahouts (keepers) entered. The stables are accessed via the Zenana enclosure. There's a free sound-and-light show here at 7pm, weather permitting.

Mahanavami-diiba RUINS
(Map p116) The Mahanavami-diiba is a 12m-high, three-tiered platform with intricate carvings and panoramic vistas of the walled complex of ruined temples, stepped tanks and the king's audience hall. The platform was used as a royal viewing area for festivities, allowing the Vijayanagar royals (and visiting nobility from other regions) to preside over military parades, sporting contests and musical performances in a show of power, tradition and celebration. Admission is included with Vittala Temple (p115) admission.

Hazarama Temple HINDU TEMPLE
(Map p116) Features exquisite carvings that depict scenes from the Ramayana, and polished black-granite pillars.

Archaeological Museum MUSEUM
(Map p116; Kamalapuram; 10am-5pm Sat-Thu) Boasts a fine collection of sculpture from local sites, plus neolithic tools, 16th-century weaponry and a large floor model of the Vijayanagar ruins. Don't miss the information panels: one details the king's daily rituals, which included drinking 400ml of sesame oil, followed by a wrestling match and then a horse ride, all before daybreak!

There's also a photographic record of the site dating back to 1856. Site admission included with Vittala Temple (p115) admission.

Activities

Hampi Waterfalls WATERFALL
About a 2km walk west of Hampi Bazaar, past shady banana plantations, you can scramble over the boulders to reach the attractive Hampi 'waterfalls', a series of small whirlpools among the rocks amid superb scenery.

Bouldering

Hampi is the undisputed bouldering capital of India. The entire landscape is a climber's adventure playground made of granite crags and boulders, some bearing the marks of ancient stonemasons. *Golden Boulders* (2013), by Gerald Krug and Christiane Hupe, has a tonne of info on bouldering in Hampi.

Thimmaclimb CLIMBING
(Map p116; 8762776498; www.thimmaclimb.wix.com/hampi-bouldering; Virupapur Gaddi; classes from ₹500) Established operation run by local pro Thimma, who guides, runs lessons and stocks professional equipment for

hire and sale. He also runs three-day trips (₹5000) to Badami for sandstone climbing.

Tom & Jerry CLIMBING
(Map p116; ☑ 8277792588, 9482746697; http://climbingshop.hampivillage.com; Virupapur Gaddi; 2½hr classes ₹600) Two local lads who are doing great work in catering to climbers' needs, providing quality mats, shoes and regional knowledge, and running climbing sessions. They also offer rappelling and slacklining classes (each ₹500).

🎪 Festivals & Events

Vijaya Utsav CULTURAL
(Hampi Festival; ☉ Jan) Hampi's three-day extravaganza of culture, heritage and the arts.

Golden Boulders SPORTS
(☑ 9482746697; http://goldenbouldersfestival.hampivillage.com; ☉ Jan) Golden Boulders is a noncompetitive 10-day outdoor climbing festival. Organised by local climbing outfit Tom & Jerry, it also features yoga, bouldering on new routes and slacklining.

Virupaksha Car Festival RELIGIOUS
(☉ Mar/Apr) This big event features a colourful procession characterised by a giant wooden chariot (the temple car from Virupaksha Temple) being pulled along the main strip of Hampi Bazaar.

🛏 Sleeping

Most guesthouses are cosy, family-run digs, perfect for the budget traveller. Walk-in rates are usually much better than those found online. More upmarket places are located further from the centre. Some tour operators base their clients in Hosapete, a grim town that's a world away from Hampi in terms of ambience. Nearby Anegundi also has good accommodation.

🛏 Hampi Bazaar

This little enclave is a classic travellers' ghetto. However, its existence is under threat as there are plans to demolish it.

★**Manash Guesthouse** GUESTHOUSE $
(Map p115; ☑ 9448877420; manashhampi@gmail.com; r with fan/AC ₹1350/1600; ❇ 🛜) This place consists of just two rooms set off a little yard, but they're the best in Hampi Bazaar, each with quality mattresses, attractive decorative touches and fast, free wi-fi. It's owned by the Mango Tree people just along the lane, so if no one is around ask in the restaurant.

Thilak Homestay GUESTHOUSE $
(Map p115; ☑ 9449900964; www.facebook.com/thilak.homestay; r with fan/AC ₹1300/2000; ❇ 🛜) A step up from most places in the bazaar, this clean, orderly place has eight well-presented rooms (and more in another block) that have spring mattresses and hot water. Owner Kish is very helpful and can arrange a reliable autorickshaw driver or make other transport arrangements.

Pushpa Guest House GUESTHOUSE $
(Map p115; ☑ 9448795120; pushpaguesthouse99@yahoo.in; d from ₹1000, with AC from ₹1700; ❇ 🛜) A decent all-rounder with comfortable, attractive and well-presented rooms that have mosquito nets. It has a lovely roof terrace and a reliable travel agency.

Padma Guest House GUESTHOUSE $
(Map p115; ☑ 08394-241331; padmaguesthouse@gmail.com; d ₹900-2000; ❇ 🛜) Slightly more upmarket than many guesthouses in the bazaar area, this place has a choice of basic, decent rooms, many with views of Virupaksha Temple, though facilities and bathrooms could do with an upgrade. Still, the owners are helpful and can arrange autorickshaw drivers, bikes and onward transport.

Ganesh Guesthouse GUESTHOUSE $
(Map p115; vishnuhampi@gmail.com; r ₹600-900, with AC from ₹1500; ❇ 🛜) The small, welcoming, family-run Ganesh has been around for over 20 years and has four tidy rooms. Also has a nice rooftop restaurant.

★**Shankar Homestay** HOMESTAY $$
(Map p116; ☑ 9482169619; hanumayana@gmail.com; Ballari; r incl breakfast with fan/AC ₹2000/2300; ❇ 🛜) Lovely family-run homestay in a tranquil rural location around 2km west of the Royal Centre (bikes are available). The five spacious rooms are furnished with handmade textiles and crafts, and the ever-helpful, welcoming hosts' cooking is superb: be sure to try dinner here.

Gopi Guest House GUESTHOUSE $$
(Map p115; ☑ 08394-241695; www.facebook.com/gopiguesthouse; r with fan/AC ₹2000/2500; ❇ @ 🛜) A dependable, welcoming place split over two properties on the same street. Gopi offers friendly service and has good-quality rooms that are almost upscale by Hampi standards. There are fine views from its rooftop cafe.

Virupapur Gaddi

The rural tranquillity of village-like Virupapur Gaddi, across the river from Hampi Bazaar, has real appeal for long-term travellers. Its many nicknames include 'The Island', 'Hippy Island', and 'Little Jerusalem' as it's particularly popular with Israelis.

Sunny Guesthouse GUESTHOUSE **$**
(Map p116; 9448566368; www.sunnyguesthouse.com; Virupapur Gaddi; r ₹600-1500;) Sunny both in name and disposition, this popular guesthouse is a hit among backpackers for its characterful huts, very well-maintained tropical garden, hammocks and chilled-out restaurant.

Shanthi GUESTHOUSE **$**
(Map p116; 8533287038; http://shanthihampi.com; Virupapur Gaddi; cottages ₹1300-1850;) Shanthi offers attractive, earth-themed thatched cottages with couch swings dangling in their front porches. The location is stunning, with a row of cottages directly overlooking rice fields. The only drawback is that the restaurant's food is below par, but with many alternatives on your doorstep that's not a huge concern.

Hampi's Boulders LODGE **$$$**
(9480904202, 9448034202; www.hampisboulders.com; Narayanpet; r incl full board from ₹7100;) This 'ecowilderness' resort is 10km west of Virupapur Gaddi by the Tungabhadra River. It's an isolated but supremely relaxed place to escape, with a choice of cottages that have elegant furnishings and river views. There's a stunning natural pool for chlorine-free swims. Rates include a guided walk, and the restaurant's food uses ingredients from its organic farm. Limited wi-fi.

Eating

Due to Hampi's religious significance, meat is mainly off the menu, and no alcohol is supposed to be sold, though some restaurants flout the ban.

Gouthami MULTICUISINE **$**
(Map p116; mains ₹80-250; 8am-11pm) A well-run place with cushion seating (or dining tables) and an excess of psychedelic wall hangings. Serves tasty Indian, Israeli and Western classics. There's an espresso machine (cappuccinos ₹120), and it also offers good Turkish coffee and cardamom tea.

Moonlight MULTICUISINE **$**
(Map p115; mains ₹80-160; 7.30am-10pm) A family-owned place right behind Virupaksha Temple that serves good breakfasts, pancakes, curries and espresso coffee.

Laughing Buddha MULTICUISINE **$**
(Map p116; Virupapur Gaddi; mains from ₹80; 8am-10pm;) Down a lane off the main drag in Virupapur Gaddi, this well-regarded place has serene river views that stretch over to Hampi's temples. Its menu includes curries, burgers and pizzas; you dine on low tables and cushions. Cash only.

Ravi's Rose MULTICUISINE **$**
(Map p115; mains from ₹100; 8am-10.30pm;) A social hang-out, with a good selection of dosa and thalis, but most folks are here for the, erm, special lassis (cough).

★ **Mango Tree** MULTICUISINE **$$**
(Map p115; mains ₹130-310; 7.30am-9.30pm) Hampi's most famous restaurant has relocated to an atmospheric tented restaurant in the bazaar but is still run by three generations of the same local family. It's an efficiently managed place with good service and delicious Indian cuisines served on banana leaves. Try a thali.

Nargila MULTICUISINE **$$**
(Map p116; Virupapur Gaddi; mains ₹110-270; 8am-1am;) Spacious, sociable place where you can lounge around for hours sampling items from a global menu and slurping beer (₹220). Stays open late in the evening, when there's often live music.

Information

DANGERS & ANNOYANCES

Hampi is generally a safe, peaceful place. However, exercise standard precautions and don't wander around the ruins after dark. Women should avoid being alone in the more remote parts of the site. Note that alcohol and narcotics are illegal in Hampi, and possession can get you into trouble.

MONEY

There's no ATM in Hampi or Virupapur Gaddi, but both have moneychangers. You'll find three ATMs in Kamalapuram (3km away) and one in Anegundi, on the other side of the river.

Getting There & Away

Hosapete is the gateway to Hampi. There's only one daily direct (very slow) bus from Hampi Bazaar to Goa (₹725, 11 hours, 7pm). Travel agents can book bus tickets to Bengaluru (from ₹600, seven hours, several at 11pm), Hyderabad (from ₹820, nine hours, four nightly), Mumbai (from ₹950, 14 hours, many nightly), Mysuru (₹750, 12 hours, 9.30pm) and other destinations; many of these include a minibus transfer from Hampi to Hosapete.

Local buses departing from the **stand** connect Hampi with Hosapete (₹18, 30 minutes, half-hourly) between 5.45am and 7.30pm. An autorickshaw costs around ₹180. For Badami, travel via Hosapete.

Hosapete is Hampi's nearest train station. **Sunny Travels** (☑ 9448969809; hampisunny travels@gmail.com; ⊙ 9.30am-7pm) can help with bookings.

Jindal Vijaynagar Airport, 35km south of Hampi, has recently been upgraded and has daily TruJet flights to Bengaluru and Hyderabad.

❶ Getting Around

Bicycles cost ₹30 to ₹50 per day in Hampi Bazaar. Mopeds (₹250 to ₹500 per day) can only be hired 'over the river' in Virupapur Gaddi or Anegundi. Traffic is very light around Hampi, except on the road to Hosapete.

A small boat shuttles frequently across the **river crossing** (person/bicycle/motorbike ₹20/20/20; ⊙ 6am-6pm) to Virupapur Gaddi. After dark it costs ₹50 to ₹100 per person, depending on how late you cross. There are also boats to **Anegundi** (person/bicycle/motorbike ₹10/10/20; ⊙ 6am-5.30pm) and **Hunuman Halli** (person/bicycle ₹10/10; ⊙ 6am-5.45pm). Note that boats don't cross the river during high water (usually July/August, monsoon season).

Walking the ruins is possible, but expect to cover at least 7km just to see the major sites. The beautiful river section between Hampi Bazaar and Vittala Temple is a delight to stroll. Autorickshaws and taxis are available for sightseeing; an autorickshaw for the day costs around ₹750.

Tours (☑ 08394-241339; ⊙ 10am-5.30pm) depart from Hosapete and Hampi.

There's no public transport to Jindal Vijaynagar airport; a taxi costs ₹1600 and the journey takes an hour.

Anegundi
☑ 08394 / POP 5300

Anegundi is an ancient fortified village that's part of the Hampi World Heritage Site, but it predates Hampi by way of human habitation. The settlement has been spared the blight of commercialisation, and retains a delightfully rustic feel: the seasons dictate the cycle of change and craft traditions endure.

It's accessed by a river crossing or via a long loop from Virupapur Gaddi.

Mythically referred to as Kishkinda, the kingdom of the monkey gods, Anegundi retains many of its historic monuments, such as sections of its defensive wall and gates, and the **Ranganatha Temple** (Map p116; ⊙ dawn-dusk) devoted to Rama. Also worth visiting is the **Durga Temple** (Map p116; ⊙ dawn-dusk), an ancient shrine closer to the village, and the hilltop Hanuman Temple. Royal residences are steadily being renovated here.

🛏 Sleeping & Eating

Anegundi has fantastic homestays in restored heritage buildings. It's ideal for experiencing Indian village life.

Peshegaar Guest House GUESTHOUSE $
(Map p116; ☑ 9449972230; www.urammaheritage homes.com; Hanumanahalli; d ₹1344; ☜) This heritage house has five simple yet stylish rooms decorated with tribal textiles around a pleasant common area with a courtyard garden. Bathrooms are shared, but there are four.

★**Uramma Cottage** COTTAGE $$
(Map p116; ☑ 9448284658; www.urammaheritage homes.com; s/d incl breakfast ₹2688/5310; ☜) A wonderfully atmospheric lodge with rustic-chic cottages scattered around a large, grassy plot. The attention to detail is evident in the chunky wooden furniture, lovely bed linen and handmade textiles that add a splash of colour. Staff members couldn't be more helpful, and the restaurant serves very fine food (meals ₹400) and beer. Rates drop in low season.

Uramma House GUESTHOUSE $$$
(Map p116; ☑ 9449972230; www.urammaheritage homes.com; s/d per person ₹2688/5310; ☜) This 4th-century heritage house is a gem, with traditional-style rooms featuring exposed beams and boutique touches. It has two bedrooms and a dining room, and is ideal for a family or small group.

❶ Getting There & Away

Anegundi is 7km from Hampi, and reached by crossing the river on a boat (₹10) from the pier east of the Vittala Temple (p115). From Hampi, get here by moped or bicycle (if you're feeling energetic). An autorickshaw to the Anegundi crossing costs ₹100 from Hampi.

North Goa

Includes ➡

Best Places to Eat

- ➡ Go With the Flow (p134)
- ➡ Thalassa (p151)
- ➡ Villa Blanche Bistro (p143)
- ➡ Café Chocolatti (p128)
- ➡ Choco Cream Gelati (p140)

Best Places to Stay

- ➡ Dreams Hostel (p147)
- ➡ Happy Panda (p158)
- ➡ Mandala (p156)
- ➡ Marbella Guest House (p126)
- ➡ Alidia Beach Cottages (p133)

Why Go?

North Goa is the Goa you might have heard all about: crowded beaches, upbeat nightlife, Goan trance, cosmopolitan cuisine, hippie markets and yoga retreats. If you like a fast pace and plenty of things to do, this is the place.

The region is framed by two great rivers – the Mandovi in the south and the Terekhol in the north – with some 35km of golden beaches in between. Calangute and Baga are the epicentre of the region, one of the few beach strips still humming in the off-season. Anjuna, with its famous Wednesday market, and Vagator still exude some hippie cool and party vibe, while the laid-back beaches of Morjim, Asvem and Mandrem are burgeoning family-friendly, Russian-heavy resorts with some flashy beachfront huts. In the far north, Arambol returns a bit of hippie-chic as a budget traveller enclave with cheap clifftop accommodation.

When to Go

Anjuna

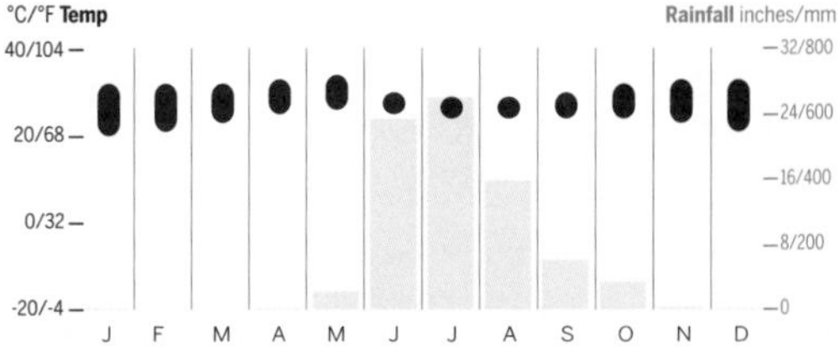

Nov–Mar High season; fine weather, beach shacks and yoga classes in full swing.

Mid-Dec–early Jan Crowds and prices peak but Christmas and NYE parties are legendary.

Oct & Apr Shoulder season; good weather, fewer crowds and cheaper rooms.

North Goa Highlights

1 **Mandrem** (p155) Sleeping in style, practising yoga and enjoying a good book.

2 **Anjuna flea market** (p140) Haggling for a bargain at this fun Wednesday market.

3 **Assagao** (p142) Cruising the country lanes and sampling fine restaurants.

4 **Arambol** (p157) Sleeping on a budget and paragliding above Sweetwater Lake.

5 **Vagator** (p145) Dining at one of the clifftop restaurants then partying into the night.

6 **Fort Aguada** (p125) Climbing to the old fort for views along the coast.

7 **Baga** (p135) Hitting the neon lights and food stalls at the Saturday night market.

8 **Dolphin trips** (p126) Taking a boat trip down the Nerul River.

9 **Asvem** (p153) Learning to surf, kitesurf or paddleboard at this broad beach.

10 **Anjuna** (p136) Dancing to Goa trance at Curlies or one of the Morjim clubs.

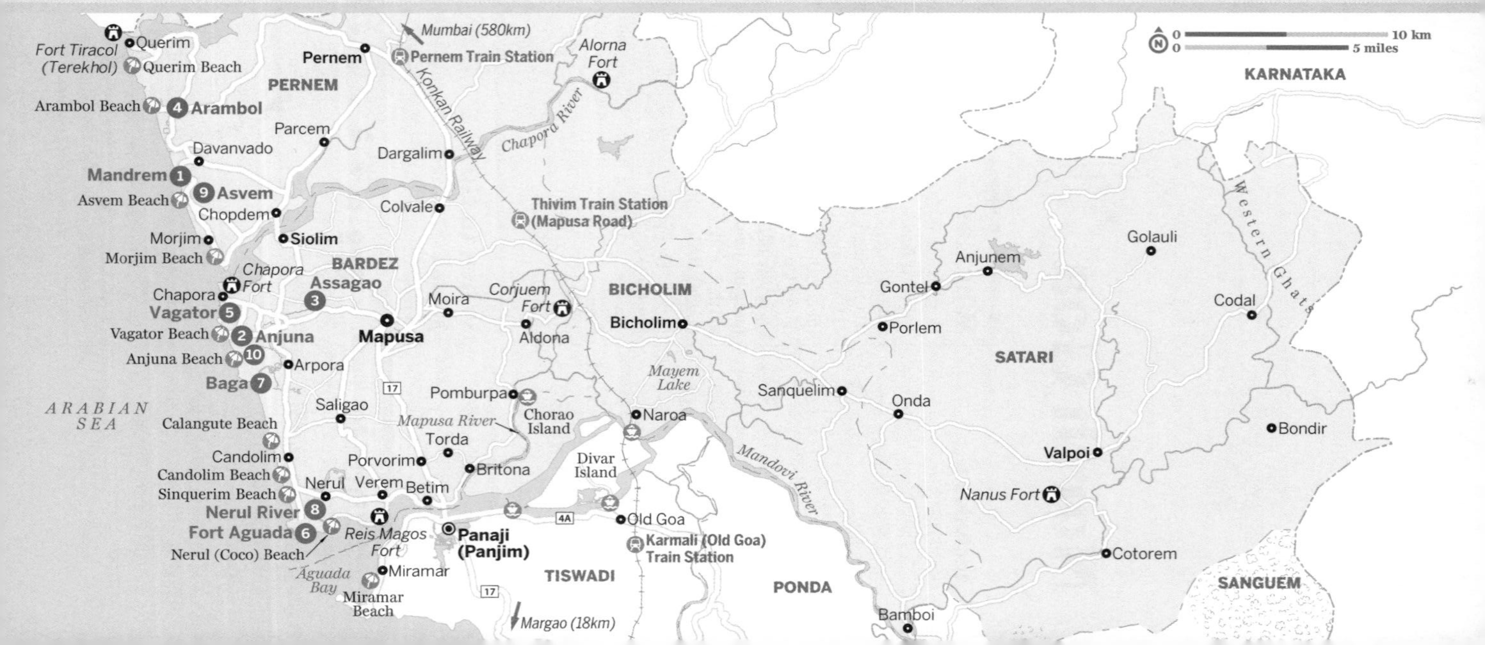

Along the Mandovi

The Mandovi River forms the southern boundary of the region. A useful shortcut from Panaji is the free vehicle ferry to Betim, from where you can explore some interesting sights on the way to Fort Aguada and Candolim.

Reis Magos & Nerul Beach

Tiny Reis Magos (Three Wise Men) village, across the Mandovi River from Panaji, is notable for its 16th-century church and Goa's oldest and best-preserved fort.

About 3km west of the fort, Nerul Beach (known locally as Coco Beach), where the Nerul River meets the Mandovi, affords a great view across to Miramar and Panaji and is popular with day trippers. The beach itself and the murky tidal waters are not much to look at, but it has a slight air of isolation as it's reached by a narrow one-way road through paddy fields.

Boat operators hang out at the beach, ready to take you on dolphin-spotting trips along the estuary, and there are a couple of restaurants on the beachfront.

Sights

Reis Magos Fort FORT

(8275025195; www.reismagosfort.com; adult/child ₹50/free; 9.30am-5pm Tue-Sun) Opened to the public in 2012 as a cultural centre, Reis Magos Fort overlooks the narrowest point of the Mandovi River estuary, making it easy to appreciate the strategic importance of the site. It was originally built in 1551, after the north bank of the river came under Portuguese control, and rebuilt in 1703, in time to assist the desperate Portuguese defence against the Hindu Marathas (1737–39).

It was then occupied by the British army in 1799 when they requisitioned Reis Magos, Cabo Raj Bhavan and Fort Aguada in anticipation of a possible attack by the French.

After the British withdrawal in 1813 the Reis Magos fort gradually lost importance, and was eventually abandoned. Like Fort Aguada nearby, the fort was turned into a prison in 1900 until it was abandoned again in 1993.

In 2011 the fort underwent extensive restoration and is now a cultural and heritage centre with exhibition spaces, a room devoted to the history of the fort and its restoration, and an excellent exhibition on Goan history and independence. You can wander the ramparts for great views and inspect the original cannons pointing out over the Mandovi.

Reis Magos Church CHURCH

(6am-noon Mon-Sat, service 8am Sun) Reis Magos Church was built below the fortress walls in 1555, shortly after the construction of the fort itself. A Franciscan seminary was later added, and over the years it became a significant seat of learning. The seminary is gone but the church is well worth a look, with its steep steps up from the road and fine views of the Mandovi River from the main doors. Outside the church, the lions portrayed in relief at the foot of the steps show signs of Hindu influence, and a crown tops off the facade. The colourful interior contains the tombs of three viceroys, including Dom Luis de Ataide, famous for holding 100,000 Muslim attackers at bay for 10 months in 1570, with his own force of just 7000 men.

Sleeping

There are several guesthouses and hotels in the village area, but most people day trip to Reis Magos. A few resorts and hotels line the coast between Reis Magos and Coco Beach.

Coco Shambhala BOUTIQUE HOTEL **$$$**

(9372267182; www.cocoshambhala.com; villas ₹46,000;) The award-winning Coco Shambhala is a luxurious retreat with just four two-bedroom villas in a lush tropical garden, each with their own private jetpool, kitchen and complimentary car and driver. The resort prides itself on a personalised experience from the chef-prepared meals to the deluxe spa.

Candolim & Fort Aguada

POP 8600

Candolim's long and languid beach, which curves to join smaller **Sinquerim Beach** to the south, is largely the preserve of charter tourists from the UK, Russia and, more than ever, elsewhere in India. It's fringed with a line of beach shacks, all offering sunbeds and shade in exchange for your custom.

In all it's an upmarket, happy holiday strip with less congestion than Calangute and Baga, but independent travellers may find it a little soulless. The post office, supermarkets, travel agents, pharmacies and plenty of banks with ATMs are all located on the main Fort Aguada Rd, running parallel to the beach.

Candolim, Sinquerim & Fort Aguada

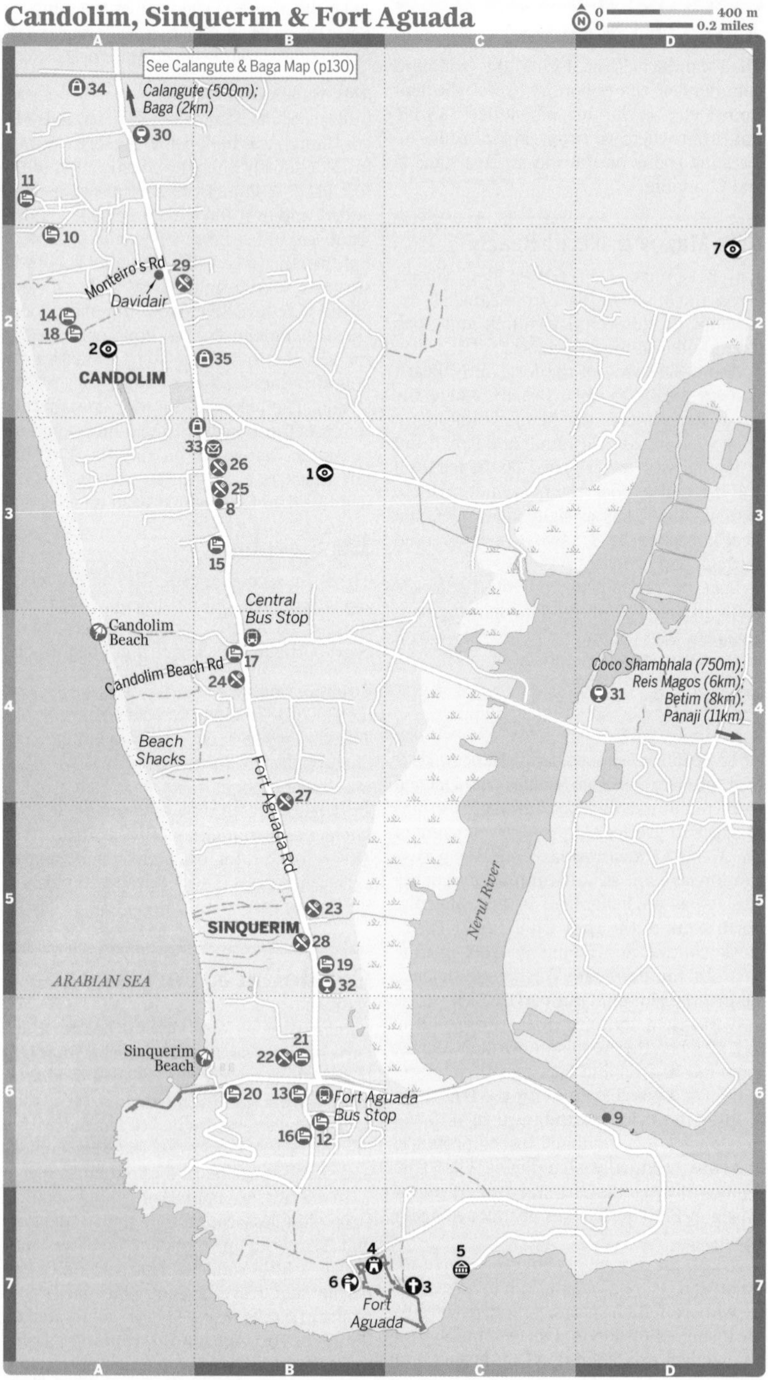

0 400 m
0 0.2 miles
See Calangute & Baga Map (p130)
Calangute (500m); Baga (2km)
Monteiro's Rd
Davidair
CANDOLIM
Candolim Beach
Central Bus Stop
Candolim Beach Rd
Beach Shacks
Fort Aguada Rd
SINQUERIM
ARABIAN SEA
Sinquerim Beach
Fort Aguada Bus Stop
Fort Aguada
Nerul River
Coco Shambhala (750m); Reis Magos (6km); Betim (8km); Panaji (11km)

Candolim, Sinquerim & Fort Aguada

Sights
1 Casa dos Costa-Frias ... B3
2 Casa dos Monteiros ... A2
3 Church of St Lawrence ... C7
4 Fort Aguada ... B7
5 Fort Aguada Jail ... C7
6 Fort Aguada Lighthouse ... B7
7 Museum of Goa ... D2
New Lighthouse ... (see 6)

Activities, Courses & Tours
Dive Goa ... (see 32)
8 John's Boat Tours ... B3
9 Sinquerim Dolphin Trips ... D6

Sleeping
10 Aashyana Lakhanpal ... A2
11 Backpacker Panda ... A1
12 Bougainvillea Guest House ... B6
13 D'Hibiscus ... B6
14 D'Mello's Sea View Home ... A2
15 Lemon Tree Amarante Beach Resort ... B3
16 Marbella Guest House ... B6
17 Ruffles Beach Resort ... B4
18 Shanu's Seaside Inn ... A2
19 Villa Ludovici Tourist Home ... B5
20 Vivanta by Taj Fort Aguada ... B6
21 Vivanta by Taj Holiday Village ... B6

Eating
22 Banyan Tree ... B6
23 Bomra's ... B5
24 Café Chocolatti ... B4
25 Fisherman's Cove ... B3
26 Newton's ... B3
Republic of Noodles ... (see 15)
27 Stone House ... B4
28 Tuscany Gardens ... B5
29 Viva Goa! ... A2

Drinking & Nightlife
30 Bob's Inn ... A1
31 LPK Waterfront ... D4
32 SinQ ... B5

Shopping
33 Fabindia ... B3
34 Literati Bookshop & Cafe ... A1
35 Sotohaus ... B2

Sights

Fort Aguada FORT

(8.30am-5.30pm) FREE Standing on the headland overlooking the mouth of the Mandovi River, Fort Aguada occupies a magnificent and successful position, confirmed by the fact it was never taken by force. A highly popular spot to watch the sunset, with uninterrupted views both north and south, the fort was built in 1612, following the increasing threat to Goa's Portuguese overlords by the Dutch, among others. Like Reis Magos and Cabo Raj Bhavan, the British occupied the fort in 1799 to protect Goa from possible French invasion.

Today visitors flock to the bastion that stands on the hilltop – though when compared with the overall area surrounded by defences, this is only a fraction of the original fort. To get to the hilltop fort, take the 4km winding road that heads east from Sinquerim Beach and loops up around the headland. Otherwise there's a steep 2km walking trail to the fort that starts just past Marbella Guest House. You can also walk out to the sea level fort walls at Sinquerim along the road past the Taj Hotel.

Fort Aguada Lighthouse LIGHTHOUSE

The old Portuguese lighthouse, which stands in the middle of Fort Aguada, was built in 1864 and once housed the great bell from the Church of St Augustine in Old Goa, before it was moved to the Church of Our Lady of the Immaculate Conception in Panaji. The lighthouse is the oldest of its sort in Asia, but is usually not open to the public.

New Lighthouse LIGHTHOUSE

(Indian/foreigner ₹10/50, camera ₹25; 10am-5.30pm) Outside the Fort Aguada bastions, the new lighthouse, built in 1976, can usually be visited; climb to the top for good views along the coast.

Church of St Lawrence CHURCH

A short way to the east of the bastion is the pretty Church of St Lawrence, which also occupies a magnificent viewpoint. The church was built in 1643 to honour St Lawrence, the patron saint of sailors, whose image stands on the gilded reredos (ornamental screen), holding a model ship.

Fort Aguada Jail HISTORIC BUILDING

Below the fort is Fort Aguada jail, once Goa's largest prison. It closed in 2015, with inmates moved to a new jail in Colvale, and there are now proposals to turn the historic buildings into a heritage site and museum. The cells stand on the site that once formed the square-shaped citadel of the hilltop Fort Aguada.

The road down to the jail's entrance passes a weird and wonderful compound known as Jimmy's Palace, home to reclusive tycoon

Jimmy Gazdar. Designed by Goan architect Gerard de Cunha, it's a closely guarded froth of fountains, foliage and follies, of which you'll catch glimpses as you whizz past.

Activities

Candolim's water sports are concentrated on Sinquerim Beach in front of the Taj.

John's Boat Tours TOURS
(9822182814, 0832-6520190; www.johnboattours.com; Fort Aguada Rd; 10am-9pm) A respected and well-organised Candolim-based operator offering a wide variety of boat and jeep excursions, as well as overnight houseboat cruises (₹6500 per person including meals). The standard half-day dolphin-watching cruise is ₹1200 (no dolphins, no pay) or join the renowned 'Crocodile Dundee' river trip (₹1400), to catch a glimpse of the Mandovi's mugger crocodile. Boat to Anjuna market is ₹1000.

Sinquerim Dolphin Trips BOATING
(per person ₹300; 8.30am-5.30pm) The boat operators on the Nerul River below Fort Aguada have banded together, so trips are fixed price. A one-hour dolphin-spotting and sightseeing trip costs ₹300 per person with a minimum of 10 passengers. Trips pass Nerul (Coco) Beach, Fort Aguada Jail and the fort.

Dive Goa DIVING
(9325030110; www.divegoa.com; Fort Aguada Rd) Based at SinQ Beach Club, this established scuba-diving outfit offers PADI and SSI courses, and boat dives to Netrani Island, Grande Island and more.

Sleeping

Though Candolim is largely frequented by package tourists and five-star luxury guests bussed straight in from Dabolim Airport, there's a surprising range of accommodation for the independent traveller. Laneways spread like tendrils from the main Fort Aguada Rd to the beach and are lined with midrange hotels and restaurants.

Backpacker Panda HOSTEL $
(9172313995; www.backpackerpanda.com; 1116, Anna Vaddo; dm from ₹500;) Down a winding lane and very close to the beach, this is Candolim's best bet for backpackers. Clean four- to eight-bed air-con dorms (some mixed, one female-only) have attached bathrooms. It has an open-sided cafe with loungy seating, and bike hire is available. Follow sign to Sonesta Inns and take the lane to the north.

Shanu's Seaside Inn GUESTHOUSE $
(9823016187; www.shanu.in; Escrivao Vaddo; d ₹1000, with AC ₹1500-3400;) Shanu is one of several large guesthouses in this little grove just behind the dunes of Candolim Beach and it's a fine choice. The 18 rooms vary from basic but comfortable to deluxe rooms with sea views, air-con, king-sized beds and fridge. The owners also run the popular Pete's Shack on the beach.

Villa Ludovici Tourist Home GUESTHOUSE $
(0832-2479684; Fort Aguada Rd; d incl breakfast ₹1000) For over 30 years Ludovici's has been welcoming travellers into its well-worn, creaky rooms in a fading old Portuguese villa. Four-poster beds on a budget; the four rooms are large and the hosts (and ghosts) are kind and amiable.

★ **Bougainvillea Guest House** GUESTHOUSE $$
(9822151969, 0832-2479842; www.bougainvillea-goa.com; Sinquerim; r incl breakfast ₹4200-5400, penthouse ₹7800;) A lush, plant-filled garden leads the way to this gorgeous family-run guesthouse, located off Fort Aguada Rd. The eight light-filled suite rooms are spacious and spotless, with fridge, flat-screen TV and either balcony or private sit-out; the top-floor penthouse has its own rooftop terrace. This is the kind of place guests come back to year after year. Book ahead.

★ **Marbella Guest House** BOUTIQUE HOTEL $$
(0832-2479551, 9822100811; www.marbellagoa.com; Sinquerim; r ₹4200-4900, ste ₹6100-7800;) This beautiful Portuguese villa, filled with antiques and enveloped in a peaceful courtyard garden, is a romantic and sophisticated old-world remnant. Rooms are individually themed, including Moghul, Rajasthani and Bougainvillea. The penthouse suite is a dream of polished tiles, four-poster bed with separate living room, dining room and terrace. The kitchen serves up some imaginative dishes. No kids under 12.

D'Hibiscus BOUTIQUE HOTEL $$
(0832-2479842; www.dehibiscus.com; 83 Sinquerim; d ₹4200, penthouse ₹6600;) Huge modern rooms with balconies are the draw at this Portuguese home off Sinquerim Beach. The top-floor penthouse rooms, with spa bath, big-screen TV and balcony sunbeds, are worth a splurge.

D'Mello's Sea View Home HOTEL $$
(0832-2489395; www.dmellos.com; Monteiro's Rd, Escrivao Vaddo; d with/without AC ₹3500/2500,

CANDOLIM'S MANSIONS

Despite the development of this once-sleepy seaside village, some intriguing architectural remnants of a rather different past remain hidden in Candolim's quiet back lanes.

In the 17th and 18th centuries, Candolim saw the arrival of a number of wealthy Goan families, fleeing from the capital at Old Goa due to the ravages of typhoid, cholera and malaria epidemics. The homes they built were lavish and ornate, filled with oyster-shell windows, fine materials from Macau and China, and scrolling carved stonework.

Though it's not open to the public, seek out the beautiful **Casa dos Costa-Frias**, down a side road just opposite Candolim's football field, which belonged to relatives of the influential Pinto family. It was built in the early 18th century, and stands behind a white, cross-topped gateway, with a family chapel tucked behind it.

Casa dos Monteiros is an example of the peak of Candolim's architectural splendour. Built by Goa's most powerful family, the Monteiros, it has the pretty 1780 Nossa Senhora dos Remedios (Our Lady of Miracles) chapel standing opposite the entrance to the house. Still occupied by descendants of the Monteiros, the house is not open to visitors, but is worth a look from the outside.

sea view ₹4750/4150;) D'Mello's has grown up from small beginnings, but is still family-run and occupies four buildings around a lovely garden just back from the beach. The front building has the premium sea-view rooms so check out a few, but all are clean and well maintained with balconies, four-poster beds and shuttered windows. Wi-fi is available in the central area.

Ruffles Beach Resort HOTEL $$
(9850752662; www.rufflesgoa.com; Fort Aguada Rd; d ₹2700-3500;) A pleasant courtyard pool and well-equipped rooms make this a reliably good midrange choice. There's a good little restaurant and bar facing the road.

Aashyana Lakhanpal VILLA $$$
(0832-2489225; www.aashyanalakhanpal.com; Fort Aguada Rd; villas 4 nights from ₹84,000;) A five-bedroom villa filled with art, another three-bedroom villa, three two-bedroom *casinhas* (little houses) and other cottages, set amid 1.6 hectares of lush, landscaped grounds spilling down to the beach, make Aashyana one of Candolim's – if not Goa's – most exclusive retreats. This is high-society luxe at its best and it puts the nearby Taj hotels in the shade for both style and price.

Vivanta by Taj Fort Aguada HOTEL $$$
(1800-111825, 0832-6645858; www.vivantabytaj.com; Sinquerim; d incl breakfast from ₹23,500, villa from ₹41,000;) Dominating the headland above Sinquerim Beach, the Taj Group's sprawling beach resort looks a little dated, but its service is still top-notch and the location impressive. Its Jiva Spa offers numerous soothing balms and palms, and the resort has a gym, pool, and three quality restaurants.

Lemon Tree Amarante Beach Resort HOTEL $$$
(0832-3988188; www.lemontreehotels.com; Fort Aguada Rd; r from ₹8400;) This boutiquey, luxe place on the main strip conjures up a strange mixture of Thai-spa style and medieval motifs. It works, though, with swish rooms equipped with wi-fi and DVD players, a luxurious spa and a roomy courtyard pool with swim-up bar.

Vivanta by Taj Holiday Village HOTEL $$$
(1800-111825, 0832-6645858; www.vivanta.tajhotels.com; Fort Aguada Rd; cottages ₹21,800-35,200;) The Taj's garden complex comprises 142 cottages and villas in a smart variation on a five-star theme, with all the luxuries you'd expect from this top-end chain. The palm-filled garden spills down to the beach, and its Banyan Tree (p128) restaurant is well regarded for good Thai food in beautiful al fresco surroundings.

Eating

Candolim has a high concentration of international restaurants. Then there's the seafront beach shacks serving world cuisine and fresh seafood. Much of the best on offer is along Fort Aguada Rd, though if you take the side streets towards the beach you'll find a few gems, along with local joints serving a cheap and tasty breakfast *bhaji-pau* (onion or potato fritters in Indian bread) or lunchtime thali.

Newton's SUPERMARKET $
(Fort Aguada Rd; ⏲9.30am-1am) If you're desperately missing Edam cheese or Marmite, or just want to do some self-catering, Newton's is Goa's biggest supermarket. There's a good line in toiletries, wines, children's toys and luxury food items. The downside is that it's often packed and security guards won't allow bags inside.

Viva Goa! GOAN $
(Fort Aguada Rd; mains ₹100-210; ⏲11am-midnight) This inexpensive, locals-oriented little place, also popular with in-the-know tourists, serves fresh fish and Goan seafood specialities such as a spicy mussel fry. Check the market price of seafood before ordering.

★**Café Chocolatti** CAFE $$
(409A Fort Aguada Rd; sweets ₹50-200, mains ₹250-450; ⏲9am-5pm Mon-Sat; 📶) The lovely garden tearoom at Café Chocolatti may be on the main Fort Aguada Rd, but it's a peaceful retreat where chocolate brownies, waffles and banoffee pie with a strong cup of coffee or organic green tea taste like heaven. Also has a great range of salads, paninis, crepes and quiches for lunch. Take away a bag of chocolate truffles, homemade by the in-house chocolatier.

Fisherman's Cove SEAFOOD $$
(☎9822143376; Fort Aguada Rd; mains ₹160-350; ⏲9am-4.30pm & 6-11.30pm) The corner streetside Fisherman's Cove is always busy thanks to a strong reputation for its seafood and Indian dishes. The food is good but its popularity can mean slow service or a wait for a table. Regular live music and a good bar area.

Stone House STEAK $$
(Fort Aguada Rd; mains ₹200-800; ⏲11am-3pm & 7pm-midnight) Surf 'n' turf's the thing at this venerable old Candolim venue, inhabiting a stone house and its leafy front courtyard, with the improbable-sounding 'Swedish Lobster' topping the list, along with some Goan dishes. It's also a popular blues bar with live music most nights of the week in season.

★**Bomra's** BURMESE $$$
(☎9767591056; www.bomras.com; 247 Fort Aguada Rd; mains ₹520-650; ⏲noon-2pm & 7-11pm) Wonderfully unusual food is on offer at this sleek little place serving interesting modern Burmese cuisine with a fusion twist. Aromatic dishes include Bomra's mussel curry, chicken pho or Burmese rice and noodle salad. Decor is palm-thatch-style huts in a lovely courtyard garden.

Tuscany Gardens ITALIAN $$$
(☎0832-6454026; www.tuscanygardens.in; Fort Aguada Rd; mains ₹300-500; ⏲1-11pm) You can easily be transported to Tuscany at Candolim's cosy, romantic Italian restaurant with check tablecloths and imported wine. Perfect antipasti, pasta, pizza and risotto are the order of the day; try the seafood pizza or buffalo mozzarella salad.

Republic of Noodles ASIAN $$$
(Lemon Tree Amarante Beach Resort; mains ₹425-650; ⏲11.30am-3pm & 7-11pm) For a sophisticated dining experience, the RoN at the Lemon Tree Amarante delivers with its dark bamboo interior, Buddha heads and floating candles. Seeking to re-create Southeast Asian street food, you'll get delicious, huge noodle plates, including a fabulous pad thai and some exciting options for vegetarians.

Banyan Tree THAI $$$
(☎0832-6645858; Vivanta by Taj Holiday Village; mains ₹760-1300; ⏲12.30-2.30pm & 7.30-10.30pm) Refined Thai food is the trademark of the Taj's romantic Banyan Tree, its swish courtyard set beneath the branches of a vast old banyan tree. If you're a fan of green curry, don't miss the succulent, signature version on offer here. Ambience, and dress, is formal.

🍷 Drinking & Nightlife

Candolim's drinking scene is largely hotel-based, but its plentiful beach shacks are a popular place for a relaxed beer or sunset cocktail. A couple of big-name nightclubs are in the area; solo males (or groups of men) might have trouble gaining entry.

Bob's Inn BAR
(Fort Aguada Rd; ⏲noon-4pm & 7pm-midnight) The African wall hangings, palm-thatch, communal tables and terracotta sculptures are a nice backdrop to the *rava* (semolina) fried mussels, but this Candolim institution is really just a great place to drop in for a drink.

LPK Waterfront CLUB
(couples ₹1700; ⏲9.30pm-4am) The initials stand for Love, Peace and Karma: the whimsical, sculpted waterfront LPK across the Nerul River from Candolim is the biggest club in the area, attracting mainly Indian party-goers from all over with huge indoor and outdoor dance areas. Most popular on

Thursday, Friday and Saturday nights, when cover prices vary and include drink coupons.

SinQ CLUB
(☎8308000080; www.sinq.co.in; Fort Aguada Rd; couples ₹1500, women ₹500; ⊙10pm-3am) The SinQ entertainment scene, almost directly opposite Taj Holiday Village, is one for the cool people but it has expanded to include the Showbar gastropub plus the beach lounge-bar with cabanas by the pool and a nightclub, so it has something for everyone. Events vary but Wednesday is usually ladies' night.

Shopping

Fabindia HOMEWARES
(www.fabindia.com; Fort Aguada Rd; ⊙10.30am-9pm) Popular nationwide chain selling fair-trade bed and table linens, home furnishings, clothes, jewellery and toiletries. Fabindia makes for a great, colourful browse, and is perfect for picking up high-end gifts or treating yourself to a traditional kurta (long shirt) or *salwar kameez* (traditional dresslike tunic and trouser combination for women).

Sotohaus DESIGN
(☎0832-2489983; www.sotodecor.com; Fort Aguada Rd; ⊙10am-6pm Mon-Sat) Offering cool, functional items dreamed up by a Swiss expat team, this is the place to invest in a natural-form-inspired lamp, mirror or dining table, to add a twist of streamlined India to your pad back home.

Information

TRAVEL AGENCIES

Davidair (☎0832-2489303; www.com2goa.com; Fort Aguada Rd; ⊙9am-6pm) Reputable, long-running travel agency specialising in flights out of Goa and organised tours throughout India.

POST

Post Office (Fort Aguada Rd)

Getting There & Away

Buses run about every 10 minutes to and from Panaji (₹20, 35 minutes), and stop at the **central bus stop** (Fort Aguada Rd) near John's Boat Tours. Some continue south to the **Fort Aguada bus stop** (Fort Aguada Rd) at the bottom of Fort Aguada Rd, then head back to Panaji along the Mandovi River road, via the villages of Verem and Betim.

Frequent buses also run from Candolim to Calangute (₹10, 15 minutes) and can be flagged down on Fort Aguada Rd.

Calangute & Baga

POP 16,000

For many visitors, particularly cashed-up Indian tourists from Bengaluru (Bangalore) and Mumbai plus Europeans on package holidays, this is Goa's party strip, where the raves and hippies have made way for modern thumping nightclubs and wall-to-wall drinking. The Calangute market area and the main Baga road can get very busy but everything you could ask for – from a Thai massage to a tattoo – is in close proximity and the beach is lined with an excellent selection of increasingly sophisticated restaurant shacks with sunbeds, wi-fi and attentive service.

Stretching between the blurred lines of Candolim and Baga, Calangute is centred on the busy market road leading to the beachfront. To the north, Baga beach consists of jostling shacks, peppered with water sports, and late-night clubs along infamous Tito's Lane, and one very busy road to the Baga River. The north side of the river is an altogether more serene experience.

Sights

Museum of Goa ARTS CENTRE
(☎7722089666; www.museumofgoa.com; 79, Pilerne Industrial Estate, Calangute; Indian/foreigner ₹100/300; ⊙10am-6pm) Not so much a museum as a gallery for contemporary art, MOG features artworks, sculptures, exhibitions, workshops, courses, sitar concerts and an excellent cafe and shop. It's the brainchild of well-known local artist and sculptor Dr Subodh Kerkar, with the philosophy of making art accessible to all. A return taxi with waiting time from the market should cost around ₹500.

Benz Celebrity Wax Museum AMUSEMENT PARK
(Calangute-Anjuna Rd, Baga; ₹200) This quirky attraction features a wax museum with reasonably accurate figures of Hollywood and Bollywood celebrities, action heroes and sports stars. There's also a 9D cinema (₹200) and bumper cars (₹150). Good for kids or a rainy day.

Church of Nossa Senhora, Mae de Deus CHURCH
(Church of Our Lady, Mother of God; Chogm Rd, Saligao) As you explore the countryside, don't miss a peek into the Church of Nossa Senhora, Mae de Deus, with its unusual neo-Gothic Christmas-cake style topped with a row of fanciful turrets. Built in 1873,

Calangute & Baga

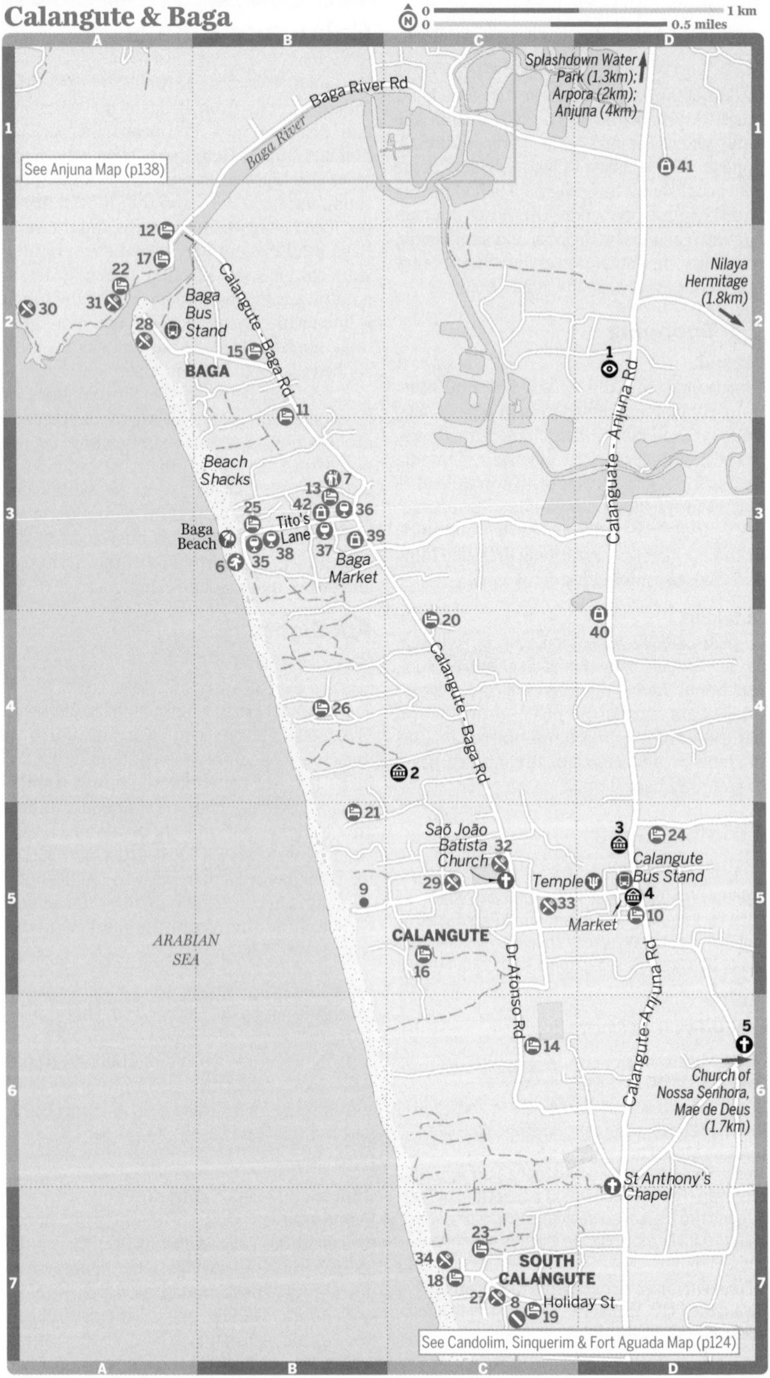
0 1 km
0 0.5 miles
Splashdown Water Park (1.3km); Arpora (2km); Anjuna (4km)
Baga River Rd
Baga River
See Anjuna Map (p138)
Nilaya Hermitage (1.8km)
Calangute - Baga Rd
Baga Bus Stand
BAGA
Calanguate - Anjuna Rd
Beach Shacks
Tito's Lane
Baga Beach
Baga Market
Calangute - Baga Rd
São João Batista Church
Temple
Calangute Bus Stand
Market
CALANGUTE
ARABIAN SEA
Dr Afonso Rd
Calangute-Anjuna Rd
Church of Nossa Senhora, Mae de Deus (1.7km)
St Anthony's Chapel
SOUTH CALANGUTE
Holiday St
See Candolim, Sinquerim & Fort Aguada Map (p124)

Calangute & Baga

Sights

1 Benz Celebrity Wax Museum D2
2 Casa Braganza C4
3 Casa dos Proença D5
4 Old Customs Post D5
5 St Alex's Church D6

Activities, Courses & Tours

6 Atlantis Watersports B3
7 Baga Snow Park B3
8 Goa Aquatics C7
9 GTDC Tours B5

Sleeping

10 Aerostel D5
11 Alidia Beach Cottages B2
12 Beach Box A2
13 Casa Baga B3
14 Casa de Goa C6
15 Cavala Seaside Resort B2
16 Coco Banana C5
17 Divine Guest House A2
18 Hotel Golden Eye C7
19 Hotel Seagull C7
20 Indian Kitchen C4
21 Johnny's Hotel B5
22 Melissa Guest House A2
23 Ospey's Shelter C7
24 Pousada Tauma D5
25 Resort Fiesta B3
26 Vila Goesa B4

Eating

27 A Reverie C7
28 Britto's A2
Cafe Sussegado Souza .... (see 10)
29 Casandré C5
30 Cliff's Beach Restaurant A2
Fiesta .... (see 25)
31 Go With the Flow A2
32 Infantaria C5
33 Plantain Leaf C5
34 Pousada by the Beach C7

Drinking & Nightlife

35 Café Mambo B3
36 Cape Town Cafe B3
37 Keventers B3
38 Tito's B3

Shopping

All About Eve .... (see 40)
39 Baga Tibetan Market B3
40 Karma Collection D4
41 Saturday Night Market D1
42 Star Magic Shop B3

it houses a rather technicolor, and allegedly 'miraculous', statue of the Mother of God herself, rescued from the ruins of an old convent at Old Goa. It's situated 2km from Calangute, on the road towards the village of Saligao.

Activities

Yoga classes pop up around Calangute and Baga each season, though it's not as organised as it is in the resorts and retreats further north. Look out for up-to-date flyers and noticeboards for the latest. You don't have to go far to find beach water sports along the Calangute–Baga strip.

Baga Snow Park SNOW SPORTS

(☎9595420781; www.snowparkgoa.com; Tito's Lane 2, Baga; ₹495; ⏲11am-7pm; 👪) This giant fridge is a mini wonderland of snowmen, igloos, slides and ice sculptures. You get kitted out with parka, pants and gloves (included) – it's novel being this cold in India! Good for kids.

Goa Aquatics DIVING

(☎9822685025; www.goaaquatics.com; 136/1 Gaura Vaddo, Calangute; dive trip/course from ₹5000/22,000) This professional dive resort offers a range of PADI courses and boat dives to Grande and Netrani Islands. An introductory dive for beginners is ₹5000 and a four-day PADI Open Water course is ₹22,000.

Atlantis Watersports WATER SPORTS

(☎9767213311; www.atlantiswatersports.com) A long-running water sports operator on Baga beach offering parasailing (₹950), banana boat rides and tubing, as well as kayak and paddleboard rental.

Barracuda Diving DIVING

(☎9822182402, 0832-2279409; www.barracudadiving.com; Sun Village Resort, Baga; dive trip/course from ₹5000/18,000) This long-standing dive school offers a vast range of PADI and SSI classes, dives and courses, including a 'Bubblemakers' introduction to scuba class of 1½ hours for children eight years and older (₹1500), Discover Scuba for ₹6500 and PADI Open Water for ₹22,000. For qualified divers, a two-tank dive to Grande Island is ₹5000 (snorkellers ₹1500).

Barracuda Diving is also notable for working with Coastal Impact (coastalimpact.in), which undertakes marine-conservation initiatives and annual underwater and beach clean-ups.

Tours

GTDC Tours TOURS
(Goa Tourism Development Corporation; ☎0832-2437132; www.goa-tourism.com) Goa Tourism's tours can be booked online or at the GTDC Calangute Residency hotel beside the beach or at the Goa Tourism visitor centre in Baga. The full-day North Goa tour (₹225, 8.45am to 6pm daily) departs from Calangute or Mapusa and takes in the Mandovi estuary, Candolim, Calangute, Anjuna and inland to Mayem Lake.

Sleeping

Calangute and Baga's sleeping options are broad and varied, though it's not a particularly budget-friendly destination, except in the off-season. Quite a few places here remain open year-round.

★**Indian Kitchen** GUESTHOUSE $
(☎0832-2277555,9822149615; www.indiankitchen-goa.com; off Calangute-Baga Rd, Baga; s/d from ₹770/880, AC chalet/apt ₹2100/3500;) Don't be fooled by the name – there's no longer a restaurant here but there is a great little budget guesthouse. Family-run Indian Kitchen has a range of rooms from basic to more spacious, comfy apartments and wooden chalets by the pool. There's a neat central courtyard and well-stocked library. Each room has its own terrace.

Johnny's Hotel HOTEL $
(☎0832-2277458; www.johnnyshotel.com; Khobra Vaddo, Calangute; s ₹800, d ₹1000-1500, with AC ₹1600-2000;) The 12 simple rooms at this backpacker-popular place make for a sociable stay, with a downstairs restaurant-bar and regular yoga and reiki classes. A range of apartments and houses are available for longer stays. It's down a lane lined with unremarkable midrange hotels and is just a short walk to the beach.

Aerostel HOSTEL $
(☎9833345744; 2/201 Naikawaddo, Calangute; dm ₹500-750) This basic backpackers' hostel is a welcome budget addition to Calangute in a super-central location behind the main market (it's actually down a quiet lane opposite KFC). The six-/eight-/10-bed dorms are air-conditioned with en suite and there's a basic kitchen.

Ospey's Shelter GUESTHOUSE $
(☎7798100981, 0832-2279505; ospeys.shelter@gmail.com; Calangute; d ₹1000) Tucked away between the beach and St Anthony's Chapel, in a quiet, lush little area full of palms and sandy paths, Ospey's is a traveller favourite and only a two-minute walk from the beach. Spotless upstairs rooms have fridges and balconies and the whole place has a cosy family feel. Take the road directly west of the chapel – but it's tough to find, so call ahead.

Divine Guest House GUESTHOUSE $
(☎9370273464; www.indivinehome.com; Baga River Rd, Baga; d ₹1200, with AC ₹1600, apt ₹3000;) Long-running Divine still sits prettily behind a plant-covered wall on the relatively quiet headland north of the Baga River. The 'Praise the Lord' gatepost offers a little gentle proselytising from the friendly family, while the rooms are homey and bright with the odd individual touches.

Melissa Guest House GUESTHOUSE $
(☎9822180095; Baga River Rd, Baga; d ₹1000;) Across the Baga River, Melissa Guest House has just four neat little rooms, all with at-

COLONIAL CALANGUTE

It's hard to find traces of the old, gentile or 'authentic' Calangute among the holiday mayhem, but it's still there. On the road to Saligao, don't miss **St Alex's Church** (Post Office Rd), with its magnificently golden and ornamented reredos (ornamental screen) and pulpit. Next, look out for the stately 18th-century *palácio* (palace) **Casa Braganza**, and **Casa dos Proença** (Calangute-Anjuna Rd), a grand mansion built in the early 18th century by Calangute's then-wealthiest family. The grand, tower-shaped verandah is screened off with oyster-shell windows, while the mansion's pitched roof was designed to create a natural air-conditioning system, channelling in cool air from the building's doors and windows.

Another relic of Calangute's past can be found at the **old customs post** (Calangute-Anjuna Rd) at the market crossroads. Several of these posts were built during Portuguese rule to monitor the coming and going of goods, and to deter smuggling. Nearby, the **covered market** makes for good local wandering, among a crush of Goans all here to buy fresh produce, spices, coffee, meat and fish – still a very local Calangute experience.

tached bathrooms and hot-water showers, in a tatty garden. Good value for the location.

Coco Banana GUESTHOUSE $

(9960803790; Baga; d with/without AC ₹1500/1200;) Among the palms south of the main entrance to Calangute Beach, low-key Coco Banana has been providing a retreat for travellers for many years. Rooms are spacious and spotless and the vibe mellow.

★ **Alidia Beach Cottages** GUESTHOUSE $$

(9822876867, 0832-2279014; Calangute-Baga Rd, Saunta Waddo; d ₹2400, with AC from ₹3900;) Set back behind a whitewashed chapel off busy Baga Rd, this convivial but quiet place has beautifully kept Mediterranean-style rooms orbiting a gorgeous pool. The cheaper non-AC rooms at the back are not as good, but all are in good condition, staff are eager to please, and there's a path leading directly to Baga Beach.

Beach Box BOUTIQUE HOTEL $$

(9607473627; http://boxhotels.in; Baga River Rd, Baga; d ₹4200-5400;) About time someone in Goa thought of recycling old shipping containers. The rooms here are pretty cosy and they're a bit of a novelty in fully equipped half or full-size shipping containers with en suite and air-con. The in-ground pool is also a shipping container and the restaurant-bar is made up of various recycled materials.

Vila Goesa HOTEL $$

(0832-2277535; www.vilagoesa.com; d with/without AC from ₹4500/3000, cottage ₹4200-4700;) Nicely situated between south Baga and north Calangute, and hidden in the palm thickets 200m back from the beach, this is a great place for lingering with a good book by the pool. Rooms are simple but pleasantly furnished; the higher the tariff, the closer you get to the beach.

Hotel Golden Eye HOTEL $$

(0832-2277308, 9822132850; www.hotelgoldeneye.com; Holiday St, Calangute; d ₹2800-4500;) This popular beachfront hotel at the end of 'Holiday St' has a fine range of rooms and apartments, from cheaper but tidy ones at the back to the boutique sea-facing rooms with modern decor, AC and cable TV. Unlike some midrangers, it's welcoming to independent walk-in travellers, though you'll need to book ahead in season. The Flying Dolphin beach restaurant is out front.

Casa de Goa HOTEL $$

(0832-6717777; www.casadegoa.com; Dr Afonso Rd, Tivai Vaddo; d/ste/villa incl breakfast from ₹5200/7000/8900;) The beautiful Casa de Goa is popular with Indian families and books up months in advance for weekends and high season. Portuguese-style yellow ochre buildings orbit a pretty pool courtyard. Decor is bright and fresh, and the big, clean rooms have safes, flat-screen TVs and new fridges, with other high-end and thoughtful touches. It's a good deal from April to October when rates are less than half.

Hotel Seagull HOTEL $$

(0832-2179969; www.seagullgoa.com; Holiday St, Calangute; d ₹3500;) Seagull's rooms, set in a cheerful blue-and-white house in south Calangute, are light and airy with air-con, and a small pool out back. Downstairs is a streetside bar-restaurant serving Goan, Indian and continental dishes.

Cavala Seaside Resort HOTEL $$

(0832-2276090; www.cavala.com; Calungute-Baga Rd, Baga; s/d incl breakfast from ₹2300/3900, d & ste with AC ₹5400-8000;) Idiosyncratic, ivy-clad Cavala has been harbouring Baga-bound travellers for over 25 years and is often full, especially the cheaper rooms. Perhaps as a result, the service is indifferent, but there's a big range of rooms, a pool (across the road at Banana Republic) and a bar-restaurant with frequent live music.

Resort Fiesta BOUTIQUE HOTEL $$$

(9822104512; www.fiestagoa.com; Tito's Lane, Baga; d & ste incl breakfast ₹8000-10,200;) Large, light-filled rooms are the signature at this beautifully designed resort behind the beachfront restaurant of the same name. The labour of love by owner Yellow Mehta is stylishly appointed with a lovely garden and pool, large verandas and modern touches like TV, minibar and dual wash basins.

Nilaya Hermitage HOTEL $$$

(0832-2269793; www.nilaya.com; Arpora; r & tent incl breakfast ₹17,300;) The ultimate in Goan luxury, set 3km inland from the beach at Arpora, a stay here will see you signing the guestbook alongside Bollywood stars and other celebrity types. Eleven beautiful red-stone Moorish rooms undulate around a swimming pool, along with two luxury 'Arabian Nights' tents. The food is as dreamy as the surroundings, and the spa will spoil you.

Pousada Tauma BOUTIQUE HOTEL $$$
(0832-2279061; www.pousada-tauma.com; Calangute; ste incl meals US$360-530;) If you're looking for luxury with your ayurvedic regime, this gorgeous little boutique hotel in busy Calangute is appropriately shielded from the outside world. Spacious, nicely furnished suites are set around a super fountain-fed pool. Rates include all meals at the romantic little open-air Copper Bowl restaurant, though ayurvedic treatments in the private centre are extra. There's also a shuttle to its beach restaurant.

Casa Baga BOUTIQUE HOTEL $$$
(0832-2253204, 0832-6517779; www.casaboutiquehotels.com; Tito's Lane 2, Baga; d ₹8400-11,200; @) The 24 luxury Balinese-style rooms, some with huge four-poster beds, make for a classy and tranquil stay in the midst of Baga's action, with all the little stylish touches the Casa boutique team is so adept at providing.

Eating

Calangute and Baga boast probably the greatest concentration of dining options anywhere in Goa, with everything from the simplest street food to the finest fillet steak, though it generally skews to high prices.

The beach shacks are an obvious go-to, but there are some interesting gems along the 'Strip' and a few excellent upmarket offerings on the north side of the Baga River.

Plantain Leaf INDIAN $
(0832-2279860; Calangute Beach Rd, Calangute; veg thali ₹150, mains ₹130-270; 11am-5pm & 7-11.45pm) In the heart of Calangute's busy market area, 1st-floor Plantain Leaf has consistently been the area's best pure veg restaurant for many years, with classic South Indian banana leaf thalis and dosas, along with more North Indian flavours. Most dishes sneak into the budget category.

Cafe Sussegado Souza GOAN $$
(09850141007; Calangute-Anjuna Rd, Calangute; mains ₹230-480; noon-11pm) In a little yellow Portuguese house just south of the Calangute market area, Cafe Sussegado is the place to come for Goan food such as fish curry rice, chicken *xacuti* (a spicy coconut dish) and pork *sorpotel* (a vinegary stew made from liver, heart and kidneys), with a shot of feni (Goan liquor) to follow. Authentic and busy with a good atmosphere.

Infantaria ITALIAN $$
(Calangute-Baga Rd, Calangute; pastries ₹80-200, mains ₹200-780; 7.30am-midnight;) Once Calangute's best bakery, Infantaria is still a popular Italian-Indian, fondue-meets-curry restaurant. The bakery roots are still there, though, with homemade cakes, croissants, little flaky pastries and real coffee. Get in early for breakfast before the good stuff runs out. Regular live music in season and it's a popular bar in the evening.

Cliff's Beach Restaurant INDIAN $$
(Baga; mains ₹180-400; 9am-11pm;) The best way to get away from the Baga beach crowd is to walk around the cliff edge north of the Baga River to secluded Cliff's. The menu is typical beach shack but it's just a great location for a cold beer and a swim in the calm waters off the beach. After dark, staff will help walk you back around the cliff.

Casandré MULTICUISINE $$
(Calangute Beach Rd, Calangute; mains ₹190-400; 6pm-midnight) Housed in an old Portuguese bungalow, this dim and tranquil taverna seems a little out of place amid the tourist tat of Calangute's main beach drag. With a long and old-fashioned menu encompassing everything from 'sizzlers' to Goan specialities, and a cocktail list featuring the good old gimlet, this is a lovable time warp.

★ **Go With the Flow** INTERNATIONAL $$$
(7507771556; www.gowiththeflowgoa.com; 614 Baga River Rd, Baga; small plates ₹180-420, mains ₹430-840; noon-10.30pm;) Stepping into the fantasy, neon-lit garden of white-wicker furniture is impressive and the food is consistently good. With a global menu leaning towards European, African and Asian flavours, this remains one of Baga's best dining experiences. Try some of the small bites (ask about a tasting plate) or go straight for the signature pork belly or African-inspired spicy prawn rice.

If you don't get vertigo, request a table high on the tower deck. Very charitably, according to management, all profits go towards the Samarpan Foundation, a not-for-profit Delhi-based charity supporting disadvantaged people, particularly children.

★ **A Reverie** INTERNATIONAL $$$
(8380095732; www.areverie.com; Holiday St, Calangute; mains ₹450-800; 7pm-late;) A gorgeous lounge bar, all armchairs, cool jazz and whimsical outdoor space, this is the place to spoil yourself, with the likes

of Spanish tapas, truffle bombs, grilled asparagus, French wines and Italian cheeses. A Reverie likes to style itself as 'fun dining' and doesn't take itself too seriously. Though it takes its cocktails seriously.

Pousada by the Beach GOAN **$$$**
(Holiday St, Calangute; mains ₹700-3500; ⏲11am-7pm) This permanent beachfront restaurant is simple in appearance but the daytime menu is bona fide fine dining – the chef also oversees Pousada Tauma's upmarket Copper Bowl. The menu is kept uncluttered with just a handful of expertly prepared Goan and seafood specialities.

Fiesta ITALIAN **$$$**
(☎8669964512; www.fiestagoa.in; Tito's Lane, Baga; mains ₹400-950; ⏲3pm-late; 📶) Overseen by local style queen Yellow Mehta, Fiesta is an intimate candlelight-by-the-pool dining experience that starts with homemade pizza and pasta and extends to French-influenced seafood dishes and tiramisu. Come early for a drink and a starter by the pool to soak in the atmosphere.

Britto's MULTICUISINE **$$$**
(☎0832-2277331; Baga beach; mains ₹330-860; ⏲8.30am-midnight) Long-running Britto's is an arena-sized Baga institution at the north end of the beachfront. It's a good spot for breakfast or Sunday roast lunch (₹410) but is pricey and impersonal the rest of the time. The drinks list is longer than the food menu and young Indian tourists are fond of ordering the iced Kingfisher mini-kegs. Live music most nights in season.

Drinking & Nightlife

Baga's boisterous club scene, centred on Tito's Lane, has long been well known among the tourist crowd looking for a good time. Some find the scene here a little sleazy and the bar staff indifferent. Solo women are welcomed into clubs (usually free) but should exercise care and take taxis to and from venues.

★Keventers MILKSHAKES
(Tito's Lane, Baga; milkshakes ₹80-230; ⏲11am-3am) Had enough of the Kingfisher? Keventers, the famous Delhi milkshake maker, has set up in Goa and on Tito's Lane no less. The hole-in-wall joint serves up classic milkshakes in its signature glass bottles, or sample the more exotic Oreo, bubblegum or salted caramel. It's the perfect antidote to a big night out.

WORTH A TRIP

SATURDAY NIGHT MARKETS

There are two well-established evening markets, **Saturday Night Market** (Calangute-Anjuna Rd; ⏲from 6pm Sat late Nov-Mar) in Arpora and **Mackie's** (Baga River Rd; ⏲from 6pm Sat Dec-Apr) in Baga, that make an interesting evening alternative to the Anjuna flea market.

The attractions here are as much about food stalls and entertainment as shopping, but there's a big range of so-so stalls, flashing jewellery, spices, clothing and textiles.

Both are occasionally known to be cancelled at short notice, so check locally or with taxi drivers.

Café Mambo CLUB
(☎7507333003; Tito's Lane, Baga; cover charge couples ₹1000; ⏲6pm-3am) Part of the Tito's empire, Mambo is one of Baga's busiest clubs with an indoor/outdoor beachfront location and nightly DJs pumping out house, hip hop and Latino tunes. Couples or women only; Friday is the popular Bollywood night.

Cape Town Cafe BAR
(www.capetowncafe.com; Tito's Lane, Baga; ⏲6pm-1am; 📶) The most laid-back of the Tito's venues, Cape Town has a street-front lounge bar with wi-fi and live sports on big screens, while inside international DJs play until late. Goan food, bar snacks and hookah pipes available.

Tito's CLUB
(☎9822765002; www.titos.in; Tito's Lane, Baga; cover charge varies; ⏲8pm-3am) The long-running titan of Goa's clubbing scene, Tito's has done its best to clean up its act and organises regular event nights that take on a distinctly Indian club scene. Saturday is Bollywood night. It's generally couples or ladies only – solo men (stags) get in on certain nights at an inflated cover charge, depending on the mood of door staff.

Shopping

In line with its status as the tourist capital of Goa, Calangute has likewise grown to become the shopping capital. Flashy neon-lit international brand shops line the main Calangute-Candolim road. Upmarket gold and jewellery shops, boutique fashion stores and dozens of arts-and-craft emporia are also here. Check out the market on Baga Rd near Tito's Lane to compare prices.

Literati Bookshop & Cafe BOOKS

(☎0832-2277740; www.literati-goa.com; Calangute; ⏰10am-6.30pm Mon-Sat) A refreshingly different bookstore, in the owners' South Calangute home, and a very pleasant Italian-style garden cafe. Come for a fine espresso and browse the range of books by Goan and Indian authors as well as antiquarian literature. Check the website for readings and events.

Baga Tibetan Market MARKET

(Calangute-Baga Rd, Baga; ⏰9am-9pm) Jewellery and semiprecious stones are the stock at this Baga market. Sold by weight, but bargaining is expected.

Star Magic Shop MAGIC

(Tito's Lane, Baga; ⏰9am-late) Learn magic tricks in just two minutes (that's the claim!) at this little Baga shop in Tito's Lane. Also has a stall at the Anjuna flea market.

Karma Collection GIFTS & SOUVENIRS

(☎9890361659; www.karmacollectiongoa.com; Calangute-Arpora Rd, Calangute; ⏰9.30am-10.30pm) Beautiful home furnishings, textiles, ornaments, bags and other enticing stuff – some of it antique – has been sourced from across India, Pakistan and Afghanistan and gathered at Karma Collection. Fixed prices mean there's no need to bargain, though it's not cheap.

All About Eve FASHION & ACCESSORIES

(☎0832-2275687; Calangute-Arpora Rd, Calangute; ⏰10am-8pm) Attached to Karma Collection, All About Eve stocks unusual clothes, bags and accessories, many designed by the owners themselves and which are unlike the usual array you'll find on a beach-road stall.

Getting There & Away

Frequent buses go to Panaji (₹20, 45 minutes) and Mapusa (₹15, 30 minutes) from both the Calangute (Calangute Beach Rd, Calangute) and Baga (Baga) bus stands.

Kadamba runs a shuttle bus between Calangute bus stand and the airport four times a day (₹150, 1½ hours).

A taxi from Calangute or Baga to Panaji costs around ₹600 and takes about half an hour. A prepaid taxi from the airport to Calangute is ₹1200.

Getting Around

Motorcycle and scooter hire is easy to arrange in Calangute and Baga (ask at your accommodation). Prices are fairly steady at around ₹300 for a gearless Honda Kinetic and ₹350 to ₹400 for an Enfield, but high demand means you might have to pay much more in peak season. Definitely try bargaining in quieter times or for rentals of more than a week.

A local bus runs between the Calangute and Baga stands every few minutes (₹5); catch it anywhere along the way, though when traffic is bad it might be quicker to walk.

Taxis between Calangute and northern Baga beach charge an extortionate ₹100.

Anjuna

POP 9640

Anjuna has been a stalwart of the hippie scene since the 1960s and still drags out the sarongs and sandalwood each Wednesday (in season) for its famous flea market. Though it continues to pull in droves of backpackers, midrange and domestic tourists are increasingly making their way here for a dose of hippie-chic. Anjuna is continuing to evolve, with a heady beach party scene and a constant flowering of new restaurants, bars and backpacker hostels. If anything, Anjuna is having a renaissance.

The village itself is a bit ragged around the edges and is spread out over a wide area, but that's part of the charm. Do as most do: hire a scooter or motorbike and explore the back lanes and southern beach area and you'll find a place that suits. Anjuna will grow on you.

Sights & Activities

Anjuna's charismatic, narrow **beach** runs for almost 2km from the rocky, low-slung cliffs at the northern village area right down beyond the flea market in the south. In season there are water sports here, including jet skis, banana boats and parasailing.

Lots of yoga, ayurveda and other alternative therapies and regimes are on offer in season; look out for noticeboards at popular cafes such as Artjuna Cafe (p140).

Goa Muay Thai MARTIAL ARTS

(☎9767479486; www.goamuaythai.com; Tito's White House, Aguada-Siolim Rd; class ₹500, weekly pass ₹2000; ⏰9-10.30am & 5-6.45pm Mon-Fri) These morning and afternoon classes are designed with fitness and technique in mind rather than full-on sparring, so are good for beginners. The boxing ring and gym at Tito's White House sets up in November.

Splashdown Water Park SWIMMING

(☎0832-2273008; www.splashdowngoa.com; Anjuna-Baga Rd, Arpora; adult/child ₹520/420, spectators ₹350; ⏲10.30am-6pm) This collection of pools, fountains and waterslides in Arpora will keep kids (and adults) happy all day long. It's marginally cheaper after 4pm. A cafe and bar overlook the action.

Brahmani Yoga YOGA
(☎9545620578; www.brahmaniyoga.com; Tito's White House, Aguada-Siolim Rd; class ₹700, 10-class pass ₹5000; ⏲classes 9.30am) This friendly drop-in centre offers daily classes from late November to April in ashtanga, vinyasa, hatha and dynamic yoga, as well as pranayama meditation. No need to book: just turn up 15 minutes before the beginning of class.

Sleeping

Anjuna has a good range of budget, backpacker and midrange accommodation spread over a wide area. Dozens of basic rooms are strung along Anjuna's northern clifftop, while pricier places front the main beach. Plenty of small, family-run guesthouses are also tucked back from the main beach strip, offering nicer double rooms for a similar price; look out for signs announcing 'rooms to let' or 'house to let'.

Wonderland Hostel HOSTEL $
(☎8692993770; www.wonderlandhostel.com; 69/6, Govekar Vaddo; dm ₹500-600, d ₹2000-2500, without bathroom ₹1200-1500; ❄📶) Superchilled Wonderland, off the path behind Anjuna Beach near Lilliput, has a lineup of cabins comprising en suite dorms and a few private rooms (some with AC), as well as a couple of old-school basic bamboo tree houses and space for tents. Owner Sandeep welcomes travellers into his loungy chill-out area with a small kitchen and cafe. Free yoga classes daily at 9am.

Red Door Hostel HOSTEL $
(☎0832-2274423; reddoorhostels@gmail.com; dm with/without AC from ₹500/400, d with/without AC ₹2200/1900; ❄📶) Red Door is a welcoming backpacker place close to Anjuna's central crossroads with clean four- and six-bed dorms plus a few private rooms. Facilities include lockers, free wi-fi, a garden, good communal areas – including a well-equipped kitchen – and a sociable cafe-bar.

Florinda's GUESTHOUSE $
(☎9890216520; s/d ₹800/1000, with AC ₹1500; ❄📶) One of the better budget places near the beach and a bit hidden next to Janet & John's, Florinda's has clean rooms, with 24-hour hot water, window screens and mosquito nets, set around a pretty garden. The few air-con rooms fill up fast.

Paradise GUESTHOUSE $
(☎9922541714; janet_965@hotmail.com; Anjuna-Mapusa Rd; d ₹1000-1200, with AC ₹1500-2000; ❄@📶) This friendly place is fronted by an old Portuguese home and offers neat, clean rooms with well-decorated options in the newer annexe. The better rooms have TVs, fridges and hammocks on the balcony. Friendly owner Janet and family also run the pharmacy, general store, restaurant, internet cafe, Connexions travel agency and money exchange.

Lazy Lama HOSTEL $
(☎9717000955; lazylamagoa@gmail.com; dm ₹300-500) A laid-back hostel down a quiet lane in Anjuna village, Lazy Lama offers six- and 10-bed dorms in a partly converted Portuguese house. Attracts a chilled crowd.

INLAND YOGA RETREATS

The Anjuna/Vagator/Assagao area has a number of yoga retreats where you can immerse yourself in courses, classes and a Zen vibe during the October to March season.

Purple Valley Yoga Retreat (☎0832-2268363; www.yogagoa.com; 142 Bairo Alto; dm/s 1 week £770/850, 2 weeks £1150/1400) Popular yoga resort in Assagao offering one- and two-week residential and nonresidential courses in Ashtanga yoga.

Swan Yoga Retreat (☎8007360677, 0832-2268024; www.swan-yoga-goa.com; drop-in classes ₹500, 1 week s/d from ₹42,000/52,000) In a peaceful jungle corner of Assagao, Swan Retreat is a very Zen yoga experience. Daily drop-in classes are available, or minimum week-long yoga retreats start every Saturday.

Yoga Magic (p139) Solar lighting, vegetable farming and compost toilets are just some of the worthy initiatives practised in this luxurious yoga resort.

Brahmani Yoga Drop-in classes at Tito's White House.

Anjuna

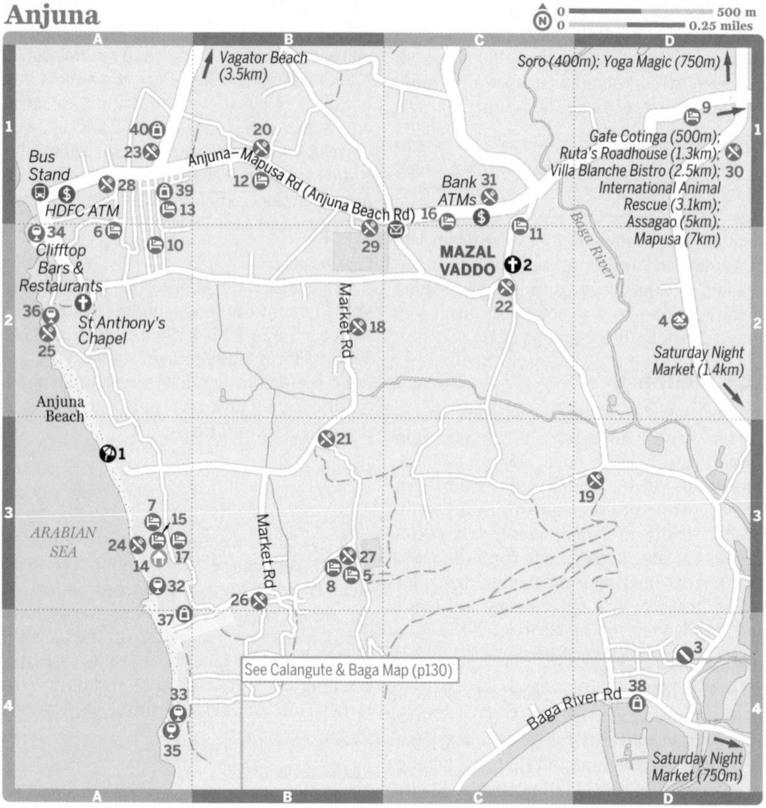

Headquarters HOSTEL $
(☎0832-2274510; dm with/without AC ₹500/400; ❄📶) Near the German Bakery, Headquarters ticks all the budget boxes for cleanliness and comfort with upstairs dorms, kitchen and common areas downstairs and a garden with some potential out back.

Vilanova GUESTHOUSE $
(☎9820232058, 9225904244; mendonca90@rediffmail.com; Anjuna Beach Rd; d ₹900-1000, with AC ₹1200; ❄📶) Big, clean rooms have a fridge, TV, 24-hour hot water and window screens and are set in three Portuguese-style bungalows in a cute little compound. Good vibes and a comfortable family atmosphere, with friendly staff and a good restaurant.

Village COTTAGE $$
(☎9988882021; d ₹3800-4500) The solid timber and rendered concrete cottages here are some of the best-designed on the beachfront. Set in a pleasant garden, they feature large beds and bathrooms, and air-con to justify the price. It's behind Elephant Art Cafe (p141).

Sea Horse HUT $$
(☎9764465078; www.vistapraiaanjuna.com; ⊙hut with/without AC ₹3500/2000; ❄📶) A lineup of timber cabins behind the beach restaurant of the same name, Sea Horse offers a good location and decent value. The huts are small and get a little hot – ask for the air-con remote control if it's uncomfortably humid. Staff are friendly and accommodating. The same owners have a pricier beachfront setup nearby called Vista Praia Anjuna.

Banyan Soul BOUTIQUE HOTEL $$
(☎9820707283; www.thebanyansoul.com; d ₹3000; ❄📶) A slinky 12-room option, tucked down the lane off Market Rd, and lovingly conceived and run by Sumit, a young Mumbai expat. Rooms are chic and well equipped with AC and TV, and there's

Anjuna

Sights
1 Anjuna Beach A3
2 Our Lady of Good Health C2

Activities, Courses & Tours
3 Barracuda Diving D4
Brahmani Yoga (see 30)
Goa Muay Thai (see 30)
4 Splashdown Water Park D2

Sleeping
5 Banyan Soul B3
6 Casa Anjuna A2
7 Florinda's A3
8 Headquarters B3
9 Hotel Bougainvillea D1
10 Lazy Lama A2
11 Palacete Rodrigues C2
12 Paradise B1
13 Red Door Hostel A1
14 Sea Horse A3
15 Vilanova C1
16 Village A3
17 Wonderland Hostel A3

Eating
18 Artjuna Cafe B2
19 Baba Au Rhum D3
20 Burger Factory B1
21 Café Diogo B3
22 Choco Cream Gelati C2
23 Eatopia A1
24 Elephant Art Cafe A3
25 Eva Cafe A2
26 FlourPower Bakeria B3
27 German Bakery B3
28 Goan Hub A1
29 Goa's Ark B2
30 Lila Café D1
31 Oltremarino C1

Drinking & Nightlife
32 Cafe Lilliput A3
33 Curlies A4
34 Purple Martini A2
35 Shiva Valley A4
36 UV Bar A2

Shopping
37 Anjuna Flea Market A4
38 Mackie's Saturday Nite Bazaar D4
39 Manali Guest House A1
40 Oxford Arcade A1

a lovely library and shady seating area beneath a banyan tree.

Palacete Rodrigues HERITAGE HOTEL $$
(0832-2273358; Mazal Vaddo; d ₹2800-3500;) This lovely family-run mansion, filled with antiques and ornate furniture, is as quirky as you could hope for in Anjuna – perhaps too over-the-top for some. Some of the 14 rooms and suites are themed and decorated along ethnic cultural lines: French, Chinese, Japanese and Goan. Outside is a neat garden and pool area.

Hotel Bougainvillea HERITAGE HOTEL $$
(Granpa's Inn; 0832-273270; www.granpasinn.com; Anjuna-Mapusa Rd; d/ste incl breakfast from ₹5700/7500;) An old-fashioned heritage hotel housed in a pretty, yellow 200-year-old ancestral mansion, 'Granpa's Inn' offers charm and a touch of luxury with a lovely pool and well-decorated cottages. The grounds are lush, shady and make for a cool retreat, though some find it a little far from the beach for this price.

Yoga Magic RESORT $$$
(0832-6523796; www.yogamagic.net; Mapusa-Chapora Rd; share/single ₹7700/11,600;) Solar lighting, compost toilets and local building materials (including cow dung and rammed earth) are some of the worthy initiatives practised in this ultra-luxurious village of Rajasthani tented lodges and bamboo-villa suites. Offers organic gourmet vegetarian food and daily yoga and meditation. Prices include breakfast and afternoon tea; daily yoga classes cost extra, or you can opt for one of the all-inclusive week-long yoga holidays. It's about 2km from Vagator Beach.

Casa Anjuna HERITAGE HOTEL $$$
(0832-2274123; www.casaboutiquehotels.com; D'Mello Vaddo 66; d incl breakfast ₹7900-16,400;) This heritage hotel is enclosed in lovely plant-filled gardens set around an inviting pool, managing to shield itself from the hype of central Anjuna. All rooms have antique furnishings and period touches; like many upmarket places it's better value out of season, when rates halve.

Eating

Anjuna has always had a reasonably good range of eating options, from clifftop restaurant-bars and cafes hidden in the back lanes to the big beachfront places near the market site. New places are popping up all the time, keeping things fresh.

Self-caterers will love Oxford Arcade (p142), an expat-oriented supermarket.

DON'T MISS

ANJUNA FLEA MARKET

Anjuna's weekly Wednesday **flea market** (⊙8am-sunset Wed Nov-Apr) is as much part of the Goan experience as a day on the beach. More than three decades ago, it was conceived and created by hippies smoking jumbo joints, convening to compare experiences on the heady Indian circuit and selling jeans or handmade jewellery to help fund their stay.

Nowadays things are far more mainstream and the merchandise comes from all over India: sculptures and jewellery courtesy of the Tibetan and Kashmiri traders; colourful Gujarati tribal women selling T-shirts; richly colourful saris, bags and bedspreads from Rajasthan; sacks of spices from Kerala; and the hard-to-miss bejewelled tribal girls from Karnataka pleading passers-by to 'come look in my shop'. Weaving in among this syrupy blend of stalls are the remaining hippies, backpackers, weekenders from Mumbai, and bus- and taxi-loads of package tourists from Russia and Europe.

Such purchasing power has inevitably pushed market prices up but you can still find some good bargains if you know the right price. These days the market sprawls back from the beach to the entrance road in the paddy fields; the endless stalls can become repetitive after a while. For a rest from the shopping there are chai stalls and a couple of restaurant-bars with live music. **Cafe Looda** has a fabulous sunset beachfront location and live music from 5pm, while **Seabreeze** packs them in with live music in the afternoon.

You might still find Westerners trading goods and services (tattoos, piercings and the like) but it's much more a souvenir market. Despite changes over the years, the market shows no sign of waning in popularity, so dive in and enjoy the ride. The best time to visit is early (from 8am) or late afternoon (around 4pm till close just after sunset).

★**Choco Cream Gelati**　　ICE CREAM **$**
(Mazal Vaddo; ice cream & gelato ₹120-180; ⊙9am-midnight) This may well be the best Italian-style gelato and ice cream in Goa and regulars know it. Scoops in a cup or waffle cone, shakes, juices and espresso coffee are all available and there's a regular parade of flavours from lemon cheesecake to salted caramel and tiramisu. There's al fresco eating out front.

FlourPower Bakeria　　BAKERY **$**
(☑9867276541; Market Rd; bread & baked goods from ₹80; ⊙11am-8pm Wed, 7-11pm Fri-Sun) This artisanal bakery produces fresh sourdough bread loaves with loads of love, along with croissants, cakes, cookies and fabulous pizzas.

Eatopia　　MULTICUISINE **$**
(Anjuna-Vagator Rd; mains ₹130-300; 🕾) In the thick of Anjuna, near Starco Crossroads, Eatopia is often overlooked but has a full menu of Indian, Goan and Western dishes at prices noticeably lower than restaurants closer to the beach. Credit cards accepted.

Café Diogo　　CAFE **$**
(Market Rd; snacks ₹80-250; ⊙8.30am-3pm) Excellent fruit salads are sliced and diced at Café Diogo, a small family-run cafe on the way down to the market. The generous avocado, cheese and mushroom toasted sandwiches and the range of lassis are also worth a try.

★**Artjuna Cafe**　　CAFE **$$**
(☑0832-2274794; www.artjuna.com; Market Rd; mains ₹130-480; ⊙7.30am-10.30pm; 🕾) Artjuna is right up there with our favourite cafes in Anjuna. Along with all-day breakfast, outstanding espresso coffee, salads, smoothies, sandwiches and Middle Eastern surprises like baba ganoush, tahini and falafel, this sweet garden cafe has an excellent craft and lifestyle shop, yoga classes, movie nights and a useful noticeboard. Great meeting place.

Eva Cafe　　CAFE **$$**
(☑7350055717; Cliff Walk; mains ₹210-350; ⊙9am-8pm; 🕾) Oceanfront Eva Cafe is a small but cosy place for healthy sandwiches, salads and sublime breakfasts featuring fresh-baked bread and good coffee. The evening menu includes nachos and a cheese platter with wine. Great sunset spot.

Goa's Ark　　MIDDLE EASTERN **$$**
(☑9145050494; www.goas-ark.com; Anjuna Beach Rd; mains ₹150-670, meze from ₹50; ⊙10am-11pm; 🕾) Set in a pleasant garden, Goa's Ark breaks the mould of most same-same restaurants, specialising in Middle Eastern and Mediterranean cuisine with meze, barbecued meat and falafel. Chargrilled steaks and fish and chips contribute to a meat-heavy menu but vegetarians are not overlooked with baba ganoush, veg burgers and lentil salads.

Elephant Art Cafe CAFE $$
(9970668845; mains ₹250-450; 8am-10pm;) A standout among the many restaurants lining Anjuna's beach, Elephant Art Cafe does a thoughtful range of tapas, sandwiches, fish and chips and pasta. Breakfasts are a highlight, with fruit bruschetta or shakshuka potato pesto eggs among the offerings.

German Bakery MULTICUISINE $$
(www.german-bakery.in; breakfast ₹60-240, mains ₹190-570; 8.30am-11pm;) Leafy and adorned with lanterns, cushioned seating, occasional live music and garden lights, this is a long-standing favourite for hearty and healthy breakfasts, fresh-baked bread, organic food and tofu balls, but the menu also runs to Indian dishes, pasta, burgers and seafood. Has healthy juices (for example wheatgrass and kombuchas) and espresso coffee.

Lila Café CAFE $$
(www.lilacafegoa.com; Tito's White House, Aguada-Siolim Rd; mains ₹100-290; 8.30am-6pm) This German cafe has been a traveller favourite for many years, first in Baga and now at Tito's White House. It serves great home-baked breads, croissants, rösti and perfect frothy cappuccinos, and specialises in buffalo cheese and smoked ham.

Goan Hub INDIAN $$
(0832-227 3765; Anjuna-Mapusa Rd; mains ₹180-350; 9am-midnight;) From the same owner as Mango Tree and Hilltop in Vagator, Goan Hub is a new bar-restaurant with that familiar streetside bar feel with beers on tap and a broad menu of Indian, Goan and Western food. It hasn't yet gained the following of Mango Tree but it's well located on the main road to the beach so anything could happen.

★ **Baba Au Rhum** FRENCH $$$
(9657210468; Anjuna-Baga Rd; baguettes ₹210-300, mains ₹480-550) It's tucked away on the back road between Anjuna and Baga but Baba Au Rhum's reputation (it was previously in Arpora) means it's always busy. Part bakery, part French cafe, this is the place for filled baguettes, croissants, crostini or quiche, as well as creamy pastas or a filet mignon. Craft beer on tap and a relaxed, open garden–restaurant vibe.

Burger Factory BURGERS $$$
(Anjuna-Mapusa Rd; burgers ₹300-500; 11.30am-3.30pm & 6.30-10.30pm Thu-Tue) There's no mistaking what's on offer at this little open-sided diner. The straightforward menu of burgers isn't cheap, but the buns are big and they are interesting and well crafted. Choose between beef or chicken burgers and toppings such as blue cheese, bacon and avocado.

Oltremarino ITALIAN $$$
(8412967105; Anjuna Beach Rd; mains ₹450-800; 1pm-midnight;) It's high-end Italian dining but the homemade pasta and speciality wood-fired pizzas are worth the splurge at this sweet garden restaurant in the grounds of a fine Portuguese mansion. Helpful staff will walk you through the lengthy menu and will insist you finish your meal with a complimentary shot of homemade Baileys.

Drinking & Nightlife

Anjuna vies with Vagator and Morjim as the trance party capital of Goa and the southern end of the beach has several nightclubs that are the most happening places in North Goa when the night is right. Market day is always fun, with live music at one or both of the two bars there.

Cafe Lilliput CLUB
(0832-2274648; www.cafelilliput.com; 8am-1am, to 4am on party nights;) Hovering over the beach near the flea-market site, Lilliput has built itself a reputation as one of the go-to nightspots, but it also has a good all-day restaurant and some interesting accommodation at the back.

Curlies BAR
(www.curliesgoa.com; 9am-3am) Holding sway at South Anjuna Beach, Curlies mixes laid-back beach-bar vibe with sophisticated nightspot – the party nights here are notorious, legendary and loud. There's a rooftop lounge bar and an enclosed late-night dance club. Thursday and Saturday are big nights, as are full-moon nights.

Shiva Valley CLUB
(9689628008; 8am-3am) At the very southern end of Anjuna Beach, past Curlies, Shiva Valley has grown from small beach shack to fully fledged trance club, with Tuesday the main party all-nighter.

UV Bar CLUB
(9822153440; from 6pm) UV Bar flies under the radar compared with the likes of Curlies and Vagator's Hilltop but its becoming known for wild trance parties, with two dance floors and a central location near the Anjuna beachfront.

Purple Martini COCKTAIL BAR
(☎9823772890; Sunset Point; ⌚9am-midnight) The clifftop sunset views, blue-and-white colour scheme and swanky bar at this beautifully situated restaurant could easily transport you to Santorini. Come for a sundowner cocktail: the downside is that drinks are pricey and there's no happy hour.

Shopping

Oxford Arcade SHOPPING CENTRE
(Anjuna-Vagator Rd; ⌚9am-9pm) Oxford Arcade, 100m from the Starco crossroads on the road to Vagator, is a fully fledged two-storey supermarket, complete with shopping trolleys and checkout scanners. It's an awesome place to stock up on toiletries, cheap booze and all those little international luxuries.

Manali Guest House BOOKS
(⌚9.30am-8.30pm) Long-running bookshop and travel agency.

Information

MONEY

Anjuna has a group of ATMs clustered together on Anjuna Beach Rd, and two close to the bus stand.

TRAVEL AGENCIES

There are plenty of reliable travel agents in town that can book train tickets, flights and local tours.

Getting There & Away

Buses to Mapusa (₹15, 30 minutes) depart every half-hour or so from the main bus stand at the end of the Anjuna–Mapusa Rd near the beach; some buses coming from Mapusa continue on to Vagator and Chapora.

A couple of direct daily buses head south to Calangute; otherwise, take a bus to Mapusa and change there.

Plenty of motorcycle taxis and autorickshaws gather at the main crossroads and you can also easily hire scooters and motorcycles here from ₹250 to ₹400 – most Anjuna-based travellers get around on two wheels.

Assagao

Snuggled in the countryside between Mapusa and Anjuna, Assagao is one of North Goa's prettiest villages, with almost traffic-free country lanes passing old Portuguese mansions and whitewashed churches. The area is inspiringly peaceful enough to be home to some of North Goa's best yoga retreats and a growing number of excellent restaurants.

Local organisation El Shaddai, a child protection charity, has several schools based here.

Activities

International Animal Rescue VOLUNTEERING
(Animal Tracks; ☎0832-2268272; www.internationalanimalrescuegoa.org.in; Madungo Vaddo; ⌚9am-4pm) The well-established International Animal Rescue collects and cares for stray dogs, cats and other four-legged animals in distress, carrying out sterilisations and vaccinations. Volunteers are welcome to help with dog walking and playing with puppies and kittens, but must have evidence of rabies vaccination.

El Shaddai VOLUNTEERING
(☎0832-2461068, 0832-6513286; www.childrescue.net; El Shaddai House, Socol Vaddo) El Shaddai is a British-founded charity that aids impoverished and homeless children throughout Goa; it has a number of schools in Assagao. Volunteers who are able to commit to more than four weeks' work with El Shaddai can apply through the website. There's a rigorous vetting process, so start well in advance. You can also help with donations and fundraising activities. For more information, there's a stall at the Anjuna flea market.

Spicy Mama's COOKING
(☎9623348958; www.spicymamasgoa.com; 517, Bouta Vaddo; 1-day course veg/nonveg ₹2000/3000, 3-day ₹5000/7000, 5-day ₹10,000/12,000) For cooking enthusiasts, Spicy Mama's specialises in spicy North Indian cuisine, from butter chicken to *aloo gobi* (cauliflower and potato curry) and *palak paneer* (cheese in a puréed spinach gravy), prepared at the country home of Suchi. The standard one-day course is four hours; book online for in-depth multiday masterclasses and for directions.

Sleeping & Eating

Assagao has some lovely guesthouses tucked away in the back lanes, as well as excellent residential yoga retreats.

Namaste Jungle Garden GUESTHOUSE $$
(☎9850466105; 138/3 Bairo Alto; cottage & apt incl breakfast ₹3500; ❄📶) There's a real feeling of communing with nature in these slick and spacious timber cottages set back in a jungly Assagao garden. It also has two apartment-style rooms with kitchen in the main building and massage and yoga available.

GREEN GOA

Goa's environment has suffered from an onslaught of tourism over the last 40 years, but also from the effects of logging, mining and local customs (rare turtle eggs have traditionally been considered a delicacy). Construction proceeds regardless of what the local infrastructure or ecosystem can sustain, while plastic bottles pile up in vast mountains. However, many tourist businesses – including five-star resorts – are recognising the need for sustainability and taking steps to be eco-minded. As a traveller, there are a few easy ways to minimise your impact on Goa's environment.

Take your own bag when shopping and refill water bottles with filtered water wherever possible. Rent a bicycle instead of a scooter, for short trips at least; bicycle rentals are declining as a result of our scooter infatuation and the bikes are poor quality, but they'll bounce back if the demand is there. Goa Tourism now employs cleaners to comb the beaches each morning picking up litter, but all travellers should do their part by disposing of cigarette butts and any litter in bins. The Goan government banned single-use plastic bags (in shops and markets) in 2018 and most shacks and bars have switched from plastic straws to paper or bamboo. Also in 2018, Kadamba introduced an all-electric bus, with plans to introduce more to the fleet.

Turtles are protected by the Forest Department (www.forest.goa.gov.in), which operates information huts on beaches such as Agonda, Galgibag and Morjim, where turtles arrive to lay eggs. Also doing good work over many years is the **Goa Foundation** (☎0832-2256479; www.goafoundation.org; St Britto's Apartments, G-8 Feira Alta), the state's main environmental pressure group based in Mapusa. It has spearheaded a number of conservation projects since its inauguration in 1986, including pressure to stop illegal mining, and its website is a great place to learn more about Goan environmental issues. The group's excellent *Fish Curry & Rice*, a sourcebook on Goa's environment and lifestyle, is sold at Mapusa's Other India Bookstore. The Goa Foundation occasionally runs volunteer projects.

Sunbeam BOUTIQUE HOTEL **$$$**
(www.justjivi.com/goa.html; Anjuna-Mapusa Rd; ste from ₹10,000; ❄📶🏊) This pair of creative suites is one of North Goa's most idiosyncratic properties. Owned and overseen by Jivi Sethi, a well-known and flamboyant Indian stylist, it's all heirlooms, high theatrics, and lots of understated luxury – as well as fabulous food.

Cafe Cotinga CAFE **$$**
(☎8605010949; www.cafecotinga.com; 1286 Kumar Vaddo; mains ₹210-550; ⏲8.30am-11pm) The garden cafe at the Tamarind Hotel on the Assagao/Anjuna fringe is a fabulous place for all-day breakfasts, pizzas and Indian dishes, but many come just for the homemade desserts from the in-house bakery – New York cheesecake and apple crumble for starters. Also a good bar.

Gunpowder MULTICUISINE **$$**
(mains ₹200-475; ⏲8-10.30am, noon-3.30pm & 7-10.30pm Tue-Sun; 📶) This garden restaurant behind the People Tree boutique exemplifies the Assagao trend in quality countryside dining, efficient service and wholesome, fresh food. Classic curries and stir-fries, both veg and nonveg, are the stars of the menu, along with tempting desserts (walnut, rum and raisin brownie) and cocktails.

Ruta's Roadhouse INTERNATIONAL **$$**
(☎8380025757; www.rutas.in; Mapusa Rd; breakfast ₹300, small/big plates ₹200/300; ⏲8.30am-6.30pm Mon-Sat) Ruta's has made a home in an old Portuguese house in Assagao, serving up excellent set breakfasts and global culinary offerings from jambalaya to spicy laksa.

★**Villa Blanche Bistro** CAFE **$$$**
(www.villablanche-goa.com; 283 Badem Church Rd; breakfast ₹100-380, mains ₹350-480; ⏲9am-11pm Thu-Tue Nov-May; 📶🌿) This lovely, German-run, chilled garden cafe draws diners to the back lanes of Assagao. Salads, sandwiches, filled bagels and cakes are specialities, but you'll also find Thai curry and German sausages, as well as lots of vegetarian and vegan options. For an indulgent breakfast or brunch try the waffles and pancakes. Sunday brunch (from 10am) is legendary.

🍷 Drinking & Nightlife

Soro PUB
(☎9881934440; Siolim Rd, Badem junction; ⏲6pm-2am) The 'village pub' is a welcome addition to the back lanes of sleepy Assagao,

with pumping live music on weekends, salsa dancing on Sunday and a fun atmosphere whenever there's a crowd. Decor is part English pub, part American bar, with exposed brick walls, barrel tables and a pool table. There's bar food but this is more for drinking and dancing.

Getting There & Away

Local buses between Mapusa and Anjuna (about 15 minutes from each) or Siolim pass through Assagao, but the village is best explored on a rented scooter or by taxi from your beach resort.

Mapusa

POP 40,500

Mapusa (pronounced 'Mapsa') is the largest town in northern Goa, and is most often visited for its busy market, which attracts scores of buyers and sellers from neighbouring towns and villages. It's a good place to pick up the usual range of embroidered bed sheets and the like, at prices far lower than in the beach resorts.

Many travellers pass through Mapusa anyway as it's the major transport hub for northern Goa buses. Most amenities are arranged around the Municipal Gardens, just north of the Kadamba bus station and main market site.

Sights & Activities

Maruti Temple HINDU TEMPLE
(Anjuna-Mapusa Rd) In the centre of town, the small, pastel-coloured Maruti temple was built in the 1840s at a site where the monkey god Hanuman was covertly worshipped during the more oppressive periods of Portuguese rule. After temples had been destroyed by the Portuguese, devotees placed a picture of Hanuman at the fireworks shop that stood here, and arrived cloaked in secrecy to perform their *pujas* (prayers).

In April 1843 the picture was replaced by a silver idol and an increasing number of worshippers began to gather here. Eventually the business community of Mapusa gathered enough funds to acquire the shop, and the temple was built in its place.

Church of Our Lady of Miracles CHURCH
Founded in 1594 and rebuilt several times since, this church (also known as St Jerome's), around 600m east of the Municipal Gardens, is famous more for its annual festival than for its architecture. It was built by the Portuguese on the site of an old Hindu temple, and thus the Hindu community still holds the site as sacred.

Mango Tree Goa VOLUNTEERING
(☎9604654588; www.mangotreegoa.org; The Mango House, near Vrundavan Hospital, Karaswada) Offers one- to three-month placements for volunteers providing teaching support for disadvantaged children around Mapusa.

MAPUSA MARKET

The **Mapusa market** (⏲8am-6.30pm Mon-Sat) goes about its business daily except Sunday, but it really gets going on Friday morning. It's a raucous affair that attracts vendors and shoppers from all over Goa, with an entirely different vibe to the Anjuna flea market. Here you'll find locals haggling for clothing and produce, and you can also hunt out antiques, souvenirs and textiles.

Sleeping & Eating

With the northern beaches so close and most long-distance buses departing in the late afternoon or early evening, it's hard to think of a good reason to stay in Mapusa, but there are a few options if you do.

Hotel Vilena HOTEL $$
(☎0832-2263115; hotelvilena@gmail.com; Feira Baixa Rd; d ₹1700-2000; ❄📶) The once budget Vilena has had a refurb and all rooms are now air-conditioned with bathroom, but it's still good value and the rooms are well kept. There's a restaurant and bar on the 1st floor and a rooftop restaurant called Goan & Grills.

Hotel Satyaheera HOTEL $$
(☎0832-2262949; Anjuna-Mapusa Rd; d with/without AC from ₹2500/2200; ❄📶) Next to the little Maruti temple in the town centre, this is Mapusa's best central midrange hotel, which isn't saying much. Rooms are comfortable enough and Ruchira, the roof-garden restaurant, is a decent place to eat.

Hotel Vrundavan SOUTH INDIAN $
(thalis from ₹100; ⏲7am-10pm Wed-Mon) This pure-veg place bordering the Municipal Gardens is a busy local spot for a hot chai, *pav bhaji* (bread with curried vegetables) or a quick breakfast.

Ruchira Restaurant MULTICUISINE $$

(Hotel Satyaheera; mains ₹150-320; ⏰11am-11pm) On the top floor of Hotel Satyaheera, this rooftop garden restaurant and bar is popular with tourists and widely deemed one of Mapusa's better family restaurants, serving tasty Goan, Indian and continental dishes (including seafood) at lower prices than the beach shacks.

Drinking & Nightlife

Pub PUB

(Market Rd; ⏰10am-4.30pm & 6.30-11pm Mon-Sat) Don't be put off by the dingy entrance or stairwell: once you're upstairs, this breezy place opposite the market is great for watching the milling crowds over a cold beer or feni. Eclectic daily specials make it a good spot for lunch.

Shopping

Other India Bookstore BOOKS

(☎0832-2263305; www.otherindiabookstore.com; Mapusa Clinic Rd; ⏰9am-5pm Mon-Fri, to 1pm Sat) This friendly and rewarding little bookshop, at the end of an improbable, dingy corridor, specialises in books about Goa and India with a focus on spirituality, environment, politics and travel. It's signposted near the Mapusa Clinic, a few hundred metres up the hill from the Municipal Gardens.

Information

MEDICAL SERVICES

Mapusa Clinic (☎0832-2263343; www.mapusaclinic.com; Mapusa Clinic Rd; ⏰consultations 9.30am-1pm & 4-8pm Mon-Sat) A well-run private medical clinic with 24-hour emergency services. Look for signs to the 'new' Mapusa Clinic, behind the 'old' one.

Getting There & Away

BUS

If you're coming to Goa by bus from Mumbai, Mapusa's **Kadamba bus stand** (☎0832-2232161; Calangute-Mapusa Rd) is the jumping-off point for the northern beaches. Local bus services run every few minutes; just look for the correct destination on the sign in the bus windshield. For buses to the southern beaches, take one of the frequent buses to Panaji, then Margao, and change there.

Local services:

Anjuna ₹15, 30 minutes
Arambol ₹40, one hour
Calangute ₹15, 30 minutes
Candolim ₹20, 35 minutes
Panaji ₹30, 30 minutes
Thivim ₹15, 20 minutes

Long-distance services are run by both government and private bus companies. Private operators' services are more frequent and have more choice of bus type. Fares are variable based on the season and even day of the week. Private operators have booking offices outside the bus stand (opposite the Municipal Gardens). There's generally little difference in price, comfort or duration between them, but shop around for the best fare. You can check fares and timings for government buses at www.goakadamba.com.

Most long-distance buses depart in the late afternoon or evening. Sample fares:

Bengaluru ₹900, with AC ₹1200; 13 to 14 hours
Hampi sleeper ₹1000; 9½ hours
Mumbai ₹850, with AC ₹900; 12 to 15 hours
Pune ₹700, with AC ₹900, 11 to 13 hours

TAXI

There's a prepaid taxi stand in the town square with a signboard of fixed prices. Cabs to Anjuna or Calangute cost ₹300; Candolim ₹400; Panaji ₹350; Arambol ₹700; Margao ₹1100; Dabolim Airport ₹1150. An autorickshaw to Anjuna or Calangute should cost ₹200.

TRAIN

Thivim, about 12km northeast of town, is the nearest train station on the Konkan Railway. An autorickshaw to or from Thivim station costs around ₹250.

Vagator & Chapora

Dramatic red stone cliffs, thick palm groves and a crumbling 17th-century Portuguese fort give Vagator and its diminutive village neighbour Chapora one of the prettiest settings on the North Goan coast. Once known for their wild trance parties and heady, hippie lifestyles, things have slowed down considerably these days and upmarket restaurants are more the style, though Vagator has some of Goa's best clubs. Chapora – reminiscent of the Mos Eisley Cantina from *Star Wars* – remains a favourite for hippies and long-staying smokers, with the smell of charas (resin of the marijuana plant) clinging heavily to the light sea breeze.

Sights

Ozran Beach BEACH

(Vagator) With shacks occupying the sands, Goa trance heavy on the sound systems, and cows thronging among the people, there's a distinctly laid-back vibe here, overseen by

Vagator & Chapora

0 400 m
0 0.2 miles

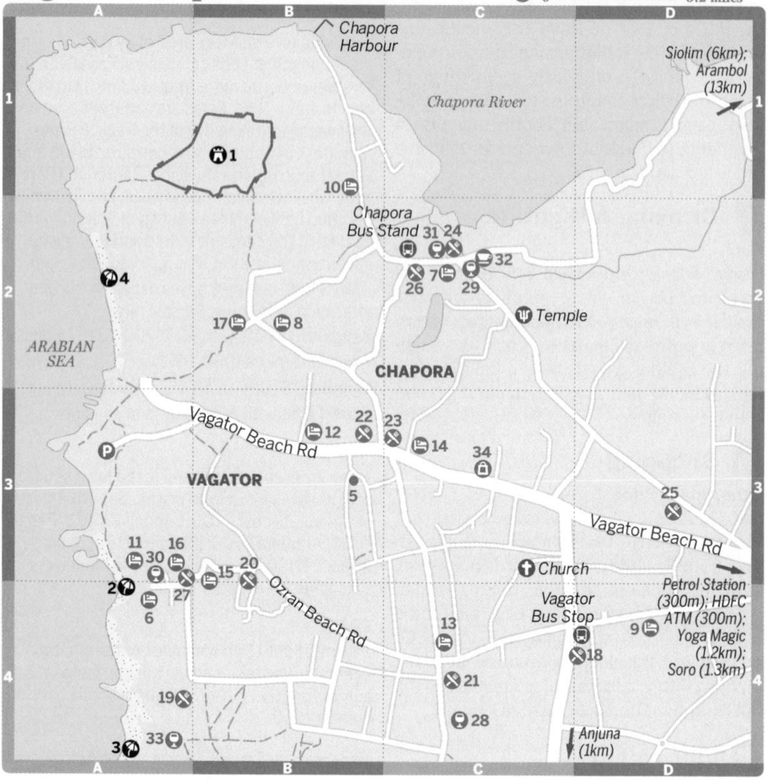

Vagator & Chapora

Sights

1 Chapora Fort B1
2 Little Vagator Beach A4
3 Ozran Beach A4
4 Vagator Beach A2

Activities, Courses & Tours

5 Mukti Kitchen B3

Sleeping

6 Alcove Resort A4
7 Baba Guesthouse & Villa C2
8 Baba Place B2
9 Bean Me Up Guest House D4
10 Casa de Olga B1
11 Casa Vagator A3
12 Dreams Hostel B3
13 Julie Jolly C4
14 Jungle Hostel C3
15 Pappi Chulo B3
16 Shalom A3
17 W Goa B2

Eating

18 AJ Supermarket D4
19 Antares A4
Bean Me Up .... (see 9)
20 Bluebird B3
21 Food Chord C4
22 Jaws B3
23 Mango Tree Bar & Cafe C3
24 Midnight Toker C2
25 Piccolo Roma D3
26 Sunrise Restaurant C2
27 Yangkhor Moonlight A3

Drinking & Nightlife

28 Hilltop C4
29 Jai Ganesh Fruit Juice Centre C2
30 Nine Bar A3
31 Paulo's Antique Bar C2
32 Scarlet Cold Drinks C2
33 Waters Beach Lounge A4

Shopping

34 Rainbow Bookshop C3

the huge, happy carved Shiva face that gazes out serenely from the rocks. Accessible by a steep footpath.

Vagator Beach BEACH

The most northerly and largest beach is a beautiful stretch of sand, which fills up for a few hours each afternoon when domestic coach tours unload their swift-clicking tourist hordes to make the most of its good swimming. Avoid this time of day and you'll have plenty of room for lounging on its pretty, boulder-studded sands.

Little Vagator Beach BEACH

Accessed by a steep footpath, this beach is less busy than Vagator's main beach.

Chapora Fort FORT

FREE Chapora's old laterite fort, standing guard over the mouth of the Chapora River, was built by the Portuguese in 1617, to protect Bardez taluk (district), in Portuguese hands from 1543 onwards. Today it is a crumble of picturesque ruins with only the outer walls remaining, though you can still pick out the mouths of two escape tunnels. The main reason to make the climb up the hill is for the sensational views along the coast from atop the fort walls.

It was built over the remnants of an older Muslim structure, hence the name of the village itself – from 'Shahpura', meaning 'town of the Shah'. Though heavily fortified, Chapora Fort was nevertheless captured several times by invaders: first by several groups of Hindu raiders, and next, in 1684, when it was reportedly conquered without a shot being fired. On this occasion the Portuguese captain of the fort decided to surrender to the Maratha forces of the chieftain Sambhaji, his decision perhaps stemming, if legend is to be believed, from the manner in which Sambhaji's forces managed to breach the fort's defences: it's said that they clung tight to tenacious 1.5m-long monitor lizards, who were able to scale the rocky walls with ease.

The Portuguese rebuilt the fort in 1717, adding features such as tunnels that led from the bastion down to the seashore and the river bank to enable resupply or escape in times of trouble, but Chapora fell again to the Marathas in 1739. Soon the northerly taluk of Pernem came into Portuguese hands, forming part of the Novas Conquistas (the 'New Conquests', the second wave of Portuguese conquests in Goa), and the significance of Chapora faded. The fort was finally abandoned to the ravages of the elements in 1892.

Courses

Mukti Kitchen COOKING

(8007359170; www.muktikitchen.com; off Vagator Beach Rd, Vagator; veg/nonveg/Goan class ₹2000/2500/3000; 11am-2pm & 6-9pm) Mukti shares her cooking skills twice daily at these recommended classes. Courses include around five dishes that can be tailored – veg or nonveg, Goan, Indian or ayurvedic. Minimum four people, maximum six; book one day ahead. You'll find Mukti's opposite Leoney Resort in Vagator.

Sleeping

Budget accommodation, much of it in private rooms, ranges along Ozran Beach Rd and Vagator Beach Rd; you'll see lots of signs for 'rooms to let'. Head down the road to the harbour at Chapora and you'll find lots of rooms – and whole homes – for rent, mainly for long-term stays from around ₹15,000 per month. Vagator also has a range of backpacker hostels and more upmarket accommodation.

★**Jungle Hostel** HOSTEL $

(0832-2273006; www.thehostelcrowd.com; Vagator Beach Rd, Vagator; dm with/without AC ₹650/550, s/d from ₹1100/1800;) One of the original backpacker hostels in North Goa, Jungle brought the dorm experience and an international vibe to Vagator and has expanded to three properties. It's still among the best around and offers cheap transfers to its other properties in Panaji and Palolem. There are clean and bright four- to six-bed dorms and private rooms. Lockers, wi-fi, breakfast and communal kitchen.

★**Dreams Hostel** HOSTEL $

(9920651760; www.dreams-hostel.goa-india-hotels-resorts.com; off Vagator Beach Rd, Vagator; dm ₹400-550, AC cabins ₹2400;) With a philosophy of 'art, music, wellness', former backpacker and local DJ Ravi has established a great little creative space for like-minded travellers with a spacious garden, clean dorms, deluxe timber cabins and chilled common areas. The hostel also acts as an artistic residency – the murals and artworks are all done by guests.

Pappi Chulo HOSTEL $

(9075135343; pappichulohostel@gmail.com; Ozran Beach Rd, Vagator; dm with/without AC ₹550/450, d ₹2000) Unashamedly Vagator's party hostel, Pappi's has a bar in the garden, movie nights and an international vibe of travellers just hanging out. Themed dorms have lockers and bunk beds.

Casa de Olga
GUESTHOUSE $

(☑9822157145, 0832-2274355; eadsouza@yahoo.co.in; Harbour Rd, Chapora; r ₹800-1350, without bathroom from ₹500) This welcoming family-run homestay, set around a nice garden on the way to Chapora harbour, offers spotless rooms of varying sizes in a three-storey building. The best are the top-floor rooms with swanky bathrooms, TV and balcony.

Baba Guesthouse & Villa
GUESTHOUSE $

(☑9822161142; babavilla11@yahoo.in; Main St, Chapora; d with/without AC ₹1000/700; ☎) With its laid-back Chapora location, Baba is often full with long-stayers but you might be lucky as a walk-in. The 14 rooms are clean and simple but serviceable.

Shalom
GUESTHOUSE $

(☑919881578459, 0832-2273166; www.shalomguesthousegoa.com; Ozran Beach Rd, Vagator; d ₹900-1500, with AC ₹2000; ✳☎) Arranged around a placid garden not far from the path down to Little Vagator Beach, this established place is run by a friendly family and offers a variety of extremely well-kept rooms and a two-bedroom apartment for long-stayers.

Bean Me Up Guest House
GUESTHOUSE $$

(☑7769095356; www.beanmeup.in; 1639/2 Deulvaddo, Vagator; d incl breakfast ₹1500-2500; ✳☎) Set around a leafy, shaded courtyard that's home to Bean Me Up, Vagator's best vegan restaurant, rooms here look simple but are themed with individual exotic decor, earthy shades, mosquito nets and shared verandahs. The mellow yoga-friendly vibe matches the clientele and the included breakfast is decadent. Morning yoga classes.

Baba Place
GUESTHOUSE $$

(☑9822156511; babaplace11@yahoo.com; Chapora Fort Rd, Chapora; d ₹2500; ✳☎☀) Baba Place, in the shadow of Chapora Fort, continues to improve with immaculate, decent-sized rooms with verandah, a small pool and a bar-restaurant.

Julie Jolly
HOTEL $$

(☑0832-2273620, 0832-2274897; www.hoteljollygoa.com; Ozran Beach Rd, Vagator; d from ₹1750, with AC ₹1950-2400; ✳@☀) Rooms are neat and spacious, like little Spanish villas surrounding a small pool. It's back from the beach action but has its own resort-style atmosphere. The owners also run two cheaper guesthouses in Vagator worth checking out – Jolly Jolly Lester and Jolly Jolly Roma.

Alcove Resort
HOTEL $$

(☑0832-2274491; www.alcovegoa.com; Little Vagator Beach; d ₹5400-8500; ✳☎☀) The location overlooking Little Vagator Beach is hard to beat at this price. Attractively furnished rooms, slightly larger cottages, and four suites surrounding a decent central pool, restaurant and bar, make this a good place for those who want a touch of affordable luxury near the beach. Add ₹500 for air-con.

W Goa
HOTEL $$$

(☑0832-6718888; www.marriott.com; Vagator Beach; r ₹34,000-60,000; ✳☎☀) Below Chapora Fort and terracing down to Vagator Beach, W Goa is the newest and swankiest hotel in North Goa with a price tag to match. This is luxury all the way with plush seaview suites and villas with sea or fort views and expansive gardens where golf carts ferry guests from pool to restaurant to beach. Even if you can't afford to stay here it's worth considering a splurge at one of the restaurants, Rock Pool or Spice Traders, or the loungy Woobar.

Casa Vagator
HOTEL $$$

(☑0832-2416738; www.casaboutiquehotels.com; Vagator; d incl breakfast ₹12,200-18,600; ✳☎☀) Down the steps past Nine Bar and opening out onto craggy Vagator Beach, this is a successfully rendered outfit in the deluxe Casa boutique mould, and one of Vagator's most stylish accommodation options. Cosy rooms and lush gardens offer gorgeous views out across the wide blue horizon. Two pools and a spa complete the picture.

🍴 Eating

Vagator has a handful of outstanding dining spots along its clifftop, along with the usual range of shacks down on the beach.

The dining scene at tiny Chapora isn't as evolved as Vagator, but that's what the people who hang out there like about it. With a couple of popular juice joints and a handful of nondescript restaurants, Chapora stays cool while the fine dining is elsewhere.

Jaws
INDIAN $

(Vagator Beach Rd, Vagator; mains ₹50-300; ☉9am-9.30pm) With a bakery counter and inexpensive dosas and South Indian thalis, unassuming Jaws is an old-timer but one of the best-value eateries in Vagator. Good for a lazy breakfast or afternoon beer.

TRANCE PARTIES

Goa has a far longer and more vibrant history of hosting parties than most people realise. As far back as the 16th century, the Portuguese colony was notorious as an immoral outpost where drinking and dancing lasted till dawn, and, despite a more strait-laced interlude at the hands of the notorious Goan Inquisition, the tradition was finally resurrected full-force when the 'Goa Freaks' arrived on the state's northern beaches in the 1960s.

But the beach parties and full-moon raves of the 1970s and '80s came to seem like innocent affairs compared with the trance parties that replaced them in the '90s. At the peak of Goa's trance period, each high season saw thousands of revellers choosing synthetic substances such as ecstasy over marijuana and dancing to techno beats in Day-glo stupors, sometimes for days at a time.

In 2000 a central government 'noise pollution' ban on loud music in open spaces between 10pm and 6am was handed down. This, combined with increasing crackdowns on drug possession, seriously put the brakes on the trance-party scene, with police teams swooping in to close down parties before they even began. This was largely greeted with relief from locals, who were becoming increasingly worried at the peak of the trance-party phenomenon about the effects of drug dealing and alcohol on Goa's own youth population.

With a tourist industry to nurture and the potential for baksheesh (bribes), the police still tend to turn a blind eye to a handful of parties during the peak Christmas and New Year period or on full-moon nights. Indoor venues, including clubs in Baga and Candolim, remain pumping till 4am or later, but entry rules are restrictive, particularly for men. In Vagator and Anjuna, several clubs still carry on by partying indoors after 10pm. Down south in Palolem, 'silent discos' are the new thing. Other parties simply take place during the day.

If you're determined to experience the remnants of Goa's true trance scene, hang around long enough in Anjuna or Vagator and you'll likely be handed a flyer for a party (many with international DJs). Taxi drivers are one of the best sources of information as it's in their interests to ferry party-goers around. Other locals get involved setting up chai and omelette stands, and selling cigarettes and laser pointers.

At the time of writing some of the best parties were happening at Shiva Valley (Tuesday), Curlies (Thursday and Saturday), Hilltop (Sunday), Re:Fresh (Morjim), Sinq (Asvem and Candolim). Download the excellent 'Party Hunt' app to see what's happening.

AJ Supermarket SUPERMARKET **$**
(☎0832-2274555; Anjuna-Vagator Rd, Vagator; ⏰9am-8.30pm Mon-Sat) Vagator's best supermarket. Full range of groceries and alcohol.

Sunrise Restaurant CAFE **$**
(Main St, Chapora; mains ₹100-300; ⏰7am-10.30pm; 📶) Sunrise doesn't pretend to be anything special but it does open early for breakfast and has good food and a little garden on the main road out of Chapora.

★ **Bean Me Up** VEGAN **$$**
(www.beanmeup.in; 1639/2 Deulvaddo, Vagator; mains ₹200-400; ⏰8am-11pm; 📶) Bean Me Up is vegan, but even nonveg travellers will be blown away by the taste, variety and filling plates on offer in this relaxed garden restaurant. The extensive menu includes vegan pizzas, ice creams, housemade tofu curry and innovative salads. Ingredients are as diverse as coconut, cashew milk and cashew cheese, quinoa, tempeh and lentil dhal. Breakfast is a treat with scrambled tofu, buckwheat pancakes and killer coconut milk smoothies.

Piccolo Roma ITALIAN **$$**
(☎7507806821; Anjuna-Chapora Rd, Vagator; pizza & pasta ₹210-520; ⏰10am-11pm; 📶) With an Italian chef in the kitchen, some say the wood-fired pizzas and house-made pasta is the best in Vagator and there's an undeniably pleasant atmosphere in the garden cafe, with its cushions and fairy lights. Starters of antipasto, crostini, soups and salads also grace the menu.

Mango Tree Bar & Cafe MULTICUISINE **$$**
(Vagator Beach Rd, Vagator; mains ₹190-510; ⏰24hr; 📶) With loud reggae, crappy service, dark-wood furniture, a sometimes rambunctious bar scene, ancient expats leaning over the bar, draught beer and an overall great vibe, the Mango Tree is a classic Vagator meeting place. It's open late (allegedly 24 hours if it's busy enough) with a menu from Goan to European, pizza and Mexican.

Bluebird GOAN $$
(www.bluebirdgoa.com; Ozran Beach Rd, Vagator; mains ₹280-480; ⏲8.30am-11pm; 📶) Bluebird specialises in Goan cuisine, with genuine vindaloos, chicken *cafreal* (marinated in a sauce of chillies, garlic and ginger), fish curry rice and Goan sausages among the temptations, as well as some delicately spiced seafood dishes. Dine in the lovely open garden cafe.

Food Chord DINER $$
(☎0832-6745000; 544/2, Ozran Beach Rd, Vagator; mains ₹175-550; ⏲7am-11.30pm; ❄📶) At the crazy retro I Love Bellbottoms hotel, this American-style diner has booth seating, Arctic air-con and a menu of club sandwiches, burgers, hot dogs and pizzas. The inner window looks out to the violin-shaped pool (nonguests can swim for ₹1500, redeemable on food and drinks). Full bar with draught beer. Vagator or Vegas?

Midnight Toker MULTICUISINE $$
(Main St, Chapora; mains ₹140-240; ⏲9am-1am; 📶) The usual array of Indian, Chinese and Russian food is on the menu but this welcoming open-fronted restaurant is also a good place to watch the Chapora scene over a cold beer.

Yangkhor Moonlight TIBETAN $$
(Ozran Beach Rd, Vagator; mains ₹170-400; ⏲8am-11pm; 📶) Well known locally for its fresh Tibetan food such as *momos* (Tibetan dumplings), *thukpa* (soup) and the rarely seen Tibetan thali (₹250), as well as pasta dishes and even sushi. The decor is simple but most travellers enjoy the food and the ambience.

Antares INDIAN $$$
(☎7350011528; www.antaresgoa.com; Ozran Beach Rd, Vagator; mains ₹395-1295; ⏲11.30am-midnight) Perched on Vagator's southern clifftop, Antares is the project of Australian Masterchef contestant Sarah Todd. The atmosphere is beachfront chic meets nightclub and the food pricey Modern Australian meets Indian, with some Goan dishes such as crab *xacuti*.

On a good night it works but those expecting fine dining may be disappointed. Down below is the daytime Beach Club with a cheaper menu and pizzas, as well as rooms.

Drinking & Nightlife

Hilltop CLUB
(www.hilltopgoa.in; Vagator; ⏲sunset-3am) Hilltop is a long-serving Vagator trance and party venue that's deserted by day but comes alive from sunset. Its edge-of-town, neon-lit coconut grove location allows it, on occasion, to bypass noise regulations to host indoor and outdoor concerts, parties and international DJs. Sunday sessions (5pm to 10pm) are legendary.

Nine Bar BAR
(Little Vagator Beach; ⏲5pm-4am) Once the hallowed epicentre of Goa's trance scene, the open-air Nine Bar terrace, on the clifftop overlooking Little Vagator Beach, is fading but stills pumps out beats in its soundproof indoor space. It generally doesn't start until December; look out for flyers and local advice to see when the big party nights are on.

Paulo's Antique Bar BAR
(Main St, Chapora; ⏲3-11pm) In season this hole-in-the-wall bar on Chapora's main street overflows with good music and cold beer. In the late afternoon the few tables on the verandah are a fine spot to watch the world in miniature go by.

Waters Beach Lounge CLUB
(☎9767200012; Ozran Beach, Vagator; ⏲noon-4am) Terracing down the hillside on the Vagator cliffs, this restaurant, bar and club is known for its loud party nights, with open-air dance floors overlooking the Arabian Sea and a soundproof room for late at night – as late as 5am. Top DJs come to play.

Jai Ganesh Fruit Juice Centre JUICE BAR
(Main St, Chapora; ⏲8.30am-midnight) Thanks to its corner location, with views up and down Chapora's main street, this may be the most popular juice bar in Goa. It's a prime meeting spot and, once parked, most people are reluctant to give up their seat. Juices ₹60 to ₹80.

Scarlet Cold Drinks CAFE
(Main St, Chapora; juices & snacks ₹30-100; ⏲8.30am-midnight) Selling juice, lassis, fruit salads and muesli, Scarlet is the second-most popular of Chapora's juice bars. There's a useful noticeboard with news of the latest local yoga classes, reiki courses and the like.

Shopping

Rainbow Bookshop BOOKS
(Vagator Beach Rd, Vagator; ⏲10am-7pm) Small but long-running shop stocking a good range of secondhand and new books.

Getting There & Away

Fairly frequent buses run to both Chapora and Vagator from Mapusa (₹15, 30 minutes) throughout the day, many via Anjuna. There are bus stops in **Chapora** (Main St) and on Vagator Beach Rd and **Anjuna-Vagator Rd** (Vagator). Practically anyone with legs will rent you a scooter/motorcycle from ₹300/500 per day.

Vagator has North Goa's most popular **petrol station** (Mapusa-Chapora Rd).

Siolim

POP 12,000

The large market town of Siolim straddles the Chapora River and is a major road junction between Anjuna, Chapora, Mapusa and the road north to Arambol. Though all travellers heading north will pass through Siolim, it's often overlooked due to its riverside location some way from the nearest beach. If you're looking for a change from sea and sand, it makes an interesting place to stay with quite a few budget and midrange guesthouses for rent, and some fine top-end heritage hotels.

Courses

Cozy Corner Cooking School COOKING
(☎7720980678; Cozy Corner Restaurant; 4hr class ₹2500; ⏲9am-1pm Tue-Wed & Fri-Sun) At the nondescript Cozy Corner Restaurant off the main road in Siolim village, this reputable cooking school (formerly at Siolim House) specialises in Goan cuisine. Visit the market to select produce then learn to cook four dishes.

Sleeping & Eating

★**Siolim House** HERITAGE HOTEL $$$
(☎9822584560, 0832-2272138; www.siolimhouse.com; Wadi; ste €135-175; ❄📶🏊) Comprising the seven-suite Siolim House hotel and the three-bedroom Little Siolim, Siolim House is one of North Goa's boutique treats. Situated in an old *palácio* (palace) that was once home to the Governor of Macau, the hotel is elegant and carefully restored and, though it has a lovely pool and air-con, is devoid of many modern trappings such as TV.

Teso Waterfront RESORT $$$
(☎0832-2270096; www.tesogoa.com; Vaddy Siolim; luxury tents ₹18,200-23,300; ❄📶🏊) This loungy upmarket party place has a cool location looking out on the lake-like mouth of the Chapora River, and is the new home of Thalassa restaurant. The safari Rajasthani tents are pricey but deluxe with air-con, fluffy beds, fridge, flat-screen TV, wardrobe and dresser. Muslin-wrapped cabanas make a great place to sip a cocktail overlooking the waterfront.

Noi Varo VILLA $$$
(☎9011071911; www.shunyachi.com; Siolim-Chapora Rd; ste ₹10,300-13,500; ❄📶🏊) This wonderful villa, ideal for families or groups looking to book the whole place, is uber exclusive. It's a spacious, stunning refurbished Portuguese mansion with three double bedrooms and a variety of extra sleeping spaces. You can kick back amid antiques, hang out in its river-view tree house, consult with its gourmet chef and float in a cool swimming pool.

★**Thalassa** GREEK $$$
(☎9850033537; www.thalassaindia.com; Teso Waterfront; mains ₹300-750; ⏲4pm-midnight) North Goa's most famous Greek restaurant was forced out of its long-running Vagator location in 2018 but has found a new waterfront home at Teso in Siolim. Still authentic and awesomely good Greek food is served al fresco overlooking the Chapora River. Kebabs, souvlaki and seafood dishes are the speciality, but this is also a great bar and it usually fills up late in the evening when you might see some Greek dancing and plate smashing. Come early, order a jug of sangria and enjoy the sunset over Chapora harbour.

Shopping

Swiss Happy Cow Cheese FOOD
(☎9923326310; www.swisshappycowchees.wixsite.com/cheese; ⏲9am-7pm Mon-Fri, 9am-5pm Sat) Artisanal Swiss and French cheeses, including brie and feta, are made on-site here by a Swiss cheesemaker using local cow, buffalo and goat's milk. Cheeses are sold by weight from ₹500 to ₹1500 per kilogram.

Getting There & Away

Siolim is on the main Calangute-Arambol road and is well served by local buses in either direction. If you have your own wheels, the road from Vagator along the Chapora River is a pleasant ride.

Morjim

Morjim Beach was once very low-key – almost deserted – and the southern end is still protected due to the presence of rare olive ridley marine turtles, which come to lay their annual clutches of eggs between November and February.

These days Morjim is super popular with Russian tourists – it's locally known as 'Little Russia' – and consequently there's a bit of a clubbing scene in season and a growing number of restaurants and beach shacks. Though

Morjim & Mandrem

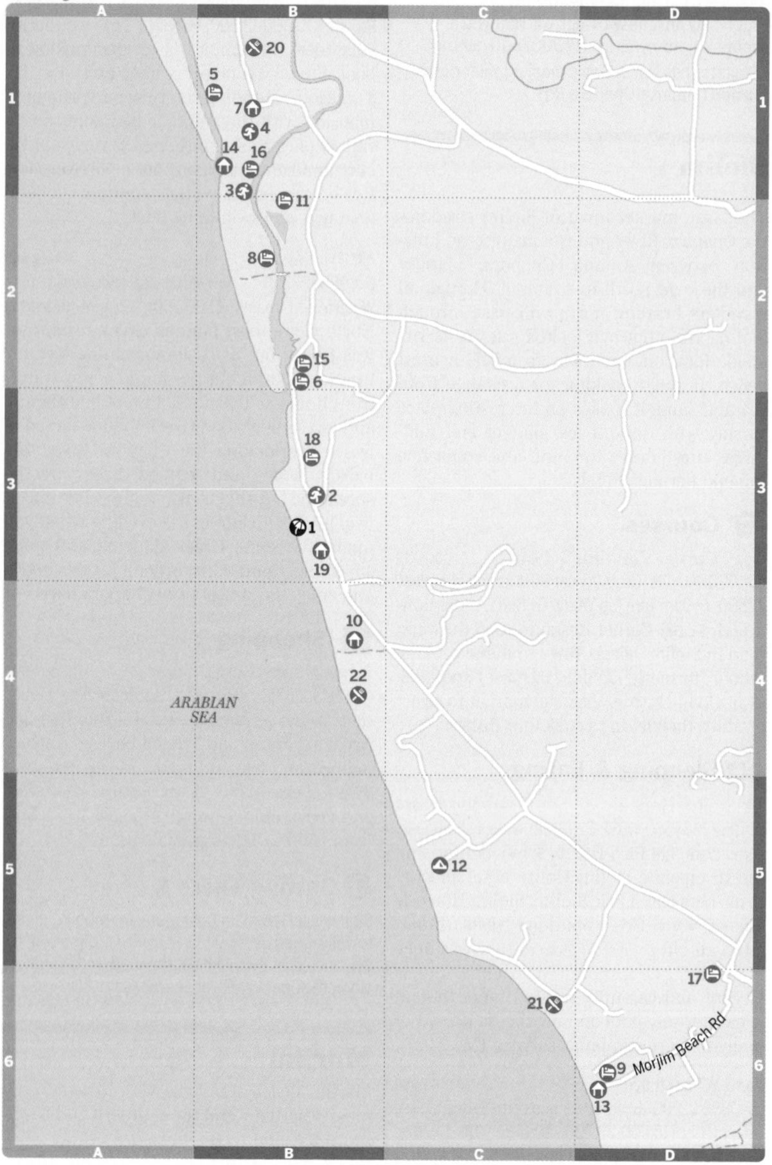

there are lovely views down the headland to Chapora Fort, the southern beach is more black sand than golden due to river runoff.

Morjim is also emerging as the beach party capital along this coast with EDM and trance parties popping up regularly in season and clubs such as Re:fresh and Sinq Beach gaining a large following.

At Marbela Beach Resort, **Banana Surf School** (☎7218063571; www.goasurf.com; Marbela Beach; 2-hour surf lesson US$70, 3-day course US$180, board hire per hour/day US$25/60) rents

Morjim & Mandrem

boards and offers beginner lessons, from two hours to five days.

Sleeping & Eating

Morjim has become extremely popular with Russian tourists, so many little guesthouses and beach huts have set up here with Cyrillic signs and menus.

★ **Wanderers Hostel** HOSTEL $
(9619235302; www.wanderershostel.com; Morjim Beach Rd; dm with fan/AC ₹400/500, shared tents ₹300, luxury tents d ₹1500;) About five minutes' walk back from Morjim Beach, Wanderers is a real find for budget travellers. The main building, decorated with original travellers' murals, has spotless dorms with lockers, bed lights and wi-fi, full kitchen, cosy communal areas and a pool table. In the garden next door is a tent village with swimming pool, yoga retreat centre and outdoor cinema.

Rainbow Cafe HUT $
(huts ₹1200;) Rainbow has some colourful, decent-value huts behind its convivial beachfront restaurant (mains ₹110 to ₹400) and bar. It's at the end of Morjim Beach Rd, right on the beach.

Goan Café & Resort RESORT $$
(0832-2244394; www.goancafe.com; apt & cottages from ₹1800, with AC ₹2200, tree houses ₹2200, without bathroom ₹1200;) Fronting Morjim Beach, this excellent family-run resort has a fine array of beachfront stilted 'tree house' huts and more solid rooms (some with AC) at the back. The beachfront restaurant is good and breakfast is included.

Marbela Beach Resort TENTED CAMP $$$
(9158881185, 9158881180; www.marbelabeach.com; 782 Gawdewada; tents & villas/ste ₹13,800/20,700;) The luxury tents and 'Spanish-style' villas at this slick resort are pricey but fitted out like five-star hotel rooms. Even if you don't stay here, the beachfront cabanas are a divine spot for a drink and the Euro fusion restaurant is destination dining. 'White parties' frequently draw a crowd. Naturally, there's a spa and yoga classes.

Bora Bora MULTICUISINE $$$
(8888558614; mains ₹270-550; 24hr) Part restaurant, part club, part beach bar, Bora Bora is the only place in this area open 24 hours. Food runs to everything from pizza to Russian, Thai and Indian with seafood nights, but most people come here to chill out and enjoy a drink or one of the DJ nights. It's at the start of Morjim's little 'eat street'.

Getting There & Away

Occasional local buses run between Siolim and Morjim village (₹10, 15 minutes), but most travellers taxi to their chosen accommodation, then hire a scooter/motorbike or use taxis from there.

Asvem

Asvem is a wide stretch of beach, growing busier each year but still a little overshadowed by Mandrem to the north. Beach-hut accommodation and beach-shack restaurants spring up each season on a very broad stretch of clean, white-sand with few hawkers. The main Morjim–Mandrem road is set some way back from the sands.

THE TURTLE WIND

Each November, a strong breeze known as the 'turtle wind' heralds the arrival of olive ridley marine turtles to lay eggs on a clutch of Goan beaches. It's believed that these females – who live for over a century – return to the beach of their birth to lay eggs, courtesy of an incredible in-built 'homing device', often travelling thousands of kilometres to do so.

One such beach is Morjim, but turtle numbers over the last century have slowly dwindled to dangerous levels due to poaching. On investigation, it was found that locals were digging up the eggs and selling them as delicacies at the market, and any turtle found out of the water was generally killed for its meat and shell. Increased tourism to Goa has also taken its toll; eggs were, for years, trampled unwittingly at rave parties, while sea and light pollution continue to threaten the survival of those that manage, against the odds, to hatch. Since nesting is influenced by lunar cycles, some environmentalists believe increasing unnatural lighting contributes to the turtles' confusion.

In 1996 the Goa Foundation, on the urging of several concerned local residents, finally stepped in and enlisted the help of the Goa Forest Department to patrol the beach and instigate a turtle conservation program. Locals who once profited from selling the eggs are now paid to guard them at several turtle protection sites (at Morjim, Agonda and Galgibag beaches) established for this very purpose. Drop into one of the forest department information huts in season, or contact the Goa Foundation (www.goafoundation.org), to learn more.

Activities

★ Vaayu Waterman's Village SURFING
(☎9850050403; www.vaayuvision.com; surfboard hire per hour/day ₹500/1500, lessons ₹2500) Goa's premier surf shop is also an activity and art centre where you can arrange lessons and hire equipment for surfing, kiteboarding, stand-up paddleboarding (SUP), kayaking and wakeboarding. A highlight is the full-day SUP tour to Paradise Lagoon in Maharashtra. The enthusiastic young owners also run an art gallery, cafe and accommodation across the road from Asvem Beach.

Arti Spa AYURVEDA
(☎9049209597; www.artifabulousbodycare.com; massage & ayurvedic treatments ₹500-2000; ⏲8am-9pm) Arti and Dinesh run this well-regarded ayurvedic spa in Asvem (on the main road behind Sea View Resort). Treatments include Keralan massage, aromatherapy and *shirodhara* (an ayurvedic massage treatment where liquids are poured over the forehead).

Sleeping & Eating

Asvem boasts a stylish and growing range of beach huts. Most places are steadily moving upmarket, but you can still find basic beach huts and rooms back from the beach for ₹1000 (less out of high season), depending on the view, facilities and proximity to the water. There are plenty of standard restaurant shacks along the beach.

Beachside by Bombay Backpackers HOSTEL $
(☎9781040244; Asvem Beach Rd; dm ₹400-450, d ₹1650; wifi) Down a lane off the main road opposite the beach, this hostel in a converted old house makes a decent budget stay with four- to six-bed dorms with individual fans and lockers. There's a distinct lack of traveller vibe compared with some of north Goa's hostels but the location and price are good.

Vaayu Waterman's Village BOUTIQUE HOTEL $$
(☎9850050403; www.vaayuvision.com; hut ₹2500-4400, d with AC ₹4500; AC wifi) The excellent boutique rooms at this water-sports outfit are stylish with the sort of artistic and soulful vibe that goes with the attached gallery, wholefood Prana Cafe, yoga *shala* (studio) and surf shop. Across the road, facing the beach, are beautifully designed Keralan-style bamboo and thatch huts.

Wellness Inn GUESTHOUSE $$
(☎9075006776; www.wellnessinn.in; d/f from ₹3200/4800; AC wifi) This 13-room guesthouse will suit yoga practitioners with daily drop-in classes, yoga training on the rooftop terrace and a health-conscious veg restaurant. Rooms are spacious, airy and all have aircon. It's often busy with travellers on yoga retreats so book ahead.

Yab Yum HUT $$$
(☎0832-6510392; www.yabyumresorts.com; hut/cottage from ₹10,600/12,050; AC wifi) 🍃 This top-notch choice has unusual, stylish, dome-

shaped huts – some look like giant hairy coconuts – made of a combination of all-natural local materials, including mud, stone and mango wood, as well as more traditional AC cottages. A host of yoga and massage options is available, and it's set in one of the most secluded beachfront jungle gardens you'll find in Goa.

Leela Cottages HUT $$$
(☎0832-22822874; www.leelacottage.com; cottage ₹5900-10,000, ste from ₹11,300;) These luxury designer beach cottages (deluxe, luxury, grand and suite) are enveloped in a gorgeous leafy garden, just steps from the beach. Stand-out touches include antique bits and pieces in each cottage, ornate furniture, individually named rooms and lots of cute throw pillows, plus air-con and minibars. There's a quality Satsanga Spa and drop-in yoga classes.

Prana Cafe HEALTH FOOD $$
(☎9850050403; www.vaayuvision.com; Asvem Beach Rd; mains ₹220-460; 9am-10pm;) There's a healthy vibe in this open-air cafe, part of the excellent Vaayu Village complex, and it naturally extends to the food. From the superfood smoothies and chia bowls to zucchini quinoa fritters, there's a wholesome freshness to the menu. It's not all vegetarian, though, with tacos and basil chicken burgers.

La Plage MEDITERRANEAN $$
(☎9822121712; Asvem Beach; mains ₹200-450; 8.30am-10pm, to 4pm Tue, Thu, Fri Dec-Apr;) Renowned in these parts, La Plage takes beach shack to the next level with its inspired gourmet French-Mediterranean food. Along with excellent salads, seafood and fabulous desserts, La Plage stocks great wines. It's usually open from late November or early December to April.

Getting There & Away

Buses run between Siolim and Asvem, but it's easier to get a taxi straight to your chosen accommodation, then either hire a scooter/motorbike or use taxis from there.

Mandrem

Mellow Mandrem is something akin to beach bliss, with its miles of clean, white sand separated from the village by a shallow creek. The beach and village has developed in recent years from an in-the-know bolthole for those seeking respite from the relentless traveller scene of Arambol and Anjuna to a fairly mainstream but still very lovely beach hang-out. There's plenty of yoga, meditation and ayurveda on offer here, plus a growing dining scene and plenty of space to lay down with a good book. Many believe there's no better place in North Goa.

Sights & Activities

Mandrem is something of a Spiritual Central, and there's plenty of yoga on offer. Many classes and courses change with the season, but there are a few places that reappear year after year.

Mandrem Beach BEACH
The beach here is wide and whiter than those further south. An unusual feature of Mandrem is the narrow river inlet separating the white-sand beach from most of the accommodation strip and road – rickety bamboo bridges connect you to the beach, where seasonal beach shacks set up.

Kite Guru WATER SPORTS
(☎8788314974; www.kiteguru.co.uk; 2/6/8hr course ₹7000/14,000/21,000, SUP lessons ₹2000) Based at Riverside in Mandrem, this is the best place in Goa to learn to kitesurf. Professional instructors offer group or solo IKO certified lessons and provide all the gear. Also stand-up paddleboard lessons and tours. Board hire for independent SUPers is ₹1000 an hour.

Shanti Ayurvedic Massage Centre AYURVEDA
(☎8806205264; 1hr massage from ₹1000; 9am-9pm) Ayurvedic massage is provided here by the delightful Shanti. Try the rejuvenating 75-minute massage and facial package, or go for an unusual 'Poulti' massage, using a poultice-like cloth bundle containing 12 herbal powders. You'll find her place on the right-hand side as you head down the beach road.

Oceanic Yoga YOGA
(☎9049247422; Junas Waddo; week-long yoga retreat from US$400) Oceanic offers yoga and meditation retreats, and yoga teacher-training courses.

Himalaya Yoga Valley YOGA
(☎9960657852; www.yogagoaindia.com; Mandrem Beach) HYV specialises in hatha and ashtanga residential, 200-hour teacher-training courses (€1475) in Goa, Dharamsala and Ireland.

Ashiyana Retreat Centre YOGA
(☎9850401714; www.ashiyana-yoga-goa.com; Junas Waddo; drop-in class ₹600) This 'tropical retreat centre' fronting Mandrem Beach and stretching back to the jungle has a long list of classes and courses available from October to April, from retreats and yoga holidays to spa, massage and 'massage camp'. Accommodation (includes free yoga) is in one of its gorgeous, heritage-styled rooms and huts.

Amalia Camp MEDITATION
(www.neeru.de; 10-day intensive life training incl meals €700) Learn the spiritual art of 'Open Clarity' at Amalia Camp, where local guru Neeru hosts *satsangs* (devotional speech and chanting sessions) to help ease you towards ever-elusive enlightenment. Check the website for a schedule of events. Registration is at Dunes Holiday Village.

Sleeping

Mandrem has a growing number of beach huts fronting the beach or river inlet for around ₹1500, though many of the operations are moving more upmarket. As with most destinations in Goa, the huts change appearance, owner and prices seasonally. You'll also find plenty of houses and rooms for rent throughout the village; just look for signs.

Riverside HUT $
(☎9049503605; www.riversidemandrem.com; Junas Waddo; huts ₹800-1200;) At the southern end of Mandrem Beach, overlooking the creek, Riverside is an excellent, two-level open-sided restaurant with a collection of well-designed but affordable palm-thatch and timber huts at the back and side. These are some of the best-value beachfront huts in Mandrem and there's a kitesurfing school here and stand-up paddleboards for rent.

★ **Dunes Holiday Village** HUT $$
(☎0832-2247219; www.dunesgoa.com; huts ₹1500-1750, d with AC ₹2200;) The pretty huts here are peppered around a palm-filled lane leading to the beach; at night, lamps light up the place like a palm-tree dreamland. Huts range from basic to more sturdy 'tree houses' (huts on stilts) and there are some guesthouse rooms with air-con. It's a friendly, good-value place with a decent beach restaurant, yoga classes and a marked absence of trance.

★ **Mandala** RESORT $$
(☎9158266093; www.themandalagoa.com; r & huts ₹1600-7000;) Mandala is a very peaceful and beautifully designed eco-village with a range of huts and a couple of quirky air-con rooms in the 'Art House'. Pride of place goes to the barn-sized two-storey villas inspired by the design of a Keralan houseboat. The location, overlooking the tidal lagoon, is serene, with a large garden, daily yoga sessions, an organic restaurant and juice bar.

Beach Street RESORT $$
(Lazy Dog; ☎9403410679; Mandrem Beach; huts ₹4300-6900, chalets ₹8600-11,800;) The beachfront huts are adorable at Beach Street, where the adjacent building encloses an inviting pool. Well-designed huts range from simple with bathroom and verandah to two-storey palm-thatch family 'chalets' sleeping five. The Lazy Dog beachfront restaurant here has five-star aspirations with waiters dressed in cruise uniforms.

Riva Beach Resort RESORT $$
(☎0832-2247612; www.rivaresorts.com; d ₹5000-9500;) This sprawling complex of hotel-style rooms and seasonal cottages tumbles down from the main road to the inlet, where bamboo bridges provide access to the beach. Spring mattresses, ocean-view balconies, a good restaurant and on-site yoga retreats. It's also a bit of a party spot – Sunday is the pool party.

Villa River Cat GUESTHOUSE $$
(☎9823610001, 0832-2247928; www.villarivercat.com; 438/1 Junas Waddo; d ₹3800-4800, without bathroom ₹3100;) This fabulously quirky circular guesthouse – filled with art, light, antiques, and an owner with a decidedly creative inclination – is popular with arty types, potential screenwriters and return guests. Animal lovers will enjoy the resident cats and dogs.

Elsewhere COTTAGE $$$
(www.aseascape.com; tents ₹8500, beach houses ₹15,600-28,200;) The exact location of this heavenly place, on some 500m of beachfront, is a closely guarded secret. Choose from four beautiful beachfront houses, intriguingly named the Piggery, Bakery, Priest's House and Captain's House, or from three luxury tents, and revel in the solitude that comes with a hefty price tag and a 60m walk across a bamboo bridge.

Eating

Karma Kitchen MULTICUISINE $$
(☎8894204735; Junas Waddo; mains ₹220-650; 9am-10pm;) This cruisey courtyard cafe offers a bit of everything but specialises in

thalis, tandoor kebabs and seafood, or a combination such as the seafood souvlaki kebab. It's also a good place to come for a drink, with wine by the glass and regular live music, including Sunday sessions.

Bed Rock MULTICUISINE $$
(Junos Vaddo; mains ₹150-400; ⌚8am-11pm; 📶) Bed Rock is a welcome change from the beach shacks with a reliable menu of Indian and continental faves (pizza, pasta etc), a cosy chill-out lounge upstairs, welcoming staff and a loyal following of regulars. Look out for live music in season.

Shopping

Arambol Hammocks HOMEWARES
(☎9619175722, 7798906816; www.arambol.com; 327 Junas Waddo) Now in Mandrem, Arambol Hammocks designs and sells hammocks, including 'flying carpets' and 'flying chairs'.

Getting There & Away

Buses run between Siolim and Mandrem village (₹10, 20 minutes) hourly, but it's hard work trying to get anywhere in a hurry on public transport. Most travellers taxi to their chosen accommodation, then either hire a scooter/motorbike or use taxis from there.

Arambol (Harmal)

POP 5320

Arambol (also known as Harmal) is the most northerly of Goa's developed beach resorts and is still considered the beach of choice for many long-staying budget-minded travellers in the north.

Arambol first emerged in the 1960s as a mellow paradise for long-haired long-stayers escaping the scene at Calangute. Today things are still cheap and cheerful, with budget accommodation in little huts and rooms clinging to the cliffsides, though the main beach is now an uninterrupted string of beach shacks, many with accommodation operations stacked behind.

The main beach is gently curved and safe for swimming but often crowded and sometimes a bit dirty – head south towards Mandrem for a quieter beach scene. A short walk around the northern headland brings you to little Kalacha Beach, another popular place thanks to the 'Sweetwater Lake' back from the beach. The headland above here is the best place in Goa for paragliding.

Activities

Aside from yoga and beach lounging, the most popular pursuits in Arambol are paragliding from the headland above Kalacha Beach (Sweetwater Lake) and kitesurfing and surfing down at the southern end. Several operators give lessons and rent equipment; look out for flyers and noticeboards.

Surf Wala SURFING
(☎9011993147; www.surfwala.com; Arambol Beach; 1½hr lesson from ₹2500, 3-/5-day course ₹7000/11,500) If you're a beginner looking to get up on a board, join the international team of surfers based at Arambol's Surf Club. Prices include board hire, wax and rashie. Check the website for instructor contact details – between them they speak English, Russian, Hindi, Konkani and Japanese! Board-only rental is ₹500/1500 per hour/day.

Arambol Paragliding PARAGLIDING
(10min flight ₹2000; ⌚11am-6pm) The headland above Kalacha Beach (Sweetwater Lake) is an ideal launching point for paragliding. There are a number of independent paragliders: ask around at the shack restaurants on the beach, arrange a pilot, then make the short hike to the top of the headland. Most flights are around 10 minutes, but if conditions are right you can stay up longer.

Himalayan Iyengar Yoga Centre YOGA
(www.hiyogacentre.com; Madhlo Vaddo; 5-day yoga course ₹5500; ⌚9am-6pm Nov-Mar) Arambol's reputable Himalayan Iyengar Yoga Centre, which runs five-day courses in hatha yoga from mid-November to mid-March, is the winter centre of the Iyengar yoga school in Dharamkot, near Dharamsala in north India. First-time students must take the introductory five-day course, and can then continue with more advanced five-day courses at a reduced rate. Booking and registration must be done in person at the centre. Accommodation is available for students in simple huts or tents (single/double ₹750/1200).

Sleeping

Arambol accommodation has expanded from basic huts along the clifftop and guesthouses in the village to a mini-Palolem of beach huts along the main beach and a selection of backpacker hostels. Enter at the 'Glastonbury St' entrance and walk north to find plenty of places clinging to the headland between here and Kalacha Beach, or enter at the south end and ask at any of the beach shacks.

Arambol

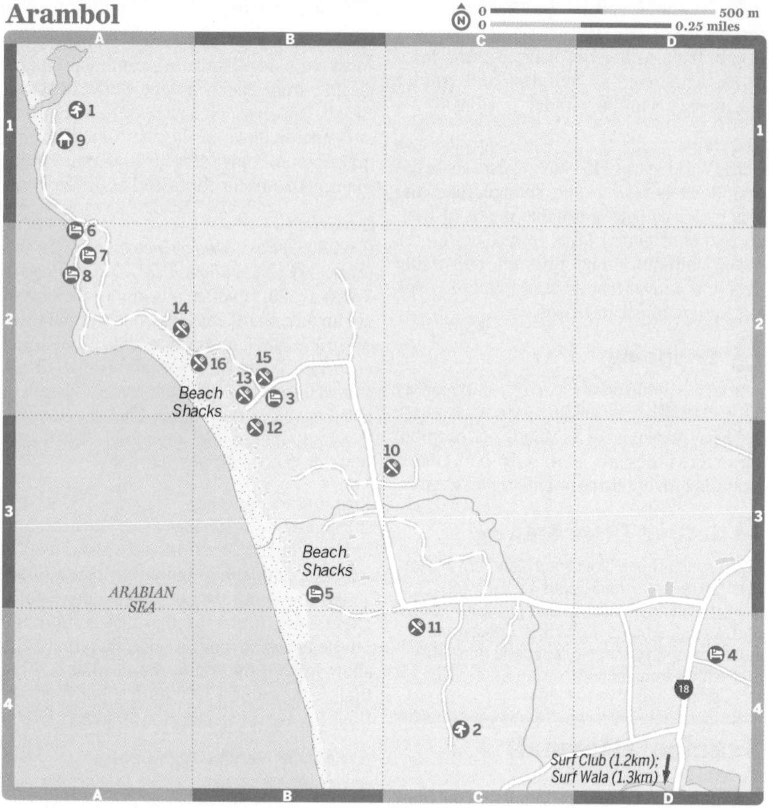

Arambol

Activities, Courses & Tours
1 Arambol Paragliding ... A1
2 Himalayan Iyengar Yoga Centre ... C4

Sleeping
3 Chilli's ... B2
4 Happy Panda ... D4
5 Lotus Sutra ... B3
6 Ludu Guest House ... A2
7 Om Ganesh ... A2
8 Pitruchaya Cottages ... A2
9 Shree Sai Cottages ... A1

Eating
10 Double Dutch ... C3
11 Dylan's Toasted & Roasted ... C4
12 Fellini ... B3
13 German Bakery ... B2
14 Rice Bowl ... A2
15 Shimon ... B2
16 This Is It ... B2

★ **Happy Panda** HOSTEL $
(☎9619741681; www.happypanda.in; dm ₹500-650, tent from ₹400;) Traveller-painted murals cover the walls in this very chilled backpacker place near the main village. Young owners have worked hard making the dorms, neon common area, bar and garden a well-equipped and welcoming budget place to crash. Artists, cooks and other skilled travellers are encouraged to lend a hand. Bikes for hire and tent accommodation available.

Surf Club GUESTHOUSE $
(www.thesurfclubgoa.com; d ₹1000-1800;) In a quiet space at the end of a lane, on the southern end of Arambol Beach, the Surf Club is one of those cool little hang-outs that offer a bit of everything: simple but clean

rooms, a fun bar with live music and surf lessons and board hire.

Pitruchaya Cottages COTTAGE $
(☑ 9404454596; r ₹700-800; 🛜) The sea-facing timber cottages here are among the best on the cliffs, with attached bathrooms, fans and verandahs.

Chilli's HOTEL $
(☑ 9921882424; Glastonbury St; d ₹700, apt with AC ₹1200; ❄🛜) Near the beach entrance on Glastonbury St, this friendly canary-yellow place is one of Arambol's better nonbeach-front bargains. There are 10 decent, no-frills rooms, all with attached bathroom, fan and a hot-water shower. The top-floor apartment with AC and TV is good value. Motorbikes and scooters available for hire.

Shree Sai Cottages HUT $
(☑ 9420767358; shreesai_cottages@yahoo.com; hut ₹800; 🛜) At the north end of the cliffs, simple, cute, sea-facing huts overlook Kalacha Beach. Alongside a good restaurant.

Ludu Guest House GUESTHOUSE $
(☑ 9404434332; r ₹500-1000; 🛜) Better than some similarly priced Arambol options, Ludu offers simply decorated, clean and bright cliffside rooms with attached cold-water showers.

Om Ganesh GUESTHOUSE $
(☑ 9404313206; r ₹600-800; 🛜) Halfway along the cliff, Om Ganesh has been around for a while and has solid rooms in a building on the hillside, and seasonal huts-with-a-view on the rooftop.

Lotus Sutra RESORT $$
(☑ 9146096940; www.lotussutragoa.com; d & cottages ₹4000-5500; ❄🛜) The fanciest place on Arambol's beachfront has a series of bright rooms in a quirky two-storey building and cute individual timber cottages facing a garden-lawn setting or towards the seafront. The Zen Oasis restaurant-bar is a popular spot and features live music.

Fort Tiracol Heritage Hotel BOUTIQUE HOTEL $$$
(☑ 7720056799; www.forttiracol.in; d incl breakfast ₹11,500-15,000, ste ₹20,000; ❄🛜) The five rooms and two suites (all named after days of the week) are part of the refurbished heritage hotel within the walls of the Portuguese Fort Terekhol. It's really a stunning location and while the rooms aren't ultra-luxurious, they're furnished in keeping with the colonial flavour and come with modern bathrooms and TV.

The Tavern restaurant and bar, with colonial-style indoor dining room and an outdoor verandah with views down the coast towards Arambol is a superb spot for a lazy lunch and is open to nonguests.

🍴 Eating

Arambol hasn't escaped the beach shack invasion, and you'll find about two dozen of them wall-to-wall along the main beach in season, complete with sunbeds and beach umbrellas (which should be free of charge if you're eating or drinking there). The northern cliff walk has a string of long-running budget restaurants with good views, and the village road down to the beach also has some interesting dining options.

Dylan's Toasted & Roasted CAFE $
(☑ 9604780316; www.dylanscoffee.com; coffee & desserts ₹80-200; ⏰ 9am-11pm late Nov-Apr; 🛜) The Goa (winter) incarnation of a Manali institution, Dylan's is a fine place for an espresso, chocolate chip cookies and old-school dessert. It's a nice hang-out, just back from the southern beach entrance, with occasional live music and open-mic nights.

German Bakery BAKERY $
(☑ 9822159699; Welcome Inn, Glastonbury St; pastries ₹30-100; ⏰ 8am-midnight) This popular little cafe bakes a good line in cakes and pastries, including lemon cheese pie and chocolate biscuit cake, as well as coffee and breakfast. It's a cool meeting spot close to the beach but away from the beach shacks.

★ Shimon MIDDLE EASTERN $$
(☑ 9011113576; Glastonbury St; mains ₹160-250; ⏰ 9am-11pm; 🛜) Just back from the beach, and understandably popular with Israeli backpackers, Shimon is the place to fill up on exceptional falafel or *sabich* (crisp slices of eggplant stuffed into pita bread along with boiled egg, boiled potato and salad). The East-meets-Middle-East thali (₹450) comprises a little bit of almost everything on the menu. Follow up with a strong Turkish coffee or its signature iced coffee. No alcohol.

This Is It MULTICUISINE $$
(☑ 7775078620; mains ₹160-370; ⏰ 8am-11pm; 🛜) Many travellers rate this the coolest place on the northern beachfront. A big menu of well-prepared Indian staples, Goan dishes, Chinese, seafood, *momos* and pasta is complemented by a laid-back, traveller-friendly

vibe, generous happy hours and regular live music. Holy Cow Backpackers is behind.

Fellini ITALIAN $$
(☎9881461224; Glastonbury St; mains ₹200-450; ⏰from 6.30pm) On the left-hand side just before the beach, this long-standing, evening-only Italian joint is perfect if you're craving a carbonara or calzone. More than 40 wood-fired, thin-crust pizza varieties are on the menu, but save space for a very decent rendition of tiramisu. Live music in season.

Rice Bowl ASIAN $$
(☎9822748451; mains ₹110-290; ⏰8am-11pm; 📶) Rice Bowl specialises in Chinese and Japanese cuisine and does it well. With a good view down to Arambol Beach, this is a great place to settle in with a plate of gyoza and a beer, or play a game of pool.

Double Dutch MULTICUISINE $$
(mains ₹120-450, steaks ₹420-500; ⏰8am-10pm) In a peaceful garden set back from the main road to the Glastonbury St beach entrance, Double Dutch has long been popular for its steaks, salads, Thai and Indonesian dishes, and famous apple pies. It's a relaxed meeting place with secondhand books, newspapers and a useful noticeboard for current Arambolic affairs.

Information

There's an ATM on the main highway in Arambol's village, about 1.5km back from the beach. If it's not working there's another about 3km north in Paliyem or about the same distance south in Mandrem.

Getting There & Away

Frequent buses to and from Mapusa (₹40, one hour) stop on the main road at the 'backside' (as locals are fond of saying) of Arambol village, where there's a church, a school and a few local shops. From here, it's a 1.5km trek down through the village to the main beach drag (head straight for the southern beach entrance or bear right for the northern 'Glastonbury St' entrance another 500m further on). An autorickshaw will charge at least ₹50 for the trip.

Plenty of places in the village advertise scooters and motorbikes for hire (per day scooter/motorbike ₹300/400).

A prepaid taxi from Mapusa to Arambol costs ₹700 but taxis on the street between Arambol and Mapusa or Anjuna/Vagator will ask closer to ₹1000. If you're heading north to Mumbai, travel agents can book bus tickets.

Inland Bardez & Bicholim

There's not as much to explore in North Goa's interior as there is in the central and southern parts of the state, but with your own wheels you can leave the beach behind for a day or two and head east into the districts of Bardez and Bicholim. There are some fine old churches, sleepy villages, forts, little traffic and it is a part of the Goan countryside that relatively few tourists see.

On the Mandovi, east of the national highway, is the pretty riverside village of Britona, with its grand old parish church. In nearby Pomburpa and Aldona villages are two more notable churches worthy of a visit.

Sights

Church of St Thomas CHURCH
Around 5km north of Pomburpa, the large and picturesque village of Aldona is home to the Church of St Thomas, built in 1596, and a grand sight on the banks of the Mapusa River.

Church of Nossa Senhora de Penha de Franca CHURCH
(Our Lady of the Rock of France; Britona) Britona's parish church, Nossa Senhora de Penha de Franca, is a grand old dame, occupying a fine location at the confluence of the Mandovi and Mapusa Rivers, looking across to Chorao Island on one side and to the Ribandar Causeway on the other.

Houses of Goa Museum MUSEUM
(☎0832-2410711; www.archgoa.org; Torda; adult/child ₹100/25; ⏰10am-7.30pm Tue-Sun) This multilevel museum was created by well-known local architect Gerard da Cunha to illuminate the history of Goan architecture. Interesting displays on building practices and European and local design will change the way you see those old Goan homes. The triangular building is an architectural oddity in itself, and the museum traces Goan architectural traditions, building materials, and styles in an in-depth but accessible way. From Panaji, a taxi or rickshaw will cost you about ₹400 one way.

Corjuem Fort FORT
On Corjuem Island around 2km northeast of Aldona, now linked by modern road bridges, you'll find the remains of Goa's only still-intact inland fort, the abandoned and atmospheric Corjuem Fort. Around 1705 Corjuem came to mark the easternmost boundary of

WORTH A TRIP

QUERIM & FORT TEREKHOL (TIRACOL)

Just a few kilometres north of Arambol, quiet **Querim Beach** (also called and signposted as Keri Beach) is a little-visited patch of sand where you can while away the hours in peace, with just a few beach shacks in residence from mid-November. Backed by a shady cover of fir and casuarina trees and the Hindu Ajoba Temple, there's not much to do here except have a leisurely swim, settle back with a book and enjoy the tranquillity that's missing from Arambol these days. You can reach Querim the long way by scooter or taxi (₹500), or tackle the headland walk (about one hour) from Kalacha Beach.

To get to Terekhol (the most northerly point in Goa) and its fort, it's fun to hop on board Querim's free **ferry** (7am-10pm, every 15-30min) that chugs passengers and vehicles across the Terekhol River from the ferry landing at the very end of the village road.

Not far from the ferry landing, you'll find **Terekhol Fort** (9am-7pm), perched high above the banks of the river of the same name. Originally built by the Marathas in the early 17th century, the fort was captured by viceroy Dom Pedro de Almeida in 1746 and was rebuilt; the little Chapel of St Anthony, which takes up almost all of the available space within it, was added at that time. The fort is currently operated as a heritage hotel (p159), but you can ask to look at the chapel or dine in the restaurant.

Portugal's colonial conquest, and the small fort was quickly built to protect the territory from raids by the Rajputs and Marathas.

Mayem Lake LAKE

Southwest of Bicholim and about 35km from Panaji, glistening Mayem Lake is a pleasant sort of place that's popular among local picnickers and families. In 2018 Goa Tourism opened a new reception centre here with a cafe, shops, parking and boating, and its North Goa bus stops here for lunch.

Shri Saptakoteshwara Temple HINDU TEMPLE

Just 2km from the ferry point in Naroa, the Shri Saptakoteshwara Temple is tiny, tucked away in a narrow emerald-green valley and undisturbed by anything apart from a few mopeds and the occasional tour bus. The deity worshipped at the temple is a lingam (a phallic symbol of Shiva, the destroyer), which underwent considerable adventures before arriving here.

After being buried to avoid early Muslim raids, the revered lingam was recovered and placed in a great Kadamba temple on Divar Island, but when the Portuguese desecrated the spot in 1560 it was smuggled away and subsequently lost. Miraculously rediscovered in the 17th century by Hindus, who found it being used as part of a well shaft, it was smuggled across the Mandovi River to safety in the temple.

To find the temple, follow the road from the ferry point at Naroa (from Divar Island) for approximately 2km, before forking right down a small tarmac lane. You'll find the temple about 1.5km along, to your left; follow the red and green archaeology arrows until you arrive. You'll know it from its shallow, Mughal-style dome, tall lamp tower and vaulted arches.

Sleeping & Eating

With Panaji and the northern beach resorts so close, few people look for accommodation east of the highway but there are a few choices.

Mayem Lake View HOTEL $

(0832-2362144; www.goa-tourism.com; Mayem Lake; d ₹1100, with AC ₹1350-1700, ste ₹2200;) Although a bit rundown, Goa Tourism's Mayem Lake View is almost certainly the nicest of all the GTDC's hotels and the lakeside location is peaceful. Its rooms are clean enough and good value and there's a restaurant serving breakfast, lunch and dinner.

Casa Britona BOUTIQUE HOTEL $$$

(0832-2416737; www.casaboutiquehotels.com; Britona; d from ₹10,300; @) Casa Britona is a gorgeous 300-year-old converted customs warehouse on the water, with luxurious antique-filled rooms, fine outdoor dining beneath the stars and a lovely riverside swimming pool.

Getting There & Away

Local buses run between Bicholim and the Divar ferry but this area is best explored with your own transport. The best access for Aldona and beyond is via Mapusa.

South Goa

Includes ➡

Best Places to Eat

- Ourem 88 (p190)
- Kopi Desa (p183)
- Jaali Cafe (p192)
- Karma Cafe & Bakery (p191)
- Zeebop by the Sea (p174)

Best Places to Stay

- Ciarans (p187)
- Blue Lagoon Resort (p180)
- Agonda White Sand (p182)
- Blue Corner (p176)
- Vivenda Dos Palhacos (p173)

Why Go?

South Goa is the more serene half of the state, and for many travellers that's the attraction. There are fewer activities and not as many bars, clubs or restaurants, but overall the beaches of the south are cleaner, whiter and not as crowded as those in the north.

Bounded to the north by the wide Zuari River and to the south by the neighbouring state of Karnataka, South Goa's coast is a series of resorts that range from the five-star hotel strips of Cavelossim and the village feel of Benaulim, to the backpacker-friendly beach-hut bliss of Palolem, Patnem and Agonda.

When to Go

Palolem

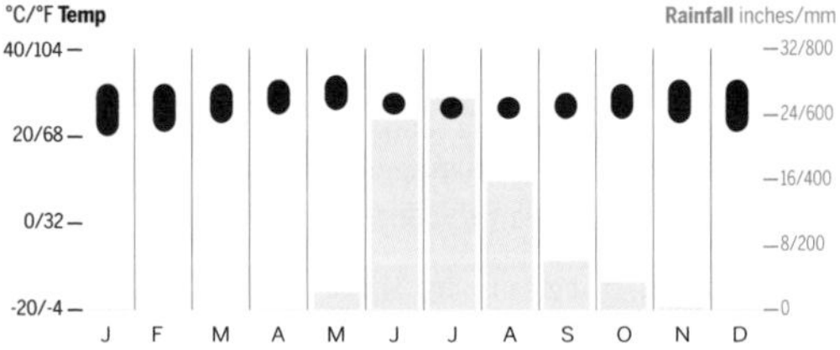

Dec–Mar High season; brilliant cloudless days, beach huts, yoga, festivals in full swing.

Apr, May, Oct & Nov Shoulder season; prices much lower, fewer crowds, humid weather.

Mid-Dec–early Jan Peak season; prices sky-high, crowds, lots of parties.

Margao

POP 122,500

Margao (also known as Madgaon) is the capital of South Goa, a busy – at times traffic-clogged – market town of a manageable size for getting things done. As the major transport hub of the south, lots of travellers pass through Margao's train station or Kadamba bus stand; fewer choose to overnight here, but it's a useful place for market shopping, catching a local sporting event or simply enjoying the busy energy of big-city India in small-town form.

Margao's compact town centre ranges around the oblong Municipal Gardens, with shops, restaurants, ATMs and the covered market all within easy reach. To the north of town is the old Portuguese-influenced Largo de Igreja district; about 1km north further is the main (Kadamba) bus station, and 1.5km southeast of the Municipal Garden is Margao's train station.

Sights & Activities

Church of the Holy Spirit CHURCH

Margao's whitewashed main church (1675) remains in use as a parish church and is finely decorated inside. The impressive reredos (ornamental screen) is dedicated to the Virgin Mary, rising from ground level to the high ceiling, made more distinguished by the gilded and carved archway that stands in front of it. The church doors are usually unlocked throughout the day, and access is via the side entrance on the northern side.

Municipal Library LIBRARY

(Abade Faria Rd; 8am-8pm Mon-Fri, 9am-noon & 4-7pm Sat & Sun) On the west side of the canary-yellow Secretariat Building, you'll find respite from the sun in the prim Municipal Library, which houses some good books about Goa. Don't miss the library's newspaper reading room, in which you're required to collect your newspaper at the counter and then sit in the seat designated only for readers of that particular paper – it's popular enough that it's often full.

Sat Burnzam Ghor HISTORIC BUILDING

(Seven Gabled House) The most famous of the traditional old Portuguese mansions in Largo de Igreja is the grand 1790 Sat Burnzam Ghor. Originally, as its name suggests, there were seven of the distinctive high-peaked gables, of which only three remain, though it remains an impressive edifice. It's currently not open to the public.

Mount Church CHURCH

Located about 500m southeast of Sat Burnzam Ghor and a fair climb up Monte Hill, Margao's only hill, Mount Church is a simple whitewashed building, faced by a similarly diminutive cross. A detour up here is worth it for the view, all the way out to Colva.

Fatorda Stadium SPORTS

(0832-2743050) With a capacity of almost 28,000, Margao's modern Fatorda Stadium (officially known as Jawarharlal Nehru Stadium) is Goa's premier sports venue. State and international football (soccer) and cricket matches are staged here. It's 2km northeast of the Municipal Gardens.

Tours

Canopy Ecotours TOURS

(8407954664, 9764261711; www.canopygoa.com; 8 Sapna Arcade, Malbhatt) This eco-operation based in Margao offers birdwatching, butterfly-spotting and wildlife photography trips into the Western Ghats. Canopy also runs Nature's Nest (www.naturesnestgoa.com), a set of rustic cottages on the outskirts of Bhagwan Mahavir Wildlife Sanctuary, with packages including meals and treks.

Sleeping

Unlike Panaji, Margao doesn't have the range of accommodation that you'd expect in a town of this size. But with the beaches of the south so close, there's really no pressing reason to stay here.

Hotel Tanish HOTEL **$$**

(0832-2735858; www.hoteltanishgoa.com; Reliance Trade Centre, Valaulikar Rd; s/d ₹1200/1700, with AC ₹1500/2000;) Oddly situated inside a modern mall, this top-floor hotel offers good views of the surrounding countryside, with stylish, well-equipped rooms. Try for an outside-facing room, as some overlook the mall interior.

Nanutel Margao HOTEL **$$**

(0832-6722222; www.nanuhotels.in; Padre Miranda Rd; s/d incl breakfast ₹5300/5900;) Margao's best business-class hotel by some margin, Nanutel is modern and slick with a lovely pool, good restaurant, bar and coffee shop, and clean air-con rooms. The location, between the Municipal Gardens and Largo de Igreja district, is convenient for everything.

South Goa Highlights

❶ **Palolem Beach** (p184) Checking into a beach hut on beautiful Palolem Beach, where you can kayak, learn to cook local dishes or just relax.

❷ **Chandor** (p170) Marvelling at the colonial-era mansions in this rural village near Margao.

❸ **Goa Chitra Museum** (p176) Learning about Goa's traditional past at this museum in Benaulim.

❹ **Cola Beach** (p180) Trekking down to secluded Cola, one of the prettiest beaches in Goa.

❺ **Galgibag & Talpona Beach** (p192) Hiring a bike and taking the pretty country ride from Patnem to Galgibag's near-deserted beach

❻ **Tanshikar Spice Farm** (p194) Cruising out to remote countryside and stopping in at the bizarre Bubble Lake along the way.

❼ **Agonda Beach** (p181) Booking into a luxurious beachfront hut and learning to surf at this serene beach.

❽ **Margao** (Madgaon; p163) Getting away from the beach in South Goa's busy capital, visiting the market, Municipal Library and church.

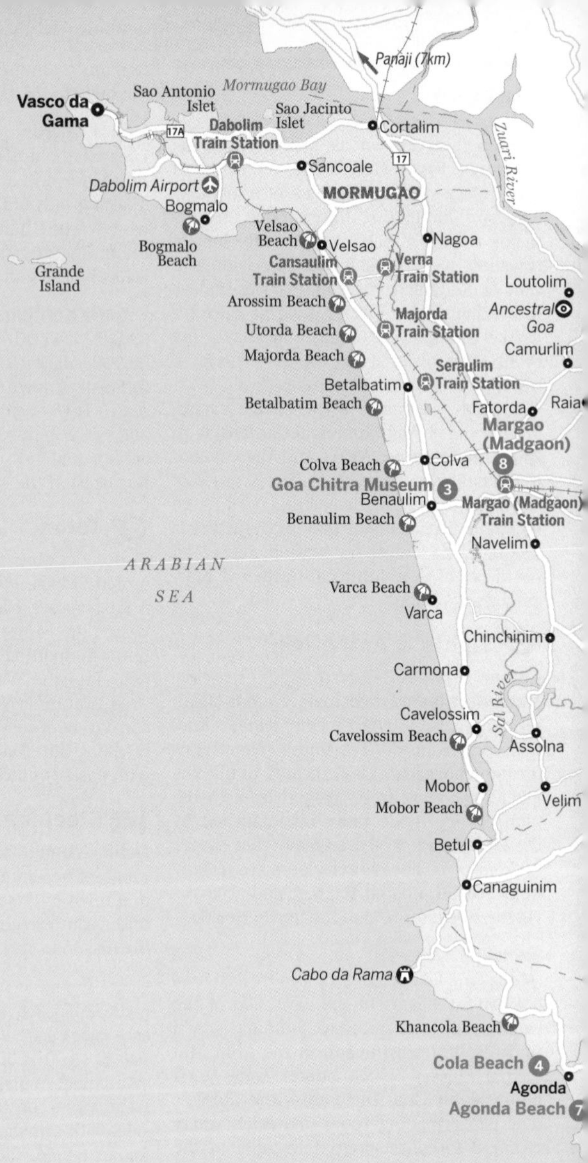

Ponda
PONDA
4A
Londa (111km);
Dharwar (146km);
Belgaum (155km)
Colem
Rachol Seminary & Church
SALCETE
Bhagwan Mahavir Wildlife Sanctuary
Curtorim
South Central Railway
Chandorgoa Train Station
Sanvordem Train Station
Sanvordem
2 Chandor
Curchorem
Sanguem River
Darguina
Paroda
Sanguem
Shri Chandreshwar (Bhutnath) Temple
2 Quepem
Salaulim Dam & Botanical Gardens
Seraulim Train Station
Zambaulim
Shri Damodar Temple
SANGUEM
Cuncolim
Rivona Buddhist Caves
Rivona
Bali Train Station
Fatorpa
Usgalimal Petroglyphs
Konkan Railway
Netravali Protected Area
QUEPEM
Pareda River
Netorli
Barcem Train Station
Quisconda
6 Tanshikar Spice Farm
Savare Waterfall
Netravali Bubble Lake
17
Savare
Animal Rescue Centre
Shri Malikarjun Temple
Honeymoon Beach
Butterfly Beach
Cotigao Wildlife Sanctuary
Palolem Beach
CANACONA
1
Char Rasta
Salginim
Canacona Island
Patnem
Chaudi
Canacona Train Station
Colomb Bay
Talpona River
Rajbag
Rajbag Beach
5 Talpona Beach
Poinguinim
Entrance to Cotigao Wildlife Sanctuary
5 Galgibag
Masher
KARNATAKA
Matem
Polem
Karwar (21km);
Gokarna (68km)
Polem Beach
0 10 km
0 5 miles

Margao (Madgaon)

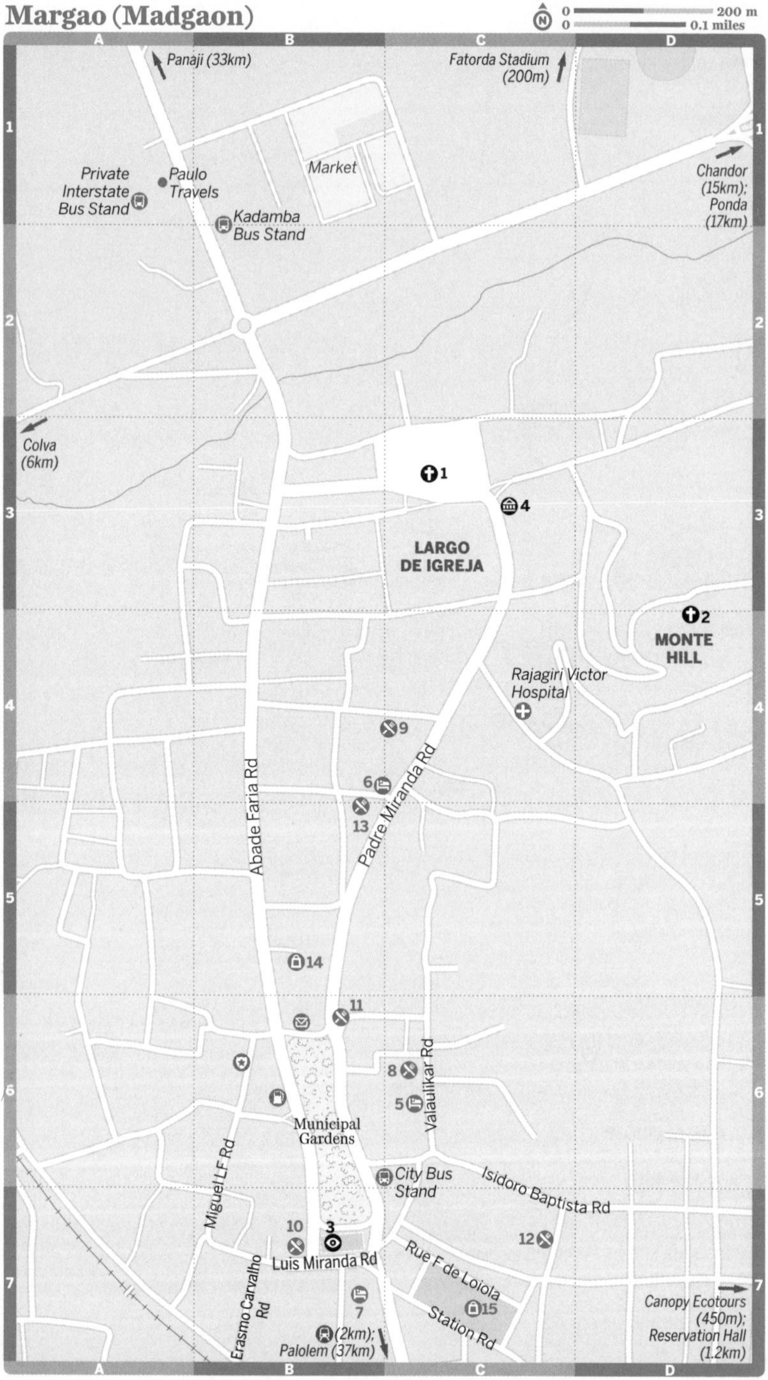
0 200 m
0 0.1 miles
A
B
C
D
1
2
3
4
5
6
7
Panaji (33km)
Fatorda Stadium (200m)
Market
Private Interstate Bus Stand
Paulo Travels
Kadamba Bus Stand
Chandor (15km); Ponda (17km)
Colva (6km)
1
4
LARGO DE IGREJA
2
MONTE HILL
Rajagiri Victor Hospital
9
6
13
Abade Faria Rd
Padre Miranda Rd
14
11
8
5
Valaulikar Rd
Municipal Gardens
Miguel LF Rd
City Bus Stand
Isidoro Baptista Rd
10
3
12
Luis Miranda Rd
Rue F de Loiola
Erasmo Carvalho Rd
7
15
Station Rd
(2km); Palolem (37km)
Canopy Ecotours (450m); Reservation Hall (1.2km)

Margao (Madgaon)

Sights

1 Church of the Holy Spirit C3
2 Mount Church D4
3 Municipal Library B7
4 Sat Burnzam Ghor C3

Sleeping

5 Hotel Tanish C6
6 Nanutel Margao B4
7 Om Shiv Hotel B7

Eating

8 Café Tato C6
9 Chikoo Tree Project C4
10 Longhuino's B7
11 Martin's B6
12 Swad C7
13 Viva Goa B5

Shopping

14 Golden Heart Emporium B5
15 MMC New Market C7

Om Shiv Hotel HOTEL **$$**
(☎0832-2710294; www.omshivhotel.com; Cine Lata Rd; s/d ₹2400/2700; ❄📶) In a lemon-yellow multistorey building tucked away behind the Bank of India, Om Shiv does a decent line in fading 'executive' rooms, all of which have air-con and balcony. There's a gym and the 7th-floor Rockon Pub. Attractive online rates can make it worthwhile.

Eating

Café Tato INDIAN **$**
(Valaulikar Rd; thalis ₹100; ⏰7am-10pm Mon-Sat) A favourite local lunch spot: tasty vegetarian fare in a bustling backstreet canteen, and delicious all-you-can-eat thalis.

Swad INDIAN **$**
(New Market; mains ₹60-120; ⏰7.30am-8pm; ❄) Some of Margao's best veg food is dished up at the family-friendly, lunch-break favourite Swad, across from Lotus Inn. The thalis, South Indian tiffins and other mains are all reliably tasty.

★**Longhuino's** GOAN **$$**
(☎0832-2739908; Luis Miranda Rd; mains ₹180-320; ⏰8.30am-10pm) A local institution since 1950, quaint old Longhuino's serves up tasty Indian, Goan and Chinese dishes, popular with locals and tourists alike. Go for a Goan dish like *ambot tik* (a slightly sour but fiery curry dish), and leave room for the retro desserts such as rum balls and tiramisu.

Chikoo Tree Project MULTICUISINE **$$**
(☎9920064597; 85 Dr Miranda Rd; mains ₹150-300; ⏰9am-10pm Tue-Sun) Breakfast on masala dosas and lunch on chicken *momos* or giant *kathi* wraps at this arty, eclectic but casual cafe that's made a welcome addition to Margao's dining scene. Good coffee and fresh-made juices.

Viva Goa GOAN **$$**
(mains ₹150-400; ⏰11am-3pm & 7-11pm) Upstairs in Clube Harmonia, South Goa's oldest cultural club venue, Viva Goa is a new iteration of the long-running Colva restaurant, serving genuine Goan cuisine, seafood and a full bar.

Martin's INTERNATIONAL **$$$**
(mains ₹360-900; ⏰11am-3.30pm & 7-11pm) It's a welcome feeling to step off Margao's hot and busy street into the cool and classy interior of Martin's. There's just 10 tables, attentive service and an eclectic menu of tapas starters, pan-Indian dishes, steaks and fish cooked on Canadian cedar wood. Just off the north end of the Municipal Gardens.

Shopping

Golden Heart Emporium BOOKS
(Confidant House, Abade Faria Rd; ⏰10am-2pm & 4-7.30pm Mon-Sat) One of Goa's best bookshops, Golden Heart is crammed with fiction, nonfiction, children's books, and illustrated volumes on the state's food, architecture and history. It also stocks otherwise hard-to-get titles by local Goan authors. It's down a little lane off Abade Faria Rd.

MMC New Market MARKET
(Rua F de Loiola; ⏰8.30am-9pm Mon-Sat) Margao's crowded, covered canopy of colourful stalls is a fun but busy place to wander around, sniffing spices, sampling soaps and browsing the household merchandise.

Information

MONEY

There are plenty of banks offering currency exchange and 24-hour ATMs ranged around the Municipal Gardens.

POST

Main Post Office (⏰9am-1.30pm & 2.30-5pm Mon-Sat) On the north side of the Municipal Gardens.

Getting There & Away

BUS

Local and long-distance buses use the Kadamba bus stand, on the highway about 2km north of the Municipal Gardens. Buses to Palolem (₹40, one hour), Colva (₹15, 20 minutes), Benaulim (₹15, 20 minutes) and Betul (₹25, 40 minutes) stop both at the Kadamba bus stand and at informal bus stops on the east and west sides of the Municipal Gardens. For Panaji (Panjim), take any local bus to the Kadamba bus stand and change to a frequent express bus (₹40, one hour). From there you can change for buses to Mapusa and the northern beaches.

Daily AC state-run buses go to Mumbai (₹900, 16 hours), Pune (₹735, 13 hours) and Bengaluru (₹660 to ₹1200, 12 hours), which can be booked online at www.goakadamba.com. Non-AC buses are about one-third cheaper but are becoming rare on long-distance routes. For greater choice and flexibility but similar prices, private long-distance buses depart from the stand opposite Kadamba. You'll find booking offices all over town; **Paulo Travels** (☎0832-2702405; www.paulobus.com; NH66) is among the best, and also has the only buses to Hampi (seat/sleeper ₹900/1500, 11 hours), but the best booking site is Red Bus (www.redbus.in).

TAXI

Taxis are plentiful around the Municipal Gardens and Kadamba bus stand, and are a quick and comfortable way to reach any of Goa's beaches. Prepaid taxi stands are at the train station and main bus stand. Fares include the following: Panaji (₹1050), Palolem (₹1050), Calangute (₹1355), Anjuna (₹1500) and Arambol (₹2000), though you'll pay up to double these fares by hiring a taxi off the street.

For Colva and Benaulim, autorickshaws should do the trip for around ₹150, but taxis ask an inflated ₹500.

TRAIN

Margao's well-organised train station (known as Madgaon on train timetables), about 2km south of town, serves both the Konkan Railway and local South Central Railways routes, and is the main hub for trains from Mumbai to Goa and south to Kochi and beyond. Its **reservation hall** (☎0832-2712790; ⏲8am-2pm & 2.15-8pm Mon-Sat, 8am-2pm Sun) is on the 1st floor and there's a foreign tourist quota counter upstairs.

Outside the station you'll find a useful prepaid taxi stand; use this to get to your beachside destination and you'll be assured a fair price. Alternatively, a taxi or autorickshaw to or from the town centre to the station should cost around ₹100.

Getting Around

Central Margao is easily navigated on foot but getting to the main bus stand or train station requires a taxi or local bus. For the bus stand take any Panaji-bound bus from the Municipal Gardens. Taxis gather at the south side of the Municipal Gardens. Motorcycle taxis are still common in Margao and are good for short trips.

Around Margao

As tempting as it is to head directly west to the beach from Margao, the area to the east and northeast of town is a rich patchwork of rice paddy fields, lush countryside, somnolent rural villages, superb colonial houses, and a smattering of historical and religious sites. With a day or two to spare and a hired motorcycle, car or taxi, you can cover most of the sights of interest and experience a rewarding side of Goa that has nothing to do with beaches.

Sights

Palácio do Deão PALACE

(☎0832-2664029, 9823175639; www.palaciododeao.com; ⏲10am-5pm Sat-Thu) About 8km southeast of Chandor is the busy small town of Quepem. Here the Palácio do Deão, the renovated 18th-century palace built by the town's founder, Portuguese nobleman Jose Paulo de Almeida, sits across from the Holy Cross Church on the banks of the small Kushavati River.

Today the restored house and its beautiful, serene gardens are open to the public. Call ahead to book a tour or arrange a delicious Portuguese-inspired lunch or afternoon tea on its lovely terrace. All donations are used to continue restoration work and eventually create a cultural centre here.

Shri Chandreshwar Temple HINDU TEMPLE

Approximately 14km southeast of Margao near the village of Paroda, a number of hills rise out of the plain, the highest of which is Chandranath Hill (350m). At the top, in a small clearing stands the Shri Chandreshwar (Bhutnath) Temple, a small but attractive 17th-century building in a lovely, solitary setting.

Although the present buildings date from the 17th century, legend has it that there has been a temple here for almost 2500 years, since the moment a meteor hit the spot. The site is dedicated to Chandreshwar, an incarnation of Shiva who is worshipped here as

'Lord of the Moon'. Consequently it's laid out so that the light of the full moon shines into the sanctum and illuminates the glittering gold deity. At the rear of the shrine, two accessory stone deities keep Chandreshwar company: Parvati (Shiva's consort) to the west, and Ganesh (his son) to the east. It's said that when the moonlight falls on it, the shrine's lingam (phallic symbol of Shiva) oozes water.

Leaving through the side entrance there is another small shrine standing separately that is dedicated to the god Bhutnath, who is worshipped in the form of a simple stone pinnacle that sticks out of the ground.

To get here, you'll need your own transport, since buses don't service this road. Head to Paroda, and ask there for the turn-off that takes you up the narrow, winding hillside road. There's a small parking area near the top, from which the approach to the temple is via a steep flight of steps.

Usgalimal Petroglyphs ROCK ART

(Colamb) One of Goa's least visited but most fascinating sights is deep in the countryside at Usgalimal: a series of prehistoric petroglyphs (rock art), carved into the laterite-stone ground on the banks of the Kushavati River, and depicting various scenes including bulls, deer and antelope, a dancing woman, a peacock and 'triskelions' – a series of concentric circles thought by some archaeologists to have been a primitive means of measuring time.

These underfoot carvings are thought to be the work of one of Goa's earliest tribes, the Kush, and were only discovered by archaeologists in 1993, after being alerted to their existence by locals. The images are thought to have been created some 20,000 to 30,000 years ago, making them an important, if entirely unexploited, prehistoric site. In order for you to make out the carvings better, you'll likely have a helping hand from a local, who sits patiently at the site waiting to drizzle water from a plastic bottle into the grooves; he appreciates a tip for his efforts.

To get here, continue past Rivona for about 6km and keep an eye out for the circular green-and-red Archaeological Survey of India signs. An unsealed road off to the right of the main road leads 1.5km down to the river bank and carvings.

Rachol Seminary & Church CHURCH

Built in 1580 atop an old Muslim fort, the Rachol Seminary and Church stands near the village of Raia, 7km from Margao. It's not officially open to visitors, but you might find a trainee priest to show you around its beautiful church and cloistered theological college.

The seminary, built by the Jesuits, soon became a noted centre of learning, graced with one of India's first printing presses.

Work on the church began in 1576, four years before the founding of the seminary, and it has been maintained in excellent condition. Its splendid gilded reredos (ornamental screen) fills the wall above the altar, featuring an image of St Constantine, the first Roman emperor to convert to Christianity; fragments of St Constantine's bones are on display near the main doorway. One of the side altars also displays the original Menino Jesus, which was first installed in the Colva church, before being taken up to Rachol amid much controversy (p171).

Shri Damodar Temple TEMPLE

Approximately 12km southeast of Chandor and 22km from Margao, on the border of Quepem and Sanguem *talukas,* is the small village of Zambaulim, home to the Shri Damodar Temple. Though the temple itself is uncompromisingly modern, the deity in its sanctum is anything but, having been rescued in 1565 from the main temple in Margao, which was destroyed by the Portuguese to make way for the Church of the Holy Spirit.

Rivona Buddhist Caves CAVE

Around 3km south of the village of Zambaulim, the road passes through Rivona, which consists of little more than a few houses spread out along the roadside. The Rivona Buddhist caves (also called Pandava caves) are rock-cut caves thought to have been used by Buddhist monks in the 7th century. Look out for strips of red cloth, hung auspiciously from an old tamarind tree nearby.

Salaulim Dam & Botanical Gardens DAM

(Curdi; adult/child ₹20/10; ⌚9am-6pm) About 26km southeast of Margao, Salaulim Dam is a major reservoir supplying irrigation and drinking water to South Goa. For visitors the dam wall is quite a sight, especially when the water level is high enough for the duck-bill spillway to be surging. Of equal interest is the lush ornamental botanical gardens at the base of the dam wall. Security is tight; you'll need photo ID to enter and photography is technically prohibited.

Getting There & Away

Local buses run from Margao to Quepem, Chandor and Loutolim, but to really explore this region in a day you'll need your own transport or a car and driver.

Chandor

The small village of Chandor, about 15km east of Margao, is an important stop for its collection of once-grand Portuguese mansions, exemplified by the wonderful Braganza House. It's a photogenic place, with fading but still grand facades and gables – many topped with typically Portuguese carved wooden roosters – and the looming white Nossa Senhora de Belem church.

Between the late 6th and mid-11th centuries Chandor was better known as Chandrapur, the most spectacular city on the Konkan coast. This was the grand seat of the ill-fated Kadamba dynasty until 1054, when the rulers moved to a new, broad-harboured site at Govepuri, at modern-day Goa Velha. When Govepuri was levelled by the Muslims in 1312, the Kadambas briefly moved their seat of power back to Chandrapur, though it was not long before Chandrapur itself was sacked in 1327, and then its glory days were finally, definitively, over.

Sights

Braganza House HISTORIC BUILDING

Braganza House, built in the 17th century and stretching along one whole side of Chandor's village square, is the biggest Portuguese mansion of its kind in Goa and the best example of what Goa's scores of once-grand and glorious mansions have today become. Granted the land by the King of Portugal, the Braganza family built this oversized house, which was later divided into the east and west wings when it was inherited by two sisters from the family.

Both sides are open to the public daily. There are no set tour times, but if you enter either side a family member or representative should give you a guided tour and regale you with a few stories of the lifestyles of the landed gentry during Goa's years of Portuguese rule. The entry fee at each side is a suggested donation and goes towards the considerable upkeep of the homes, which receive no official funding.

The **West Wing** (0832-2784201; donation ₹150; 9am-5pm) belongs to one set of the family's descendants, the Menezes-Braganças. It's well maintained and more like a museum than a home, filled with gorgeous Belgian glass chandeliers, Italian marble floors and antique treasures from Macau, Portugal, China and Europe. Also here is the extensive library of Dr Luís de Menezes Bragança, a noted journalist and leading light in the Goan Independence movement. No photography.

Next door, the **East Wing** (0832-2784227; donation ₹200; 9am-6pm) is owned by the Pereira-Braganza family, descendants of the other half of the family. It's not as grand and well-maintained as its counterpart but is beautiful in its own lived-in way and is also crammed with antiques and collectables from around the world. It features a large ballroom with marble floor, but the high point is the small family chapel, which contains a carefully hidden fingernail of St Francis Xavier.

Fernandes House HISTORIC BUILDING

(0832-2784245; donation ₹100-200; 9am-6pm) A kilometre east past the church, and open to the public, is the Fernandes House, whose original building dates back more than 500 years, while the Portuguese section was tacked on by the Fernandes family in 1821. The secret basement hideaway, full of gun holes and with an escape tunnel to the river, was used by the family to flee attackers. Admission includes a guided tour.

Festivals & Events

Feast of the Three Kings RELIGIOUS

(6 Jan) Chandor hosts this colourful festival, during which local boys re-enact the arrival of the three kings from the Christmas story.

Getting There & Away

Local buses run infrequently from Margao to Chandor (₹10, 30 minutes) but the best way to get here is with your own transport. A taxi from Margao should cost ₹500 round trip, including waiting time.

Loutolim

Architectural relics of Goa's grand Portuguese heritage can be seen around the unhurried village of Loutolim, some 10km northeast of Margao.

The centre of the village is the brooding whitewashed Church of Salvador do Mundo.

Sights

Casa Araujo Alvares HISTORIC SITE
(☎0832-2750430; adult/child ₹100/50, camera ₹20; ⏰9am-5.30pm) Loutolim is home to a number of impressive Portuguese mansions but just one, Casa Araujo Alvares, opposite Ancestral Goa, is officially open to the public. You can tour the interior of the 250-year-old house on an informative automated half-hour 'sound-and-light show' that illuminates rooms and furnishings to accompanying commentary.

Ancestral Goa AMUSEMENT PARK
(☎0832-2777034; www.ancestralgoa.com; adult/child ₹50/25, camera ₹20; ⏰9am-6pm) Ancestral Goa is a high kitsch park with a series of sculptures depicting traditional Goan lifestyle. Follow the numbered trail to the mysterious 'Big Foot', a footprint in the rock that you can touch and make a wish on, and Sant Mirabai, the largest laterite sculpture in India.

Sleeping

Casa Susegad GUESTHOUSE $$$
(☎0832-6483368; www.casasusegad.com; s/d ₹7500/9000; ❄📶🏊) With just five lovely, antique-filled rooms, this British-run place makes a wonderful upmarket retreat. An organic vegetable garden supplies the ingredients for delicious dinners, and a menagerie of parakeets, monkeys, cats and dogs inhabit the extensive gardens, complete with terrace swimming pool. It's about 1km from the church.

Colva

POP 3140

Once a sleepy fishing village, and in the sixties a hang-out for hippies escaping the scene up at Anjuna, Colva is still the main town-resort along this stretch of coast, but these days it has lost any semblance of the beach paradise vibe.

A large concrete roundabout marks the end of the beach road and the entrance to the beach, filled with day-trippers, package tourists and listless hawkers. The main beach drag is lined with dreary stalls and shabby cafes. Travel a little way north or south, though, and you'll find some of the peace missing in central Colva.

Colva's beach entrance throngs with water-sports operators keen to sell you parasailing (₹1400), jet-skiing (15 minutes single/double ₹400/600) and dolphin-watching trips (per boat ₹2500). Rates are fixed, but ensure that life jackets are supplied.

COLVA'S MENINO JESUS

Colva's 18th-century **Our Lady of Mercy Church** (⏰mass in Konkani 7am daily, in English 9.30am Sun) is home to a little statue known as the 'Menino' (Baby) Jesus, which is said to miraculously heal the sick. Legend has it that the statue was discovered by a Jesuit priest named Father Bento Ferreira in the mid-17th century, after he was shipwrecked somewhere off the coast of Mozambique. The plucky missionary swam to shore, to see vultures circling a rocky spot. On closer inspection, he discovered the statue, apparently washed ashore after having been tossed overboard by pirates.

When he was posted to Colva in 1648, Father Ferreira took the Menino Jesus along with him, and had it installed on the high altar, where it promptly began to heal the sick. It wasn't long before it was worshipped with its own special Fama de Menino Jesus festival (p26).

Sleeping

Sam's Guesthouse HOTEL $
(☎0832-2788753; r ₹800; 📶) Away from the fray, north of Colva's main drag on the road running parallel to the beach, Sam's is a big, cheerful place with friendly owners and spacious rooms that are a steal. Rooms are around a pleasant garden courtyard and there's a good restaurant and whacky 'cosy cave'. Wi-fi in the restaurant only.

★**Skylark Resort** HOTEL $$
(☎0832-2788052; www.skylarkresortgoa.com; d with AC ₹3350-4500, f ₹5000; ❄📶🏊) A serious step up from the budget places, Skylark's clean, fresh rooms are graced with bits and pieces of locally made teak furniture and block-print bedspreads, while the lovely pool makes a pleasant place to lounge. The best (and more expensive) rooms are those facing the pool.

La Ben HOTEL $$
(☎0832-2788040; www.laben.net; Colva Beach Rd; r with/without AC ₹1800/1650; ❄📶) Neat, clean and not entirely devoid of atmosphere, La Ben is a traveller hang-out in the middle of the action with decent, good-value rooms,

Colva

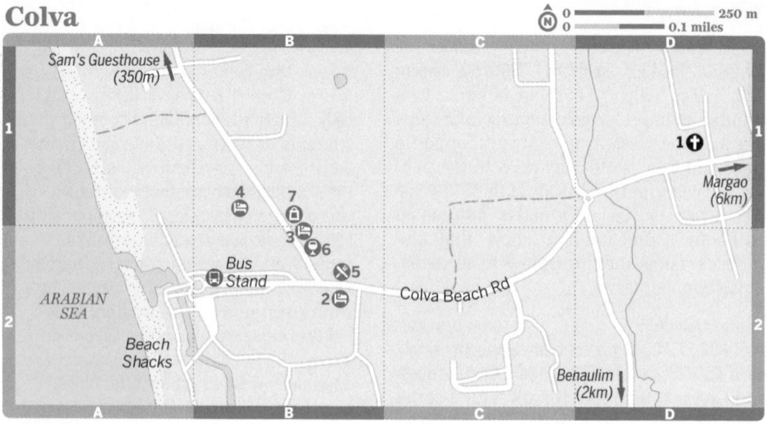

Colva

Sights
1 Our Lady of Mercy Church D1

Sleeping
2 La Ben B2
3 Skylark Resort B2
4 Soul Vacation B1

Eating
Garden Restaurant .... (see 2)
5 Sagar Kinara B2

Drinking & Nightlife
6 Leda Lounge & Restaurant B2

Shopping
7 Goa Animal Welfare Trust Shop B1

and has been around for ages. There's a rooftop bar and, at street level, the very good **Garden Restaurant** (Colva Beach Rd; mains ₹170-370; ⏲7.30am-11.30pm; ☎).

Soul Vacation HOTEL $$$
(☎0832-2788147; www.soulvacation.in; 4th Ward; d incl breakfast ₹6300-8300, f villas from ₹10,400; ❄☎≋) Thirty sleek white rooms arranged around nice gardens and a neat pool are the trademarks of Soul Vacation, set 400m back from Colva Beach. This is central Colva's most upmarket choice and, though pricey, there's a nice air of exclusivity about it. There's an ayurvedic spa, garden cafe and bar.

Eating & Drinking

Numerous beach shacks line the Colvan sands between November and April, offering the extensive standard range of fare and fresh seafood, and there are some decent cafes on the road leading to the beach.

Sagar Kinara INDIAN $
(Colva Beach Rd; mains ₹70-190; ⏲7am-10.30pm) A pure-veg restaurant upstairs (nonveg is separate, downstairs) with tastes to please even committed carnivores, Sagar Kinara is clean, efficient and offers cheap and delicious North and South Indian cuisine all day.

Leda Lounge & Restaurant BAR
(⏲noon-3pm & 7-11pm) Part sports bar, part music venue, part cocktail bar, Leda is Colva's best nightspot, though it operates as much as a restaurant, and even the bar closes in the afternoon. There's live music from Thursday to Sunday, fancy drinks (mojitos, Long Island iced teas) and good food at lunch and dinner.

Getting There & Away

Buses from Colva to Margao run roughly every 15 minutes (₹15, 20 minutes) from 7.30am to about 7pm, departing from the parking area at the end of the beach road. A taxi/autorickshaw to Margao is ₹500/150.

Scooters can be hired around the bus stand (with some difficulty) for ₹300 per day.

North of Colva

The far northern section of South Goa's coastline extends from Colva, the main beach resort along this strip, to Bogmalo, a few kilometres south of Dabolim Airport. The north end of the beach is marred by the Zuari Agro chemical plant, but further south around Arossim and Majorda things get a little livelier with the odd beach shack and water sports.

North of Bogmalo is the industrial port of Vasco da Gama and the harbour of Mormugao.

Local buses ply the coast road between Colva and Arossim and there are direct buses between Margao and Vasco.

The South Central Railway passes through this area, terminating in Vasco da Gama, but the village stops are of limited use to travellers – you're better off picking up trains in Margao or Vasco.

Betalbatim, Majorda & Utorda

Though the beaches along this entire strip are really just different patches of one long and continuous stretch of sand, some places have more character than others. Betalbatim Beach, just to the north of Colva, is a good example of what a difference a few hundred metres can make; it's as calm, quiet and pastoral as Colva is crowded and is itself divided into the romantically named Lover's Beach and Sunset Beach. A handful of beach shacks crowd around the various entrances.

Majorda Beach is separated from the laneways by a stream, forded by rickety bamboo bridges. Further north again, Utorda is a clean, if slightly characterless, stretch of beach, approached on rickety bridges over a series of creeks. It's mostly popular with holidaymakers from the surrounding swish resorts, as well as for Indian beach weddings at places like Royal Orchid and Zeebop.

Majorda is the only place in South Goa where you can ride a horse on the beach with **Greenland Horse Riding** (☑9822586502; Majorda Beach; 10min around ₹500). Bookings are helpful, or call in to Greenland Restaurant where the horses are stabled.

🛏 Sleeping

Shalom Homestay HOMESTAY $
(☑0832-2881016, 9822586596; 81/4 Gomes Vaddo, Majorda; s/d ₹500/700) This homestay at the beginning of the lane to Majorda Beach is a real bargain, with three clean rooms (two rooms share a bathroom). Enquire at Suzanne's Cafe across the street.

Dom Pedro's Haven GUESTHOUSE $$
(☑9890191147; www.dompedroshaven.com; Utorda; r incl breakfast with/without AC ₹2200/2000; ❄🔊) A down-to-earth option (unusual on this strip of coast) on the left-hand side at the entrance to Utorda Beach road,

Dom Pedro's is a lovely blue-and-white Mediterranean-style place with 20 rooms, some cottages in the garden and a small pool. Upstairs is a popular bar-restaurant.

Rainbow's End GUESTHOUSE $$
(☑9833099014; www.majordaguesthouse.com; 81 Gomes Vaddo, Majorda; d cottages ₹3500; ❄🔊🏊) A good-value family-run place on the road back from Majorda Beach, Rainbow's End has four air-conditioned timber cottages orbiting a small pool and a lovely garden. If it's full, ask about rooms in the Portuguese house that shares space with Carpe Diem Art Cafe.

★**Vivenda Dos Palhacos** BOUTIQUE HOTEL $$$
(☑9881720221; www.vivendagoa.com; Majorda; d ₹7650-12,950; ❄🔊🏊) This lovely boutique hotel, run by a well-travelled Indian-born British brother-and-sister team, is a gem of the South Goan coast and strictly for seriously discerning travellers who value quality accommodation and privacy. It's back from the beach and the road, in an unsignposted cul-de-sac and is an oasis of calm in a heavily touristed world.

Alila Diwa HOTEL $$$
(☑0832-2746800; www.alilahotels.com; Majorda; r ₹17,700-26,000; ❄🔊🏊) The Alila is South Goa's standout boutique design hotel resort with an awesome infinity pool overlooking the rice paddies. Rooms are modern and minimalist and the excellent restaurants include poolside VIVO and the intimate Spice Studio. Naturally there's a swanky spa.

Kenilworth HOTEL $$$
(☑0832-6698888; www.kenilworthhotels.com; Utorda Beach; d ₹14,500-17,500, ste from ₹21,000; ❄🔊🏊) This ritzy resort is an upmarket affair backing onto the beach with all the standard five-star bells and whistles including a massive swimming pool, gym, tennis courts and luxury spa. Its Salute Cucina restaurant offers traditional Italian cooking, while the Liquid Lounge is a cocktail bar with DJs on weekends.

🍴 Eating

Half a dozen beach shacks set up on each beach stretch in season and there are a scattering of good restaurants in the lanes back from the beach.

★**Carpe Diem Art Cafe** CAFE $
(☑8888862462; 81/2 Gomes Vaddo, Majorda; dishes ₹100-370; ⊙10am-7pm Tue-Sun) Carpe Diem is an art gallery showcasing local

WORTH A TRIP

THREE KINGS CHAPEL

It's the hilltop views, rather than the plain little chapel itself, that should entice you to take the steep road east off the coastal road up to **Three Kings Chapel** (Cuelim; ⏲8am-sunset). On clear days, you'll have a gorgeous, camera-friendly view south across thick palm groves, paddy fields, beaches and the Arabian Sea.

Local legend has it that the church (also called Church of Our Lady of Remedios) is haunted by the ghosts of three Portuguese kings, one of whom plotted to poison the others but died himself in the process. Villagers supposedly buried the three in the church and since then haunted happenings have been reported. To get here, follow the road for 4km north from Cansaulim and take the right fork uphill at Cuelim.

artists and a creative learning centre housed in a beautiful old Portuguese mansion, but for the average passing traveller it's also an excellent cafe. Admire the artworks over espresso coffee, sweet and savoury waffles, sandwiches, wraps or chicken wings. Nice change from the beach shacks!

Martin's Corner GOAN **$$**
(☎0832-2880413; www.martinscornergoa.com; Betalbatim; mains ₹250-400; ⏲11.30am-3pm & 6.30-11pm; 📶) An award-winning local legend, Martin's Corner, near Sunset Beach, is a great place to sample upmarket Goan cuisine and seafood in a relaxed setting back from the beach. The *xacutis* and vindalhos are superb, and there are plenty of tasty vegetarian options on offer. Live music most nights from 8pm.

Raj's Pentagon Restaurant & Garden Pub INDIAN **$$**
(☎0832-2881402; www.goapentagon.com; Majorda; mains ₹180-490; ⏲noon-midnight) Raj's is as much a place to come for the live music as to eat, though the food is pretty good and the ambience welcoming. Decent garden setting, great seafood and Goan favourites, and regular musos on stage in season.

Greenland Bar & Restaurant MULTICUISINE **$$**
(Majorda; mains ₹200-550; ⏲8am-10pm; 📶) Just back from Majorda's southern 'Cabana Beach' you'll find cute long-running Greenland, with a faux garden and a couple of horses. It serves up some great Goan specialities including *xacutis* (a spicy chicken or meat dish incorporating coconut milk and flesh) and vindaloo (fiery curry in a marinade of vinegar and garlic), along with the usual beach-shack fare.

★**Zeebop by the Sea** SEAFOOD **$$$**
(☎0832-2755333; www.zeeboprestaurantgoa.com; Utorda Beach; mains ₹200-500; ⏲10.30am-11pm) The most famous beachfront restaurant north of Colva, Zeebop is renowned for its excellent seafood and party nights. Stylish and award-winning Zeebop is set a little back from Utorda's main beach but still has a sandy floor. It's a firm favourite with locals and is popular for weddings and parties so you might need to book ahead in season.

Cansaulim, Arossim & Velsao

Only about 3km north of Utorda, the coast road passes though the busy market village of Cansaulim, crossing the train line a couple of times. From here lanes lead down to the beaches of Arossim, Cansaulim and, at the northern end, Velsao. Despite the gloomy presence of the vast and looming Zuari Agro chemical plant to the north, this stretch of beach makes a quiet place to get away from it all, in the company of just a lifeguard, a few beach shacks and a flock or two of milling seabirds.

The coast road travels some way back from the beach, through thick coconut groves past dozens of old bungalows and paddy fields, while occasional laneways lead you down to the beach.

Sleeping & Eating

ITC Grand Goa Resort & Spa HOTEL **$$$**
(☎0832-2721234; Arossim; d ₹22,400-39,000; ❄@🏊) Probably the swankiest resort on the beach strip north of Colva, the sprawling 18-hectare ITC Grand (formerly Park Hyatt) dominates the Arossim beach area. Rooms are lavish and large, and the resort has plenty of features, from its Kaya Kalp Royal Spa spread over a series of stunning outdoor pavilions to lagoons, pools and its signature restaurants.

Starfish Beach Shack INDIAN **$$**
(Arossim Beach; mains ₹200-350) This simple beach shack is, unusually, the only one on Arossim Beach so you'll find it popular with British and Russian package holidaymakers

staying nearby, who are on first-name terms with the staff. Sun beds and beach umbrellas occupy an otherwise very quiet patch of sand.

Tempero GOAN $$$
(☎0832-2721234; ITC Grand Hotel; mains from ₹650; ⏰noon-3pm & 6-11pm) Gorgeous upmarket Goan cuisine is crafted at this fabulous ITC Grand restaurant, which offers the piquant flavours of the region's specialities in all their glory. Unsurprisingly pricey, but try the vindalho or the kingfish curry and you won't be disappointed. It's one of five upmarket restaurants at the resort.

Bogmalo

Only 4km from the Dabolim Airport, Bogmalo Beach is a thin crescent of sand with a scruffy village and a slightly isolated air, given there are no other beaches around it. One end of the bay is marred by the '70s-style Bogmalo Beach Resort, which somehow evaded the restriction requiring all hotels to be built at least 500m from the high-tide line.

Bogmalo rarely feels too crowded, and has a reputable dive outfit with easy access to Grande Island.

Sights & Activities

Naval Aviation Museum MUSEUM
(☎0832-5995525; adult/child ₹20/5, camera/video ₹25/50; ⏰10am-5pm Tue-Sun) The Naval Aviation Museum, at the naval base on the road above Bogmalo Beach, makes an interesting diversion if you're interested in ships and planes. The museum offers a neat and interesting presentation of India's naval history, including an outdoor exhibit of fighter aircraft and naval helicopters.

★**Goa Diving** DIVING
(☎9049442647; www.goadiving.com; courses from ₹11,000, 1-/2-tank dive ₹3000/5000) Mainland India's original dive operator, with 25 years' experience, Goa Diving is an internationally respected outfit and a good place to earn your PADI certificate. It has an office on the road into Bogmalo but usually maintains a booth at the entrance to the beach in season.

Full Moon Cruises BOATING
(☎9764625198; rahul54293@gmail.com; Full Moon Cafe, Bogmalo Beach Rd; boat trip per couple ₹6500) Rahul, at the Full Moon Cafe, operates these daily half-day boat trips, tailored to customers' requirements but usually involving a spot of dolphin-watching, a bit of fishing and a visit to Bat Island just off the Bogmalo coast. Boats can carry up to six – add ₹1500 per person after the first two.

Sleeping & Eating

Joets Guest House GUESTHOUSE $$
(☎0832-2538036; www.joets.in; d incl breakfast ₹6200; ❄📶) At the northern end of the beachfront, this clean and simple guesthouse offers seven spacious rooms behind the popular, sometimes rowdy bar and restaurant. Rates include free use of the swimming pool at Coconut Creek.

Sarita's Guest House GUESTHOUSE $$
(☎0832-2538965; www.saritasguesthouse.com; d/ste ₹2500/3500; ❄📶) Beachfront Sarita's has clean but unremarkable rooms with air-con and TV, and a common balcony offering an unimpeded view of the beach. Also has a bar and restaurant.

Coconut Creek COTTAGE $$$
(☎0832-2538090, 0832-2358100; www.coconutcreekgoa.com; cottages ₹10,000; ❄📶🏊) Stylish cottages are set around an inviting pool in a coconut grove just back from the northern end of the beach. Coconut Creek is easily the nicest place to stay in Bogmalo but it's aimed squarely at package tourists and is a little pricey for independent walk-ins. The in-house restaurant and bar are worth a visit, even for nonguests.

Full Moon Cafe MULTICUISINE $$
(Bogmalo Beach Rd; mains ₹130-600; ⏰8am-11pm; 📶) At the entrance to Bogmalo Beach, Full Moon is a good place to survey the beach action over a Kingfisher and some of the best food in Bogmalo. Fresh seafood is a highlight and owner Rahul organises boat trips.

Getting There & Away

Local buses run along the coast road between Colva and Cansaulim, some continuing north to Dabolim. Buses also run direct from Margao to Cansaulim. A taxi from Colva to Cansaulim should cost around ₹200.

Colva to the Sal River

The beach and coast road stretches about 15km south from Colva to the Sal River at Betul, via the beach resorts of Benaulim, Varca, Cavelossim and Mobor. From there a huge bridge spans the river to Assolna (it replaced the vehicle ferry in 2014) and you can continue on along the beautiful forest road, past the turn-offs to windswept Cabo da Rama fort and secluded Cola Beach, to Agonda.

This trip is the scenic alternative to the main road (NH66) between Margao and Palolem – perfect on a scooter or Enfield.

Benaulim

A long stretch of largely empty sand peppered with a few beach shacks and water-sports enthusiasts, the beaches of Benaulim and nearby Sernabatim to the north are much quieter than Colva, partly because the village is a good kilometre back from the beach.

Out of season it has a somewhat desolate feel, but the lack of traffic or any serious beachfront development is an obvious attraction to many travellers, some of whom rent houses in the village and stay for the season. In many ways, this is the southern antithesis of Calangute and Baga in the north.

Benaulim has a special place in Goan tradition: legend has it that it was here that the god Parasurama's arrow landed when he fired it into the sea to create Goa.

Sights & Activities

★Goa Chitra MUSEUM
(☎0832-2772910; www.goachitra.com; St John the Baptist Rd, Mondo Vaddo; ₹300; ⊙9am-6pm Tue-Sun) Artist and restorer Victor Hugo Gomes first noticed the slow extinction of traditional objects – from farming tools to kitchen utensils to altarpieces – as a child in Benaulim. He created this ethnographic museum from the more than 4000 cast-off objects that he collected from across the state over 20 years. Admission is via a one-hour guided tour, held on the hour. Goa Chitra is 3km east of Maria Hall – ask locally for directions.

San Thome Museum MUSEUM
(☎9822363917; www.goamuseum.com; Colva Rd; ₹200; ⊙9am-6pm) This quirky museum at the Varca (southern) end of Benaulim, dubbed 'Back in Time', has three floors of carefully presented technology through the ages, from old cameras and typewriters to gramophones, clocks and projectors. Highlights include a Scheidmayer grand piano, a Raleigh bicycle and an anchor cast from the same pattern as the *Titanic*'s.

Pele's Water Sport WATER SPORTS
(☎9822686011; jet ski per 10min ₹400, parasailing per ride ₹1000, dolphin trips ₹300) Water sports in Benaulim are not as chaotic as in Colva, though some operators hang around the beach shacks. One of the best is Pele's Water Sport, which offers parasailing and dolphin-spotting trips, as well as jet skis for hire.

Sleeping

Lots of budget rooms for rent can be found along the roads towards Benaulim and Sernabatim Beach, while the big five-stars are further south. The best of the budget beachfront accommodation is at Sernabatim Beach, a few hundred metres north of Benaulim. Prices have slowly crept up, but there are still lots of family-run places with just a handful of rooms with bargain-basement prices.

★Blue Corner HUT $
(☎9850455770; www.bluecornergoa.com; huts ₹1300; wi-fi) It's rare to find good old-fashioned palm-thatch cocohuts on this stretch of beachfront but the 11 sturdy thatched huts at Blue Corner are the best in Benaulim. Each one has a veranda, fan and wi-fi. The beachfront restaurant at the front gets rave reviews from guests.

Anthy's Guesthouse GUESTHOUSE $
(☎0832-2771680, 9922854566; www.anthysguesthousegoa.com; Sernabatim Beach; d with/without AC ₹1900/1600; AC wi-fi) One of a handful of places lining Sernabatim Beach, Anthy's is a standout favourite with travellers for its good restaurant, book exchange and well-kept cottage-style garden rooms, which stretch back from the beach, surrounded by a garden. There are also a few comfortable wooden cabins.

Furtados GUESTHOUSE $
(☎0832-2770396; Sernabatim Beach; d with/without AC ₹1800/1200; AC wi-fi) Conveniently positioned at the main entrance to Sernabatim Beach, Furtados has decent, clean and pretty good-value rooms behind its popular beachfront restaurant.

D'Souza Guest House GUESTHOUSE $
(☎0832-2770583; d ₹600) With just three rooms, this traditional blue-painted house in the back lanes is run by a local Goan family and comes with bundles of homely atmosphere and a lovely garden. It's often full so book ahead.

Rosario's Inn GUESTHOUSE $
(☎0832-2770636; rosariosinn@ymail.com; r with/without AC ₹900/600; AC wi-fi) Across a football field flitting with young players and dragonflies, family-run Rosario's is a large establish-

Benaulim

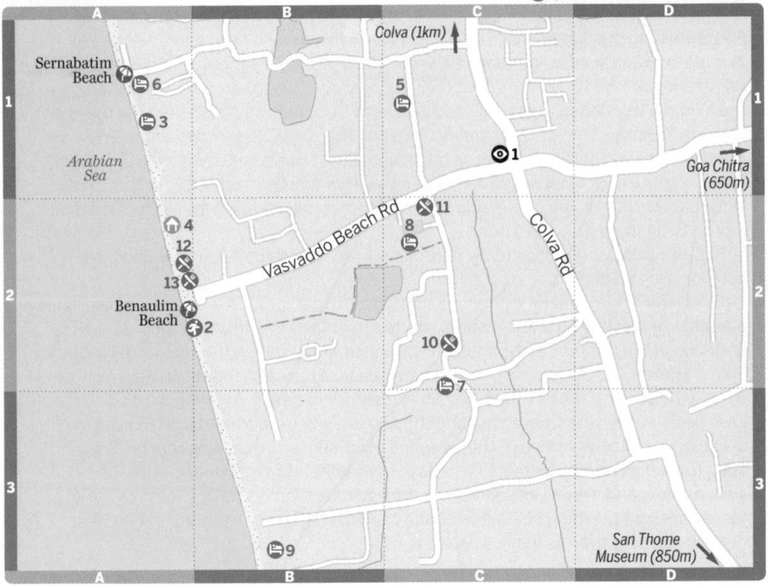

Benaulim

Sights
1 Maria Hall C1

Activities, Courses & Tours
2 Pele's Water Sport B2

Sleeping
3 Anthy's Guesthouse A1
4 Blue Corner A2
5 D'Souza Guest House C1
6 Furtados A1
7 Palm Grove Cottages C2
8 Rosario's Inn C2
9 Taj Exotica Resort & Spa B3

Eating
10 Cafe Malibu C2
11 Goodfellas C2
12 Johncy Restaurant A2
13 Pedro's Bar & Restaurant A2

ment with very clean, simple rooms and a restaurant. Excellent value for long-stayers.

Palm Grove Cottages HOTEL **$$**
(☎0832-2770059; www.palmgrovegoa.com; Vaswado; d incl breakfast ₹3800-4250;) Old-fashioned, secluded charm and Benaulim's leafiest garden welcomes you at Palm Grove Cottages, a fine midrange choice. The quiet AC rooms, some with balcony, all have a nice feel but the best are the spacious deluxe rooms in a separate Portuguese-style building. The Palm Garden Restaurant here is exceptionally good.

Taj Exotica Resort & Spa HOTEL **$$$**
(☎0832-6683333; www.tajhotels.com; d ₹34,500-63,500;) Bollywood stars and sheikhs are known to stay at the Taj Exotica, one of Goa's plushest and priciest resorts. Set in 23 hectares of tropical gardens 2km south of Benaulim, it has spas, restaurants and pools. Most travellers will be content to visit its swish restaurants, including the Goan cuisine of Miguel Arcanjo and the beachfront Lobster Village.

Eating

Benaulim and Sernabatim Beaches have a few seasonal restaurant shacks, and there are some very good restaurants along, or just off, the main road back from the beach. For a splurge head to the five-star resorts.

Cafe Malibu INDIAN **$**
(mains ₹120-200; 8am-11pm) This unpretentious little family-run cafe offers a nice dining

FADING FISHERIES

Somewhere in the region of 50,000 Goans are dependent on fishing for their family income, but Goa's once-abundant waters are today facing a serious threat from overfishing, and locals now reminisce about their younger days when *ramponkars* (fishers), in their simple wooden outriggers, would give away 60cm-long kingfish because they had so many to spare. These days it's difficult to buy fish direct from boats, and even local markets offer slim pickings because much of the best fish is sold directly to upmarket hotels, exported, or shipped to interstate markets where the best prices are fetched. Naturally this has driven up the price of seafood, not only for tourists, but for Goans who rely on their staple fish curry rice.

In the high season, Goa actually relies heavily on importing fish and seafood from neighbouring Karnataka.

Overfishing has become a phenomenon since modern motorised trawlers, owned and operated by wealthy business owners, started to eclipse the simple traditional fishing methods of the *ramponkars* in the 1970s. Despite a law limiting trawlers to beyond a 5km shoreline 'exclusion zone', trawlers stay relatively close to the shore, adversely affecting the catch of the *ramponkars,* while their use of tightly knit nets, which don't allow juvenile fish to escape (these are either thrown away or used for fertiliser) has further dwindled fish stocks. Although the *ramponkars* continue to press for change, Goan state legislature seems helpless in the face of powerful trawler owners, while the seas slowly empty and irreversible damage is done to maintaining this precious resource. Meanwhile, many fishing boats now spend as much time ferrying tourists around for dolphin-spotting trips as they do catching fish.

experience in its roadside garden setting on a back lane a short walk back from the beach. It does a good job of Goan specialities as well as Indian and continental dishes.

Farm House GOAN **$$**
(☎9822130430, 0832-2770534; Ascona, Benaulim; mains ₹180-340; ⏰11.30am-3pm & 7.30pm-midnight Tue-Sun; 📶) Beneath a large palapa-style shelter overlooking a well-stocked fish pond beside the Sal River, the Farm House is renowned locally for its Goan dishes, seafood and steaks. Weekends are enormously popular for live music and the opportunity for a spot of fishing (11am to 3pm). It's off the main road at the southern end of Benaulim village.

Johncy Restaurant MULTICUISINE **$$**
(Vasvaddo Beach Rd; mains ₹150-450; ⏰7am-midnight) Not so much a shack as a beachfront restaurant, Johncy has been around forever, dispensing standard Goan, Indian and Western favourites – and cold beer – from its location just back from the sand. Live music on weekends.

Pedro's Bar & Restaurant MULTICUISINE **$$**
(Vasvaddo Beach Rd; mains ₹120-500; ⏰7am-midnight; 📶) Set amid a large, shady garden at the beachfront car park and popular with local and international travellers, long-running Pedro's offers standard Indian, Chinese and Italian dishes, as well as Goan choices and 'sizzlers'. Regular live music in season.

Goodfellas ITALIAN **$$$**
(☎9657531631; pizzas & pasta ₹400-650; ⏰6pm-midnight; 📶) Authentic wood-fired pizza is the standout at this corner bistro where Italians run the kitchen with aplomb. Fresh pasta, lasagne and ravioli also grace the menu with imported cheeses, porcini mushrooms and deli meats. Occasional live music and Sunday lunch.

ℹ Getting There & Around

Buses from Margao to Benaulim are frequent (₹15, 20 minutes); some continue on south to Varca and Cavelossim. Buses stop at the Maria Hall crossroads, or at the junctions to Sernabatim or Taj Exotica – just ask to be let off. From Maria Hall an autorickshaw should cost around ₹60 for the five-minute ride to the sea.

If you're staying in Benaulim you'll appreciate having your own transport: look out for 'bike for rent' signs in the village or down at the beach shacks. Rental costs around ₹300 per day.

Cavelossim & Mobor

POP 1955

Cavelossim village – a straggling strip of jewellery and gem shops, souvenir shops, ATMs, one quite swish department store, and the increasingly common proliferation of cosmetic dentists – is a place of large hotels and time-share complexes strung along the main road.

Like Mobor to the south, Cavelossim is somewhat unique in that it's wedged between the Sal River and the Arabian Sea and there are a number of hotels and restaurants overlooking the river. Still, the main attraction is the beach, a gently sloping strip of clean sand with just a few beach shacks and a returning cast of regulars. By the time you reach the lush, landscaped Leela hotel, you know you're in Mobor. These days Cavelossim and Mobor attract mostly Russian holidaymakers but it's a very low-key scene and the southern end of the beach is usually deserted.

Tours

Betty's Place Boat Trips BOATING
(0832-2871456, 9226424717; www.bettysgoa.com; Mobor Beach) A decent restaurant by night, Betty's offers a wide range of boat cruises by day, including a full day combined dolphin-watching and birdwatching trip (₹1000 including lunch and drinks), fishing trips, sunset boat rides (₹500), and a two-hour birdwatching trip on the Sal River (₹500; departs daily at 4pm).

Sleeping & Eating

Cavelossim is squarely aimed at package tourists, and most midrange places have little interest in renting rooms separately to walk-in travellers. Mobor is dominated by the Leela but also has the Holiday Inn and a handful of midrange places.

Byke Old Anchor HOTEL $$
(0832-6627172; www.thebyke.com; Cavelossim Rd, Cavelossim; r ₹2700-5000;) One of Cavelossim's original resorts, the ageing Old Anchor is quaint and hard to miss – the main building is shaped like a ship. But it remains good value compared with the fancy resorts around it. Rooms are plain but comfortable, with modern amenities, and the pool, bar and veg restaurant all have an appealing holiday quality.

Leela Goa HOTEL $$$
(0832-6621234; www.theleela.com; Mobor; r ₹27,000-31,500, ste from ₹41,000;) Goa's largest and most luxurious resort, the opulent Leela is the place to indulge your five-star fantasies. Set amid 30 hectares of land, this enormous expanse of manicured Goan perfection has its own 12-hole golf course, and rooms of varying degrees of decadence.

Mike's Place MULTICUISINE $$
(0832-2871248; www.mikesplacegoa.com; mains ₹180-450; 8.30am-11pm;) Down a lane opposite Novotel's Dona Sylvia, nudging up against the Sal River, Mike's is something of an institution (as is Mike's 'Love Shack' on the beach). The menu is pretty standard Indian-Goan-Chinese-continental but it has stood the test of time and the location is great. Rooms here (₹2500) are good value.

Fisherman's Wharf SEAFOOD $$$
(9011018866; www.thefishermanswharf.in; mains ₹320-550; noon-11pm;) The original Fisherman's Wharf still sits overlooking the Sal River, a beautiful al fresco dining experience where fresh seafood and Goan specialities are the highlights. Signature Goan dishes include prawn *balchao* and rawa fried kingfish but you'll also find continental and Chinese food and kebabs. Live music on weekends.

Getting There & Away

To the south of Cavelossim and Mobor is the mouth of the Sal River. To continue down along the coast of South Goa, take the backcountry roads and the huge new bridge spanning the Sal River to Assolna, then continue on towards Betul. Hourly buses run along the coast road from Colva (₹15) or via the highway from Margao (₹15).

Cabo da Rama

The laterite spurs along the coastline of Goa, providing both high ground and ready-made supplies of building stone, were natural sites for fortresses, and there was a fortress at **Cabo da Rama** (9am-5.30pm) FREE long before the Portuguese ever reached Goa.

Today this is one of Goa's most atmospheric ruined fortresses, even though there's little to see of the old structure except for the front wall, with its dry moat and unimposing main gate, and the small church that stands just inside the walls. But the superb coastal views north and south are worth coming for and there are a few old cannons lying around. Services are still held in St Anthony's chapel every Sunday and Tuesday morning.

History

Named after Rama of the Hindu Ramayana epic, who was said to have spent time in exile here with his wife Sita, the original fortress was held by various rulers for many years. It wasn't until 1763 that it was obtained by the Portuguese from the Hindu Raja of Sonda and was subsequently rebuilt; what remains today, including the rusty cannons, is entirely Portuguese.

Although the fort saw no real action after the rebuild, it was briefly occupied by British troops between 1797 and 1802 and again between 1803 and 1813, when the threat of French invasion troubled the British enough to move in. Parts were used as a prison until 1955, before the whole thing was allowed to fall into ruin.

🛏 Sleeping & Eating

Inevitably the magnificent clifftops near Cabo da Rama would be developed and so it is that a couple of stunningly located resorts have appeared overlooking the secluded beaches north of Cabo da Rama fort.

Cape Goa   RESORT $$$
(☑ 9075843958; www.thecapegoa.com; Canaguinim; r incl breakfast ₹25,300-33,500; ❋ 🛜) Romantic getaways might not come any better than this. With just nine gorgeous thatched cottages – all sea-facing and with jacuzzi on the personal outdoor deck – there's enough privacy and a spectacular clifftop location gazing out over the Arabian Sea to make you forget the outside world. Secluded beach? Check. Sunset cocktails? Check. There's also a top-quality restaurant and bar.

Red Crab   SEAFOOD $$
(☑ 9850192064; mains ₹180-400; ⊙ 8.30am-10pm) The clifftop views alone are worthy of a stop here on the way to or from Cabo da Rama fort, around 1km away. Seafood, Goa specialities and the usual multicuisine are on offer – or just kick back with a cold beer.

❶ Getting There & Away

To get to the fort from the coast road, turn west at the red-and-green signposted turn-off about 12km north of Agonda. The road dips into a lush valley then winds steeply up to a barren plateau punctuated by farmhouses and wandering stock. The fort is at the end of this road, about 3km from the turn-off.

Local buses come here from Margao or Betul (₹15, around 40 minutes) several times daily but check times for returning buses as you might get stuck.

A return taxi to Cabo da Rama costs around ₹900 from Palolem, including waiting time. With your own transport it's an excellent ride from Palolem, Agonda or along the south coast.

Cola & Khancola

Cola Beach is one of those hidden gems of the south coast – a relatively hard-to-reach crescent of sand enclosed by forested cliffs and with a gorgeous emerald lagoon stretching back from the beach.

It has been discovered, of course, and in November and April several hut and tent villages set up here, but it's still a beautiful, low-key place and popular with day-trippers from Agonda and Palolem.

Further north around the headland is an even more remote beach known as Khancola Beach, or Kakolem, with one small resort reached via a steep set of jungly steps from the clifftop above.

🛏 Sleeping & Eating

Casa Diya   HUT $
(☑ 9158053843; kloakars@yahoo.com; Cola Beach; huts ₹1500) This is the budget offering on Cola Beach with just a few hillside huts and a basic restaurant south of the lagoon.

★ Blue Lagoon Resort   HUT $$
(☑ 9673277756; www.bluelagooncola.com; Cola Beach; cottages ₹3800-5400; 🛜) These sweet timber cottages dominate central Cola Beach, overlooking either the beach or the lagoon, and are the first place you'll find on the walk down from the car park. The highest price are those with uninterrupted sea views. The restaurant is popular with guests and day-trippers.

Palm Discoveries   HUT $$
(☑ 9820991637; www.palmdiscoveries.com; Khancola Beach; huts ₹1500) The six huts here are very simple and wonderfully isolated. It's a steep walk down laterite steps through the jungle to get here and at the bottom you're greeted with the secluded covelike Khancola Beach and the smiling staff at the small restaurant-bar. Even if you don't stay it's worth hiking down for a few hours on the beach.

Cola Beach Resort   TENTED CAMP $$
(☑ 9822061223; www.colabeach.com; Cola Beach; tents/cottages incl breakfast ₹6000/6500; 🛜) A short walk north of the lagoon, Cola Beach Resort fronts an even quieter stretch of beach, where Rajasthani safari tents and wooden cottages occupy space among the palms. The tents are spacious and comfortable enough but feel overpriced, even for Cola.

SOUTH GOA CRUISING

Take your moped, Enfield Bullet or hired taxi and hit the open road – avoiding cows, pedestrians, careening trucks, chickens, dogs, bicycles, pigs, water buffalo and the other assorted obstacles that make Goan roads something of a thrilling ride.

Palolem to the Sal River This beautiful stretch of coastal road winds from Palolem via Agonda Beach then through thick forested hills before dropping down to the Sal River. Along the way, detour to pretty Cola Beach and Cabo da Rama fort.

Chandor–Quepem–Loutolim circuit Delve deep into the world of Goan Portuguese mansions with this back-road circuit from Margao; detour to the petroglyphs of Usgalimal and the Buddhist caves at Rivona.

Colva to Velsao Head north from busy beachfront Colva, up the scenic coast road past dozens of crumbling Portuguese palaces. Stop off here and there to discover deserted stretches of beach, and climb up to Velsao's Three Kings chapel for the view back down.

Palolem to Netravali Head inland through farmland and protected forest to a spice farm, waterfalls and the mysterious Bubble Lake around Netravali.

Dwarka Beach Resort HUT $$$
(☎8551056490; www.dwarkagoa.com; Cola Beach; d huts incl meals ₹13,000;) A beach hut for ₹13,000 – no way! The huts are certainly very nice and most are sea-facing, terracing down the hillside to the beach side of the lagoon. Boutique is the word here, with only 10 huts and lots of personal attention. And meals are included. But ₹13,000? Unsurprisingly, the restaurant and bar is exclusive to guests.

Getting There & Away

Getting to Cola is not difficult but it's a rough 2km road south to the beach from the main road. A return taxi from Palolem costs around ₹500.

Agonda

POP 3800

Travellers have been drifting to Agonda for years and seasonal hut villages – some very luxurious – now occupy almost all available beachfront space in season, but it's still more low-key than Palolem and a good choice if you're after some beachy relaxation. The coast road between Betul and Palolem passes through Agonda village, while the main traveller centre is a single lane running parallel to the beach.

Sights & Activities

Agonda Beach is a fine 2km stretch of white sand framed between two forested headlands. The surf can be fierce and swimming is not as safe as Palolem, but lifeguards are on patrol.

Lots of local and foreigner-run yoga, meditation and ayurveda courses and classes set up in season, and local boats can take you on trips to other beaches or to spot dolphins.

South of Agonda are pretty Honeymoon Beach and then Butterfly Beach, two lovely coves, the latter named for its lepidopterous inhabitants. Both are accessible on foot or by boat, but there are no facilities.

Local fishing boats will take you out on sightseeing trips from ₹1500.

Aloha Surf India SURFING
(☎8605476576; 1hr/2hr/full day board rental ₹400/700/1500, group/private lesson from ₹1500/2500; ⊙8am-6pm Oct-May) The first surf school in Goa's deep south, Aloha is run by a passionate local crew. Learn to surf on Agonda's gentle 'green' waves or hire a board. Also stand-up paddleboard lessons and surf tours.

Sleeping

Agonda has gone seriously upmarket in its beach-hut operations, with the best beachfront resorts offering air-con, TV and open-sky bathrooms and all with a restaurant and bar, usually beach-facing. Between November and March you won't find sea-facing huts under ₹3000, but those behind will be cheaper. As with any seasonal accommodation, standards and ownership can change.

Back from the beach on the parallel road are a few cheaper guesthouses.

Fatima Guesthouse GUESTHOUSE $
(☎0832-2647477; www.fatimasguesthouse.com; d ₹1000-1500, with AC ₹1500-2500;) An ever-popular budget guesthouse set back from the beach, with clean rooms, a good

Agonda

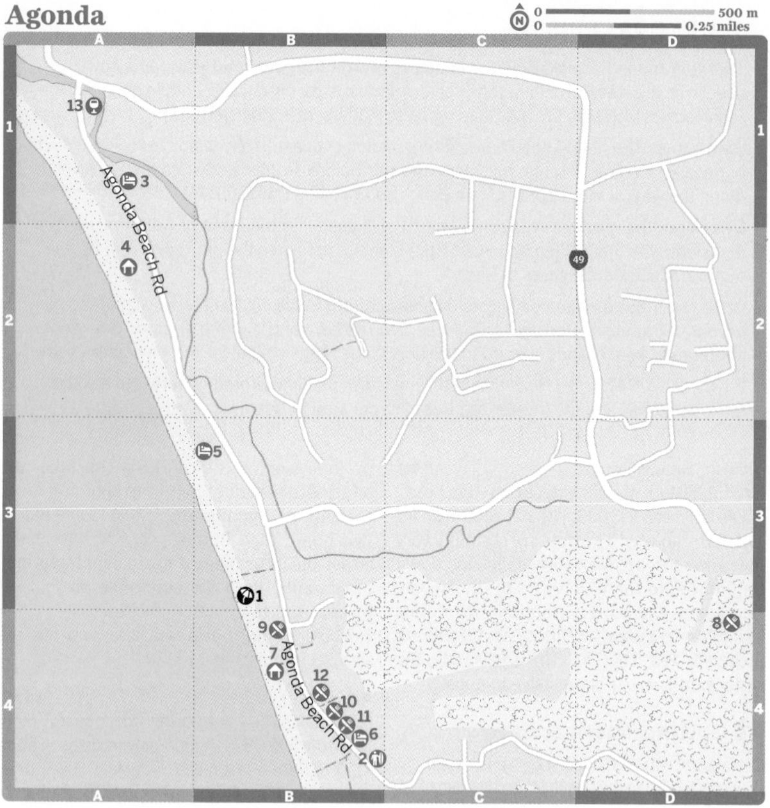

Agonda

Sights
1 Agonda Beach B3

Activities, Courses & Tours
2 Aloha Surf India B4

Sleeping
3 Abba's Gloryland A1
4 Agonda White Sand A2
5 Cuba Agonda B3
6 Fatima Guesthouse B4
7 H2O Agonda B4

Eating
8 Blue Planet Cafe D4
9 Kopi Desa B4
10 La Dolce Vita B4
11 Mandala Cafe B4
12 Zest Cafe B4

Drinking & Nightlife
13 Riverside Bar & Restaurant A1

restaurant and obliging staff. Rooftop yoga classes in season.

Abba's Gloryland GUESTHOUSE $
(☎0832-2647822, 9423412795; www.abbasgloryland.com; Agonda Beach Rd; huts ₹1200, r with AC ₹1900; ❄📶) Back from the beach, Abba's is a decent budget choice with timber cottages at the side and air-con rooms in a separate building, all in a pleasant garden.

★**Agonda White Sand** HUT $$
(☎9823548277; www.agondawhitesand.com; Agonda Beach; huts ₹4600-5200; ❄📶) Beautifully designed and constructed cottages with open-air bathrooms and spring mattresses surround a central bar and beachfront restaurant. Some have air-con.

H2O Agonda HUT $$
(☎9921836730; www.h2oagonda.com; Agonda Beach; d incl breakfast ₹5700-9300; ❄📶) With its purple and mauve muslin curtains and Arabian nights ambience, H2O is among the most impressive of Agonda's luxury cottage setups. From the hotel-style reception, walk through a leafy garden to the spacious cottages with air-con and enormous open-air bathrooms. The more expensive sea-facing cottages with king-size beds may be worth paying extra for.

Cuba Agonda COTTAGE $$$
(☎0832-2645775; www.cubagoa.com; Agonda Beach; d ₹6200-10,000; ❄📶) These blue-and-white sea-facing cottages look a bit like fancy English bathing boxes but they're well-appointed inside with air-con, TV and comfy beds, and verandas with steps straight to the beach.

Eating

All of Agonda's resorts and hotels have restaurants, but there are a few interesting places back in the village too.

Mandala Cafe CAFE $
(☎8554091819; Agonda Beach Rd; chai ₹15, dishes ₹100-250; ⏲8am-11pm; 📶) Feeling like a glass of masala chai or a vegan pancake? Slip into a cushioned alcove at this shanti little travellers' cafe for a down-to-earth antithesis to Agonda's over-the-top beach bars.

Zest Cafe VEGETARIAN $$
(☎8806607919; Agonda Beach Rd; mains ₹190-360; ⏲8am-10pm; 📶) The Agonda branch of Zest has a lush and loungy garden setting to complement the vegan and vegetarian menu of Mexican or teriyaki bowls, pizza, Balinese tofu and raw-food desserts. Great breakfast spot.

Blue Planet Cafe VEGETARIAN $$
(☎0832-2647448; mains ₹140-250; ⏲9am-3pm & 6-9.30pm; 📶) Scrambled tofu and vegan pancakes grace the menu of soul food at mostly vegan Blue Planet, a welcoming detox removed from the beach scene. You'll find salads, smoothies and innovative veg dishes and a bucolic vibe. It's in an off-track jungle location about 2km from Agonda village (follow the signs off the main Agonda–Palolem road).

La Dolce Vita ITALIAN $$
(☎90799911; mains ₹250-500; ⏲9am-10pm; 📶) Excellent Italian food is dished out at Dolce Vita, with gingham tablecloths, a long, sprawling blackboard menu, and plenty of passionate yelling and gesturing when the place gets busy. Wood-fired pizzas are authentic.

Kopi Desa EUROPEAN $$$
(☎7767831487; small plates ₹150-295, mains ₹350-695; ⏲8am-11pm; 📶) The name translates from Indonesian as 'coffee village' but this al fresco restaurant and cocktail bar has become firmly established for its imaginative Euro-centric menu, tapas-style plates, from pork-belly bites to crab and lobster tortellini, sourdough pizzas and burgers. Regular live music in season.

Drinking & Nightlife

You can get a drink at any beach shack and live music will often fire up in season, but Agonda is generally more low key than Palolem.

Riverside Bar & Restaurant BAR
(☎7517634728; Agonda Beach Rd; ⏲9am-midnight; 📶) Head on down to the north end of the beach, but on the river side of the road, for a friendly, rustic bamboo-bar hang-out with regular live music, open mic nights and fire dances.

Information

There's an HDFC ATM just beside the church crossroads.

Getting There & Away

Scooters and motorbikes can be rented from places on the beach road for around ₹300 to ₹400. Autorickshaws depart from the main T-junction near Agonda's church to Palolem (₹300) and Patnem (₹300). Taxis are around ₹50 more.

Local buses run from Chaudi sporadically throughout the day (₹15), but ask for Agonda Beach, otherwise you'll be let off in the village about 1km away.

Chaudi

Also known as Canacona, the small but busy town of Chaudi on the main highway (soon to be bypassed), is the place to come to get things done if you're staying in Palolem, Agonda, Patnem or around. Here you'll find several banks and ATMs, pharmacies, doctors, a supermarket of sorts, a post office, mobile-phone vendors, and a good fruit and vegetable market for stocking up on self-catering essentials.

Palolem

POP 12,440

Palolem is undoubtedly one of Goa's most postcard-perfect beaches: a gentle curve of palm-fringed sand facing a calm bay. But in season the beachfront is transformed into a toy town of colourful and increasingly sophisticated timber and bamboo huts fronted by palm-thatch restaurants. It's still a great place to be and is popular with backpackers, long-stayers and families. The protected bay is one of the safest swimming spots in Goa and you can comfortably kayak and paddleboard for hours here.

Just around the headland at the southern end of the beach, Colomb Bay – reached by foot or by road – is another little hideaway with several low-key resorts and restaurants.

Away from the beach you can learn to cook, drop in to yoga classes or hire a motorbike and cruise to surrounding beaches, waterfalls and wildlife parks.

Sights

Cotigao Wildlife Sanctuary NATURE RESERVE

(☎0832-2965601; adult/child ₹20/10, camera/video ₹30/150; ⌚7am-5.30pm) About 9km southeast of Palolem, and a good day trip, is the beautiful, remote-feeling Cotigao Wildlife Sanctuary, Goa's second-largest sanctuary and easily its most accessible if you have your own transport. Don't expect to bump into its more exotic residents (including gaurs, sambars, leopards and spotted deer), but frogs, snakes, monkeys, insects and blazingly plumed birds are in no short supply.

Trails are hikable; set off early morning for the best sighting prospects from one of the two forest watchtowers, 7km and 12km from the park entrance. If you're serious about spotting wildlife, it might be worth staying a night in one of the forest department **cottages** (₹800-1500), right behind the reception at the park entrance. They're no frills but clean, and meals can be arranged. From here you can make a start before the park even opens.

Butterfly Beach BEACH

Hire a local boatman from Palolem Beach to ferry you up to Butterfly Beach and back (₹2000 for the boat), relishing the views of untouched coastline along the way. The beach can also be reached by road towards Agonda and a walk from the car park.

Activities

Palolem offers no shortage of yoga, reiki and meditation classes in season. Locations and teachers change seasonally – ask around locally to see whose hands-on healing powers are hot this season.

Palolem's calm waters are perfect for kayaking and stand-up paddleboarding. Kayaks are available for hire for around ₹200 per hour, paddleboards for ₹500. Mountain bikes (₹150 per day) can be hired from **Seema Bike Hire** (Ourem Rd).

Aranya Yoga YOGA

(www.aranyayogaashram.com; off Palolem Beach Rd; drop-in class ₹400; ⌚drop-in classes 8am, 10am & 4pm Sep-Mar) Highly regarded daily drop-in yoga classes in hatha, ashtanga and

IT'S A DOG'S LIFE

South Goa has several animal welfare shelters that welcome volunteers or visitors to help walk or play with rescued stray dogs.

The **Goa Animal Welfare Trust** (☎0832-2653677, 9763681525; www.gawt.org; Curchorem; ⌚9am-5.30pm Mon-Sat, 10am-1pm & 2.30-5pm Sun), in the small inland town of Curchorem, works hard at providing veterinary help for sick animals, shelter for puppies and kittens, sterilisation programs for street dogs and low-cost veterinary care (including anti-rabies injections) for Goan pets. Volunteers are welcome, even just for a few hours on a single visit, to walk or play with the dogs. Items such as your old newspapers can be used for lining kennel floors, as can old sheets, towels and anything else you might not be taking home.

You can make contact with the shelter at the **Goa Animal Welfare Trust Shop** (☎0832-2653677; www.gawt.org; ⌚9.30am-1pm & 4-7pm Mon-Sat) in Colva, a charity shop selling souvenirs and secondhand books.

At Chapolim, a few kilometres northeast of Palolem Beach, the small Animal Rescue Centre also takes in sick, injured or stray animals. Volunteers welcome. Look out for the sign on the road to Chaudi; it's about 2km north near the Chapolim dam.

beginners, as well as five-day intensive courses (₹7500) and teacher training courses.

Anand Yoga Village YOGA
(☎7066454773; www.anandyogavillage.com; off Ourem Rd; drop-in classes ₹400, five-pass ₹1500) An international team of yoga instructors runs three daily drop-in classes in hatha, vinyasa and ashtanga disciplines at this inclusive new yoga village. Week-long yoga holidays (€330 per person) including accommodation in comfy timber cabins, breakfast and lunch and unlimited yoga and meditation. Teacher training courses (200 hours) also available.

Humming Bird Spa SPA
(1hr massage from ₹1900; ⏲9am-8pm) For sheer pampering, Palolem's best all-round spa is at Ciarans resort (p187). Choose from ayurvedic, Swedish, Balinese, Thai or aroma massage, waxing or even a full-body mud wrap.

Animal Rescue Centre VOLUNTEERING
(☎0832-2644171; www.arcgoa.in; Chapolim; ⏲10am-1pm & 2.30-5pm Mon-Sat) Opposite the Chapolim dam wall, 2km north of Chaudi, this centre treats sick, stray and injured animals and welcomes volunteers, visitors and donations. Volunteer placements are two weeks to three months.

Courses

Rahul's Cooking Class COOKING
(☎7875990647; www.rahulcookingclass.com; Palolem Beach Rd; per person ₹1500; ⏲11.30am-2.30pm & 6-9pm) Rahul's is one of the original cooking schools, with three-hour morning and afternoon classes each day. Prepare five dishes including chapati and coconut curry. Minimum two people; book at least one day in advance.

Masala Kitchen COOKING
(☎8390060421; www.aranyayogaashram.com/cooking-classes; Palolem Beach Rd; per person ₹1300) Established cooking classes at Aranya Yoga just off Palolem Beach Rd; book a day in advance. Includes South Indian thalis served on banana leaf and sattvic cooking.

Tours

You'll find plenty of local fishers keen to take you out on dolphin-spotting and fishing expeditions on their outrigger boats. They generally charge a minimum ₹2000 for a one-hour trip but bargaining is possible. They also do trips to nearby Butterfly and Honeymoon Beaches, or up to Agonda and Cola Beaches.

★ **Goa Jungle Adventure** OUTDOORS
(☎9850485641; www.goajungle.com; trekking & canyoning trips ₹2390-3990; ⏲Oct-May) This adventure company, run by experienced French guide Manu, will take you out for thrilling trekking and canyoning trips in the Netravali area at the base of the Western Ghats, where you can climb, jump and abseil into remote water-filled plunges. Trips, including jungle survival and sea-cliff jumping, run from half-day to several days. Meeting and registration is in Palolem. Shoes can be rented for ₹200 per day. Call to arrange a meeting with Manu.

Sleeping

Most of Palolem's accommodation is of the seasonal beach-hut variety, though there are plenty of old-fashioned guesthouses or family homes with rooms to rent back from the beach. It's still possible to find a basic palm-thatch hut near the beach for as little as ₹800 outside of high season, but many of the huts these days are more thoughtfully designed – the very best have air-con, flat-screen TV and sea-facing balcony.

Camp San Francisco HUT $
(☎9158057201; www.campsanfrancisco.com; huts & r ₹800-3500) This hut village and associated guesthouse (Casa San Francisco) runs all the way from the beach to Palolem Beach Rd, offering a room or hut to suit most travellers. It's a good deal in mid-season as it has some of the cheaper huts along this stretch of beach. Naturally, there's a restaurant at the front.

Rainbow Lining HOSTEL $
(☎8390248102; 76 Ourem Rd; dm ₹450-600, d ₹2500; ❄📶) This refurbished house is a good deal for backpackers with four- to 10-bed air-con dorms (bunks are curtained off) and a few private rooms. Friendly owners, rooftop yoga and breakfast available. At the time of writing, a new restaurant-bar MOG (Mad Over Goa) was about to open.

Sevas HUT $
(☎9422065437; www.sevaspalolemgoa.com; Colomb Bay; d huts ₹800-1500; 📶) Hidden in the jungle on the Colomb Bay side of Palolem, Sevas has some of the more basic palm-thatch huts around, reflected in the price. But it's a very peaceful place set in a lovely shaded garden area.

Palolem

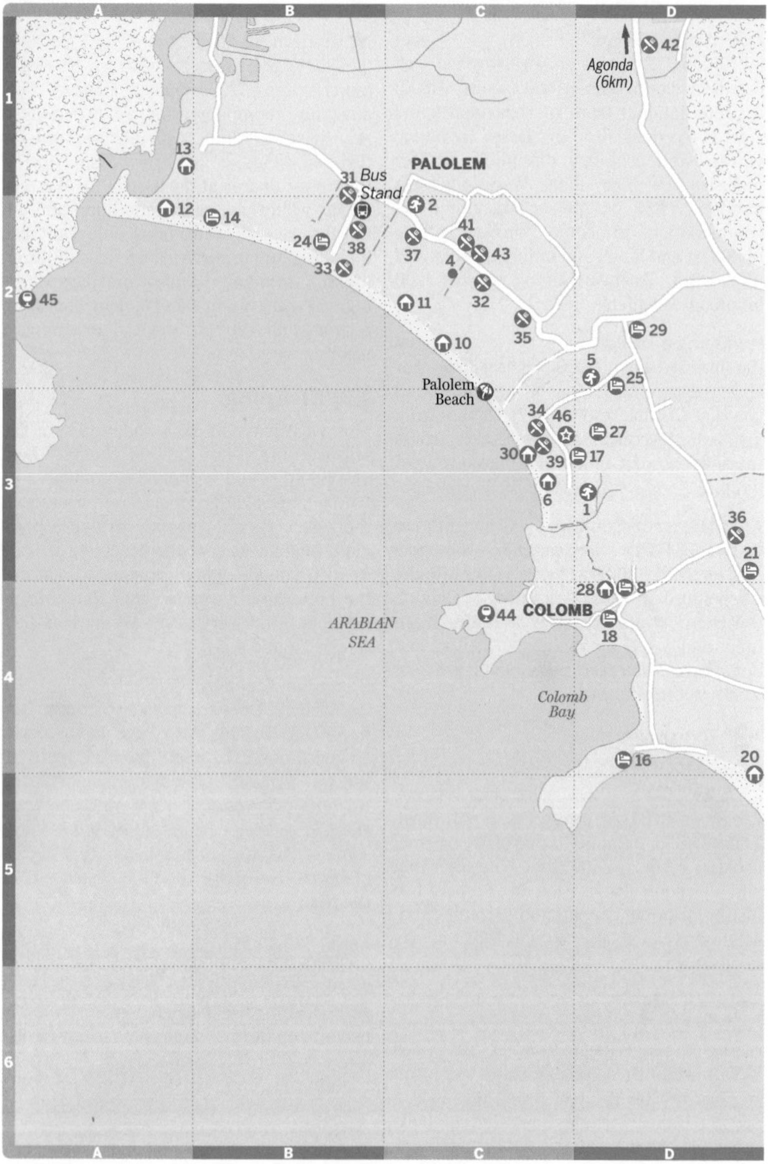

Summer HOSTEL $

(☎0832-2643406; www.thehostelcrowd.com/summerhostel; 99/1 Ourem Rd; dm with/without AC ₹550/450, d ₹1500-1900; ❄📶) The latest offering from the Hostel Crowd is minimalist in design but all the facilities are there, with free breakfast, lockers, communal kitchen and lounge, and the popular Bombay Roasters cafe.

★Cozy Nook HUT $$

(☎9822584760, 9822382799; www.cozynookgoa.com; huts ₹2500-4000) At the northern end of the beach, long-running Cozy Nook is

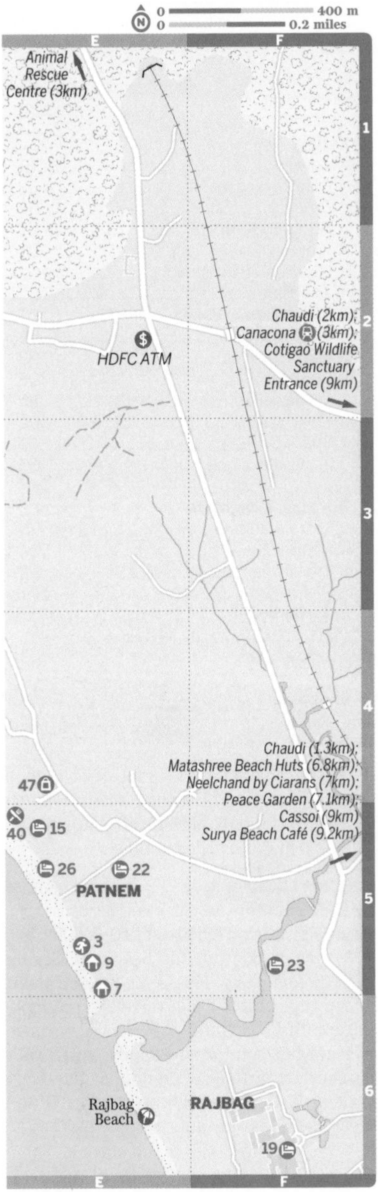

one of Palolem's originals and still builds well-designed cottages including two-storey bamboo pads with Rajasthani touches, chill-out decks, more pedestrian rooms and a bar and restaurant, all among the coconut palms. Yoga and kayak rental available.

★Ciarans HUT **$$**
(☎0832-2643477; www.ciarans.com; huts incl breakfast ₹4200-6300, r with AC ₹5500; ❄📶) Ciarans has some of the most impressive huts on the beachfront. Affable owner John has worked hard over two decades to maintain a high standard and his beautifully designed cottages around a plant-filled garden are top-notch. There's a popular multicuisine restaurant with nightly live music, tapas restaurant and quality massage and spa centre (p185).

Eco-credentials are also good here. Ciarans has a sewerage treatment plant, solar hot water and solar lighting. Ciarans also has fine hut resorts at Talpona and Galgibag beaches.

Kate's Cottages GUESTHOUSE **$$**
(☎9822165261; www.katescottagesgoa.com; Ourem Rd; d ₹4000-5000; ❄📶) The two stunning rooms above Fern's restaurant are beautifully designed with heavy timber finishes, huge four-poster beds, TV, modern bathrooms and views to the ocean from the balcony. There are also a couple of cheaper ground-floor cottages. Jack and Kate are lovely hosts.

La La Land RESORT **$$**
(☎7066129588; www.lalaland.in; cottages ₹4200-8700; ❄📶) On Colomb Bay, La La Land takes Keralan-style cottages to another level with a range of quirky but stylish huts and A-frame chalets all set in a beautiful garden. The latest venture here is an ayurvedic spa and Yoga Land (www.yokoyoga.co.uk) *shalas* set back in the jungle, making this a true retreat.

Dreamcatcher HUT **$$**
(☎9646872700, 9878550550; www.dreamcatcher.in; d huts ₹2500-6800; 📶) One of the largest hut resorts in Palolem, Dreamcatcher's 60-plus sturdy huts are nevertheless secluded, set in a coconut grove just back from the far northern end of the beach. One of the highlights here is the riverside restaurant and cocktail bar, plus the wide range of holistic treatments, massage and yoga on offer, with drop-in yoga and reiki courses available. Access it from the back road running parallel to the beach.

Bhakti Kutir COTTAGE **$$**
(☎9823627258, 0832-2643469; www.bhaktikutir.com; Colomb Bay; cottages ₹2800-4000; @) Ensconced in a thick wooded grove in the Colomb Bay area south of Palolem, Bhakti's rustic cottages are a little worn and you might find yourself sharing with local wildlife but this is still a popular eco and

Palolem

Activities, Courses & Tours

1 Anand Yoga Village D3
2 Aranya Yoga C2
Humming Bird Spa .... (see 11)
3 Kranti Yoga E5
Masala Kitchen .... (see 2)
4 Rahul's Cooking Class C2
5 Seema Bike Hire D2

Sleeping

6 Art Resort C3
7 Bamboo Yoga Retreat E5
8 Bhakti Kutir D4
9 Bougainvillea Patnem E5
10 Camp San Francisco C2
11 Ciarans C2
12 Cozy Nook A2
13 Dreamcatcher A1
14 Fernandes B2
15 Home E5
16 Kala Bahia D4
17 Kate's Cottages D3
18 La La Land D4
19 Lalit Golf & Spa Resort F6
20 Micky's D4
21 Oceanic Hotel D3
22 Palm Trees E5
23 Palm Trees Ayurvedic Heritage F5
24 Palolem Beach Resort B2
25 Palolem Guest House D2
26 Papaya's E5
27 Rainbow Lining D3
28 Sevas D4
29 Summer D2
30 The Nest C3

Eating

31 Café Inn B1
32 Cafe Sussegado C2
33 Dropadi B2
Fern's By Kate's .... (see 17)
34 German Bakery C3
35 Hira Bar & Restaurant C2
Jaali Cafe .... (see 47)
36 Karma Cafe & Bakery D3
37 Little World C2
38 Magic Italy B2
39 Ourem 88 .... C3
40 Salida del Sol E5
41 Shiv Sai C2
42 Space Goa D1
43 Zest Cafe C2

Drinking & Nightlife

Lost Paradise .... (see 44)
44 Neptunes C4
45 Sundowner A2

Entertainment

46 El Diablo - Asian Steakhouse & Movie Bar C3

Shopping

47 Jaali E4

spiritual retreat with an ayurvedic massage centre and daily drop-in yoga classes.

Nest HUT **$$**
(☎9604416142; www.thenestpalolem.com; d ₹1500-2500, with AC ₹5000; ❄📶) This very nifty village of seafront beach huts and restaurant is good value. The best huts have sea views, TV and air-con.

Fernandes COTTAGE **$$**
(☎0832-2643743, 9822151364; www.fernandeswoodenhuts.com; cottages ₹2000-3500; 📶) This smart wooden beach hut operation is one of the most eye-catching on the northern beach strip, offering premium sea-facing cottages and cheaper garden cottages behind a very chilled restaurant. A mellow option on an otherwise quite busy bit of beach.

Palolem Beach Resort RESORT **$$**
(☎9764442775; www.cubagoa.com; r with/without AC ₹4300/3400, cottages ₹5300-6000; ❄📶) The location is handy, on the beachfront at the main road entrance to the beach, but that only contributes to the lack of soul here and the rooms and huts are overpriced and devoid of character. However, it is a good value option in the fringe seasons when it's one of the only beachfront places open. There's a middling restaurant.

Palolem Guest House HOTEL **$$**
(☎0832-2644879; www.palolemguesthouse.com; Ourem Rd; d from ₹2550, with AC ₹3000-5700; ❄📶) Set back from the beach on Ourem Rd, Palolem Guest House has been around a long time and will suit travellers not looking for the beach-hut experience. A range of plain but comfortable rooms, most with air-con, are arranged around a nice leafy garden. It's a short walk to the beach and several good restaurants.

Oceanic Hotel HOTEL **$$**
(☎0832-2643059; www.oceanicgoa.com; d ₹4200-7200; ❄📶🏊) This neat white building, set a fair distance from the beach on the road between Palolem and Patnem, is a popular six-room boutique hotel, made particularly appealing by its swimming pool and patio restaurant, Baa's Kitchen. The standard rooms are compact, the upstairs deluxe ones bigger.

Art Resort HUT $$$
(☎9665982344; www.art-resort-goa.com; Ourem Rd; huts ₹6200-9500; ❄📶) The nicely designed upmarket beachfront cottages around an excellent restaurant have a Bedouin camp feel with screened sit-outs, double storeys and modern artworks sprinkled throughout. The resort hosts art exhibitions and has regular live music.

Eating

Palolem's beach doesn't have the sort of beach-shack restaurants you'll find further north but in season every hut operation lining the beach perimeter has its own restaurant, often with tables and umbrellas plonked down on the sand. They all serve fresh seafood, so just check out a few and find the ambience that suits. A range of restaurants can be found on the beach road and Ourem Rd.

Shiv Sai INDIAN $
(thalis ₹100, mains ₹100-200; ⏲9am-11pm) A thoroughly local lunch joint on the parallel beach road, Shiv Sai serves tasty thalis of the veggie, fish and Gujarati kinds, as well as Goan dishes.

Hira Bar & Restaurant INDIAN $
(breakfast from ₹25; ⏲6am-7.30pm) It looks like something from a Mumbai slum, but a simple *bhaji-pau* (bread with curried vegetables) and a glass of chai is not a bad way to start the day and budget-minded long-termers know it.

★**Magic Italy** ITALIAN $$
(☎8805767705; 260 Palolem Beach Rd; mains ₹260-500; ⏲1-11pm; 📶) On the main beach road, Magic Italy has been around since 1999 and the quality of its pizza and pasta remains high, with imported Italian ingredients like ham, salami, cheese and olive oil, imaginative 13-inch wood-fired pizzas and homemade pasta. Sit at tables, or Arabian-style on floor cushions. The atmosphere is busy but chilled.

Little World VEGETARIAN $$
(☎9887956810; Palolem Beach Rd; mains ₹200-400; ⏲8am-11pm; 📶) Little World is a sweet little vegetarian and vegan cafe with a whole-food philosophy, quirky decor and an inventive menu. Buckwheat pancakes, waffles and scrambled tofu for breakfast, homemade bread and filling salad bowls.

Zest Cafe VEGETARIAN $$
(☎8806607919; www.zestgoa.com; Palolem Beach Rd; mains ₹190-360; ⏲8am-9pm; 📶🌶) Bowls of pad Thai, plates of meze, vegan platters, raw food cakes and soy or almond milkshakes, all freshly prepared, make Zest a popular hang-out among the vegan, health-conscious crowd. There's an almost identical branch in Agonda (p183).

Dropadi INDIAN $$
(mains ₹180-400; ⏲9am-10pm; 📶) Ask locals for their favourite beach restaurant and many will say Dropadi, an ordinary looking place at the main beach entrance. The speciality here is fresh seafood, Goan and pan-Indian cuisine. It's been around long enough to justify its reputation for well-prepared food.

Space Goa CAFE $$
(☎7066067642; www.thespacegoa.com; 261 Devabag; mains ₹180-350; ⏲8.30am-5.30pm; 📶) On the Agonda road, the Space Goa combines an excellent organic whole-food cafe with a gourmet deli, craft shop and a wellness centre offering meditation, acupuncture and other healing treatments. The food is fresh and delicious and the desserts – such as chocolate-beetroot cake – are divine. Drop-in morning yoga classes are ₹500.

Fern's By Kate's GOAN $$
(☎9822165261; Ourem Rd; mains ₹250-450; ⏲8.30am-10.30pm; 📶) On the road running behind the southern beach entrance, this solid timber family-run place serves up excellent authentic Goan food such as local sausages, fish curry rice and shark *amok tik*, along with a wide range of Indian, continental and sizzler dishes. Pizzas are a new addition – one features Goan sausage.

German Bakery BAKERY $$
(Ourem Rd; pastries ₹30-80, mains ₹100-300; ⏲7am-10pm; 📶) Tasty baked treats are the stars at the established Nepali-run German Bakery, but there is also an excellent range of set breakfasts and yummy stuff like yak-cheese croissants, along with Israeli, Chinese, Italian and Indian options. It's set in a peaceful garden festooned with flags.

Café Inn CAFE $$
(☎7507322799; Palolem Beach Rd; mains ₹100-450; ⏲8am-11pm; 📶) If you're craving a strong latte or a rum-infused slushie, Café Inn, which grinds its own blend of coffee beans, is one of Palolem's more popular hang-outs off the beach. Breakfasts are filling, and

comfort-food burgers and panini sandwiches hit the spot. Regular live music and party nights.

Cafe Sussegado CAFE $$
(Palolem Beach Rd; coffees ₹70-100, mains ₹50-350; ⏲6am-10pm) This friendly streetside cafe is a good place for strong morning coffee or a lunchtime thali – the Goan fish thali is ₹250.

★ **Ourem 88** EUROPEAN $$$
(☎8698827679; mains ₹550-800; ⏲6-10pm Tue-Sun) British-run Ourem 88 is a gastronomic sensation. It has just a handful of tables and a small but masterful menu, with changing specials chalked up on the blackboard. Try baked brie, tender calamari stuffed with Goan sausage, braised lamb shank or fluffy soufflé. English roast dinner on Sunday. Worth a splurge.

Drinking & Nightlife

Palolem doesn't party like the northern beaches but it's certainly not devoid of nightlife. Some of the beach bars stay open 24 hours in season, there are silent headphone parties at least once a week and other DJ club nights are organised seasonally. Several beach bars, such as Ciarans, have live music, so you'll find someone playing every night of the week in season.

Leopard Valley CLUB
(www.facebook.com/leopardvalley; Palolem-Agonda Rd; entry from ₹600; ⏲9pm-4am Fri) South Goa's biggest outdoor dance club is a sight (and sound) to behold, with 3D laser light shows, pyrotechnics and state-of-the-art sound systems blasting local and international DJs on Friday nights. It's in an isolated but easily reached (by taxi) location between Palolem and Agonda. Check the Facebook page to see what's on.

Neptunes CLUB
(www.facebook.com/neptunesgoa; Neptune Point, Colomb Bay; ₹800; ⏲9pm-4am Sat Nov-Apr) On a rocky headland just south of Palolem Beach, this was Palolem's only remaining silent disco at the time of writing. Don your headphones and tune into three DJ channels. No entry unless you're dancing.

Lost Paradise CLUB
(Neptune Point, Colomb Bay; ⏲from 4pm Thu) Palolem's latest club/dance event is a day-into-night event, where disco and funk meet house and techno at the popular Neptune Point venue.

Sundowner BAR
(www.sundowner-palolem.com; ⏲9am-midnight; 📶) At the far northern end of the beach, across the narrow estuary (easy to cross at low tide), Sundowner is indeed a cool place to watch the sunset. The seasonal bar is nicely isolated with views across the rocks to forested (and inaccessible) Canacona (Monkey) Island. Also serves pizzas and has a few cottages.

Entertainment

Free movies are shown nightly at a couple of restaurants in Palolem, including **El Diablo** (Ourem Rd; ⏲8pm) FREE on Ourem Rd. As long as you're eating or having a drink you can settle in and enjoy.

Information

Palolem's beach road is lined with travel agencies, internet cafes and places to change money. The nearest ATM is on the road to Chaudi about 1km from the beach entrance; there are several in Chaudi itself.

Getting There & Away

Frequent buses run to nearby Chaudi (₹8) from the **bus stand** (Palolem Beach Rd) on the corner of the road down to the beach. Hourly buses to Margao (₹40, one hour) depart from the same place, though these usually go via Chaudi anyway. From Chaudi you can pick up regular buses to Margao, from where you can change for Panaji, or south to Polem Beach and Karwar in Karnataka.

The closest train station is Canacona, 2km from Palolem's beach entrance.

An autorickshaw from Palolem to Patnem should cost ₹100, or ₹150 to Chaudi. A taxi to Dabolim Airport is around ₹2500, or ₹2000 to Margao.

Getting Around

Scooters and motorbikes can be hired on the main road leading to the beach from around ₹300, or from Seema Bike Hire (p184).

Patnem

Smaller and less crowded than neighbouring Palolem, pretty Patnem makes a much quieter and more family-friendly alternative. The waters aren't as calm and protected as at Palolem, but **Patnem Beach** is patrolled by lifeguards and it's safe for paddling.

The beach is, naturally, lined with shack restaurants and beach-hut operations in season but it has an altogether relaxed vibe, where lazing on the sand or sipping a cocktail is the order of the day. It's easy enough to walk around the northern headland to Colomb Bay and on to Palolem.

Activities & Tours

Kranti Yoga YOGA
(0832-2643007; www.krantiyoga.com) Highly regarded Kranti Yoga offers week-long intensive yoga courses from €569, along with yoga holidays and teacher training courses.

KOKOindia TOURS
(8390470980; www.kokoindia.com) This expat tour agent is based in Patnem and offers bespoke tours all over India but also some interesting day trips from Palolem and Patnem, including the popular KOKO Lunch Club (₹3200), a day trip to the countryside including a five-course lunch at Quepem's Palácio do Deão.

Sleeping

Patnem has a fairly consistent range of a dozen or so seasonal beach huts and a few hotels back from the beach.

Long-stayers will revel in Patnem's choice of village homes and apartments available for rent from ₹15,000 to ₹50,000 per month.

Micky's HUT $$
(9850484884; www.mickyhuts.com; d ₹1500-2000;) Micky's is an old-timer at the north end of Patnem Beach with a range of simple budget huts and rooms. It's run by a friendly family and open for most of the year. There's a cruisey beachfront bar and cafe among the palms.

Kala Bahia GUESTHOUSE $$
(9764863073; www.kalabahia.com; r ₹3100-4300; restaurant 8am-10pm Mon-Sat, to 4pm Sun;) At the northern end of Patnem Beach (reached by road via Colomb), Kala Bahia is a sweet guesthouse, veg restaurant and something of an event centre, with yoga, music and movie nights. Cocktails and sunset views looking back down on Patnem Beach are fabulous. Rooms are secure and comfortable and there are a few cabins.

Palm Trees Ayurvedic Heritage RESORT $$
(9673178731; www.thepalmtreesayurvedagoa.com; huts ₹5300-6800;) This ayurvedic resort has an exquisite riverside location in a thick palm grove at the southern end of Patnem village (access from Patnem–Rajbag road).

Bougainvillea Patnem HUT $$
(9822189913; www.bougainvilleapatnem.com; huts ₹2000-3500;) Simple but clean and good value rooms behind the restaurant as well as the few premium sea-facing huts at the front. Yoga retreats and drop-in classes and ayurvedic treatments available.

Palm Trees COTTAGE $$
(9673178731; www.thepalmtreesgoa.com; Patnem Beach Rd; cottages ₹2000-2800;) The 10 Keralan-style cottages here are a step up from most beach-hut accommodation – and a few steps back from the beach – with imported bamboo and palm-thatch materials from Kerala and thoughtful furniture and artworks. It's all set in a serene garden on the main road to the beach.

Papaya's COTTAGE $$
(9923079447; www.papayasgoa.com; huts ₹2000-3000, cottages with AC ₹4500;) Solid huts constructed with natural materials head back into the palm grove from Papaya's popular restaurant. These are easily some of the best cabins and rooms on Patnem Beach: each hut is lovingly built, with lots of wood, four-poster beds and floating muslin, while the one and two-bedroom air-con brick cottages are fitted out like apartments.

Home GUESTHOUSE $$
(9923944676; www.homebeachresort.com; r ₹2000-3500; 8am-10pm;) Home is a lovely family-owned guesthouse-style resort with a popular beachfront restaurant serving awesome dessert – chocolate brownies, apple tarts and cheesecake. No beach huts here but eight neatly decorated, light-filled rooms behind the restaurant and some larger family rooms around the garden at the street entrance. Minimum two-night stay.

Bamboo Yoga Retreat HUT $$$
(9637567730; www.bamboo-yoga-retreat.com; cottages per person €82-92;) This laid-back yoga retreat, exclusive to guests, has a wonderful open-sided *shala* facing the ocean at the southern end of Patnem Beach, and three more *shalas* among the village of beautifully designed timber and thatched huts. Yoga holiday rates include brunch, meditation and two daily yoga classes, but there are also training courses and ayurvedic treatments.

Eating

★**Karma Cafe & Bakery** CAFE $
(9764504253; Patnem Rd, Colomb; baked goods from ₹60, mains ₹120-230; 6.30am-9.30pm;

) Pull up a cushion at this chilled cafe and bakery opposite the Colomb road and delve into a superb range of freshly baked breads, croissants and pastries as well as coffee and smoothies. Delve further for *momos*, Nepali thalis and even Vietnamese rice paper rolls.

★ Jaali Cafe CAFE $$
(8007712248; small plates ₹180-220; 9am-6pm Tue, to 11pm Wed-Sun) The menu at this lovely garden cafe is something special, with a delicious range of tapas-style Middle Eastern and Mediterranean plates – choose two or three dishes each and share. Sunday brunch is a stellar event popular with local expats. There's also an excellent boutique and a highly regarded massage therapist on hand.

Salida del Sol MULTICUISINE $$
(7507404102; www.salida-patnembeach.com; mains ₹180-390; 8am-11pm;) Patnem's beachfront restaurants all have their own qualities and followings and Salida del Sol works on many fronts, from the friendly and attentive staff to fresh food and Arabian Nights atmosphere. Standouts are the *momos* and Nepali set meals but, of course, there's also Indian and Western food including pizza and pasta. Nice huts in the garden at the back, too.

Shopping

Jaali FASHION & ACCESSORIES
(8007712248; 9.30am-6.30pm Nov-Apr) This small boutique shop back from Patnem Beach stocks handicrafts, textiles, antiques and clothing sourced from all over India by the expat owner, as well as locally made pieces. Individual, hand-picked and interesting stuff.

Getting There & Away

The main entrance to Patnem Beach is reached from the country lane running south from Palolem, then turning right at the Hotel Sea View. Alternatively, walk about 20 minutes along the path from Palolem via Colomb Bay, or catch a bus heading south (₹5). An autorickshaw charges around ₹80 from Palolem.

Rajbag

Quiet little Rajbag is a small sandy cove, one beach south from Patnem and accessible both by road and via a nice short walk around the headland from Patnem Beach, clambering across the rocks along the way. The beach lacks any real character since the perimeter of the five-star Lalit takes up part of it, and treacherous undertows can make swimming dangerous.

Though dominated by the resort, Rajbag is a nice enough place to linger on the sands, and is usually quite quiet. The main street in the village has a growing collection of shops and eateries.

Sleeping

A number of locals have apartments and houses geared to long-stayers up for grabs in Rajbag; ask around for leads.

Lalit Golf & Spa Resort HOTEL $$$
(0832-2667777; www.thelalit.com; ste ₹16,000-20,000, villas from ₹140,000;) Rajbag is dominated by the presence of this 85-acre five-star. The hotel is particularly popular with well-heeled domestic and Russian tourists, and is notable for having Goa's only championship nine-hole golf course (nonguests ₹1550 for 18 holes), a helipad and the Rejuve Spa. The lagoon swimming pool will probably make you forget there's an ocean outside. Look out for the small Hindu temple to the left of the entrance – local pressure forced the developers to build around it rather than move it.

Getting There & Away

Rajbag village is only around 400m south of the Chaudi-Patnem Rd; get off where the highway bypass is being constructed and walk, or walk around the headland from Patnem Beach. A taxi/autorickshaw from Palolem should cost ₹150/100.

Galgibag & Talpona

Galgibag and Talpona form another of South Goa's beach gems – a broad stretch of barely touched sand framed by the Talpona River in the north and the Galgibag River to the south, all backed by swaying pines and palms. In terms of the number of people here, this is what Palolem was like 20 years ago! The only disruption to this peace is the construction of the new highway bypass, though it's far enough back from the beach to be ignored.

Near the southern end, 'Turtle Beach' is where rare, long-lived olive ridley sea turtles come to nest on the beach between November and March. This is a protected area: a

GOA'S FORTS

Goa has several surviving colonial forts that have stood watch for several centuries over strategically important estuaries. Built by the Portuguese (but frequently on the sites of older defensive structures) soon after their 16th-century arrival into Goa, the forts were made of locally mined laterite, a red and porous stone that proved, in most instances, a good match for the forces pitted against it.

Under the supervision of Italian architect Fillipo Terzi, the Portuguese developed their Goan bastions to be able to withstand the forces of gunpowder and cannonballs. Inside the strong fort walls, the buildings were often carved directly out of the stone itself, with storerooms for supplies and weaponry connected by a maze of subterranean tunnels. Sometimes these tunnels led down as far as the sea itself to supply the forts during any lengthy times of siege.

Though the forts were made to withstand attacks from the sea by Portugal's main trade rivals, the Dutch and the British, they were never the sites of full-scale warfare, and as the threat of maritime invasion slowly faded during the 18th and 19th centuries, most forts fell into disrepair. Some, such as Cabo da Rama (p179), Reis Magos (p123) and Fort Aguada (p125), found favour as prisons, while others became army garrisons or plundering sites for building materials. Today they're atmospheric relics of a bygone age, with the advantage of some picture-perfect views down over the coast they once guarded so closely.

Forest Department information hut here should be staffed during nesting season.

Undertows and currents can be strong here, so although lifeguards are stationed at either end, swimming out of your depth is not recommended.

Sleeping & Eating

There's a growing number of guesthouses and beach huts at Galgibag and Talpona, but it's all very low-key.

Matashree Beach Huts HUT $
(9823609183; matashreebeachhuts@gmail.com; Talpona Beach; huts ₹1500;) The budget offering on Talpona Beach, Matashree has 10 basic lime-green huts on the beach, with bathroom and fan. A bargain for the location.

Neelchand by Ciarans HUT $$
(7796783663, 0832-2632082; www.neelchand.com; Talpona Beach; cottages ₹4000;) The Ciarans magic from Palolem has been transported to an absolute beachfront location on near-deserted Talpona Beach. There are just seven lovely timber cottages (five with air-con) in a sweet little garden strewn with hammocks and flowering plants. There's a beachfront restaurant and bar but this is a place for peace rather than partying.

Cassoi HUT $$
(7796456453; www.cassoibyciarans.com; Galgibag Beach; huts & tents ₹3000-5000;) Woven into the palms on peaceful Galgibag Beach, this hut village has something for everyone with Rajasthani safari tents, round African-style huts, double-storey boat-shaped huts and air-con rooms in a house, all in an intimate garden. All the ecofriendly attention to detail is there and the restaurant serves great veg and nonveg food. Cassoi means 'turtle'.

Peace Garden HUT $$
(9168350727; www.peacegardengoa.com; Talpona Beach; huts ₹2100-4800;) Peace Garden is a well-constructed hut village on Talpona Beach with a focus on wellness and relaxation – there are drop-in yoga classes (₹500) daily, yoga holidays and massage and ayurvedic therapies. Accommodation ranges from garden cottages at the back to family cottages and the deluxe sea-facing huts, all with attached bathroom and fan.

Surya Beach Café SEAFOOD $$
(9923155396; Galgibag Beach; mains ₹200-350; 9am-10pm) Surya Beach Café, nestled at Galgibag's southern end in the pine trees, specialises in fresh oysters, clams, mussels and crabs caught from the Galgibag River. Surya himself will show you the live catch and prepare it 'rava' fried or spicy Goan-style. It's a simple place, but they claim that celebrity chef Gordon Ramsay has dined here and recommended it. Surya also has two rooms (₹3500) for rent.

WORTH A TRIP

TANSHIKAR SPICE FARM

One of the best day trips you can make away from the coast in Goa's far south is the winding 35km drive to the village of Netravali in search of an excellent spice farm, the mysterious bubble lake and jungle treks to hidden waterfalls. The ride out from Palolem alone makes this trip worthwhile, passing farms then the hilly forest of the Netravali Protected Area.

Tanshikar Spice Farm (☎9421184114, 0832-2608358; www.tanshikarspicefarm.com; Netravali; tours incl lunch ₹500; ⏰10am-4pm) is a working, family-run organic spice farm with crops including vanilla, cashews, pepper, nutmeg and chillies, as well as beekeeping. There are no tour buses out here and the amiable young owners give you personalised tours of the plantation and nearby bubble lake. They can also offer guided jungle treks to nearby waterfalls. If you really want to feel the serenity, book into one of the excellent mud-walled eco-cottages (₹1500) with bamboo sit-outs, a lovely elevated stilt tree house (₹3000) or a room in the Hindu-style house.

Near the spice farm (about 500m before the T-junction), the **Netravali Bubble Lake** is actually the bathing tank of the small Hindu Gopinath temple. Tiny streams of bubbles constantly bob up to the lake's surface, appearing to get faster if you clap your hands close to the water. The cause is trapped methane gas escaping from the sandy bottom. Eyeing the temple and tank as a tourist attraction, the local authorities brought the bulldozers in and built a parking lot around it.

The other highlight of a day trip out here is the series of **waterfalls** that can be reached by jungle hikes. Treks to the falls vary from 45 minute to three hours. Ask for directions or a guide at Tanshikar Spice Farm.

From Palolem or Chaudi on the NH66, turn off at the Forest Checkpoint on the left-hand side (before Cotiago Sanctuary) and follow the road for about 30km to the T-junction, turn right and look out for the signs to Tanshikar.

Santosh Family Beach Restaurant SEAFOOD $$
(Galgibag Beach; mains ₹150-400; 📶) At the end of the road near the Galgibag River, Santosh is a family-run place back from the beach specialising in locally caught seafood but offering the usual veg and nonveg menu. Not to be outdone by it's neighbour, Santosh claims to be recommended by Jamie Oliver.

ℹ Getting There & Away

With your own transport, getting to Talpona and Galgibag is half the fun. From Palolem or Chaudi, a wonderfully scenic back road follows the Talpona River then skirts behind the beach to Galgibag. From here you can continue along the Galgibag River to join up with NH66 at Poinguinum. Note that the new national highway bypass runs through this area.

Polem

In the very far south of the state, 25km south of Palolem and a couple of kilometres from the Karnataka border, Polem Beach is set around a small bay on the seafront of the tiny village of Polem. With no beach shacks or development of note, it has a real castaway feel, pristine, litter-free sand and a beautiful view of a cluster of rocky islands out towards the horizon. There's one family-run place to stay and eat on the beach, but otherwise it retains a local feel, with a few fishers bringing in their catch to the northern end and nothing much else to keep you company except scuttling crabs and circling seabirds.

Kamaxi Beach Resort (☎9141615846, 9341367429; www.kamaxibeachresort.com; cottages ₹2000, d ₹1500, without bathroom ₹1000, with AC ₹3500; ❄), the sole place to stay in Polem, has some pretty earthy rooms but you're paying for the seclusion, and the friendly brothers work hard at keeping the place clean and very low-key. Basic wooden huts are at the southern end of the beach and simple rooms in a pair of buildings at the northern beach entrance. A basic restaurant serves fresh seafood and cold drinks.

ℹ Getting There & Away

To get to Polem, take a bus from Chaudi (₹30, 50 minutes) towards Karwar and get off at the Polem bus stop, around 3km after the petrol station. The stop is directly opposite the turn-off to the beach, then it's a 1km walk to the village and beach. An easier option is to hire a motorbike in Palolem.

Beyond Goa

The most popular interstate excursion from South Goa is into Karnataka to the holy town and hippie beaches of Gokarna, around 50km from the border.

Gokarna

08386 / POP 29,200

A regular nominee among travellers' favourite beaches in India, Gokarna attracts a crowd for a low-key, chilled-out beach holiday and not for full-scale parties. Most accommodation is in thatched bamboo huts along the town's several stretches of blissful coast.

In fact there are two Gokarnas. For most Indian visitors Gokarna is a sacred pilgrimage town of ancient temples that are the focus of important festivals such as **Shivaratri** (Feb/Mar) and **Ganesh Chaturthi** (Sep). International travellers flock to the 'other' Gokarna: a succession of ravishing sandy beaches south of town.

Sights

This is a deeply holy town and foreigners should be respectful in and around its many temples: do not try to enter their inner sanctums, which are reserved for Hindus only. It's customary for pilgrims to bathe in the sea and fast, and many shave their heads, before entering Gokarna's holy places.

The best beaches are due south of Gokarna town: first, Kudle Beach (5km by road from Gokarna), then Om Beach (6km by road). Well hidden away south of Om Beach lie the small, sandy coves of Half Moon Bay and Paradise Beach, which don't have road access. A lovely coastal trail links all the beaches, but as there have been (very occasional) reports of muggings, it's probably best not to walk it alone.

★**Mahabaleshwara Temple** HINDU TEMPLE
(Car St; 6am-8.30pm) This is a profoundly spiritual temple, built of granite by Mayurasharma of the Kadamba dynasty and said to date to the 4th century. It's dedicated to Lord Shiva. Hindus believe it brings blessings to pilgrims who even glimpse it, and rituals are performed here for the deceased. A *gopuram* (gateway tower) dominates the complex, while inside a stone statue of Nandi (Shiva's bull) faces the inner chamber, home to Shiva's lingam. Foreigners may enter the complex but not the inner sanctum.

★**Mahaganapati Temple** HINDU TEMPLE
(Car St; 6am-8.30pm) Deeply atmospheric temple complex, encircled by lanes but peaceful inside. Here there's a (rare) stone statue of an upright, standing Ganesh, said to be over 1500 years old, who is depicted with a flat head - said to mark the spot where the demon Ravana struck him. This is the second-most holy site in Gokarna and it's customary for pilgrims to visit here first before heading to the neighbouring Mahabaleshwara Temple. Foreigners are not allowed inside the inner sanctum.

Activities

Cocopelli Surf School SURFING
(8105764969; www.cocopelli.org; Gokarna Beach; lessons per person ₹2000, board rental per 2hr ₹750; mid-Oct–May) This reputable surf school offers lessons by internationally certified instructors. It also rents boards and kayaks.

Shankar Prasad YOGA
(08386-256971; www.shankarprasad.org.in; Bankikodla Village) A beautiful ashram in a century-old heritage house, set in huge grounds dotted with coconut palms. Weekly and monthly courses of yoga are well structured and good value; teacher training (200 hours costs from ₹59,000 including full board) is also offered. Accommodation is in dorms or private rooms. It's 5km north of Gokarna town.

Sleeping

Nirvana Café GUESTHOUSE $
(9742466481, 8386257401; suresh.nirvana@gmail.com; Om Beach; cottages ₹750-1200;) These attractive cottages, towards the eastern end of the beach, are some of Om's best, all with front porches that face a slim central garden. You'll find a good beachfront restaurant, a laundry and a travel agency.

Zostel Gokarna HOSTEL $
(in Dehli 011-39589002; www.zostel.com; Kudle Beach Rd; dm/cottages ₹800/2600;) Some of the best dorms in Karnataka, with AC, lockers and sea views, await at this efficiently managed hostel. The cottages are also very inviting, perfect for couples, and there are cool common rooms and a restaurant. Located a 10-minute walk from Gokarna town, or a bit further away from Kudle Beach.

Arya Ayurvedic Panchakarma Centre SPA HOTEL $$

(☎9611062468; www.ayurvedainindien.com; Kudle Beach; r from ₹1900; ❄📶) At the southern end of **Kudle**, this ayurvedic centre has some of the best rooms on the beach. It offers simple yet elegant accommodation with quality furnishings a few steps from the shore. Priority is given to those booking ayurvedic packages. There's a fine in-house cafe.

White Elephant GUESTHOUSE $$

(Arnav Cottages; ☎7090332555; http://whiteelephanthampi.com; cottages ₹2000-3000; ❄📶) Well-constructed, spacious cottages and fine sea views are the main draws at this established place (previously called Arnav) above Kudle Beach. It's run by hospitable folk and there's an elevated deck perfect for yoga.

★**SwaSwara** HOTEL $$$

(☎08386-257132; www.swaswara.com; s/d 5 nights from €1780/2390; ❄@📶🏊) 'Journeying into the self' is the mantra at SwaSwara and you certainly have the infrastructure to achieve that here, as this is one of South India's finest retreats. Yoga, ayurvedic treatments, a meditation dome, and elegant private villas with open-sky showers and lovely sitting areas await. No short stays are possible. It's inland from Om Beach.

Eating

In Gokarna town it's all about Indian food. On the beach most places offer (over-) long menus taking in seafood, curries, Italian and Israeli food.

★**Prema** INDIAN $

(Gokarna Beach Rd; mains ₹100-200; ⏰8am-10pm) Always packed, this humble-looking place has a prime location just before the town beach. It offers Western food, but it's best to stick to the South or North Indian classics. Finish your meal with a rose or coconut ice cream (₹15).

Sunset Point INDIAN $

(Om Beach; mains ₹120-200; ⏰7.30am-10pm) Family-run place at the eastern end of Om Beach with a great perch overlooking the waves. The long menu takes in breakfasts, sandwiches, and Indian and Chinese dishes; grilled prawns are around ₹200.

Chez Christophe FRENCH $$

(☎9901459736; www.facebook.com/chezchristoff; Gokarna Town Beach; mains from ₹150; ⏰Nov-May; 📶) For a very different vibe, stroll up the shore to this chilled French place, a 10-minute walk north from the main section of beach. You'll find authentic salads, fresh pasta, French desserts and wine by the glass. There's low seating, beach swings, and live music some nights.

Arya Ayurvedic Panchakarma Centre INDIAN $$

(www.ayurvedainindien.com; Kudle Beach; mains ₹130-220; ⏰8am-10pm; 📶) Modish beachfront restaurant that boasts an open kitchen and a fine menu of vegetarian dishes freshly prepared using ayurvedic principles.

Getting There & Away

BUS

Local and private buses depart daily to Bengaluru (₹510 to ₹724, 12 hours) and Mysuru (from ₹578, 12 hours), as well as Mangaluru (from ₹266, 6½ hours) and Hubballi (₹198, four hours).

For Hampi, **Paulo Travels** (☎08394-225867; www.paulobus.com) is a popular choice (November to April only); its buses head via Hosapete (fan/AC ₹1400/1650, nine hours). Note that if you're coming from Hampi, you'll be dropped at Ankola, from where there's a free transfer for the 26km journey to Gokarna.

There are also regular buses to Panaji (Panjim; ₹135, three hours) and Mumbai (₹768 to ₹1035, 12 hours).

TRAIN

Many express trains stop at Gokarna Rd station, 9km from town. There are other options from Ankola, 26km away. Hotels and travel agencies in Gokarna can book tickets.

Of the three daily trains to Mangaluru the 3.12pm Bengalaru Express (sleeper/2AC ₹235/780, 5½ hours) is the most convenient. Heading to Margoa (Madgaon) there are three daily trains; the 8.42am (sleeper/2AC ₹170/745, 2½ hours) continues on to Mumbai (sleeper/2AC ₹460/1750, 12 hours).

Autorickshaws charge ₹230 to go to Gokarna Rd station (₹450 to Ankola); a bus from Gokarna town charges ₹30 and leaves every 30 minutes.

Understand Goa & Mumbai

Goa Today

Growth is the buzz word in Goa right now. You can see it in visitor numbers, infrastructure projects, housing prices and the increasing interest being shown by outside developers. Politically Goa might not match the more powerful Indian states, but Goa's tourism rupee – both foreign and domestic – is far from underestimated and, for better or worse, much of Goa's population relies more than ever on the annual influx of holidaying visitors. The question is: how much is too much?

Best in Print

Shantaram (Gregory David Roberts; 2003) Gripping tale of a fugitive in Mumbai, with Goa featuring.

Goa and the Blue Mountains (Richard Burton; 1851) Classic account of Goa.

Goa Traffic (Marissa de Luna; 2011) Thriller set in Goa's party scene.

Reflected in Water: Writings on Goa (Jerry Pinto; 2006) Collected writings by literary luminaries.

Houses of Goa (Pandit/Mascarenhas; 1999) Beautifully illustrated book on Goa's mansions.

Goa Freaks: My Hippie Years in India (Cleo Odzer; 1995) A disturbing tale of the drug-crazed, hippie 'freak' days of the 1960s and '70s, by one who lived it.

Best on Film

Baga Beach (2013) Tackles tricky subjects such as the seedy side of tourism, migrants in Goa and child sexual abuse.

Dum Maaro Dum (2011) This hit crime-thriller proved controversial in Goa for just one line: 'Over here, liquor is cheap but women are even cheaper'.

My Brother...Nikhil (2005) Set in Goa in the late 1980s this film explores the sensitive themes of HIV and homosexuality.

Goa (2015) Romantic comedy set in Goa and starring British actress Rachel Wise.

The Tourism Factor

Goa was a solitary Portuguese outpost in India for more than 450 years and the influence of colonial rule can still be seen everywhere: in the exquisite, crumbling architecture; in the East-meets-West cuisine; and in the siesta-saturated joie de vivre that Goans themselves call *susegad*.

Western travellers, hippies, freaks and backpackers have been dropping into Goa since the 1960s but in the past decade the tourism landscape has changed radically, with domestic tourists far outweighing foreign tourists and the overall industry adapting and developing as a result. It's fair to say the growth in tourism in the past five years has surprised even the locals. In 1985, total tourist arrivals were just a tick over 775,000; in 2013 it was over 3.12 million and in 2017 there were 7.79 million visitors – more than doubling in just five years. Of these, only 890,000 were foreign tourists, about 55% of whom were Russian and 19% from the UK.

Young male Indian tourists, singles, couples and families, often middle class with disposable incomes, are now making Goa their holiday destination of choice. While most tourism operators rely on the brief November to February tourist trade, domestic tourists are increasingly visiting in the summer (monsoon) season and weekends are now considered high season at virtually any time of year.

All of this is generally good news for those involved in a saturated tourist trade and for the state's GDP, but a little bemusing for the rest of the population who deal with the annual invasion and the overstretching of precious resources.

Infrastructure Boom

The increasing traffic into and out of Goa and the importance of Mormugao as a seaport has inevitably led to a construction boom. A new greenfield international airport is expected to open at Mopa (North Goa) in 2020, and years of road and bridge construction should also be operational, at least in part, by 2020 – a four to six-lane national highway bypass that could cut north-south travel time to under an hour.

New hotels and resorts are going up across the coastal belt but locals complain that basic infrastructure – water, power, local roads – is struggling to meet the demands, especially in the Candolim-Calangute-Baga belt.

The Darker Side

Despite its charms Goa is not a perfect paradise. The state's large homeless population is mostly made up of migrants from Karnataka and Maharashtra, driven from their homes by water shortages and lured to Goa's coast hoping life will treat them more kindly. Almost inevitably, it doesn't. Locals also complain of uncontrolled foreign investment with wealthy buyers snapping up prime real estate, and 'mafia-run' businesses paying off corrupt authorities leading to some legitimate businesses being denied licences or rental space.

Meanwhile Goa suffers from a sorely stressed environment, burdened by the effects of logging, iron-ore mining, relentlessly expanding tourism and uncontrolled industrial growth. Rare turtle eggs have traditionally been considered a delicacy but are now precariously protected on increasingly busy beaches, plastic bottles pile up, and vagrant cows feast on refuse from noisome rubbish bins.

Poverty, prostitution, a shady underworld drugs trade, violent crime, including assaults and murders of tourists, and police corruption also remain pressing issues.

Looking to the Future

Goa enjoys one of India's highest per-capita incomes and comparatively high health and literacy rates, factors which attract migrants and traders from other parts of India. Goa's active economy has given rise to a healthy gross domestic product of around US$11 billion annually.

Enterprising locals are slowly leading the way toward to a cleaner, more sustainable future, instigating local recycling initiatives, volunteering on turtle-egg protection duties, or working with local green organisations, such as the Goa Foundation, on campaigns such as stopping illegal mining. Such efforts, along with luck, persistence and political will, may ensure Goa's charms retain their place on travel itineraries for centuries to come.

POPULATION: **1.8 MILLION**

AREA: **3700 SQ KM**

TOURIST ARRIVALS: **TOTAL 7.79 MILLION; FOREIGNERS 890,459 (2017)**

LITERACY RATE: **GOA 87%; NATIONAL AVERAGE 74%**

if Goa were 100 people

62 would be urban dwellers
38 would be rural dwellers

belief systems

(% of population)

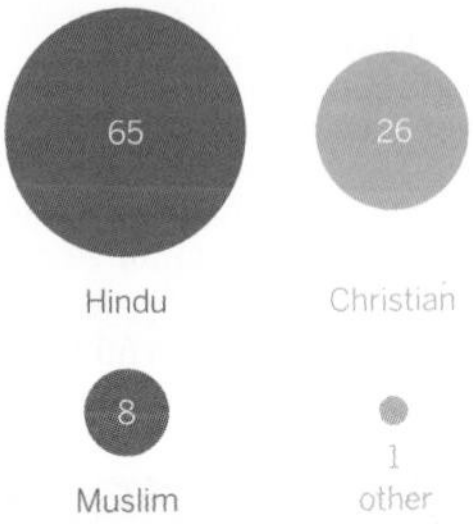

population per sq km

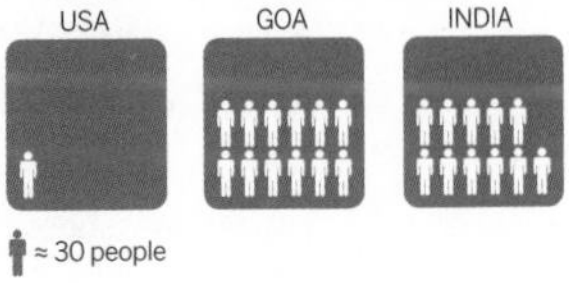

History

Goa has been through a dizzying array of rulers from Ashoka's Mauryan empire in the 3rd century BC to the long-ruling Kadambas from the 3rd century AD, and the Hindu Vijayanagar empire to the Adil Shahs of Bijapur in the 15th century. But it was the arrival of the Portuguese in 1510 that changed the course of Goan history, religion and culture forever. The 450-year Portuguese occupation only came to an end in 1961 when they were ousted by the Indian Army.

Prehistoric Beginnings

According to Hindu legend, Goa was created by Parasurama, the sixth incarnation of the Hindu god Vishnu, who shot an arrow into the Arabian Sea and commanded the tide to retreat, to create a peaceful spot for his Brahmin caste to live.

A trip out into the Goan hinterland, however, to the riverside rock carvings of Usgalimal offers an alternative picture of the first Goans, hunter-gatherer tribes who inhabited the hinterland sometime between 100,000 BC and 10,000 BC. No one really knows where they originally came from; some believe they were migrants from Africa, others that they hailed from eastern Asia, or were a northern tribe forced southwards by instability in their homeland.

Head out to remote Usgalimal in South Goa to examine the petroglyphs (rock art), including images of a peacock and a dancing woman inscribed into the laterite river rocks by the earliest Goans.

Early Wranglings

In the 3rd century BC Goa became part of the mighty Buddhist Mauryan empire. Ashoka, probably the greatest Mauryan emperor, sent a Buddhist missionary to convert the locals; the monk set up shop in a rock-cut cave near modern-day Zambaulim, preaching nonviolence and urging the tribes to give up their nasty habit of blood sacrifice. Though he had some success, introducing the plough and spreading literacy, his liturgy fell largely on deaf ears, and following the rapid demise of the Mauryans after the death of Ashoka in 232 BC, Goa turned to Hinduism, commingled with its old tribal practices.

The next seven centuries saw Goa ruled from afar by a succession of powerful Hindu trading dynasties, which sent Goan goods and spices to

TIMELINE

2400–700 BC

Goa experiences at least two waves of Aryan immigration from the north, bringing with them improved farming techniques and the first elements of what would become Hinduism.

AD 420

Goa's home-grown Hindu rulers, the Kadambas, rise to power over their distant overlords, and install their own royal family, ushering in a period of religious tolerance, prosperity and innovation.

1054

Goa's capital shifts from Chandrapur (modern-day Chandor) to Govepuri (now Goa Velha). Wealth and trade skyrocket, with locals building vast homes and places of worship with the profits from the spice trade.

Africa, the Middle East and Rome. However, continued wrangling between these dynasties offered the opportunity for a homespun dynasty to quietly emerge: in AD 420 the local Kadamba clan declared independence, and created their very own 'royal family'.

Kadamba Prosperity

Under the Kadamba royal family, Goa finally had some stability. By the late 6th century, the Kadambas had found their stride, and in contrast with what was to come, the Kadamba rule was a period of tolerance. Muslim merchants from Arabia and East Africa were encouraged to settle, Hindu temples were constructed statewide and prestigious academic institutions were inaugurated.

Yet, like all good things, it was not to last. The success of the Kadambas signalled their own downfall, as Muslim Bahmani sultans from the Deccan in South India, keen on getting their hands on Kadamba wealth, began pouring into Goa from the 10th century onwards. Today, the sole Kadamba structure to survive the troubled years to follow is the melancholy Tambdi Surla Mahadeva temple, saved from a grisly fate only by its remote jungle location.

In 1352 the Bahmanis triumphed, and years of religious tolerance were brought to an abrupt and painful end. The new rulers immediately set about a harsh regime of Hindu persecution, destroying the grand Kadamba temples and killing their priests. They reigned intermittently, ousted by rival kingdoms from time to time, until the late 1400s, when a force far bigger than their own was to sail merrily over the horizon.

The 'Inquisition Table', around which sat its dreaded interrogators, is now housed at the Goa State Museum in Panaji. A crucifix that once stared down, with open eyes, at the Inquisitors' victims, now also lives in Panaji, at the Chapel of St Sebastian.

The Portuguese Arrive

In 1498 Vasco da Gama, a Portuguese sea captain, landed south of Goa at Calicut (present-day Kozhikode) on the Malabar Coast, 'seeking Christians and spices', with a view to superseding the Arab monopoly of the overland spice trade. He didn't have much luck finding Christians, but there were certainly spices in abundance.

However, it was to take 50 years of Muslim-Christian fighting before Portugal was able to claim those spices as its own, establishing firm territorial borders in Goa – now known as the Velhas Conquistas (Old Conquests) – that stretched from Chapora Fort in the north to Cabo da Rama Fort in the south.

The Inquisition Arrives

Initially, Portugal's approach to its new subjects was relatively enlightened: Hindus were considered friends against Portugal's Muslim foe, and 'conversion' was largely confined to allowing Portuguese soldiers to marry local women, so that their children would be raised Christian.

1352

After suffering three centuries of Muslim raids, Goa comes under the rule of Muslim Bahmanis and almost all trace of the Kadambas' Hindu legacy is quickly destroyed, except for the Tambdi Surla Mahadeva temple.

1498

Portuguese captain Vasco da Gama arrives in Goa, making him the first European to reach India via the Cape of Good Hope. The Portuguese hope this will allow them to dominate Eastern trade routes.

1534

Portugal gains the islands that form modern-day Mumbai from the Muslim sultans of Gujarat. They name the area 'Bom Bahia'. A century later, the British government takes possession.

1543

Goa's Muslim sultan cedes areas of Goa to Portugal, to stop it from supporting a rival contender for the throne. Portugal now owns land from Chapora Fort in the north to Cabo da Rama Fort in the south.

But in 1532 Goa's first Vicar General arrived, and the age of tolerance was over. Increasingly stringent laws were passed to forbid Hindu worship, and to allow only Christians rights to land. Then, in 1560, the terrifying Portuguese Tribunal of the Holy Office – otherwise known as the Goan Inquisition – came to Goa.

Establishing itself at the old sultan's palace in what is now Old Goa, the tribunal soon began flexing its ecclesiastical muscles, but astonishingly the subsequent two centuries of Portuguese religious terrorism failed to completely eradicate Hinduism from Goa. Many Hindus fled across the Mandovi River, into the region around modern-day Ponda, smuggling their religious statuaries to safety and secretly building temples to house them.

GOAN HOUSE OF HORRORS

Of all Portugal's alleged abuses of its Goan subjects, the terrors to which the population was subjected to under the iron rule of the Inquisition – also known as the Holy Office or Santo Officio – were undoubtedly the worst.

The Inquisition was dispatched to Goa on royal command, originally conceived to target 'New Christians' (Cristianos Nuevos), the forcibly converted Jews and Muslims of Portugal who had fled to the country's colonies and 'lapsed' back to their original faiths. By the time the Inquisition arrived, life was already becoming increasingly difficult for the region's Hindus, who for some years had been enduring a slowly eroding official tolerance to their faith. Idols had already been banned, temples closed and priests banished. Now, with the arrival of the Inquisitors, matters went from bad to worse: refusing to eat pork became a crime punishable by imprisonment, as was possession of turmeric, incense and other items used in traditional Hindu worship.

Once a 'confession' of heresy had been extracted, the prisoner then languished in a windowless cell, awaiting one of the Inquisition's famous *autos-da-fé* (trials of faith). During these morbidly theatrical 'trials', dozens of prisoners, dressed in tall mitres and robes emblazoned with macabre images of human beings engulfed in flames, would be marched across the city of Old Goa, from the Palace of the Inquisition to the Church of St Francis of Assisi, amid crowds of onlookers and to the solemn tolling of the Sé Cathedral bell.

The luckiest ones were to endure slavery abroad. Victims who refused to recant their 'heresy' were usually burned at the stake; those willing to admit to it were thoughtfully strangled before the pyre was lit.

In the period between 1560 and 1774 (after which records become sketchy) a total of 16,176 people were arrested by the Inquisition, mostly Hindus, though more than two-thirds of those burned alive were Jews who had been forcibly converted as Cristianos Nuevos. In 1814 the Inquisition was finally repealed, as part of an Anglo-Portuguese treaty, and most of its later records destroyed.

1560

Portugal's Tribunal of the Holy Office (the Goan Inquisition) arrives in Goa to begin its brutal 200 years of suppression of religious freedoms, executing hundreds of 'heretics', and instilling fear into Goan hearts.

1612

British East India Company ships defeat a Portuguese fleet off the coast of Western Gujarat, starting the end of Portuguese hold. The Dutch soon outmanoeuvre Portuguese ships with their superior technology.

1664

The Hindu Marathas, under the leadership of legendary, fearsome warrior Shivaji, temporarily take parts of Goa, alerting the Portuguese to the dangers lurking in Eastern, as well as Western, powers.

1739

The Portuguese sign a treaty with the Marathas, handing over large tracts of their northern territory near Mumbai in exchange for full Maratha withdrawal from Goa.

Goa's Golden Age

Not all religious orders, however, came tarred with the same cruel and zealous brush as the Inquisitors. By the mid-16th century, Franciscan, Dominican and Augustinian missionaries, along with Jesuits and others, were present in Goa, establishing hospitals and schools, and teaching alternative methods of farming and forestry.

When they weren't busy converting the masses, they were masterminding much of Goa Dourada's (Golden Goa's) glorious ecclesiastical building boom. Levies from the lucrative international spice trade financed work on the Sé Cathedral and the Basilica of Bom Jesus, and soon Old Goa's population stood at 300,000, larger than London or Lisbon itself. Though life remained perilous – many would-be immigrants perished at sea en route, or succumbed to bouts of malaria, typhoid or cholera that swept the city – in Goa it seemed truly golden.

On encountering Francis Xavier's 'incorrupt' body in 1634, a Portuguese noblewoman named Dona Isabel de Caron was allegedly so anxious to obtain a relic that she bit off the dead saint's little toe... and it gushed fresh blood into her mouth.

Portuguese Struggles

Just as 'Goa Dourada' and its magnificent edifices were in their ascendancy, Portugal's own fortunes were beginning to wane.

In 1580 bankrupted by a disastrous campaign in North Africa, Portugal was annexed by Spain, and it wasn't until 1640 that the Portuguese regained independence. Wranglings followed over Goa, both with Britain and with the last of the mighty Maratha Empire, led by Shivaji, whose homeland lay in the Western Ghats of southern Maharashtra. In 1739, following a two-year siege, a treaty between the Portuguese and the Marathas forced the Portuguese to hand over large tracts of their northern territory, near Mumbai (then Bombay), in exchange for a full Maratha withdrawal from Goa.

And though Portugal succeeded in adding more territory to Goa during the 18th century – *talukas* (districts) including Bicholim Ponda, Quepem and Canacona, known as the Novas Conquistas, or New Conquests – the grand age of Portuguese Goa was on the decline. The effects of the Inquisition, coupled with plague after horrendous plague sweeping Old Goa, meant that by 1822 Old Goa had been completely abandoned, its monuments lost in a tangle of jungle. The senate moved to Panjim (present-day Panaji) in 1835, which soon after became Goa's official capital.

Meanwhile Portugal continued to struggle with troublemakers within and without. In 1787 the short-lived Pinto Revolt, whose conspirators were largely Goan clerics, sought to overturn their overlords' rule. The revolt was discovered while it was still in the planning, and several of the leaders were tortured and put to death, while others were imprisoned or shipped off to Portugal.

1781–88

The Novas Conquistas (New Conquests) sees Portugal add to its Goan territory, delineating, by 1788, the confines of the state as we know it today.

1787

The first serious local attempt to overthrow the Portuguese, the Pinto Revolt, is attempted; it's unsuccessful and its leaders are either tortured and executed, or shipped to Portugal.

1843

Panjim becomes Goa's new capital, and Old Goa is left almost uninhabited. British adventurer Richard Burton soon describes Old Goa as a place of 'utter devastation'.

1955

On 15 August a huge satyagraha is called. Portuguese troops open fire on protesters; many are arrested, beaten, imprisoned and exiled to Africa.

INCORRUPTIBLE OLD ST FRANCIS

Goa's patron saint, Francis Xavier, was born in Spain in 1506. A founding member of the Society of Jesus (the Jesuits), he embarked on a number of missionary voyages from Goa between 1542 and 1552, before dying off the coast of China just before Christmas in 1552.

After his death (so the story goes) several sackfuls of quicklime were emptied into his coffin, to consume Xavier's flesh in preparation for the return of the mortal remains to Goa. Two months later, the body remained in perfect condition – 'incorrupt' despite all that quicklime. The following year, it arrived back in Goa and its preservation was declared a miracle.

It took until 1622 for Francis Xavier to be canonised for his posthumous efforts. But by then, holy relic hunters had corrupted the incorruptible: his right arm had been removed and divided between Jesuits in Japan and Rome (where it could allegedly still sign its name), and by 1636 parts of one shoulder blade and internal organs had been scattered throughout southeast Asia. Even his diamond-encrusted fingernail was removed, and is now squirrelled away at the Pereira-Braganza house in Chandor.

At last, at the end of the 17th century, the body reached an advanced state of desiccation and the miracle appeared to be over. Nowadays the parched remains of Francis Xavier are kept in a glass coffin in the Basilica of Bom Jesus in Old Goa.

End of an Empire

The 19th century saw increasing calls for Goan freedom from Lisbon. Uprisings and rebellions became common, and by the 1940s the Goan leaders were taking their example from the Independence movement across the border in British India. But despite widespread demonstrations, on 10 June 1947 the Portuguese Minister of Colonies, Captain Teofilo Duarte, warned that the 'Portuguese flag will not fall down in India without some thousands of Portuguese, white and coloured, shedding their blood in its defence'.

The March to Independence

When overtures by the newly independent Indian government were made to the Portuguese in 1953, it became clear that the Portuguese had no intention of withdrawing. On 11 June 1953 diplomatic relations between the two countries were broken off.

Within Goa, protests continued, often met with violent retaliation from Portuguese forces. Meanwhile India manoeuvred for international support. However, Indian Prime Minister Jawaharlal Nehru found himself pushed to the brink when, in November 1961, Portuguese troops stationed 10km south of Goa opened fire on Indian fishing boats. On the night of 17 December 1961 Operation Vijay saw Indian troops crossing the border. They were met with little resistance and by evening of the following day the troops reached Panaji.

A small faction within Goa still advocates independence from India; learn more at www.freegoa.com.

1961

On 17 December, Indian troops cross the border into Goa; by 19 December, an Indian flag flies atop Panaji's Secretariat Building.

1987

On 31 May, Goa is officially declared India's 25th state by Prime Minister Rajiv Gandhi, in a landmark ruling for the state's generations of armed supporters.

1996

Bombay's name is officially changed to Mumbai, the name derived from the goddess Mumba who was worshipped by early Koli fisherfolk in the area.

2008

A series of coordinated terrorist attacks by Pakistani militants rocks Mumbai in November (known as '26/11'), leaving 164 people dead, including 10 in the Leopold Cafe.

At 8.30am on 19 December, troops of the Punjab Regiment occupied the Panaji Secretariat Building and unfurled the Indian flag, signifying the end of the 450-year Portuguese occupation of Goa. The Portuguese left quietly shortly afterwards.

Post-Independence

Initially, India's self-proclaimed 'liberation' of Goa was met with a lukewarm response from Goans themselves. Some feared a drop in their relatively high standard of living, and saw in themselves few similarities with their Indian neighbours. Others feared the loss of their cultural identity, and that Portuguese plutocrats would simply be replaced by an army of Indian bureaucrats.

Nevertheless, the first full state government was operating in Goa by the end of December 1962. On 31 May 1987 Goa was officially recognised as the 25th state of the Indian Union, and in 1992, its native tongue, Konkani, was recognised as one of India's official languages.

For most of the 1990s political instability plagued the young state: between 1990 and 2005, Goa had no fewer than 14 governments. Corruption became rife, and policy-making impossible. One of the parties to benefit from the chaos was the right-wing Hindu nationalist Bharatiya Janata Party (BJP). In March 2006 communal riots between Muslims and Hindus broke out in Sanvordem, in the interior of Goa, threatening the very religious tolerance Goans themselves are famous for.

Away from the political machinations, from the 1960s Goa began to experience a new wave of visitors – travellers on the hippie trail setting up camp and dancing on the beaches. This naturally developed into mainstream tourism, from the trance parties of the 1980s to package and charter tourists of the 1990s onwards. Over time, Goan entrepreneurs took to tourism-related industries – hotels, restaurants, beach shacks, travel agents and boat tours – and the economy shifted from mainly agriculture, fishing and commerce to tourism. Heavy industry in the form of controversial iron-ore mining and the manufacture of petrochemicals followed, forever changing the face of Goa.

Portugal's dictator Dr Antonio de Oliveira Salazar attempted to lobby world leaders into condemning India's claims over Goa: he even managed to persuade John F Kennedy to write to Nehru, advising him against the use of force on the issue.

Contemporary Goa

Goa's political landscape has changed over the years but two major parties still battle it out for governance.

In the 2017 state legislative elections the BJP won the popular vote but lost eight seats to the Congress Party and, needing 21 seats for a majority, was forced into a shaky coalition government with the Maharashtrawadi Gomantak Party (MAG), Goa Forward Party and independents on the proviso that Manohar Parrikar return as Chief Minister.

2012

Iron-ore mining in Goa is suspended by the Supreme Court following investigations into illegal and corrupt operations.

2014

Goa's popular Chief Minister Manohar Parrikar is appointed Minister of Defence in the central government. He is replaced as party leader by Laxmikant Parsekar.

2016

Prime Minister Narendra Modi unexpectedly takes ₹500 and ₹1000 notes out of circulation to rid the economy of 'black money'.

2017

The central government introduces a complex goods and services tax, increasing most hotel bills.

The Goan Way of Life

Goa's compact coastal geography and four centuries of Portuguese rule have imbued in its people a uniquely independent spirit and culture that's undeniably Indian, but unmistakably Goan. Whether working in farming, fishing or the tourist industry, life here changes with the seasons, family is all-important and festivals are celebrated with gusto.

Goan Identity

With the frequent comings and goings of the sultans, kings, governors and colonising cultures over the last several thousand years, Goans have grown adept at clinging tight to their indigenous traditions while blending in the most appealing elements of each successive visitation. Goans today take substantial pride in their Portuguese heritage – evident in their names, music, food and architecture – combining this seamlessly with Hindu festivals, Konkani chatter, Christmas parties, a keen interest in the English football leagues and, with the influx of Russian travellers, an uncanny ability to read Cyrillic and rustle up a good bowl of borscht.

Whether Catholic Goan, Hindu Goan, Muslim Goan or 'new' Goan, some things unite everyone native to this eclectic state. Everyone has a strong opinion about the constantly changing face of Goa, and of what it means, in essence, to be Goan. Everyone possesses a set of nostalgic memories of 'the way things used to be', whether this means the opulent landowning days of Portuguese dependence, the trippy free-love '60s, the calm before the package-holiday storm or before the damage of heavy industry. Above all, Goans across the state are eager to ensure, each in their own individual way, that Goa doesn't lose its alluring, endearing, ever-evolving distinctiveness in the decades to come.

Goans, like almost everyone else, are taking to the internet in search of love. Popular sites – allowing would-be brides and grooms (and their parents) to scour the whole of India for suitable matches – include www.bharatmatrimony.com and www.shaadi.com.

Lifestyle

Compared to the rest of the country, Goa is blessed with a relatively high standard of living, with healthcare, schooling, wages and literacy levels all far exceeding the national average. Its population of somewhere around 1.8 million is divided roughly down the middle between rural and urban populations, and many people continue to make their living from tilling the land, fishing or raising livestock.

However, there are still those who fall desperately far below the poverty line. You may notice slums surrounding the heavy industry installations as you drive south on the national highway from Dabolim Airport. Many migrant workers, attracted to Goa by the hopes of benefiting from its tourist trade, end up begging on its beaches, and hundreds of homeless children from surrounding states are supported by local and international charities.

Another acute social problem, linked both to poverty and Goa's liberal attitude to drinking, is alcoholism, though it's a problem shared with other south Indian states.

Traditional Culture

Though many cultural traditions overlap and mingle, particularly within Goa's Christian and Hindu communities, you'll find some traditional practices still going strong in Goa.

Marriage

Though 'love matches' are increasingly in vogue in Goa in Christian and Hindu circles alike, both communities still frequently use a matchmaker or local contacts to procure a suitable partner for a son or daughter. If all else fails, you'll find scores of ads listed in the newspaper classifieds or online sites, emphasising the professional qualifications, physical attributes and 'wheatish' complexion of each young, eligible individual.

Following Hindu marriages, generally the young wife will leave her family home to live with her husband's family. However, this is not always the case, and many young couples today are choosing to branch off to begin their own family home. Dowries are usually still required by the groom's family in both Christian and Hindu weddings, either helping facilitate a match or hindering it; a mixed-caste marriage will become much more acceptable if there's a good dowry, but a high-caste girl from a poor family can find it very difficult to secure a partner of a similar 'status'.

Hindu weddings in Goa are lengthy, gleeful and colourful, while Christian wedding ceremonies are more sombre (though the party afterwards usually kicks up a storm) and similar to those in the West, with some elements, such as the ritual bathing of the bride, borrowed from Hinduism. *Chudas,* green bracelets traditionally worn by married women, are donned by both Hindu and Christian brides, and tradition dictates that, should her husband die before her, the widow must break the bangles on his coffin.

Death

Death, as everywhere, is big business in Goa, and you'll spot plenty of coffin makers, headstone carvers and hearse services on your travels. In the Christian community, personal items are placed with the deceased in the grave, including (depending on the habits of the deceased) cigarettes and a bottle of feni, while most Hindus are cremated. Annual memorials, wakes and services for the dead are honoured by Christians and Hindus alike.

There are numerous superstitions in the Hindu and Christian communities about restless spirits – particularly of those who committed suicide or died before being given last rites – and a number of measures are undertaken at the funeral to discourage the spirit from returning. The clothing and funeral shroud are cut, and a needle and thread are placed in the coffin. The spirit of the deceased who wishes to come back must first repair its torn clothing, a task that takes until daylight, at which time departure from the grave is impossible.

SUSEGAD

You won't get far in Goa without hearing references to *susegad* or *sossegado,* a joie de vivre attitude summed up along the lines of 'relax and enjoy life while you can'. Originating from the Portuguese word *sossegado* (literally meaning 'quiet'), it's a philosophy of afternoon siestas, and long, lazy evenings filled with feni and song. On the 25th anniversary of Goan Independence, even Prime Minister Rajiv Gandhi described how 'an inherent nonacquisitiveness and contentment with what one has, described by that uniquely Goan word *sossegado,* has been an enduring strength of Goan character'.

Women in Goan Society

Generally, the position of women in Goa is better than that elsewhere in India, with women possessing property rights, education options and career prospects not shared by their sisters in other states. The result of Goa's progressive policies today is that women are far better represented than elsewhere in professions and positions of influence. While men undoubtedly still predominate and many women still choose to fulfil traditional household roles, around 15% of the state's workforce are women, many of whom fill roles as doctors, dentists, teachers, solicitors and university lecturers, and 30% of panchayat (local government council) seats are reserved for women.

The Church of Our Lady of Miracles in Mapusa was built on the site of an ancient Hindu temple. The church's annual feast day, held 16 days after Easter, is celebrated by Christians and Hindus together.

Religion

On paper, at least, it's clear: roughly 26% of Goa's population is Christian, 65% Hindu and 8% Muslim. But statistics alone don't reveal the complex, compelling religious concoction that typifies the population's belief.

Religious Hybrids

During the fierce, Inquisition-led imposition of Christianity by the Portuguese, many Hindus fled to safety in parts of the state still considered safe, while others converted to the new faith and remained in Portuguese territory. Thus, for generations, many Goan families have contained both Catholics and Hindus.

The distinction was further blurred by the ways in which Christianity was adapted to appeal to the local population. As early as 1616 the Bible was translated into Konkani, while in 1623 Pope Gregory permitted Brahmin families to retain their high-caste status after converting to Catholicism, and allowed the continuance of a number of local festivals and traditions.

Today the fusion of these religions is still extremely evident. In Goa's numerous whitewashed churches, Christ and the Virgin Mary are often adorned with Hindu flower garlands, and Mass is said in Konkani. Christians and Hindus frequently pay respects to festivals of the others' faith, with both Christmas and Diwali being a source of celebration and *mithai*-giving (sweet-giving) for all.

But that's not to say that Goa is free from religious tensions. In 2006 anti-Muslim riots, beginning with the destruction of a makeshift village mosque in Sanvordem, shook Goa's religiously tolerant to the core.

Goan Hindu homes are identifiable by the multicoloured *vrindavan* (ornamental plant container) that stands in front of the house. Growing inside it is the twiggy tulsi plant, sacred to Hindus, as in mythology the tulsi is identified as one of the god Vishnu's lovers, whom his consort, Lashmet, turned into a shrub in a fit of jealousy.

Hinduism

Though Hinduism encompasses a huge range of personal beliefs, the essential Hindu belief is in Brahman, an infinite being, or supreme spirit, from which everything derives and to which everything will return. Hindus believe that life is cyclical and subject to reincarnations *(avatars)*, eventually leading to moksha, spiritual release. An individual's progression towards that point is governed by the law of karma (cause and effect): good karma (through positive actions such as charity and worship) may result in being reborn into a higher caste and better circumstances, and bad karma (accumulated through bad deeds) may result in reincarnation in animal form. It's only as a human that one can finally acquire sufficient self-knowledge to achieve liberation from the cycle of reincarnation.

Islam

Brought to Goa in the 11th century by wealthy Arab merchants, who were encouraged by local rulers to settle here for reasons of commerce, Islamic rule predominated in the region for large chunks of medieval Goan history.

GOA'S CASTE SYSTEM: HINDU & CHRISTIAN ALIKE

Every Hindu is born into an unchangeable social class, a caste or *varna,* of which there are four distinct tiers, each with its own rules of conduct and behaviour.

These four castes, in hierarchical order, are the Brahmins (Bamons in Konkani; priests and teachers), Kshatriyas (Chardos in Konkani; warriors and rulers), Vaisyas (merchants and farmers) and Sudras (peasants and menial workers). Beneath the four main castes is a fifth group, the Untouchables (Chamars in Konkani; formerly known as 'Harijan', but now officially 'Dalits' or 'Scheduled Castes'). These people traditionally performed 'polluting' jobs, including undertaking, street sweeping and leather working. Though discrimination against them is now a criminal offence in India, it's nevertheless still an unfortunate part of life.

While the caste system doesn't play as crucial a part in life in Goa as elsewhere in India, it's still recognised and treated in a uniquely Goan way, and holders of public office remain largely of the Bamon or Chardo castes.

The Christian community also quietly adheres to the caste system, a situation that can be traced back to Portuguese rule since, as an incentive to convert to Catholicism, high-caste Goan families were able to keep their caste privileges, money and land. Even today, in village churches, high-caste Christians tend to dominate the front pews and the lower castes the back of the congregation, and both Hindus and Christians carefully consider questions of caste when selecting candidates for a suitable marriage match.

With the arrival of the Portuguese, Islam all but disappeared from Goa, and now remains only in small communities. Most Goan Muslims today live in Goa's green heartland, around Ponda, in the vicinity of the state's biggest mosque, the Safa Masjid.

Christianity

Christianity (Catholicism) has been present in Goa since the arrival of the Portuguese in the 16th century, who enforced their faith on Goa's Muslim and Hindu population by way of the Goan Inquisition. By the time Hindus and Muslims were once again able to practise freely, Catholicism had taken root and was here to stay.

For the last 30 years or so, a form of faith known as 'Charismatic Christianity' has been gaining ground in Goa. Worship involves lots of dancing, singing and sometimes 'speaking in tongues', with readings from the New Testament allegedly used to harness the power of the Holy Spirit, heal the sick and banish evil forces. Unlike mainstream Catholicism, Charismatic Christianity's services are usually in the open air, and its priests reject all notions of caste, understandably making the movement particularly popular among Goa's lower castes.

The official football (soccer) season runs from January to May; tickets to the matches generally cost less than ₹30 and can be bought at the ticket kiosks outside the Jawaharlal Nehru Stadium in Margao on match days.

Sport

Most people know how seriously Indians take the pursuit of cricket, but it may come as a surprise to learn that Goa's top sport is football (soccer), another legacy left over from the days of Portuguese rule. Every village has at least one football team, and sometimes several – one team for each *waddo* (ward) of the village – and league games are fiercely contested.

This has seen the creation of several teams that regularly perform at National Football League (NFL) level. The main Goan teams to watch are Salgaonkar SC from Vasco da Gama, Dempo SC from Panaji (Panjim), and Churchill Brothers SC from Margao. The big matches are played out at the Jawaharlal Nehru Stadium (known locally as Fatorda Stadium) in Margao, regularly attracting up to 35,000 fans.

Delicious India

Goan cuisine is a tantalising fusion of Portuguese and South Indian flavours: the quintessential Goan lunch of 'fish curry rice' is fried mackerel steeped in coconut, tamarind and chilli sauce and served with a mound of rice. *'Prodham bhookt, magi mookt',* say the locals in Konkani: 'You can't think until you've eaten well', and Goans take the sating of their appetites extremely seriously.

Staples & Specialities

Given Goa's seaside location, it's little wonder that the local lunchtime staple is 'fish curry rice'; you'll find it on any 'non-veg' restaurant's menu, and it's a cheap and tasty way to fill up for lunch.

Aside from seafood, chicken and pork are popular meat dishes in Goa, and the latter makes for a local lunchtime favourite, served up in the form of a piled plate of Goan *chouriços*. These air-dried, spicy red pork sausages (similar to Spanish chorizo) are flavoured with feni (liquor distilled from cashew fruit or palm sap), toddy (palm sap) vinegar and chillies, and strung in desiccated garlands from streetside stalls.

Another delicacy you won't find anywhere else in India is pork *sorpotel*, a spicy masala dish combining chillies, ginger, garlic, cinnamon, cloves and a dash of feni; it's often served at Christmas.

According to linguists, there's no such thing as an Indian 'curry' – the word, an Anglicised derivative of the Tamil word *kari* (black pepper), was used by the British as a term for any dish including spices.

Sauces

Uniquely Goan preparations include *xacuti* (pronounced *sha-coo-tee*), a spicy sauce combining coconut milk, freshly ground spices and red chillies. Chicken and seafood are frequently served basted with *rechead*, a spicy marinating paste. Dry-fried chicken might otherwise be served spicy *cafrial* style, marinated in a green masala paste and sprinkled with toddy vinegar. Meanwhile, the original *vindalho* – far from being the sole preserve of British curry-house lads – is a uniquely Goan derivative of Portuguese pork stew that traditionally combines *vinho* (wine vinegar) with *ahlo* (garlic) and spices.

Spices

Head to one of Goa's divinely scented spice farms to find evidence of the sought-after spices that kept conquerors coming back to Goa for centuries. South India still produces the very best of the world's black-pepper crop, an essential ingredient in savoury dishes worldwide, while locally produced turmeric, coriander and cumin, combined with garlic, chillies, tamarind and *kokum* (a dried fruit used as a spice) form the basis of many a Goan meal. Other locally grown spices include cardamom, vanilla, cinnamon, cloves, curry leaves, ginger and nutmeg.

Cooking classes (p37) are gaining popularity in Goa. You'll find them at Vagator, Palolem, Patnem and Siolim.

Rice

Rice is by far the most important staple in southern India, providing most meals for most people throughout most of their lives, and India is one of the world's largest rice producers. Apart from being boiled or steamed, rice is cooked up to make *pulao* (pilau; aromatic rice casserole), or a Muslim biryani, with a layer of vegetable, chicken or mutton curry. Naturally it also forms the basis of the Goan staple 'fish curry rice'.

Dhal

Vegetarian or omnivorous, Christian, Hindu or Muslim, India is united in its love for dhal (lentils or pulses). In Goa, you'll find three types of dhal: thin, spicy *sambar,* served with many breakfast dishes; dhal fry, which is yellow and mild with the consistency of a thick soup; and dhal makhani, richer and darker, spiked with *rajma* (kidney beans), onions and another handful or two of some of the 60 types of pulses grown in the country. Various other pulses, including *kabuli chana* (chickpeas) and *lobhia* (black-eyed beans), also turn up regularly in that delicious Goan breakfast staple, *bhaji-pau.*

Seafood

Seafood is plentiful, fresh and delicious in Goa, though not cheap compared with other dishes. Among the most famous Goan fish dishes are *ambot tik,* a slightly sour curry usually accompanied by shark; *caldeirada,* a mild seafood stew with vegetables flavoured with wine; and the Portuguese-inflected *recheiado* which sees a whole fish, usually a mackerel or pomfret, slit down the centre, stuffed with a spicy red sauce, and fried up in hot oil. Another regular on Goan menus is *balchão,* a rich, tangy tomato and chilli sauce, often cooked with tiger prawns or fish.

In typical South Indian restaurants, rice and curry dishes are often eaten with the hands. Try to eat only with your right hand; the left is considered unclean and for the purposes of ablution only. If you're invited to dine with a family, always take off your shoes and wash your hands before dining.

Sweets

Look out for *bebinca,* the most famous of Goan sweets, a rich 16-layer coconut pancake-type cake, whipped up with sugar, nutmeg, cardamom and egg yolks. Also be sure to sample *batica,* a squidgy coconut cake best served piping hot from the oven; *doce,* made with chickpeas and coconut; and *dodol,* a gooey fudgelike treat, made from litres of fresh coconut milk, mixed with rice flour and jaggery.

Celebrations

Goan festivals and celebrations are synonymous with feasting. Weddings are occasions to indulge gastronomic fantasies, and often include dishes such as *sorpotel,* a combination of meat, organs and blood, diced and cooked in a thick, spicy sauce flavoured with feni. Seafood also features at feasts. Desserts might include *bebinca* and *leitria* (an elaborate coconut sweet covered by a lacy filigree of egg yolks and sugar syrup).

Hindu festivals, too, are big food affairs. *Karanjis,* crescent-shaped flour parcels stuffed with sweet *khoya* (milk solids) and nuts, are synonymous with Holi, the most boisterous Hindu festival, as are *malpuas* (wheat pancakes dipped in syrup), *barfis* (fudgelike sweets) and *pedas* (multicoloured pieces of *khoya* and sugar). Pongal (Tamil for 'overflowing'), the south's major harvest festival, produces a dish of the same name, made with the season's first rice, along with jaggery, nuts, raisins and spices.

BREAKFAST INDIAN-STYLE

Breakfast is an excellent meal in which to explore the delights of South Indian cuisine. A favourite is the classic *bhaji-pau,* a white bread roll *(pau)* served ready to dunk into a spicy side curry *(bhaji).*

Masala dosas (thin pancakes of rice and lentil batter, fried and folded, and often served with masala-spiced potato filling) are another breakfast staple, as are the other southern specialities of *idli* (round steamed rice cakes often eaten with *sambar* and chutney) and *vada* (also spelled *wada;* potato and/or lentil savoury doughnut, deep-fried and served with *sambar* and chutney).

Vegetarians & Vegans

South Indian cuisine is some of the best in the world for those who abstain from fish, flesh and fowl. Vegans might face some challenges, since it's sometimes hard to work out whether food has been cooked in ghee (clarified butter) but look out for the words 'pure veg'.

Goan Cookbooks

- *The Essential Goa Cookbook – Maria Teresa Menezes*
- *Savour the Flavour of India – Edna Fernandes*
- *Goan Recipes and More – Odette Mascarenhas*
- *Goan Cookbook – Joyce Fernandes*

Drinks

Nonalcoholic Drinks

Chai (tea) is the national drink, boiled for hours with milk, sugar and masala spices, and served piping hot, sweet and frothy.

Coffee is less widely consumed by Goans, but you'll have no problem finding Indian-style coffee, and espresso machines are becoming common in tourist cafes that cater to international tastes.

Fizzy drinks, fresh lime soda, lassis and shakes are standard fare at cafes and shacks. Look out for coconut street vendors – for ₹50 they'll chop the top off and poke a straw in for a refreshing, natural drink.

Alcoholic Drinks

Goans love to drink and low taxes mean alcohol is cheaper here than elsewhere in India. Beer is king (when it's cold), and Kingfisher is still the most popular local brand, though Bira, Tuborg, Simba, Heineken, Budweiser and others are muscling in on the market. More importantly for beer lovers, craft beer is making an appearance in Goa, with two microbreweries currently operating. Goa Brewing Co in Sangolda produces small-batch seasonal beers such as Eight Finger Eddie IPA. Susegado Brewing (www.susegado.com) produces Dorado IPA and a mango wheat beer.

The fiery local liquor is feni, made either from fermented cashew fruit or palm sap (toddy), which is distilled to around 30% to 35% proof. Feni first-timers mix it with a soft drink or soda water, or just close your eyes and take your medicine.

Hard liquor, known in India as IMFL – Indian-made foreign liquor – is very cheap (if purchased at a liquor store) and the rum, brandy and whisky versions are reasonably palatable.

Wine, though not India's strong point, is slowly gaining ground, but you'll pay dearly for choosing the grape over the grain: bought at a liquor store, even a mediocre bottle of local wine costs from ₹500 (safe bets are Sula, Chateau Indage and Grover).

Cooking Online

- *www.goanfoodrecipes.com*
- *www.hildastouchofspice.com*
- *www.thegoanfoodie.com*

Where to Eat & Drink

Goa's eating-out options are divided into the 'local' and 'nonlocal' varieties: the local serving up Indian or Goan cuisine of one sort or another, and the nonlocal encompassing everything from Tibetan kitchens and pizza restaurants to French fine dining.

The simplest local restaurants, often known as 'hotels' come either in 'veg' or 'non-veg' varieties, and are the best places for a cheap breakfast or a filling lunch.

Street Food

Street food carts are not as common in Goa as elsewhere in India, but you will find them around markets, at Miramar Beach in Panaji and at the main beach entrances to Calangute and Colva. A good rule of thumb is that if locals are eating at a streetside stand, it's a pretty safe bet, but make sure your food is freshly cooked – don't eat anything that looks like it has been sitting around for a while.

Markets & Shopping

Shopping is a big part of any exotic holiday and India is a shoppers' paradise. From colourful markets to traditional handicrafts, in Goa you'll find souvenirs, textiles, jewellery, carpets and one-off bargains from all over India.

Where to Shop

Tourism lures market traders to Goa from all over India. While this means that you're unlikely to take home much that is genuinely Goan – apart from decorative bottles of cashew feni, packets of locally grown spices and perhaps hand-painted tiles – it also means that you can find almost anything from Kashmiri carpets to Karnatakan carvings.

Panaji has a growing number of upscale 'lifestyle boutiques' vending high-end household goods and gorgeous Goan coffee-table books. Craft shops, department stores and clothes shops line the 18th June Rd and MG Rd, while Caculo Mall is a modern multistorey department store. Calangute and Candolim, too, host a selection of sleek boutiques, souvenir shops and big-name brands. Most stores are situated on the roads leading down to their beaches, and on the main Fort Aguada road.

Markets

In Goa the markets are either aimed specifically at tourists or specifically at locals. For local shopping, try the municipal markets in Panaji and Margao, offering plenty of colour and a good line in spices, bangles and posters of Indian gods, or head to Mapusa, where the daily morning market is busiest and most vibrant on Fridays.

Anjuna's Wednesday flea market, though somewhat commercialised and predictable, is still a major weekly attraction and good fun to wander around. The two Saturday night markets – Mackie's in Baga and the Saturday Nite Market (formerly Ingo's) in Arpora – are also good fun, with food stalls, entertainment, neon-lit stalls and lots of flashing jewellery. The three tourist markets operate only during the high season from November to the end of March.

The roads leading to the beach in Palolem and Arambol are packed with stalls selling silver jewellery, drums, hammocks, embroidered bedsheets, sandals, and all the usual lines in Indian souvenirs. But if you prefer the goods to come to you, never fear: sit for 15 minutes on almost any stretch of beach, and migrant salespeople will appear bearing jewellery, fabrics, and an excellent well-practised hard sell.

Mumbai is India's great marketplace, with some of the country's best shopping. Spend a day at the markets north of CSMT for the classic Mumbai shopping experience. Booksellers set up daily on the sidewalks along the main thoroughfare between Colaba and Fort.

Mumbai's main market district is one of Asia's most fascinating, a working-class district stretching north of Crawford Market up as far as Chor Bazaar, a 2.5km walk away.

Best Bookshops

Golden Heart Emporium (p167), Margao

Other India Bookstore (p145), Mapusa

Singbal's Book House (p95), Panaji

Rainbow Bookshop (p150), Vagator

Best Goan Markets

Anjuna Flea Market (p140), Anjuna

Mapusa Market (p144), Mapusa

Saturday Night Market (p135), Arpora

Municipal Market (p94), Panaji

MMC New Market (p167), Margao

THE ART OF HAGGLING

The friendly art of haggling is an absolute must in most parts of Goa and Mumbai, unless you don't mind paying above market value. Traders in towns and markets are accustomed to tourists who have lots of money and little time to spend it, meaning that a shopkeeper's 'very good price' might in fact be a rather bad one.

If you have absolutely no idea what something should really cost, a good rule of thumb is to bank on paying half of what you're originally quoted. The vendor will probably look aghast and tell you that this is impossible, as it's the very price they had to pay for the item themselves. This is when the battle for a bargain begins and it's up to you and the salesperson to negotiate a price. You'll find that many shopkeepers lower their so-called final price if you head out of the shop and tell them that you'll think about it.

Don't lose your sense of humour and sense of fairness while haggling – it's not a battle to squeeze every last rupee out of a poor trader, and not all vendors are out to make a fool of you. In essence, the haggle itself is often the very spirit, and the fun, of the Indian shopping experience. Don't forget to smile – and never get angry.

What to Buy

Antiques

In Goa you'll find a couple of knick-knack-style antique shops in Mapusa, near the Municipal Gardens, along with antique-furniture shops scattered here and there across the state. Most shops can organise shipping.

To protect India's cultural heritage, the export of certain antiques is prohibited, especially those which are verifiably more than 100 years old. Reputable antique dealers know the laws and can make arrangements for an export-clearance certificate for old items that are OK to export. Detailed information on prohibited items can be found on the Archaeological Survey of India (ASI) website (www.asi.nic.in).

For an unusual gift for that budding Houdini, or to provide means to pass time on a long bus journey, seek out rabbits in hats and enchanted handkerchiefs at Shamin Khan's Star Magic Shop (p136) in Baga, which also has a weekly stall at the Anjuna Flea Market.

Carpets

It may not surprise you that India produces and exports more handcrafted carpets than Iran, but it probably comes as more of a surprise to find that some of them are of virtually equal quality. India's best carpets come from Kashmir, and can be found in Kashmiri-run shops throughout Goa.

Leatherwork

Indian leatherwork is not made from cowhide but from buffalo, camel, goat or some other form of animal. *Chappals,* the basic sandals found all over India, are the most popular buy.

Papier-Mâché

Probably the most characteristic Kashmiri craft, basic papier-mâché articles are made in a mould, then painted and polished in layers until the final intricate design is produced. Items include bowls, jewellery boxes, tables and lamps.

Textiles

This is still India's major industry and 40% of the total production is at village level, where it is known as *khadi* (homespun cloth). Bedspreads, tablecloths, cushion covers or fabric for clothing are popular *khadi* purchases. In Gujarat and Rajasthan heavy material is embroidered with tiny mirrors and beads to produce everything from dresses to stuffed toys to wall hangings; tie-dye work is popular in Rajasthan and Kerala; and in Kashmir embroidered materials are turned into shirts and dresses. All of this is available in Goan shops and markets.

Arts & Architecture

Goa's traditional art forms, much of its architecture, and even its sporting passions are strongly influenced by its colonial legacy. Goans display an infectious love of music, festivals, dance, poetry and literature, and a rich artistic and cultural heritage, seamlessly blending Indian and Portuguese elements.

Music & Dance

Listen carefully beyond the Bob Marley, lounge and techno jumble of the beach shacks, and you'll hear Goa's own melodies, a heady concoction of East and West.

The most famous kind of Goan folk song is the *mando,* also known as the 'love song of Goa', a slow melody with accompanying dance, which sees its largely Catholic participants dance in parallel lines, flourishing paper fans and handkerchiefs. You might catch a glimpse of this if you pass a Christian wedding or feast day in progress.

Though increasingly rare, the melancholy, haunting fado can still be heard here and there in Goa, the songs of which lament lost love, or the longing for a Portuguese home that most singers, in fact, have never seen. Listen out for the late, great folk singer Lucio de Miranda, or Oslando, another local folk and fado favourite.

Aside from local celebrations (to which tourists are often extended a warm welcome), the best place to find traditional music and dance performances is at Panaji's Kala Academy (p94).

Local Konkani pop is a strange and sometimes wonderful combination of tinny, trilly musical influences – African rhythms and Portuguese tunes, with a bit of calypso thrown in. You'll catch its twangy melodies from passing cars, buses and taxis, and in local Goan lunch spots. A classic, old-school performer to look out for, who has influenced a whole new generation of local musicians, is the much-loved Lorna, the 'Goan nightingale'.

Goa Trance

The Western electronic music scene in Goa still thumps – albeit less incessantly than in past years – to the hypnotic rhythms of Goa trance and psy-trance, a uniquely Goan sound that came to prevalence on the beaches of Anjuna in the early 1990s.

Its most famous exponent is Goa Gil, who still DJs trance parties worldwide. Go to www.goagil.com to see where he's next appearing – the schedule usually includes gigs in Goa or elsewhere in India. Other well-known artists include Hallucigen, Astral Projection and Cosmosis. You can pick up Goa trance CDs at the Anjuna flea market.

Literature

Although it can be difficult to get hold of Goan literature (books go out of print very quickly), a decent amount of Konkani literature is available in English translation.

Some mainstays of Goan literature include *Angela's Goan Identity,* a 1994 fictional work by Carmo D'Souza, which offers a fascinating insight into a girl's struggle to define her Goan identity towards the final years

REMO FERNANDES

Goan singer, musician and producer Remo Fernandes is famous in India for his ability to fuse cultural influences in both his music and his image.

Remo was born in Siolim in 1953. After studying architecture in Bombay and hitch-hiking around Europe and Africa (busking along the way), he returned to Goa. Several rejections from Indian labels made him record his first (and arguably one of his best) albums, *Goan Crazy*, at home in Siolim. From there, Remo shot to success with more hit albums, film-score offers, awards, product endorsements and titles such as the 'Freddie Mercury of India'.

Remo is loved in Goa, not only for the versatility of his talent but also for never cutting his Goan roots along his path to fame. When Remo turned 50 in May 2003, he celebrated with a free 4½-hour concert in Goa.

Look out for *Old Goan Gold* as well as *Forwards into the Past*, which has arrangements by Remo and vocals by the late, fado-famed Lucio de Miranda. Remo lives and records in Siolim.

of the Portuguese era in Goa, while Frank Simoes' engaging *Glad Seasons in Goa* offers an affectionate account of Goan life.

Perhaps the greatest classic of Goan literature, though, is *Sorrowing Lies My Land*, by Lambert Mascarenhas, first published in 1955, which deals with the struggle for Goan Independence launched in Margao in 1946. Meanwhile, Victor Rangel-Ribeiro weaves together Goan vignettes in his award-winning first novel *Tivolem*. Mario Cabral E Sa's *Legends of Goa*, illustrated by one of Goa's best-known artists, Mario de Miranda, is a colourful reworking of some of Goa's best folk tales and historical titbits.

Architecture

Goa's most iconic architectural form is likely the slowly crumbling bungalow mansion, with its wrought-iron balconies, shady front *balcãos* (pillared porches), oyster-shell windows and central *saquãos* (inner courtyards), around which family life traditionally revolved.

For an especially good selection of the most up-to-date local Goan literary releases, drop in to Margao's Golden Heart Emporium (p167), Mapusa's Other India Bookstore (p145), or the numerous book stores around Panaji's Municipal Gardens.

Most were built in the early 18th century, as rewards to wealthy Goan merchants and officials for their services to the Portuguese. The architecture was inspired by European tastes, but the materials – red laterite stone, wood and terracotta, and oyster shells used instead of glass for windows – were all local. The wealthiest of these homes also contained a locally crafted wooden chapel or oratory, which housed gilded and golden relics, altars and images of Catholic saints as the focal point for family prayers.

Churches, too, bear the hallmark of Portugal, many of them cruciform and constructed of whitewashed laterite stone. Even the humblest of village churches usually sports a sumptuous interior, with an elaborate gilt reredos (ornamental altarpiece or screen), and lots of carving, painting and chandeliers.

Goan temples are yet another form of architectural hybrid, enfolding both Muslim and Christian elements into traditional Hindu designs. Domed roofs, for example, are a Muslim trait, while balustraded facades and octagonal towers are borrowed from Portuguese church architecture. Their most unusual and distinctive features, however, are their 'light towers', known as *deepastambhas*, which look a little like Chinese pagodas and are atmospherically decorated with oil lamps during festival periods.

Painting

Although there's no painting style particular to Goa, some of the state's most historically significant artistic output can be seen in the murals at Rachol Seminary, in the ornately decorated churches across Goa, and adorning the portraiture-heavy walls of Goa's grand mansion homes.

Internationally, one of Goa's best-known artists was Francis Newton Souza (1924–2002), whose expressionist paintings can be found in galleries worldwide. Out and about in Goa, the two artists you're most likely to come across are installation artist Dr Subodh Kerkar, and the late, much-loved artist and illustrator Mario de Miranda, who died in 2011 but whose distinctive style continues to adorn everything from books to billboards. You can see his work at the Mario Gallery (p85) in Torda.

Cinema

The Indian film industry is the largest on the planet, with around 800 movies produced annually, most of them elaborate, formulaic, melodramatic Bollywood montages that celebrate romance, violence and music, with saccharine lip-synced duets and fantastic dance routines, all performed by Indian megastars who are worshipped like deities countrywide. While in Goa, you must see at least one of these incredible creations of high camp. In Panaji head to the comfortable INOX Cinema or the far more gritty Cine Nacional.

The INOX and other venues play host to Goa's annual International Film Festival of India (p89), the country's largest such festival, which sees actors, producers and screenwriters jetting in for preening and partying all along the red carpet.

Goa is becoming an increasingly popular shooting location for Indian films (Bollywood, Tamil, Konkani, Telugu and Malayalam), either as a beach backdrop or with Goa providing an integral setting in the film's plot. Films to look out for:

Finding Fanny (2014; director Homi Adajania) Comedy road trip set in a fictional Goan village. In English and Hindi.

Husbands in Goa (2012; Saji Surendran) For something different this Malayalam (Keralan) comedy follows three men travelling to Goa to escape from their domineering wives.

Bourne Supremacy (2004; Paul Greengrass) This Hollywood action film is worth a look just to see Matt Damon jogging on Palolem Beach and out-driving the baddies (miraculously emerging in Panaji in the same scene).

Last Hippie Standing (2001; Marcus Robbin) This short documentary (find it on YouTube) traces the history of the hippie days of the 1960s and '70s, with interviews and some original Super 8 footage.

Stroll the lanes of Chandor, Siolim or the coastal villages between Velsao and Mobor for a treasure trove of Portuguese mansions in various stages of decay. Visit the Houses of Goa Museum (p160) at Torda to get up to speed on Goa's architectural heritage.

Theatre

Goa's theatre scene is dominated by the unique local street plays known as *tiatr* and *khell tiatr* (a longer form of *tiatr* performed only during festivals such as Carnival and Easter). The *tiatrs,* almost all of which are in Konkani, provide a platform for satire on politics, current affairs and day-to-day domestic issues.

Since 1974 Panaji's Kala Academy (p94) has held an annual festival (performed in Konkani) each November, showcasing the work of well-known *tiatr* writers. Throughout the year, this is also the venue for arts, drama and folk theatre.

Wildlife & the Environment

Goa may be tiny but it possesses a surprising diversity of landscape and environment. In the five decades since the Portuguese left its shores, Goa has experienced phenomenal growth in tourism, industry and population, sometimes taxing to the limit this beautiful, yet fragile ecosystem.

The Land

Goa occupies a narrow strip of the western Indian coastline, approximately 105km long and 65km wide, but within this relatively tiny area exists an incredibly diverse mixture of landscapes, flora and fauna.

To the east of the state lie the gorgeous green Western Ghats, whose name derives from the Sanskrit for 'sacred steps'. This mountain range runs along India's entire west coast, but in Goa is made up of the Sahyadri Range, comprising around one-sixth of the state's total area. The ghats are the source of all seven of Goa's main rivers, the longest of which, the Mandovi, meanders for 77km to the Arabian Sea at Panaji.

Goa – A View from the Heavens, by aerial photographer Gopal Bodhe, is a beautifully photographed book dedicated to Goa's environment and heritage.

Goa's grassy hinterland is made up mostly of laterite plateaus, with thin soil covering rich sources of iron and manganese ore. The midland has thus suffered from large-scale open-cast mining, evident in the red gashes in Goan hillsides.

Spice, fruit, cashew and areca-nut plantations predominate commercially, while terraced orchards make efficient use of limited water sources to support coconut, jackfruit, pineapple and mango groves.

Though just a fraction of the state's total area, Goa's coast is its crowning glory. Mangroves line tidal rivers, providing shelter for birds, marine animals and crocodiles, while paddy fields, coconut groves, estuaries and the sea provide the majority of the population's food.

Unfortunately, the beaches and marine waters have suffered from unfettered tourist development, overfishing, untreated sewage, pollution from sea tankers and iron-ore mining.

Wildlife

Despite Goa's diminutive size, the state is home to a surprising array of fauna and some spectacular birdlife. The most impressive mammalian species, such as wild elephants and leopards, occur only in small numbers, are incredibly shy, and are thus hard to spot. Tigers have been recorded by the forest department in Mhadei Wildlife Sanctuary.

Seven great rivers flow from the Western Ghats to Goa's coast. From north to south: Terekhol (Tiracol), Chapora, Mandovi, Zuari, Sal, Talpona and Galgibag.

Mammals

The wild animals you'll most likely encounter in Goa are the state's mischievous monkeys: most visible are smallish, scavenging bonnet macaques, and larger, black-faced, long-limbed Hanuman langurs.

Other inhabitants include common mongooses, smooth Indian otters, giant squirrels, slender lorises and shaggy sloth bears.

In Goa's wildlife sanctuaries, you may come across gaur (Indian bison), porcupines, sambars (buff-coloured deer), chitals (spotted deer) and barking deer. One of the rarer animals inhabiting Goa's forests is the nocturnal pangolin (scaly anteater). The 'mini-leopard' (known as the *vagati* in Konkani), a greyish fluffy-tailed creature about the size of a domestic cat, is also sometimes seen, along with the Indian civet.

Common dolphins can often be found frolicking offshore or in estuaries, while fruit bats and Malay fox vampire bats come out in force as the Goan sun goes down.

S Prater's *The Book of Indian Animals* and Romulus Whitaker's *Common Indian Snakes* are two reliable guides to the nonhuman residents of Goa.

Reptiles, Snakes & Amphibians

Snakes are common, though reclusive, with 23 species, of which eight are venomous. You're most likely to see nonvenomous green whip snakes, golden tree snakes, rat snakes, cat snakes, wolf snakes and Russell's sand boas. *Kusadas* (sea snakes) are common along the coastline, but generally live in deep waters, far off the coast.

Goa is also home to chameleons, monitor lizards, turtles and two species of crocodile. Flap-shell turtles and black-pond turtles are freshwater species plentiful during the monsoon, while a third species, the olive ridley sea turtle, is in grave danger of extinction (p154). There are protected nesting sites on Mandrem, Morjim and Agonda beaches.

Though crocs are also threatened, you can spot the saltwater variety in the Mandovi and Zuari estuaries, along with the less aggressive 'Mandovi mugger', which mostly inhabits Mandovi River waters around Divar and Chorao Islands.

Birds

Goa is big news for visiting birdwatchers. Top birdwatching spots include Dr Salim Ali Bird Sanctuary (p98) on Chorao Island, Bondla Wildlife Sanctuary (p111) and Mayem Lake (p161).

Birds of Southern India, by Richard Grimmet and Tim Inskipp, is a comprehensive birdwatching field guide, considered by many to be the must-have guide to the region. More focused is *Birds of Goa*, by local naturalist Rahul Alvares and Heinz Lainer. Online, check out www.birdsofgoa.com.

In open spaces, a flash of colour may turn out to be an Indian roller, identified by its brilliant blue flight feathers. Drongos are common, while pipits and wagtails strut in large flocks among the harvest stubble. Common hoopoes are often seen (or heard) in open country, while birds of prey such as harriers and buzzards soar overhead. Kites and vultures can wheel on thermals for hours; ospreys, another large hawk, patrol reservoirs and waterways for fish suppers.

Stalking long-legged at the shallow edges of ponds are various species of egret. Indian pond herons, also known as paddy birds, are small and well camouflaged in greys and browns.

Colourful kingfishers, Goa's unofficial mascot, patiently await their prey on overhanging branches. Species include black-and-white pied kingfishers, colourful common kingfishers (also known as river kingfishers), and stork-billed kingfishers, sporting massive red bills.

In the forest, woodpeckers are more often heard than seen as they chisel grubs from the bark of trees. Their colourful relatives include barbets and Indian koels, whose loud, piercing cry can be relentless in spring. Hill mynahs are an all-black bird with a distinctive yellow 'wattle' about the face.

The jewels in Goa's avian crown must be its three magnificent species of hornbill, resembling South American toucans. At the other end of the size spectrum, the iridescent, nectar-feeding purple sunbird is equally brilliant. A host of smaller birds, such as flycatchers, warblers, babblers and little tailorbirds forage for insects in every layer of vegetation.

Wildlife Sanctuaries

Roughly 12%, or 455 sq km, of Goa's total area is given over to wildlife sanctuaries and reserves, under the auspices of the Goa **Forest Department** (Map p86; ☎0832-2424352; www.goa.gov.in; Swami Vivekanand Rd). In 1999 Madei (208 sq km) in Satari taluk (district) and Netravali (211 sq km) in Sanguem taluka were declared protected areas.

The main sanctuaries are Bondla (p111), the smallest at 8 sq km, Bhagwan Mahavir (p113), the largest at 240 sq km, and Cotigao (p184), near Palolem.

Plants

The best time for wildlife watching is as soon after the monsoon as possible. October is perfect, when tourist numbers and temperatures are low and animals are attracted to still-verdant watering holes.

Flowering plants, grasses, brackens and ferns all play their part in Goa's ecology, and the Western Ghats comprise some of Asia's densest rainforest. On their lower slopes, thinner, drier soil supports semi-evergreen forest; in other places the arid landscape leads to savannah-like vegetation.

The coastal region has a wide range of flora, with saline conditions supporting mangrove swamps. In villages, banyan and peepul trees provide shade for the Hindu and Buddhist shrines that are often beneath them.

Environmental Issues

Deforestation

Over-cutting of the forested Western Ghats began at the start of the 20th century, and environmental groups estimate that more than 500 hectares of Goa's forests continue to disappear every year.

The damage caused by deforestation is far-reaching. Animal habitats are diminishing, as are the homelands of the tribal Dhangar, Kunbi and Velip peoples. In an effort to curb the damage, the government has stepped up its efforts to protect Goa's forests: felling fees now apply, licences must be obtained, and reforestation projects are under way.

Online Resources

Goa Foundation (www.goafoundation.org)

World Wildlife Fund (www.wwfindia.org)

Centre for Environment Education (http://ceeindia.org/goa.html)

Mining

In past decades nearly half the iron ore exported annually from India has come from Goa, with huge barges ferrying the ore along the Zuari and Mandovi Rivers to waiting ships.

Of the millions of tonnes of rock and soil extracted annually, only about 15% is saleable ore. Surplus is dumped on spoil tips and is washed away come the monsoon, smothering both river and marine life. Other side-effects of mining include the disruption of local water tables and the pollution of air and drinking water.

In 2010 the Shah Commission report into illegal mining – lobbied for by environmental groups such as the Goa Foundation – revealed corruptions, scams and unlicensed mining, which led to the Supreme Court suspending all mining activities in 2012.

The Goa Foundation described this victory as 'suspending more than a decade of senseless extraction and looting which irreversibly brutalised the natural environment, destroyed the peace of village communities and damaged public health'.

By 2014 the Goan government had renewed a limited number of mining licences, with a cap of 20 million tonnes of iron ore extraction, paving the way for at least partial resumption of an industry that has provided some 10% of the state's GDP.

However, in 2018 the Supreme Court again cancelled 88 mining leases, effectively shutting down the industry and leading to protests from 'mining dependants' – those working in the industry. At the time of writing, renewing of mining leases was still being thrashed out between Goa's government and the central government.

Survival Guide

Scams

India has an unfortunately deserved reputation for scams, both classic and newfangled. Of course, most can be avoided with some common sense and an appropriate amount of caution. They tend to be more of a problem in the major gateway cities (such as Delhi or Mumbai), or very touristy spots (such as Rajasthan). Chat with fellow travellers and check the India branch of Lonely Planet's Thorn Tree forum (www.lonelyplanet.com/thorntree) to keep abreast of the latest cons.

OTHER TOP SCAMS

- Gunk (dirt, paint, poo) suddenly appears on your shoes, only for a shoe cleaner to magically appear and offer to clean it off – for a price.
- Some shops are selling overpriced SIMs and not activating them; it's best to buy your SIM from an official outlet such as Airtel, Vodafone etc and check it works before leaving the area.
- Shops, restaurants or tour guides 'borrow' the name of their more successful and popular competitor.
- Touts claim to be 'government-approved' guides or agents, and sting you for large sums of cash. Enquire at the local tourist office about licensed guides and ask to see identification from guides themselves.
- 'Tourist offices' turn out to be dodgy travel agencies whose aim is to sell you overpriced tours, tickets and tourist services.

Contaminated Food & Drink

- Most bottled water is legit, but ensure that the seal is intact and the bottom of the bottle hasn't been tampered with.
- While in transit, try to carry packed food if possible, and politely decline offers of food or drink from locals on buses or trains; hygiene can be an issue and people have been drugged in the past.
- Though there have been no recent reports, the late 1990s saw a scam where travellers died after consuming food laced with dangerous bacteria from restaurants linked to dodgy medical clinics. In unrelated incidents, some clinics have given more treatment than necessary to procure larger payments from insurance companies.

Credit-Card Cons

Be careful when paying for souvenirs with a credit card. While government shops are usually legitimate, private souvenir shops have been known to surreptitiously run off extra copies of the credit-card imprint slip and use them for phoney transactions later.

Ask the trader to process the transaction in front of you. Memorising the CVV/CVC2 number and scratching it off the card is also a good idea, to avoid misuse. If anyone asks for your PIN with the intention of taking your credit card to the machine, insist on using the machine in person.

Druggings

Be extremely wary of accepting food or drink from strangers, even if you feel you're being rude. Women should be particularly circumspect. Occasionally, tourists (especially those travelling solo) have been drugged and robbed or even attacked. A spiked drink is the most common method, but snacks and even homemade meals have also been used.

Gem Scams

Don't be fooled by smooth-talking con artists who promise foolproof 'get rich quick' schemes. In this scam, travellers are asked to carry or mail gems home and then sell them to the trader's (nonexistent) overseas representatives at a profit. Without exception, the goods – if they arrive at all – are worth a fraction of what you paid, and the 'representatives' never materialise.

Travellers have reported this con happening in Agra, Delhi and Jaisalmer, but it's particularly prevalent in Jaipur. Carpets, curios and *pashmina* woollens are other favourites for this con.

Overpricing

Always agree on prices beforehand while using services that don't have regulated tariffs. This particularly applies to friendly neighbourhood guides, snack bars at touristy places, and autorickshaws and taxis without meters.

Photography

Ask for permission where possible while photographing people. If you don't have permission, you may be asked to pay a fee.

Theft

- Theft is a risk in India, as anywhere else. Keep your eye on your luggage at all times on public transport, and consider locking it, or even chaining it on overnight buses and trains. Remember that snatchings often occur when a train is pulling out of the station, as it's too late for you to give chase.
- Take extra care in dormitories and never leave your valuables unattended. Use safe deposit boxes where possible.
- Remember to lock your door at night; it is not unknown for thieves to take things from hotel rooms while occupants are sleeping.

Touts & Commission Agents

- Cabbies and autorickshaw drivers will often try to coerce you into staying at a hotel of their choice, only to collect a commission (added to your room tariff) afterward. Where possible, prearrange hotel bookings and request a hotel pick-up.
- You'll often hear stories about hotels of your choice being 'full' or 'closed' – check things out yourself and reconfirm and double-check your booking the day before you arrive.
- Be very sceptical of phrases like 'my brother's shop' and 'special deal at my friend's place'. Many fraudsters operate in collusion with souvenir stalls.
- Avoid friendly people and 'officials' in train and bus stations who offer unsolicited help, only to guide you to a commission-paying travel agent. Look confident, and if anyone asks if this is your first trip to India, say you've been here several times and that your onward travel is already booked.

Transport Scams

- Upon arriving at train stations and airports, if you haven't prearranged a pick-up, use public transport, or call an Uber or equivalent, or go to the prepaid taxi or airport shuttle-bus counters. Never choose a loitering cabbie who offers you a cheap ride into town, especially at night.
- While booking multiday sightseeing tours, research your own itinerary, and be extremely wary of anyone in Delhi offering houseboat tours to Kashmir – we've received many complaints over the years about dodgy deals.
- When buying a bus, train or plane ticket anywhere other than the registered office of the transport company, make sure you're getting the ticket class you paid for. Use official online booking facilities where possible.
- Train-station touts (even in uniform or with 'official' badges) may tell you that your intended train is cancelled/flooded/broken down or that your ticket is invalid or that you must pay to have your e-ticket validated on the platform. Do not respond to any approaches at train stations.

KEEPING SAFE

- A good travel-insurance policy is essential.
- Email copies of your passport identity page, visa and airline tickets to yourself, and keep copies on you.
- Keep your money and passport in a concealed money belt or a secure place under your shirt.
- Store at least US$100 separately from your main stash.
- Don't publicly display large wads of cash when paying.
- Consider using your own padlock at cheaper hotels.
- If you can't lock your hotel room securely from inside, stay elsewhere.

Women & Solo Travellers

Women Travellers

Reports of sexual assaults against women and girls are on the increase in India, despite tougher punishments being introduced after the notorious gang rape and murder of a female intern in Delhi in 2012. There have been several instances of sexual attacks on tourists over the last few years, though it's worth bearing in mind that the vast majority of visits are trouble free.

Unwanted Attention

Unwanted attention from men is a common problem.

➡ Being stared at is something you'll simply have to live with, so don't let it get the better of you.

➡ Be aware that men may try to take surreptitious photos with their phones – objecting loudly may discourage offenders.

➡ Refrain from returning male stares; this will be considered encouragement.

➡ Dark glasses, phones, books or electronic tablets are useful props for averting unwanted conversations.

➡ Wearing a wedding ring and saying you're due to meet your husband shortly can ward off unwanted interest.

Sexual Harassment

➡ Many women travellers have experienced provocative gestures, jeering, getting 'accidentally' bumped into and being followed, as well as more serious intrusions.

➡ Incidents are particularly common at exuberant (and crowded) public events such as the Holi festival. If a crowd gathers, find a less busy spot.

➡ Women travelling with a male partner will receive less hassle, but still be cautious.

Clothing

In big cities, you'll see local women dressing as they might in New York or London. Elsewhere women dress conservatively, and it pays to follow their lead.

➡ Avoid sleeveless tops, shorts, short skirts (ankle-length is recommended) and anything skimpy, see-through, tight-fitting or which reveals too much skin.

➡ Wearing Indian-style clothes such as the popular *salwar kameez* (traditional dress-like tunic and trousers) is viewed favourably.

➡ Drape a dupatta (long scarf) over your T-shirt to avoid stares – it also doubles as a head-covering for temple visits.

➡ Avoid going out in public wearing a choli (sari blouse) or a sari petticoat; it's like being half-dressed.

➡ Indian women tend to wear long shorts and a T-shirt when swimming; it's wise to wear a sarong from the beach to your hotel.

Staying Safe

The following tips will help you avoid uncomfortable or dangerous situations during your journey:

➡ Maintain a healthy level of vigilance, even if you've been in the country for a while. If something feels wrong, trust your instincts.

➡ Women have been drugged in the past so don't accept any food or drinks, even bottled water, from strangers.

➡ Keep conversations with unknown men short – being willing to chat can be misinterpreted.

➡ If you feel that a guy is encroaching on your space, he probably is. Protesting loudly enough to draw the attention of passers-by can stop unwelcome advances.

➡ The silent treatment can also be effective.

➡ Instead of shaking hands say *namaste* – the traditional, respectful Hindu greeting.

➡ Avoid wearing expensive-looking jewellery and carrying flashy accessories.

➡ Only go for massage or other treatments with female therapists, and go to cinemas with a companion.

➡ At hotels, keep your door locked, particularly at night; never let anyone you don't

SAFETY ON BUSES & TRAINS

- Don't organise your travel in such a way that it means you're hanging out at bus/train stations late at night.
- Solo women have reported less hassle by opting for the more expensive classes on trains, but try to avoid empty carriages.
- If you're travelling overnight by train, book an upper outer berth in 2AC; you're out of the way of wandering hands and the presence of fellow passengers is a deterrent to dodgy behaviour.
- On public transport, don't hesitate to return any errant limbs, put an item of luggage between you and others, be vocal (attracting public attention) or simply find a new spot.

know well into your hotel room.

- Avoid wandering alone in isolated areas – gallis (narrow lanes), deserted roads, beaches, ruins and forests.
- Use your smartphone's GPS maps to keep track of where you are; this will also alert you if a taxi/rickshaw is taking the wrong road.
- Try to look confident about where you are going in public; consult maps at your hotel (or at a restaurant) rather than on the street.

Taxis & Public Transport

Being female has some advantages; women can usually queue-jump for buses and trains without consequence and on trains and metros there are special ladies-only carriages. There are also women-only waiting rooms at some stations.

- Prearrange an airport pick-up from your hotel, particularly if you will arrive after dark.
- If travelling after dark, use a recommended, registered taxi service; travel with a companion where possible.
- Never hail a taxi in the street or accept a lift from a stranger.
- Never agree to have more than one man (the driver) in the car – ignore claims that this is 'just my brother' etc.
- Uber (www.uber.com) and Ola Cabs (www.olacabs.com) are useful, as you get the driver's licence plate in advance; pass the details on to someone else as a precaution.
- When taking rickshaws alone, call/text someone, or pretend to, to indicate that someone knows where you are.

Sanitary Items

Sanitary pads are widely available, but tampons are usually restricted to pharmacies in some big cities and tourist towns.

Websites

Peruse personal experiences proffered by female travellers at www.journeywoman.com and www.wanderlustandlipstick.com. Blogs such as Breathe, Dream, Go (https://breathedreamgo.com) and Hippie in Heels (https://hippie-inheels.com) are also full of tips.

Solo Travellers

Travelling solo in India may be great, because local people are often so friendly, helpful and interested in meeting new people. You're more likely to be 'adopted' by families, especially if you're commuting together on a long rail journey. If you're keen to hook up with fellow travellers, try tourist hubs such as Delhi, Goa, Rajasthan, Kerala, Manali, McLeod Ganj, Leh, Agra and Varanasi, or browse the messages on Lonely Planet's Thorn Tree forum (www.lonelyplanet.com/thorntree).

Cost

The most significant issue facing solo travellers is cost.

- Single-room accommodation rates are sometimes not much lower than double rates.
- Some midrange and top-end places don't even offer a single tariff.
- It's always worth trying to negotiate a lower rate for single occupancy.
- Ordering a thali (set-meal platter) at restaurants is an affordable way to try out a number of different dishes.

Safety

Most solo travellers experience no major problems in India, but, as anywhere else, it's wise to stay on your toes in unfamiliar surroundings.

- Some less honourable souls (locals and travellers alike) view lone tourists as an easy target for theft and sexual assault.
- Single men wandering around isolated areas have been mugged, even during the day.

Transport

- You'll save money if you find others to share taxis, autorickshaws, or a hired car and driver.
- Solo bus travellers may be able to get the 'co-pilot' seat beside the driver, handy if you've got a big bag.

Directory A–Z

Accessible Travel

There are few provisions for travellers with disabilities in Goa outside of the most top-end hotels, and thus the mobility-impaired traveller will face a number of challenges. Few older buildings have wheelchair access; toilets have certainly not been designed to accommodate wheelchairs; and footpaths are often riddled with potholes and crevices. If your mobility is restricted you will need an able-bodied companion to accompany you, and you'd be well-advised to hire a private vehicle with a driver. For more advice, contact one of the following organisations:

Accessible Journeys (www.disabilitytravel.com)

Disability Rights Association of Goa (DRAG; Map p86; ☎0832-2427160; www.disabilitygoa.org; MG Rd, c/o Star Investments)

Disability Rights UK (www.disabilityrightsuk.org)

Enable Holidays (www.enableholidays.com)

Mobility International USA (www.miusa.org)

Download Lonely Planet's free Accessible Travel guide from http://lptravel.to/AccessibleTravel.

Accommodation

Accommodation prices in Goa can vary considerably depending on the season and demand. The high season runs from November to late February, but prices climb even higher during the crowded Christmas and New Year period (around 22 December to 3 January). Mid-season is October and March to April, and low season is the monsoon (May to September). These dates can vary a little depending on the monsoon and the granting of shack licences, which are renewed every couple of years. Other peak periods include Indian holidays such as Diwali and Holi.

All accommodation rates listed are for the high season – but not for the peak Christmas period, when you'll almost certainly have to book in advance. Always call ahead for rates and ask about discounts. Listed rates also include taxes, which can range from 12% to 28% – budget places usually include taxes in their quoted rates while most top-end places do not.

BOOK YOUR STAY ONLINE

For more accommodation reviews by Lonely Planet authors, check out http://lonelyplanet.com/hotels/. You'll find independent reviews, as well as recommendations on the best places to stay. Best of all, you can book online.

Budget

Beach huts These range from basic bamboo and palm thatch to more sophisticated midrange and even top-end versions. They're most commonly found at Arambol, Mandrem, Asvem, Agonda, Palolem, Cola, Patnem and Talpona beaches.

Budget guesthouses No-frills, fan-cooled rooms set back from the beach, found all along the coast and in cities such as Panaji and Margao. Only the very cheapest places have shared bathroom.

Hostels A growing part of the accommodation market and a good deal for solo travellers. Clean dorms (some with air-con) with free wi-fi, lockers, bed lights, breakfast, fully-equipped kitchen and a good chance of meeting other travellers. The best are found in Anjuna, Vagator, Panaji, Palolem and Morjim.

Rooms and houses to let Those staying in one place from a week to six months should consider renting a local house or room(s) in a house. These can range from ₹2000 to ₹6000 per week depending on condition, length of rental, location and time of year. Signs (with a phone number) are common around places such as Anjuna, Chapora, Patnem and Benaulim but there are rooms available all along the

SLEEPING PRICE RANGES

The following price ranges refer to a double room with bathroom:

$ less than ₹1500

$$ ₹1500–7500

$$$ more than ₹7500

coastal belt. Get in early (before November) for the best deals. Online sites such as AirBnB are worth checking out.

Midrange

Apartments A more upmarket version of local houses to let, modern serviced and unserviced apartments are available for stays from a week to several months. Some include a swimming pool and security. Check sites such as www.airbnb.co.in, www.goaholidayhomes.com or www.goarooms.in.

Hotels and guesthouses In the midrange category hotels will come with TV, private bathroom, balcony or verandah, optional air-con, free wi-fi, usually an attached restaurant and services such as travel desk, housekeeping etc.

Top End

Heritage and boutique hotels The stand-out accommodation option in Goa is the range of heritage properties, often housed in restored Portuguese homes. In a similar category are boutique hotels and luxury high-class places, often with just a few rooms.

Resorts These include four- or five-star beachfront properties with swimming pools, spas, high-end restaurants, first-class service and sometimes tennis courts or golf courses.

Tented camps and villas You will also find the occasional luxury tent encampment or fabulously equipped private villa in this price range.

Booking Services

Advance booking is essential for the peak Christmas and New Year season and recommended anytime from December to March. Most places listed here can be booked directly online; if not you can usually book places through Booking.com (www.booking.com). Other useful booking services in Goa include Oyo (www.oyorooms.com), Goibibo (www.goibibo.com) and Yatra (www.yatra.com).

To compare or book beach huts in South Goa, check out www.beachhutbooking.com. For homes and rooms to let, AirBnB (www.airbnb.co.in) is gaining traction.

Customs Regulations

- Duty-free allowance is 2L of wine or spirits and 200 cigarettes (or 50 cigars, or 250g of tobacco) per person.
- Foreign currency totalling more than US$10,000 must be declared.
- Antiques more than 100 years old are not permitted to be exported from India without an export clearance certificate. See the Central Board of Excise and Customs website (www.cbec.gov.in) for more information.

Electricity

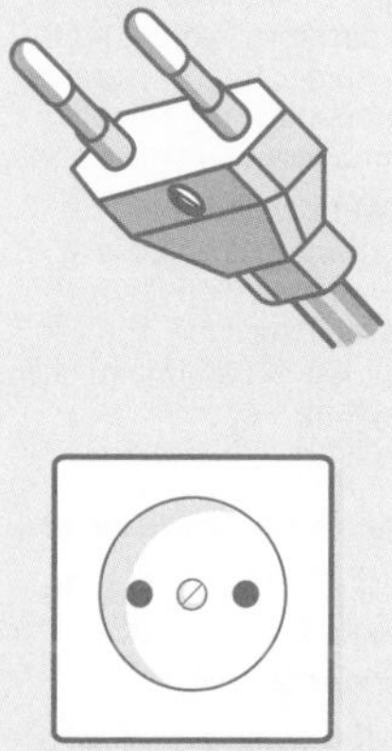

Type C
230V/50Hz

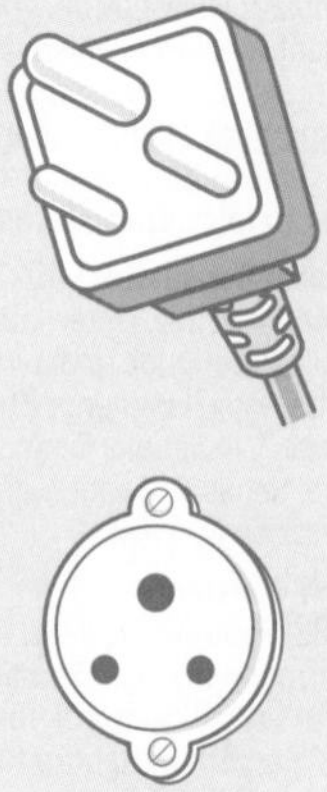

Type D
230V/50Hz

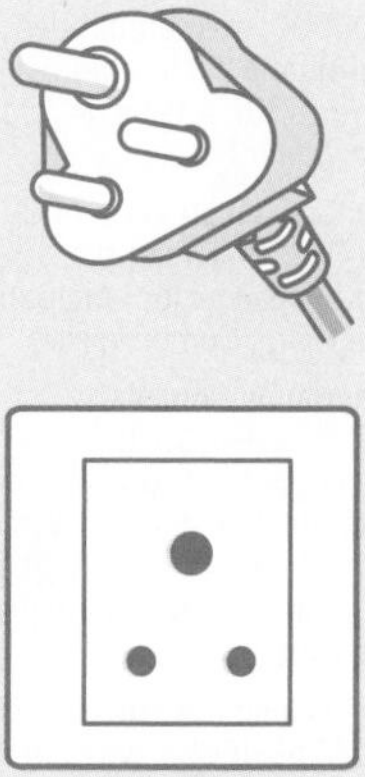

Type M
230V/50Hz

Embassies & Consulates

The following foreign diplomatic missions are based in Mumbai.

Australian Consulate (☎022-67574900; www.mumbai.consulate.gov.au; 10th fl, A Wing, Crescenzo Bldg, G Block, Plot C 38-39, Bandra Kurla Complex, Bandra East)

British Consulate (☎022-66502222; www.gov.uk/government/world/organisations/british-deputy-high-commission-mumbai; Naman Chambers, C/32 G Block Bandra Kurla Complex, Bandra East)

Canadian Consulate (☎022-67494444; https://international.gc.ca/world-monde/india-inde/mumbai.aspx?lang=eng; 21st fl, Tower 2, Indiabulls Finance Centre, Senapati Bapat Marg, Elphinstone Rd West)

French Consulate (☎022-66694000; www.ambafrance-in.org/-Consulate-in-Bombay-; Wockhardt Towers, East Wing, 5th fl, Bandra Kurla Complex, Bandra East)

German Consulate (☎022-22832422; https://india.diplo.de/in-en/vertretungen/gkmumbai; 10th fl, Hoechst House, Nariman Point)

Israeli Consulate (☎022-61600500; www.embassies.gov.il/mumbai; Marathon Futurex, 1301, A Wing, NM Joshi Marg, Lower Parel)

Japanese Consulate (☎022-23517101; www.mumbai.in.emb-japan.go.jp; 1 ML Dahanukar Marg, Cumballa Hill)

Netherlands Consulate (☎022-22194200; https://www.netherlandsworldwide.nl/countries/india/about-us/consulate-general-in-mumbai; 1st fl, Forbes Bldg, Charanjit Rai Marg, Fort)

New Zealand Consulate (☎022-61316666; www.mfat.govt.nz/en/countries-and-regions/south-asia/india/new-zealand-high-commission/new-zealand-consulate-general-mumbai-india; Level 2, Maker Maxity, 3 North Ave, Bandra Kurla Complex)

Sri Lankan Consulate (☎022-22045861; www.mumbai.mission.gov.lk; Mulla House, 34 Homi Modi St, Fort)

Thai Consulate (☎022-22823535; www.thaiembassy.org/mumbai; 12th fl, Express Towers, Barrister Rajni Patel Marg, Nariman Point)

US Consulate (☎022-26724000; https://in.usembassy.gov/embassy-consulates/mumbai; C49, G Block, Bandra Kurla Complex, Bandra East)

Food

The following price ranges refer to a standard main course:

$ less than ₹150

$$ ₹150–400

$$$ more than ₹400

Insurance

Comprehensive travel insurance to cover theft, loss and medical problems (as well as air evacuation) is strongly recommended.

- Some policies exclude potentially dangerous activities such as scuba diving, motorcycling, paragliding and even trekking: read the fine print.
- If you plan to hire a motorcycle in India, make sure the rental policy includes at least third-party insurance.
- Check in advance whether your insurance policy will pay doctors and hospitals directly or reimburse you later.
- It's crucial to get a police report in India as soon as possible if you've had anything stolen; insurance companies may refuse to reimburse you without one.
- Worldwide travel insurance is available at www.lonelyplanet.com/travel-insurance. You can buy, extend and claim online anytime – even if you're already on the road.

Internet Access

- Internet cafes are virtually nonexistent in Goa.
- USB dongles (modems) for 4G internet connections direct to your laptop are available at mobile-phone shops.
- Free wi-fi is common in cafes, beach shacks and accommodation; ask before booking.
- If you have a smart phone with a local SIM and data plan, you can use this as a personal hotspot modem with your laptop computer or tablet.

Legal Matters

It's important to realise what your own embassy can and can't do to help you if you get into trouble. Generally it won't be much help if the trouble you're in is your own fault. Your embassy will not be sympathetic if you end up in jail after committing a crime locally, even if such actions are legal in your own country.

Drugs

Acid, ecstasy, cocaine, charas (hashish), marijuana and most other forms of drugs are illegal in India (though still available in Goa), and purchasing or carrying drugs is fraught with danger. India's anti-drug laws are some of the toughest in the world, and Goa's central jail is filled with prisoners, including some foreigners, serving lengthy sentences for drug offences. Being caught in possession of even a small quantity of illegal substances, including hash, can mean a 10-year stretch.

Dealing with Police

Police corruption can be a problem in Goa, with drug use among travellers giving some poorly paid police officers opportunities for extortion, but the local Goan government has worked hard at stamping out this practice in recent years.

Probably the best way to deal with police extortion, should it happen to you, is through polite, respectful persuasion. If that fails, attempt to bargain down the 'fine' before paying up, and try to establish the identity (or at least a good mental image) of the police officer. That's assuming you're innocent. If not, pay up and be thankful.

In practical terms, the most contact the average traveller is likely to have with the law will be on the road. Police have lately started cracking down on all traffic, mainly on the NH66 at large intersections, bridges and entry/exit points into towns. If you're riding a two-wheeler, you'll possibly be flagged down and an opportunistic police officer will push to extract a 'fine', especially if you don't have the correct licence (international driving permit for foreigners) or are not wearing a helmet. The official fines are quite low (₹100 for not wearing a helmet for example) but you may be pressured to pay up to 10 times this amount. If this happens, keep your cool and try to negotiate it down.

LGBT+ Travellers

In September 2018, India's Supreme Court finally ruled consensual homosexuality legal, overturning a 2013 decision to criminalise such activity and ending almost two decades of court action to repeal section 377 of the Indian penal code.

In 2014, there was a ruling that gave legal recognition of a third gender in India, a step towards increased acceptance of the large yet marginalised transgender *(hijra)* population.

Goa's liberal reputation draws gay men, and there's a discreet scene, mainly around the Calangute/Baga and Candolim area, however, public displays of affection are frowned upon for both homosexual and heterosexual couples.

In Mumbai, Gay Bombay (www.gaybombay.org) is a great resource, with event listings including meet-ups in Bandra, and GB-hosted bar and film nights. Other resources:

Humsafar Trust (☎022-26673800; www.humsafar.org; 3rd fl, Manthan Plaza Nehru Rd, Vakola Santa Cruz East; ⏰10am-6.30pm Mon-Fri) Mumbai's most well-known LGBTQ community organisation.

Gaylaxy (www.gaylaxymag.com) India's best gay e-zine.

Gaysi (www.gaysifamily.com) Mumbai-based lifestyle e-zine.

LABIA (Lesbian & Bisexuals in Action; www.sites.google.com/site/labiacollective/home) Lesbian and bi support group based in Mumbai.

Queer Azaadi Mumbai (www.facebook.com/qam.mumbaipride) Organises Mumbai's Pride Parade (www.mumbaipride.in), which is usually held in early February.

Money

The Indian rupee (₹) is divided into 100 paise, but only 50 paise coins are legal tender and these are rarely seen. Coins come in denominations of ₹1, ₹2, ₹5 and ₹10 (the 1s and 2s look almost identical); notes come in ₹5, ₹10, ₹20, ₹50, ₹100, ₹500 and ₹2000.

ATMs

➡ There are many 24-hour ATMs in Goa, particularly in Panaji, Margao and Mapusa, but also in villages and smaller beach resorts such as Agonda, Palolem and Arambol.

➡ ATMs linked to Axis Bank, Citibank, HDFC, HSBC, ICICI and State Bank of India usually recognise foreign cards (Cirrus and Maestro). Other banks may accept major cards (Visa, MasterCard etc).

➡ Check with your home bank about foreign ATM charges. You'll often be charged for transactions at both ends (usually ₹200 at the ATM you're using), so it pays to withdraw as much cash as possible, rather than making lots of small withdrawals.

➡ ATMs dispense mostly ₹500 or even ₹2000 notes, which can be difficult to change for small purchases. Most banks have a limit of ₹10,000 to ₹15,000 per transaction.

➡ Some 'remote' beach or inland destinations still require a trek to find an ATM, so you'll need to bring cash along with you.

Credit Cards

➡ Credit cards are accepted in many hotels and guesthouses, most travel agencies, higher-end stores and an increasing number of tourist restaurants and even beach shacks.

➡ MasterCard and Visa are the most widely accepted credit cards.

Opening Hours

Outside high season (November to March) many tourist-oriented shops, restaurants and services may be closed completely. Some businesses may close for an hour or two in the afternoon or have reduced services during the low season (May to September). Hours provided are for high season.

Banks 10am to 2pm Monday to Friday, to noon Saturday

Bars noon to midnight

Clubs 10pm to 5am

Restaurants and cafes 8am to 11pm

Shops 10am to 6pm

Post

The Indian postal service (www.indiapost.gov.in), though massive, is generally pretty good. Letters sent from Goa and Mumbai almost invariably reach their destination.

It costs ₹12 to send a small postcard anywhere in the world from India, and ₹50 for a large postcard or a standard letter (up to 20g).

PRACTICALITIES

Newspapers & Magazines Goa has four English-language dailies: the *Herald* (www.oheraldo.in), the *Navhind Times* (www.navhindtimes.in), the *Goan* (http://englishnews.thegoan.net) and the local version of the *Times of India* (www.timesofindia.indiatimes.com). Local magazines include *Viva Goa* (www.vivagoamagazine.com) and *Goa Streets* (www.goastreets.com).

Radio All India Radio (AIR; www.airpanaji.gov.in) transmits local and international news. There are several private FM broadcasters and music stations.

TV The government TV broadcaster is Doordarshan. Satellite TV, which has BBC World, CNN, Star World and Star Movies, MTV, VH1 and HBO, is widely available at hotels.

Weights & Measures Although India officially uses the metric system, imperial weights and measures are still sometimes used. You may hear the term lakh (100,000) and crore (10 million) referring to rupees, people or anything else in large numbers.

Smoking Smoking is banned in many, but not all, restaurants and in government buildings and places such as railway stations, where transgressors face a ₹1000 fine.

Public Holidays

In addition to the public holidays listed below, a number of festivals and events (p23) are celebrated throughout the region at various times of year.

Republic Day 26 January

Good Friday (Easter) March/April

Buddha Jayanti April/May

May Day 1 May

Independence Day 15 August

Gandhi Jayanti 2 October

Guru Nanak Jayanti November

Feast of St Francis Xavier 3 December

Goa Liberation Day 19 December

Christmas 25 December

Safe Travel

Despite stories of violent crime, drug-related misdeeds and police corruption (some of them internationally high-profile and involving tourists) Goa remains essentially a safe destination for travellers. So long as you adhere to a few basic and common-sense safety precautions, you should stay safe and secure in Goa.

- Avoid walking along unlit back lanes or beach areas alone at night.
- Always agree on the price of a taxi or autorickshaw before getting in.
- Beware of undertows when swimming.
- Don't leave valuables in your room.
- Wear a helmet if riding a motorbike.
- Steer well clear of drugs.

Telephone

- Local and long-distance telephone calls can be made from private call offices (labelled PCO/ISD/STD).
- The area code for everywhere within the state of Goa is 0832, which you need to dial when calling from outside the state or from a mobile phone. Mumbai's area code is 022.
- To make an international call, you need to dial 00 (international access code from India), plus the country code (of the country you are calling), the area code and the local number.
- To make a call to Goa from outside the country, dial the international access code plus 91 (international country code for India), then 832 (Goa's area code omitting the initial 0) and then the local number.

Mobile Phones

Any unlocked GSM phone will work fine in Goa and most parts of India but expensive international roaming charges (for making and receiving calls) mean a better option is to buy a local SIM card and connect to a local carrier. Data charges are cheap, so you can use an internet-based service such as Skype, WhatsApp or Messenger to make international calls.

- Popular and reliable prepaid carriers in Goa include Airtel and Vodafone, though you'll also find !dea and BSNL.
- To buy a SIM card go to any shop or travel agent advertising your preferred carrier (they're everywhere) and look at the prepaid call and data plans on offer.
- Foreigners need two passport photos, photocopies of passport identity and visa pages and preferably a copy of a drivers licence or similar with your home address (the phone shop can sometimes do the photocopies for you).
- You must supply a residential address, which can be the address of your hotel or a local friend. Usually

the phone company will call your hotel (notify reception in advance) any time up to 24 hours after your application to verify that you're staying there.

- At some outlets and on certain plans tourists can bypass the paperwork and activation period but the validation is usually limited to 30 days.
- Prepaid mobile-phone kits (SIM card and phone number, plus an allocation of calls) are available from about ₹200, while internet data plans at around ₹300 offer a whopping 1.5GB per day. Once activated, you can easily top up talk-time and data at any store advertising your carrier.
- Local (India-wide) call costs from Goa are less than ₹1 a minute, and international calls are less than ₹10 a minute.

Taxes & Refunds

In 2017 the Indian government introduced a controversial Goods & Services Tax (GST) to replace a slew of other state and federal taxes. The GST is confusing as there are four main rates of taxation – 5%, 12%, 18% and 28%. For travellers this will mainly be noticed with accommodation, where rooms over ₹1000 are taxed at between 12% and 28%.

Restaurants add only the 5% tax rate to bills. Alcohol is outside the GST scheme but still attracts a VAT of between 12% and 15%.

At the time of writing the government was working on a scheme to allow tourists to get GST refunds at airports.

Time

India is 5½ hours ahead of GMT/UTC, 4½ hours behind Australia (EST) and 10½ hours ahead of the USA (EST). It is officially known as IST – Indian Standard Time, although many Indians prefer to think it stands for Indian Stretchable Time. There's no daylight saving time.

Toilets

Public toilets exist in Panaji and at some popular beach entrances (usually with a ₹1 or ₹2 fee) but they're not common. Toilet paper is even more rare. Restaurants, cafes and hotels in Goa almost always have sit-down flush toilets.

Tourist Information

Goa Tourism Development Corporation (GTDC; Map p86; ☎0832-2437132; www.goa-tourism.com; Paryatan Bhavan, Dr Alvaro Costa Rd, Panaji; ⏰9.30am-5.45pm Mon-Fri), usually called Goa Tourism these days, is the state government tourism body and it's a surprisingly progressive government organisation, acting more like a commercial business with numerous hotels and operating a host of tours and even a taxi smartphone app.

Visas

e-Visa (ETA)

Citizens of most countries, including Australia, Israel, Japan, New Zealand, Russia, United Kingdom, USA and most European nationalities, are currently able to apply online for a 60-day double-entry e-Visa, or Electronic Travel Authority (ETA), for arrival at 26 airports, including Goa, Bengaluru, Chennai, Kochi, Delhi, Hyderabad, Kolkata, Mumbai and Trivandrum.

You need to apply online at www.indianvisaonline.gov. in a minimum/maximum of four/120 days before you are due to travel. The fee varies by country (for most countries it's US$80 but for UK, USA and Russia it's $US100), and you have to upload a photograph (headshot – you can do this yourself with a smartphone camera) as well as a scanned copy of your passport. Follow online instructions carefully as your fee won't be refunded if the application is rejected for any reason. The e-Visa is valid from the date of arrival and cannot be extended.

Other Visa Types

If you want to stay longer than 60 days (up to six months), or are not covered by the e-Visa scheme, you must get a visa before arriving in India. Visas are available at Indian missions worldwide, though in many countries applications are processed by a separate private company. In some countries, including the UK, you must apply in person at the designated office as well as filing an application online.

Most people are issued with a standard six-month tourist visa, which for most nationalities permits multiple entry. Tourist visas are valid from the date of issue, not the date you arrive in India. Student and business visas have strict conditions (consult the Indian embassy for details).

Five- and 10-year tourist visas are available to US citizens only under a bilateral arrangement; however, you can still only stay in the country for up to 180 days continuously. Currently you are required to submit two passport photographs with your visa application; these must be in colour and must be 5.08cm by 5.08cm (2in by 2in; larger than regular passport photos). An onward travel ticket is a requirement for some visas, but this isn't always enforced (check in advance).

For visas lasting more than six months, you're supposed to register at the Foreigners' Regional Registration Office in Delhi or Goa within 14 days of arriving in India; enquire about these special conditions when you apply for your visa.

Transport

GETTING THERE & AWAY

Air

Goa's airport, **Dabolim** (Goa International Airport; ☎0832-2540806; NH566), is served directly by domestic flights, a handful of international flights from the Middle East, and seasonal package-holiday charters (mostly from Russia, Europe and the UK).

Unless you're on a charter, you'll generally have to fly into a major city such as Mumbai or Delhi and change to a domestic flight.

A new greenfield airport at Mopa in North Goa is expected to be completed by 2020.

Mumbai's **Chhatrapati Shivaji Maharaj International Airport** (☎022-66851010; www.csia.in; Santa Cruz East) is a major international and domestic air hub for southern India.

CHARTER FLIGHTS

Reliable charter flights into Goa from the UK or Germany include the following:

Tui (☎+44 0203 636 1931; www.tui.co.uk)

Condor Airlines (☎+49 (0) 180 6 767767; www.condor.com)

Thomas Cook Airlines (www.thomascookairlines.com)

Domestic Flights

Several budget airlines, along with the national carrier **Air India** (☎1800 1801407, 022-22023031; www.airindia.com; Air India Bldg, cnr Marine Dr & Madame Cama Rd, Nariman Point, Mumbai; ⏲9.15am-6.30pm Mon-Thu, 9.15am-6.15pm Fri, 9.15am-1pm & 1.45-5pm Sat), operate direct daily flights between Goa and Mumbai, Chennai, Delhi, Bengaluru (Bangalore), Kochi and Hyderabad. A return flight to Mumbai with a low-cost carrier such as SpiceJet can cost as little as US$100 if booked a few weeks in advance. You can book online directly with the airline or through a booking site.

Domestic airlines flying into and out of Goa include the following:

Indigo (www.goindigo.in)

GoAir (www.goair.in)

SpiceJet (www.spicejet.com)

Jet Airways (www.jetairways.com)

Vistara (www.airvistara.com)

Air Asia India (www.airasia.com)

Land

Bus

Private and state-run long-distance buses run to and from Goa daily. Tickets can be booked in advance online, at ticket agents located near the bus stands or through travel agents or tourist accommodation. Note that travel into and out of Mumbai by road is interminably slow; the train is faster and more comfortable.

Kadamba (www.goakadamba.com), the state government bus company, operates across the state and to neighbouring regions. For private or state buses you can book online with www.redbus.in.

Buses for Mumbai and other cities depart from Panaji, Margao and Mapusa between 5.30pm and 8.30pm daily; there are dozens of operators and departures, but fares are standard to/from anywhere in Goa.

Bengaluru (Bangalore; ₹600/800/1100, 14 to 15 hours)

Mumbai (express/AC/sleeper ₹450/650/1100, 12 to 14 hours)

Hampi (sleeper, ₹1000, 10 to 11 hours)

Pune (₹450/750/1000, 11 hours)

TYPES OF BUS

State-run and private companies offer 'ordinary', 'deluxe', 'superfast' and VIP services, but definitions are flexible. The most comfortable are the Volvo buses with reclining seating and air-conditioning.

Many long-distance buses travel overnight – bring earplugs if you want to block out the Bollywood movies on the video screens. The standard

CLIMATE CHANGE & TRAVEL

Every form of transport that relies on carbon-based fuel generates CO_2, the main cause of human-induced climate change. Modern travel is dependent on aeroplanes, which might use less fuel per kilometre per person than most cars but travel much greater distances. The altitude at which aircraft emit gases (including CO_2) and particles also contributes to their climate change impact. Many websites offer 'carbon calculators' that allow people to estimate the carbon emissions generated by their journey and, for those who wish to do so, to offset the impact of the greenhouse gases emitted with contributions to portfolios of climate-friendly initiatives throughout the world. Lonely Planet offsets the carbon footprint of all staff and author travel.

is air-con, which can feel too cold – wear long sleeves and pack a blanket or sarong. On some routes such as Goa–Mumbai and Goa–Hampi, flat-berth sleeper buses are available. While these may be horizontal, bus travel is not like train travel – you might wake to find yourself flying out of bed on the first sharp corner.

Train

The 760km-long Konkan Railway (www.konkanrailway.com), completed in 1998, is the main train line running through the state, connecting Goa with Mumbai to the north and Mangalore to the south.

The biggest station in Goa is Margao's Madgaon station (p168), and many trains also pass through Karmali station near Old Goa, 12km from Panaji. Smaller stations on the line include Pernem for Arambol, Thivim for Mapusa and the northern beaches, and Canacona for Palolem.

BOOKING TRAINS

For services, fares and bookings check the Konkan Railway (www.konkanrailway.com), Indian Railways (www.indianrail.gov.in; www.irctc.co.in), the excellent India Rail Info (http://indiarailinfo.com), with added offline browsing support, or the user-friendly Erail (erail.in). Cleartrip (www.cleartrip.com/trains) and Makemytrip (www.makemytrip.com/railways) are also useful travel booking sites. To register with these sites you'll need a working mobile phone number and email address.

However, online booking of train tickets has its share of glitches: travellers have reported problems with registering themselves on some portals and using credit cards.

You can only book six train tickets online per calendar month, and after that you can only buy them in person. If you book online and accept a waitlisted ticket and it isn't confirmed before the train leaves its destination, the money is refunded to the credit card and the ticket is worthless.

Man at Seat 61 (www.seat61.com) has lots of good information, and explains in detail how to register an IRCTC account if you don't have an Indian mobile number.

Children under the age of five travel for free; those between five and 12 are charged half price.

Within Goa, in-person train bookings are best made at Margao's station, at the train reservation office at Panaji's Kadamba bus stand or at any travel agent selling train tickets. Book as far in advance as possible for sleepers, as they fill up quickly – though a limited number of tickets go on sale the day before travel, so it's always worth checking. A small number of tickets are set aside for foreign travellers – enquire at the tourist quota counter at Margao station and show your passport.

Reservation fees generally range from ₹40 to ₹60, or slightly more if booking through a travel agent. Even if there are no seats, passengers cancel and there are regular no-shows. On the day of departure you can buy a 'Reservation Against Cancellation' (RAC) ticket for around ₹50 that will allow you to board the train. Once on board the conductor will usually find you a seat or sleeper berth and you pay the additional fare. If you book more than a few days in advance you may be waitlisted, which means you pay full fare and hope there are enough cancellations to get you on. This can be risky as you can't board the train if the ticket is still waitlisted, but you can get a refund.

TRAIN CLASSES

There are several different classes, but not all are available on all trains. Sleeper berths are converted to bench seats by day. In 2016, double-decker trains started operating between Mumbai and Goa.

AC First Class (1A)
Air-conditioned accommodation in simple two-berth or four-berth lockable compartments. Bedclothes and meals are provided.

AC 2 Tier (2A) Two-tier berths arranged in groups of two- and four-berth curtained compartments in an air-conditioned, open-plan carriage.

AC 3 Tier (3A) Three-tier berths arranged in groups of six in an open-plan air-con carriage.

First Class (FC) A non-AC version of AC First Class (1A).

AC Chair Car (CC) Air-conditioned carriage with reclining seats.

Sleeper (SL) Similar to AC 3 Tier (3A) but without air-conditioning. Instead there are fans and open windows.

Second Sitting (2S) Unreserved second-class seating on plastic chairs or wooden benches.

Sea

Cruise ships, mostly from the UAE or travelling between Mumbai and the Maldives, call in at Goa's Mormugao cruise ship terminal as part of their itineraries.

In 2018 a Mumbai to Goa ferry began operating three times a week.

GETTING AROUND

Bicycle

Goa offers plenty of variety for cycling, certainly in the village back lanes. A bicycle can also be a convenient and ecofriendly way of getting around beach towns.

Hire

At most beach resorts in Goa you'll find people who are prepared to rent out a local, Indian-made, single-gear rattler, though mountain bikes are sometimes also available. Expect to pay around ₹50 to ₹150 per day.

Purchase

For a longer stay of three months or more in Goa, consider buying a bicycle locally. Basic Indian road bikes (including Hero, Atlas, BSA and Raleigh) are available at bicycle shops in cities from ₹3500 and mountain bikes from ₹4000. You should be able to pick up a second-hand bike for ₹1000 to ₹1500.

If you want a quality machine for serious touring, bring your own, along with spare parts and accessories and a very strong bike lock.

Boat

Local ferries cross a number of creeks and rivers, but there are no long-distance ferry routes within Goa.

Goa's Ferries

One of the joys of day-tripping in Goa is a short ride on one of the state's few remaining vehicle/passenger ferries, which, until the recent addition of road bridges spanning Goa's wide and wonderful rivers, formed a crucial means of transport for locals. Most ferries run every half hour or so (busy routes run non-stop) from around 7am to 10pm. The ferries are free to pedestrians and two-wheelers.

Panaji to Betim (p95) The most popular ferry and a useful short cut to the northern beaches.

Ribandar to Chorao Island (p98) For Dr Salim Ali Bird Sanctuary.

Old Goa to Divar Island (p98)

Divar Island to Naroa (p99)

Querim to Terekhol Fort (p161)

Bus

➡ An extensive network of buses shuttle to and from almost every tiny town and village, though the main hubs are Panaji, Margao and Mapusa. Travelling between north and south Goa you'll generally need to change buses at Margao, Panaji or both.

➡ There are no timetables, but buses are frequent and usually have the destination posted (in English and Konkani) in the front window. Fares range from ₹5 to ₹40.

➡ Local buses are mostly old rustbuckets and can be slow, stopping frequently to drop off or pick up passengers. Between Panaji and Margao or Mapusa, look for the faster 'express' buses.

MUMBAI TO GOA FERRY

In late 2018 a new cruise ship ferry service began operating between Mumbai and Goa. **Angriya Cruises** (☎8314810440; www.angriyacruises.com; Mormugao Cruise Terminal; ⏰4pm Tue, Thu, Sun Oct-May) is a seven-deck, 130m-long luxury cruise ship with two restaurants, six bars, a spa and an infinity pool. More than just sea transport between two cities this is an overnight pleasure cruise where you get to see the sunset and sunrise from the deck.

The ship departs from Mumbai's Victoria Docks (Purple Gate) at 4pm on Monday, Wednesday and Friday, arriving at Goa's Mormugao cruise terminal around 9am the next day. It departs Goa at 4pm on Tuesday, Thursday and Sunday.

Onboard accommodation ranges from dormitory bunks (₹4300) and luxury single pods (₹4650) to spacious double rooms (₹8950 per person) and family rooms (₹5700 per person). Meals are an additional ₹2000/1000 per adult/child. At those prices it's cheaper than a business-class flight between Mumbai and Goa.

The service operates from October to May and online bookings open one month in advance.

Car & Motorcycle

➡ It's easy in Goa to organise a private car with a driver (or simply a taxi) for long-distance day trips. Expect to pay from ₹2000 for a full day out on the road (usually defined as eight hours and 80km).

➡ Self-drive hire cars start from ₹1100 per day for a small car to upwards of ₹4500 for a large 4WD, excluding fuel and usually with a per kilometre limit. Your best bet for rentals is online at sites such as www.goa2u.com.

➡ Familiarise yourself with road signs: on Goa's major NH66 national highway there are varying speed limits for different types of vehicle.

➡ You won't find the likes of Avis, Hertz etc in Goa but check out sites such as Vailankanni Car Hire (www.goacars.in) and Urban Drive (www.urbandrive.co.in).

Motorcycle

You'll rarely go far on a Goan road without seeing a local or tourist whizzing by on a scooter or motorbike, and renting one is, in theory, a breeze. You'll likely pay from ₹200 to ₹400 per day for a scooter, ₹400 to ₹500 for a smaller Yamaha motorbike (relatively rare), and ₹400 to ₹800 for a Royal Enfield Bullet, depending on supply and demand. Prices can drop considerably if you're renting for more than a few days or if it's an off-peak period – bargain if there are lots of machines around.

If you want to book a bike in advance, try www.ziphop.in.

Driving Licence

An international driving permit is now considered mandatory, certainly as far as local police looking to extract 'fines' are concerned. The first thing a policeman will want to see if he stops you is your licence, and an international permit is incontrovertible. Permits are available from your home automobile association. In any case, it must be accompanied by your home drivers licence. Although you should be able to ride an automatic scooter with only a car licence and international permit, Goan police may try to fine you for not having a 'two-wheeler' licence.

The bottom line, though, is that even if you don't have the correct documents, as long as you pay up you'll generally be allowed to ride on. Claiming not to have any cash on you is a good start at bargaining down the fine.

Fuel & Spare Parts

➡ Though subject to change, at the time of research unleaded petrol cost around ₹70 per litre.

➡ Distances are generally short and small bikes (such as the Honda Kinetic or Activa) are very economical – at least 30km per litre.

➡ There are increasing numbers of petrol stations in main towns including Panaji, Margao, Mapusa, Ponda and Vasco da Gama. There are also busy pumps near Vagator, Palolem and Arambol.

➡ Where there are no petrol pumps, general stores sell petrol by the litre (usually in recycled water bottles at ₹80 to ₹100); be aware that sometimes petrol in plastic bottles has been diluted with kerosene.

➡ Before hiring a bike, ensure that the fuel gauge, indicators and horn all work.

Road Conditions & Safety

Goan roads can be treacherous, filled with human, bovine, canine, feline, mechanical and avian obstacles, as well as a good sprinkling of potholes and hairpin bends.

➡ Be on the lookout for 'speed breakers'. Speed humps are stand-alone back breakers or come in triplets. They can be hard to spot, especially at night.

➡ Take it slowly, try not to drive at night (country lanes are poorly lit), and don't attempt a north–south day trip on a scooter.

➡ Goa's main NH66 is a highway in name only – single lane and congested in parts. However, the new north-south multilane bypass will open in stages from late 2019.

Road Rules

➡ Driving is on the left, vehicles give way to the right and road signs are universal pictorial signs.

➡ Helmets are mandatory for two-wheelers in Goa though many riders continue to ignore this away from the main highway. You can be pulled over and fined for not wearing one and the safety implications are obvious.

➡ At busy intersections, traffic police are often on hand to reduce the chaos. Otherwise, make good use of your horn.

➡ Speed limits range from 30km/h to 60km/h. The blood alcohol limit is 0.03% – the equivalent of just one standard drink for most people. Police are increasingly using 'alcometers' at traffic stops and the penalties for being drunk at the wheel can be severe.

➡ The highway code in India can be reduced to one essential truth – 'Might is Right' – meaning the bigger the vehicle, the more priority you're accorded. Motorbikes sit only above bicycles and pedestrians on the food chain.

Local Transport

Autorickshaw

An autorickshaw (also called an auto, three-wheeler or, outside of India, a tuk-tuk) is the quintessential Indian

GOA MILES

Ridesharing services such as Uber and Ola are banned in Goa, partly due to the powerful taxi unions and partly because the state government wanted a piece of the action. The latest Goa Tourism transport initiative, launched in 2018, is Goa Miles (www.goamiles.com), a taxi smartphone app that works much like Uber.

Since the service is (at least for now) subsidised by the government, the fares are roughly half what you would pay a taxi driver off the street (closer to the fares charged at the airport prepaid counter). For example, a small car from Panaji to Arambol costs just ₹900. Another advantage is security, as the drivers are registered, the cars can be tracked, and the cars themselves are modern and clean. Until more drivers/cars join the service there are likely to be lots of occasions when cars are unavailable in your area, especially at night.

Goa Miles should be a great service with fair prices and safe rides – provided the taxi unions don't find a way to stamp it out.

short-hop form of transport, a yellow-and-black three-wheeled contraption powered by a noisy two-stroke motorcycle engine. It's about a third cheaper than a taxi and generally a better option for short trips – count on a minimum ₹50 for a short journey and ₹150 for a slightly longer one.

Flag down an autorickshaw and negotiate the fare before you jump in; if the driver's charging too much, try another.

Motorcycle Taxi

Goa is the only place in India where motorcycle taxis, known as 'pilots', are a licensed form of transport. They're identified by a yellow front mudguard and, although not as common as they used to be, you'll still find them at Panaji, Mapusa and Margao and they'll magically appear at markets or parties when demand is high. They cost half the price of a taxi.

Taxi

Taxis are widely available for town-hopping, but the local union cartel means prices are often ridiculously high, especially at night and more so around expensive hotels. A day's sightseeing, depending on the distance, is likely to be around ₹1500 to ₹2500. Agree on a price beforehand.

An initiative by Goa Tourism is the **Women's Taxi Service** (☎0832-2437437), with female drivers, phone-only bookings, and only women, couples or families accepted as passengers. The vehicles are fitted with accurate meters and GPS monitoring, and the drivers are trained in first aid and self-defence. Fares can even be paid with a credit card. The problem is that there aren't enough cars/drivers to make this a reliable service.

Train

Goa's rail services, though great for getting to and from the state, aren't particularly useful for getting around it. It's usually quicker and more convenient to travel by bus, taxi or under your own steam. An exception is travelling the length of the state, say from Arambol or Mapusa to Palolem, which would otherwise require several bus changes.

➡ There are two railways in Goa: the South Central Railway runs east from Vasco da Gama, through Margao and into Karnataka. This line is most useful for day-tripping to Dudhsagar Falls via Colem station.

➡ The interstate Konkan Railway train line passes through Goa: stations from north to south in Goa are Pernem (for Arambol), Thivim (for Mapusa), Karmali (for Old Goa and Panaji), Verna, Margao (for Colva and Benaulim), Bali, Barcem and Canacona (for Palolem).

Health

There is huge geographical variation in India, so in different areas heat, cold and altitude can cause health problems. Hygiene is poor in most regions, so food- and water-borne illnesses are common. A number of insect-borne diseases are present, particularly in tropical areas. Medical care is basic in various areas (especially beyond the larger cities), so it's essential to be well prepared.

Pre-existing medical conditions and accidental injury (especially traffic accidents) account for most life-threatening problems. Becoming ill in some way, however, is common. Fortunately, most travellers' illnesses can be prevented with some common-sense behaviour or treated with a well-stocked travellers' medical kit. However, never hesitate to consult a doctor while on the road, as self-diagnosis can be hazardous.

BEFORE YOU GO

You can buy many medications over the counter in India without a doctor's prescription, but it can be difficult to find some of the newer drugs, particularly the latest antidepressant drugs, blood-pressure medications and contraceptive pills. Be circumspect about self-medicating, as travellers mixing the wrong drugs or overdosing have on occasion ended in tragedy. Bring the following:

- medications in their original, labelled containers
- a signed, dated letter from your physician describing your medical conditions and medications, including generic medication names
- a physician's letter documenting the medical necessity of any syringes you bring
- if you have a heart condition, a copy of your ECG taken just prior to travelling
- any regular medication (double your ordinary needs).

Insurance

Don't travel without health/travel insurance. Emergency evacuation is expensive. There are various factors to consider when choosing insurance. Read the small print.

- You may require extra cover for adventure activities such as rock climbing and scuba diving.
- In India, doctors usually require immediate payment in cash. Your insurance plan may make payments directly to providers or it will reimburse you later for overseas health expenditures. If you do have to claim later, make sure you keep all relevant documentation.
- Some policies ask that you telephone back (reverse charges) to a centre in your home country, where an immediate assessment of your problem will be made.

Vaccinations

Specialised travel-medicine clinics are your best source of up-to-date information; they stock all available vaccines and can give specific recommendations for your trip. Most vaccines don't give immunity until *at least* two weeks after they're given, so visit a doctor well before departure. Ask your doctor for an International Certificate of Vaccination (sometimes known as the 'yellow booklet'), which will list all the vaccinations you've received.

Required & Recommended Vaccinations

The only vaccine required by international regulations is that for yellow fever. Proof of vaccination will only be required if you have visited a country in the yellow-fever zone within the six days prior to entering India. If you are travelling to India from Africa or South America, you should check to see if you require proof of vaccination.

The World Health Organization (WHO) recommends

VACCINATIONS FOR LONG STAYS

The following immunisations are recommended for long-term travellers (more than one month) or those at special risk (seek further advice from your doctor):

Japanese B encephalitis Three injections in all. Booster recommended after two years. Sore arm and headache are the most common side effects. In rare cases an allergic reaction comprising hives and swelling can occur up to 10 days after any of the three doses.

Meningitis Single injection. There are two types of vaccination: the quadravalent vaccine gives two to three years' protection; the meningitis group C vaccine gives around 10 years' protection. Recommended for long-term backpackers aged under 25.

Rabies Three injections in all. A booster after one year will then provide 10 years' protection. Side effects are rare – occasionally headache and sore arm.

Tuberculosis (TB) A complex issue. Adult long-term travellers are usually advised to have a TB skin test before and after travel, rather than vaccination. Only one vaccine is given in a lifetime.

the following vaccinations for travellers going to India (as well as being up to date with measles, mumps and rubella vaccinations). Note that there is no vaccine for malaria, so prophylaxis is used instead.

Adult diphtheria and tetanus Single booster recommended if none in the previous 10 years. Side effects include sore arm and fever.

Hepatitis A Provides almost 100% protection for up to a year; a booster after 12 months provides at least another 20 years' protection. Mild side effects such as headache and sore arm occur in 5% to 10% of people.

Hepatitis B Now considered routine for most travellers. Given as three shots over six months. A rapid schedule is also available, as is a combined vaccination with hepatitis A. Side effects are mild and uncommon, usually headache and a sore arm. In 95% of people lifetime protection results.

Polio Only one booster is required as an adult for lifetime protection. Inactivated polio vaccine is safe during pregnancy.

Typhoid Recommended for all travellers to India, even those only visiting urban areas. The vaccine offers around 70% protection, lasts for two to three years and comes as a single shot. Tablets are also available, but the injection is usually recommended as it has fewer side effects. Sore arm and fever may occur.

Varicella If you haven't had chickenpox, discuss this vaccination with your doctor.

Medical Checklist

Recommended items for a personal medical kit include:

- Antibacterial cream, eg mupirocin
- Antibiotic for skin infections, eg amoxicillin/clavulanate or cephalexin
- Antifungal cream, eg clotrimazole
- Antihistamine – there are many options, eg cetrizine for daytime and promethazine for night
- Antiseptic, eg Betadine
- Antispasmodic for stomach cramps, eg Buscopam
- Contraceptive
- Decongestant, eg pseudoephedrine
- DEET-based insect repellent
- Diarrhoea medication – consider an oral rehydration solution (eg Gastrolyte), diarrhoea 'stopper' (eg loperamide) and antinausea medication (eg prochlorperazine); antibiotics for diarrhoea include ciprofloxacin; for bacterial diarrhoea azithromycin; for giardia or amoebic dysentery tinidazole
- First-aid items such as scissors, elastoplasts, bandages, gauze, thermometer (but not mercury), sterile needles and syringes, safety pins and tweezers
- Ibuprofen or another anti-inflammatory
- Iodine tablets (unless you are pregnant or have a thyroid problem) to purify water
- Migraine medication if you suffer from migraines
- Paracetamol
- Pyrethrin to impregnate clothing and mosquito nets
- Steroid cream for allergic or itchy rashes, eg 1% to 2% hydrocortisone
- Sunscreen (with a high SPF)
- Throat lozenges
- Thrush (vaginal yeast infection) treatment, eg clotrimazole pessaries or Diflucan tablet
- Ural or equivalent if prone to urinary-tract infections

Websites

There's a wealth of travel-health advice on the internet; www.lonelyplanet.com is a good place to start. It's a good idea to consult your government's travel-advisory website to see if there are any specific health risks to be aware of.

Further Reading

Recommended references include *Travellers' Health* by Dr Richard Dawood and *Travelling Well* by Dr Deborah Mills, which is now also available as an app; check out the website (www.travellingwell.com.au) too.

IN INDIA

Availability & Cost of Healthcare

Medical care is hugely variable in India. Some cities now have clinics catering specifically to travellers and expatriates; these clinics are usually more expensive than local medical facilities, and offer a higher standard of care. Additionally, the staff members know the local system, including reputable hospitals and specialists. They may also liaise with insurance companies should you require evacuation. It's usually difficult to find reliable medical care in rural areas.

Self-treatment may be appropriate if your problem is minor (eg traveller's diarrhoea), you are carrying the relevant medication, and you cannot attend a recommended clinic. If you suspect a serious disease, especially malaria, travel to the nearest quality facility.

Before buying medication over the counter, check the use-by date, and ensure that the packet is sealed and properly stored (eg not exposed to the sunshine).

Infectious Diseases

Malaria

This is a serious and potentially deadly disease. Before you travel, seek expert advice according to your itinerary (rural areas are especially risky) and on medication and side effects.

Malaria is caused by a parasite transmitted by the bite of an infected mosquito. The most important symptom of malaria is fever, but general symptoms, such as headache, diarrhoea, cough or chills, may also occur. Diagnosis can only be properly made by taking a blood sample.

Two strategies should be combined to prevent malaria: mosquito avoidance and antimalarial medications. Most people who catch malaria are taking inadequate or no antimalarial medication.

Travellers are advised to prevent mosquito bites by taking these steps:

- Use a DEET-based insect repellent on exposed skin. Wash this off at night – as long as you are sleeping under a mosquito net. Natural repellents such as citronella can be effective but must be applied more frequently than products containing DEET.
- Sleep under a mosquito net impregnated with pyrethrin.
- Choose accommodation with proper screens and fans (if not air-conditioned).
- Impregnate clothing with pyrethrin in high-risk areas.
- Wear long sleeves and trousers in light colours.
- Use mosquito coils.
- Spray your room with insect repellent before going out for your evening meal.

A variety of medications are available:

Chloroquine and Paludrine combination Limited effectiveness in many parts of South Asia. Common side effects include nausea (40% of people) and mouth ulcers.

Doxycycline (daily tablet) A broad-spectrum antibiotic that helps prevent a variety of tropical diseases, including leptospirosis, tick-borne disease and typhus. Potential side effects include photosensitivity (a tendency to sunburn), thrush (in women), indigestion, heartburn, nausea and interference with the contraceptive pill. More serious side effects include ulceration of the oesophagus – take your tablet with a meal and a large glass of water, and never lie down within half an hour of taking it. It must be taken for four weeks after leaving the risk area.

Lariam (mefloquine) This weekly tablet suits many people. Serious side effects can be an issue with this drug, though, and include depression, anxiety, psychosis and seizures. Unusually vivid nightmares that last months after use of the drug are not uncommon. Anyone with a history of depression, anxiety, other psychological disorders or epilepsy should not take Lariam. It is considered safe in the second and third trimesters of pregnancy. Tablets must be taken for four weeks after leaving the risk area.

Malarone A combination of atovaquone and proguanil. Side effects are uncommon and mild, most commonly nausea and headache. It is the best tablet for scuba divers and for those on short trips to high-risk areas. It must be taken for one week after leaving the risk area.

Traveller's Diarrhoea

This is by far the most common problem affecting travellers in India – between 30% and 70% of people will suffer from it within two weeks of starting their trip. It's usually caused by bacteria, and thus responds promptly to treatment with antibiotics.

Traveller's diarrhoea is defined as the passage of more than three watery

DRINKING WATER

- Never drink tap water.
- Bottled water is generally safe – check that the seal is intact at purchase.
- Avoid ice unless you know it has been made without tap water.
- Be careful of fresh juices served at street stalls in particular – they're likely to have been watered down with tap water or may be served in jugs/glasses that have been rinsed in tap water.
- Avoid fruit that you don't peel yourself, as it will likely have been rinsed in tap water. Alternatively, rinse fruit yourself in mineral water before you eat it.
- Boiling water is usually the most efficient method of purifying it.
- The best chemical purifier is iodine. It should not be used by pregnant women or those with thyroid problems.
- Water filters should also filter out most viruses. Ensure your filter has a chemical barrier such as iodine and a small pore size (less than four microns).
- In tourist areas, some guesthouses, cafes and restaurants use water filters; use your own judgment as to whether you think this water will be safe to drink.

bowel actions within 24 hours, plus at least one other symptom, such as fever, cramps, nausea, vomiting or feeling generally unwell.

Treatment consists of staying well hydrated; rehydration solutions like Gastrolyte are the best for this. Antibiotics such as ciprofloxacin or azithromycin should kill the bacteria quickly. Seek medical attention quickly if you do not respond to an appropriate antibiotic.

Loperamide is just a 'stopper' and doesn't get to the cause of the problem. It can be helpful, though (eg if you have to go on a long bus ride). Don't take loperamide if you have a fever or blood in your stools.

Amoebic dysentery Amoebic dysentery is very rare in travellers but is quite often misdiagnosed by poor-quality labs. Symptoms are similar to bacterial diarrhoea: fever, bloody diarrhoea and generally feeling unwell. You should always seek reliable medical care if you have blood in your diarrhoea. Treatment involves two drugs: tinidazole or metronidazole to kill the parasite in your gut and then a second drug to kill the cysts. If left untreated, complications such as liver or gut abscesses can occur.

Giardiasis Giardia is a parasite that is relatively common in travellers. Symptoms include nausea, bloating, excess gas, fatigue and intermittent diarrhoea. The parasite will eventually go away if left untreated, but this can take months; the best advice is to seek medical treatment. The treatment of choice is tinidazole, with metronidazole a second-line option.

Other Diseases

Avian flu 'Bird flu' or Influenza A (H5N1) is a subtype of the type A influenza virus. Contact with dead or sick birds is the principal source of infection and bird-to-human transmission does not easily occur. Symptoms include high fever and flu-like symptoms with rapid deterioration, leading to respiratory failure and death in many cases. Immediate medical care should be sought if bird flu is suspected. Check www.who.int/en.

Cholera There are occasional outbreaks of cholera in India. This acute gastrointestinal infection is transmitted through contaminated water and food, including raw or undercooked fish and shellfish. Cases are rare among travellers, but those who are travelling to an area of active transmission should consult with their health-care practitioner regarding vaccination.

Dengue fever This mosquito-borne disease is becomingly increasingly problematic, especially in the cities. As there is no vaccine available it can only be prevented by avoiding mosquito bites at all times. Symptoms include high fever, severe headache and body ache and sometimes a rash and diarrhoea. Treatment is rest and paracetamol – do not take aspirin or ibuprofen, as these increase the likelihood of haemorrhage. Make sure you see a doctor to be diagnosed and monitored.

Hepatitis A This food- and water-borne virus infects the liver, causing jaundice (yellow skin and eyes), nausea and lethargy. There is no specific treatment for hepatitis A; you just need to allow time for the liver to heal. All travellers to India should be vaccinated against hepatitis A.

Hepatitis B This sexually transmitted disease is spread by body fluids and can be prevented by vaccination. The long-term consequences can include liver cancer and cirrhosis.

Hepatitis E Transmitted through contaminated food and water, hepatitis E has similar symptoms to hepatitis A but is far less common. It is a severe problem in pregnant women and can result in the death of both mother and baby. There is no commercially available vaccine, and prevention is by following safe eating and drinking guidelines.

HIV Spread via contaminated body fluids. Avoid unprotected sex, unsterile needles (including in medical facilities) and procedures such as tattoos. The growth rate of HIV in India is one of the highest in the world.

Influenza Present year-round in the tropics, influenza (flu) symptoms include fever, muscle aches, a runny nose, cough and sore throat. It can be severe in people over the age of 65 or in those with medical conditions such as heart disease or diabetes – vaccination is recommended for these individuals. There is no specific treatment, just rest and paracetamol.

Japanese B encephalitis This viral disease is transmitted by mosquitoes and is rare in travellers. Most cases occur in rural areas and vaccination is recommended for travellers spending more than a month outside cities. There is no treatment, and the virus may result in permanent brain damage or death. Ask your doctor for further details.

Rabies This fatal disease is spread by the bite, scratch or, if you already have an open wound, possibly even the lick of an infected animal – most commonly a dog or monkey. Rabies is almost always fatal once symptoms appear, but treatment before this is very effective. You should seek medical advice immediately after any animal bite and commence postexposure treatment. Having pretravel vaccination means that postbite treatment is greatly simplified. If an animal bites you, immediately wash the wound with soap and water for several minutes, and apply iodine-based antiseptic. If you are not prevaccinated you will need to receive rabies immunoglobulin as soon as possible, ideally within a few hours. If travelling with a child, make sure they're aware of the dangers and that they know to tell you if they've been bitten, scratched or licked by an animal.

Tuberculosis While TB is rare in travellers, those who have significant contact with the local population (such as medical and aid workers and long-term travellers) should take precautions. Vaccination is usually only given to children under the age of five, but adults at risk are advised to have pre- and posttravel TB testing. The main symptoms are fever, cough, weight loss, night sweats and fatigue.

Typhoid This serious bacterial infection is also spread via food and water. It causes a high and slowly progressive fever and headache, and may be accompanied by a dry cough and stomach pain. It is diagnosed by blood tests and treated with antibiotics. Vaccination is recommended for all travellers who are spending more than a week in India. Be aware that vaccination is not 100% effective, so you must still be careful with what you eat and drink.

Zika At the time of writing, most of India had been categorised as having a moderate risk of Zika virus (except for Rajasthan, which had a high risk, especially Jaipur), though there have been recent cases in Tamil Nadu and Ahmedabad. Check online for current updates.

Environmental Hazards

Air Pollution

Air pollution is a huge problem in India. According the World Health Organization (WHO), Delhi is the most polluted major city in the world. The next six most polluted cities are also in North India. If you have severe respiratory problems, speak with your doctor before travelling to India. All travellers are advised to listen to advisories on pollution levels from the Indian press or government officials. It's worth taking a properly fitted face mask if you are affected by air quality. In North India air pollution is at its worst during the cooler winter months (November and December particularly), partly due to the stubble-burning of crops in rural regions surrounding the big cities, and not helped by all the firecrackers let off during Diwali.

Short-term exposure can lead to a sore throat, sore eyes, itchy skin and a runny nose. As well as face masks, throat lozenges can help, as can frequently rinsing your face, hands and hair. Long-term exposure is, obviously, more serious.

Diving & Surfing

Divers and surfers should seek specialised advice before they travel to ensure that their medical kit contains treatment for coral cuts and tropical ear infections. Divers should ensure that their insurance covers them for decompression illness – get specialised diving insurance through an organisation such as Divers Alert Network (www.danasiapacific.org). Certain medical conditions are incompatible with diving; check with your doctor.

Food

Dining out brings with it the possibility of contracting diarrhoea. Ways to help avoid food-related illness:

- avoid tap water, and food rinsed in it
- eat only freshly cooked food
- avoid shellfish and buffets
- peel fruit
- cook vegetables
- soak salads in iodine water for at least 20 minutes
- eat in busy restaurants with a high turnover of customers.

Heat

Many parts of India, especially down south, are hot and humid throughout the year. For most visitors it takes around two weeks to comfortably adapt to the hot climate. Swelling of the feet and ankles is common, as are muscle cramps caused by excessive sweating. Prevent these by avoiding dehydration and excessive activity in the heat. Don't eat salt tablets (they aggravate the gut); drinking rehydration solution or eating salty food helps. Treat cramps by resting, rehydrating with double-strength rehydration solution and gently stretching.

Dehydration is the main contributor to heat exhaustion. Recovery is usually rapid and it is common to feel weak for some days afterwards. Symptoms include the following:

- feeling weak
- headache
- irritability
- nausea or vomiting
- sweaty skin
- a fast, weak pulse
- normal or slightly elevated body temperature.

Treatments include:

- getting out of the heat
- fanning the sufferer
- applying cool, wet cloths to the skin
- laying the sufferer flat with their legs raised
- rehydrating with water containing a quarter of a teaspoon of salt per litre.

Heatstroke is a serious medical emergency requiring urgent attention. Symptoms include the following:

- weakness
- nausea
- a hot, dry body
- temperature of over 41°C
- dizziness
- confusion
- loss of coordination
- seizures
- eventual collapse.

Treatment:

- get out of the heat
- fan the sufferer
- apply cool, wet cloths to the skin or ice to the body, especially to the groin and armpits.

Prickly heat is a common skin rash in the tropics, caused by sweat trapped under the skin. Treat it by moving out of the heat for a few hours and by having cool showers. Creams and ointments clog the skin so they should be avoided. Locally bought prickly-heat powder can be helpful.

Altitude Sickness

If you're going to altitudes above 3000m, acute mountain sickness (AMS) is an issue. The biggest risk factor is going too high too quickly – follow a conservative acclimatisation schedule found in good trekking guides, and *never* go to a higher altitude when you have any symptoms that could be altitude related. There is no way to predict who will get altitude sickness, and it is quite often the younger, fitter members of a group who succumb.

Symptoms usually develop during the first 24 hours at altitude but may be delayed up to three weeks. Mild symptoms include the following:

- headache
- lethargy
- dizziness
- difficulty sleeping
- loss of appetite.

AMS may become more severe without warning and can be fatal. Severe symptoms include the following:

- breathlessness
- a dry, irritative cough (which may progress to the production of pink, frothy sputum)
- severe headache
- lack of coordination and balance
- confusion
- irrational behaviour
- vomiting
- drowsiness
- loss of consciousness.

Treat mild symptoms by resting at the same altitude or lower until recovery, which usually takes a day or two. Paracetamol or aspirin can be taken for headaches. If symptoms persist or become worse, immediate descent is necessary; even 500m can help. Drug treatments should never be used to avoid descent or to enable further ascent.

The drugs acetazolamide (Diamox) and dexamethasone are recommended by some doctors for the prevention of AMS; however, their use is controversial. They can reduce the symptoms, but they may also mask warning signs; severe and fatal AMS has occurred in people taking these drugs.

To prevent AMS, carry out the following steps:

- ascend slowly – have frequent rest days, spending two to three nights at each rise of 1000m
- sleep at a lower altitude than the greatest height reached during the day, if possible. Above 3000m, don't increase sleeping altitude by more than 300m daily
- drink extra fluids

CARBON MONOXIDE POISONING

Some mountain areas rely on charcoal burners for warmth, but these should be avoided due to the risk of fatal carbon-monoxide poisoning. The thick, mattress-like blankets used in many mountain areas are amazingly warm once you get beneath the covers. If you're still cold, improvise a hot-water bottle by filling your drinking-water bottle with boiled water and covering it with a sock.

- eat light, high-carbohydrate meals
- avoid alcohol and sedatives.

Insect Bites & Stings

Bedbugs Don't carry disease, but their bites can be itchy. You can treat the itch with an antihistamine.

Lice Most commonly appear on the head and pubic areas. You may need numerous applications of an antilice shampoo such as pyrethrin.

Ticks Contracted while walking in rural areas. Ticks are commonly found behind the ears, on the belly and in armpits, and bites can lead to serious infections such as Kyasanur forest disease. If you have had a tick bite and have a rash at the site of the bite or elsewhere, fever or muscle aches, see a doctor. Doxycycline prevents tick-borne diseases.

Leeches Found in humid rainforest areas. They don't transmit any disease, but their bites are often itchy for weeks and can easily become infected. Apply an iodine-based antiseptic to any leech bite to help prevent infection.

Bee and wasp stings Anyone with a serious bee or wasp allergy should carry an injection of adrenaline (eg an Epipen).

Skin Problems

Fungal rashes There are two common fungal rashes that affect travellers. The first occurs in moist areas of the body, such as the groin, the armpits and between the toes. It starts as a red patch that slowly spreads and is usually itchy. Treatment involves keeping the skin dry, avoiding chafing and using an antifungal cream such as clotrimazole or Lamisil. The second, *Tinea versicolor*, causes light-coloured patches, most commonly on the back, chest and shoulders. Consult a doctor.

Cuts and scratches These become easily infected in humid climates. Immediately wash all wounds in clean water and apply antiseptic. If you develop signs of infection (increasing pain and redness), see a doctor.

Sunburn

Even on a cloudy day sunburn can occur rapidly.

- Use a strong sunscreen (factor 30) and reapply after a swim.
- Wear a wide-brimmed hat and sunglasses.
- Avoid lying in the sun during the hottest part of the day (10am to 2pm).
- Be vigilant above 3000m – you can get burnt very easily at altitude.

If you become sunburnt, stay out of the sun until you have recovered, apply cool compresses and, if necessary, take painkillers for the discomfort. One per cent hydrocortisone cream applied twice daily is also helpful.

Women's Health

For gynaecological health issues, seek out a female doctor.

Birth control Bring adequate supplies of your own form of contraception.

Thrush Heat, humidity and antibiotics can all contribute to thrush. Treatment is with antifungal creams and pessaries such as clotrimazole. A practical alternative is a single tablet of fluconazole (Diflucan).

Urinary-tract infections These can be precipitated by dehydration or long bus journeys without toilet stops; bring suitable antibiotics.

Language

Thanks to its unusual colonial history, Goa has inherited a mixture of languages. Portuguese is still spoken as a second language by a few Goans, although it is gradually dying out. Konkani is the official language of Goa, whereas Marathi is taught as a standard subject in the state, as well as being the main language of Mumbai. Children in Goa are obliged to learn Hindi in school, and the primary language used in many schools is actually English, since both Hindi and English have official status in India. English is widely spoken in tourist areas in Goa and Mumbai.

HINDI

Hindi has about 600 million speakers worldwide, of which 180 million are in India. It developed from Classical Sanskrit, and is written in the Devanagari script. In 1947 it was granted official status along with English.

Most Hindi sounds are similar to their English counterparts. The main difference is that Hindi has both 'aspirated' consonants (pronounced with a puff of air, like saying 'h' after the sound) and unaspirated ones, as well as 'retroflex' (pronounced with the tongue bent backwards) and nonretroflex consonants. Our simplified pronunciation guides don't include these distinctions – if you read them as if they were English, you'll be understood just fine.

The pronunciation of vowels is important, especially their length (eg a and aa). The consonant combination ng after a vowel indicates nasalisation (ie the vowel is pronounced 'through the nose'). Note also that au is pronounced as the 'ow' in 'how'.

Word stress in Hindi is very light; we've indicated the stressed syllables with italics.

Basics

Hindi verbs change form depending on the gender of the speaker (or the subject of the sentence in general) – meaning it's the verbs, not the pronouns 'he' or 'she', which show whether the subject of the sentence is masculine or feminine. In these phrases we include the options for male and female speakers, marked 'm' and 'f' respectively.

Hello./Goodbye.	नमस्ते।	na·ma·*ste*
Yes.	जी हाँ।	jee haang
No.	जी नहीं।	jee na·*heeng*
Excuse me.	सुनिये।	su·ni·*ye*
Sorry.	माफ़ कीजिये।	maaf *kee*·ji·ye
Please ...	कृपया ...	kri·pa·*yaa* ...
Thank you.	थैंक्यू।	*thayn*·kyoo
You're welcome.	कोई बात नहीं।	*ko*·ee baat na·*heeng*

How are you?
आप कैसे/कैसी हैं? — aap *kay*·se/*kay*·see hayng (m/f)

Fine. And you?
मैं ठीक हूँ। आप सुनाइये। — mayng teek hoong aap su·*naa*·i·ye

What's your name?
आप का नाम क्या है? — aap kaa naam kyaa hay

My name is ...
मेरा नाम ... है। — *me*·raa naam ... hay

Do you speak English?
क्या आपको अंग्रेज़ी आती है? — kyaa aap ko an·*gre*·zee *aa*·tee hay

I don't understand.
मैं नहीं समझा/समझी। — mayng na·*heeng* sam·jaa/*sam*·jee (m/f)

Accommodation

Where's a ...?	... कहाँ है?	... ka·*haang* hay
guesthouse	गेस्ट हाउस	gest *haa*·us
hotel	होटल	*ho*·tal
youth hostel	यूथ हास्टल	yoot *haas*·tal

Do you have a ... room?	क्या ... कमरा है?	kyaa ... *kam*·raa hay
single	सिंगल	*sin*·gal
double	डबल	da·*bal*

How much is it per ...?	... के लिय कितने पैसे लगते हैं?	... ke li·*ye* *kit*·ne *pay*·se *lag*·te hayng
night	एक रात	ek raat
person	हर व्यक्ति	har *vyak*·ti

Eating & Drinking

What would you recommend?
आपके ख़्याल में क्या अच्छा होगा? — aap ke kyaal meng kyaa *ach*·chaa *ho*·gaa

NUMBERS – HINDI

1	१	एक	ek
2	२	दो	do
3	३	तीन	teen
4	४	चार	chaar
5	५	पाँच	paanch
6	६	छह	chay
7	७	सात	saat
8	८	आठ	aat
9	९	नौ	nau
10	१०	दस	das
20	२०	बीस	bees
30	३०	तीस	tees
40	४०	चालीस	*chaa*·lees
50	५०	पचास	pa·*chaas*
60	६०	साठ	saat
70	७०	सत्तर	*sat*·tar
80	८०	अस्सी	*as*·see
90	९०	नब्बे	*nab*·be
100	१००	सौ	sau
1000	१०००	एक हज़ार	ek ha·*zaar*

Do you have vegetarian food?
क्या आप का खाना शाकाहारी है? — kyaa aap kaa *kaa*·naa shaa·kaa·*haa*·ree hay

I don't eat (meat).
मैं (गोश्त) नहीं खाता/खाती। — mayng (gosht) na·*heeng* *kaa*·taa/*kaa*·tee (m/f)

I'll have ...
मुझे ... दीजिये। — mu·*je* ... *dee*·ji·ye

That was delicious.
बहुत मज़ेदार हुआ। — ba·*hut* ma·ze·*daar* hu·*aa*

Please bring the menu/bill.
मेन्यू/बिल लाइये। — *men*·yoo/bil *laa*·i·ye

Emergencies

Help!
मदद कीजिये! — ma·*dad* *kee*·ji·ye

Go away!
जाओ! — *jaa*·o

I'm lost.
मैं रास्ता भूल गया/गयी हूँ। — mayng *raas*·taa bool ga·*yaa*/ga·*yee* hoong (m/f)

Call a doctor!
डॉक्टर को बुलाओ! — *daak*·tar ko bu·*laa*·o

Call the police!
पुलिस को बुलाओ! — pu·*lis* ko bu·*laa*·o

I'm ill.
मैं बीमार हूँ। — mayng *bee*·maar hoong

I'm allergic to (antibiotics).
मुझे (एंटीबायोटिकिस) की एलरजी है। — mu·*je* (*en*·tee·baa·*yo*·tiks) kee e·*lar*·jee hay

Where's the toilet?
टॉइलेट कहाँ है? — *taa*·i·let ka·*haang* hay

Shopping & Services

I'd like to buy ...
मुझे ... चाहिये। — mu·*je* ... *chaa*·hi·ye

I'm just looking.
सिर्फ़ देखने आया/आयी हूँ। — sirf *dek*·ne *aa*·yaa/*aa*·yee hoong (m/f)

Can I look at it?
दिखाइये। — di·*kaa*·i·ye

Do you have any others?
दूसरा है? — *doos*·raa hay

How much is it?
कितने का है? — *kit*·ne kaa hay

It's too expensive.
यह बहुत महंगा/महंगी है। — yeh ba·*hut* ma·*han*·gaa/ma·*han*·gee hay (m/f)

Can you lower the price?
क्या आप दाम कम करेंगे? — kyaa aap daam kam ka·*reng*·ge

There's a mistake in the bill.
बिल में गलती है। — bil meng *gal*·tee hay

Transport & Directions

When's the ... (bus)?	... (बस) कब जाती है?	... (bas) kab *jaa*·tee hay
first	पहली	*peh*·lee
next	अगली	*ag*·lee
last	आख़िरी	*aa*·ki·ree

bicycle rickshaw	साइकिल रिक्शा	*saa*·i·kil *rik*·shaa
boat	जहाज़	ja·*haaz*
bus	बस	bas
plane	हवाई जहाज़	ha·*vaa*·ee ja·*haaz*
train	ट्रेन	tren

a ... ticket	के लिये ... टिकट दीजिये।	ke li·*ye* ... ti·*kat dee*·ji·ye
1st-class	फ़र्स्ट क्लास	farst klaas
2nd-class	सेकंड क्लास	se·*kand* klaas
one-way	एक तरफ़ा	ek ta·ra·*faa*
return	आने जाने का	*aa*·ne *jaa*·ne kaa

I'd like to hire a ...	मुझे ... किराये पर लेना है।	mu·*je* ... ki·*raa*·ye par *le*·naa hay
4WD	फ़ोर व्हील ड्राइव	for vheel *draa*·iv
bicycle	साइकिल	*saa*·i·kil
car	कार	kaar
motorbike	मोटर साइकिल	*mo*·tar *saa*·i·kil

Where's ...?
... कहाँ है? — ... ka·*haang* hay

How far is it?
वह कितनी दूर है? — voh *kit*·nee door hay

What's the address?
पता क्या है? — pa·*taa* kyaa hay

Can you write it down, please?
कृपया यह लिखिये? — kri·pa·*yaa* yeh li·*ki*·ye

Can you show me (on the map)?
(नक्शे में) दिखा सकते है? — (*nak*·she meng) di·*kaa* *sak*·te hayng

KONKANI

After a long and hard-fought battle, Konkani was recognised as the official language of Goa in 1987, becoming a national language in 1992. Before that, argument had raged that Konkani was actually no more than a dialect of Marathi, the official language of the much larger Maharashtra. Konkani is an Indo-Aryan language and has 2.5 million speakers. The Devanagari script (also used to write Hindi and Marathi) is the official writing system for Konkani in Goa. However, Konkani speakers also use the Kannada script, as given here.

A few pronunciation tips: ai is pronounced as in 'aisle', eu as the 'u' in 'nurse' (a short sound), oh as the 'o' in 'note' and ts as in 'hats'. The symbol ng (as in 'sing') indicates the nasalisation of the preceding consonant, meaning that the consonant sound is pronounced 'through the nose'.

Basics

Hello.	ಹಲ್ಲೋ.	*hal*·lo
Goodbye.	ಮೆಳ್ಯಾಂ.	*mel*·yaang
How are you?	ಕಸೊ/ಕಶಿ ಆಸಾಯ್?	*keu*·so/*keu*·shi *aa*·saay (m/f)
Fine, thanks.	ಹಾಂವ್ಂ ಬರೊಂ ಆಸಾಂ.	*haang*·ung *beu*·rong *aa*·saang
Yes.	ವ್ಹಯ್.	*weu*·i
No.	ನಾಂ.	naang
Please.	ಉಪ್ಕಾರ್ ಕರ್ನೆ.	*up*·kaar keurn
Thank you.	ದೇವ್ ಬರೆಂ ಕರುಂ.	*day*·u *bo*·reng *ko*·roong
Excuse me.	ಉಪ್ಕಾರ್ ಕರ್ನೆ.	*up*·kaar keurn
Sorry.	ಚೂಕ್ ಜ಼ಾಲಿ, ಮಾಫ಼್ ಕರ್.	tsook *zaa*·li maaf keur

What's your name?
ತುಜೆಂ ನಾಂವ್ಂ ಕಿತೆಂ? — *tu*·jeng *naang*·ung *ki*·teng

My name is ...
ಮ್ಹಜೆಂ ನಾಂವ್ಂ ... — *meu*·jeng *naang*·ung ...

Do you speak English?
ಇಂಗ್ಲಿಶ್ ಉಲೈತಾಯ್ಗೀ? — *ing*·leesh *u*·leuy·taay·gee

I don't understand.
ನಾಂ, ಸಮ್ಜೊಂಕ್–ನಾಂ. — naang *som*·zonk·naang

I understand.
ಸಮ್ಜಾಲೆಂ. — *som*·zaa·leng

NUMBERS – KONKANI

1	ಏಕ್	ayk
2	ದೋನ್	dohn
3	ತೀನ್	teen
4	ಚಾರ್	chaar
5	ಪಾಂಚ್	paants
6	ಸೊ	so
7	ಸಾತ್	saat
8	ಆಟ್	aat
9	ನೋವ್	nohw
10	ಧಾ	daa
20	ವೀಸ್	wees
30	ತೀಸ್	tees
40	ಚಾಳೀಸ್	*tsaa*·lees
50	ಪನ್ನಾಸ್	*pon*·naas
60	ಸಾಟ್	saat
70	ಸತ್ತರ್	*seut*·teur
80	ಐಂಶಿಂ	*euyng*·shing
90	ನೊವ್ವೋದ್	*no*·wod
100	ಶೆಂಭರ್	*shem*·bor
1000	ಹಝ಼ಾರ್	*ha*·zaar

Accommodation

Do you have a single/double room?
ಸಿಂಗಲ್/ಡಬಲ್ ರೂಮ್ ಮೆಳಾತ್ಗೀ? — *sin*·gal/*da*·bal room *me*·laat·gee

How much is it per night?
ಏಕಾ ರಾತೀಚೆಂ ಭಾಡೆಂ ಕಿತ್ಲೆಂ? — e·kaa *raa*·ti·cheng *baa*·deng *kit*·leng

How much is it per person?
ಏಕ್ಲ್ಯಾಕ್ ಭಾಡೆಂ ಕಿತ್ಲೆಂ? — *ek*·lyaak *baa*·deng *kit*·leng

Eating & Drinking

Can you recommend a dish?
ಬರೆಂ ಏಕ್ ನಿಸ್ತೆಂ ಝ಼ಾಲ್ಯಾರ್ ಖೈಂಚೆಂ? — *beu*·reng ayk *nis*·teng *zaa*·lyaar *keu*·ing·cheng

I'd like the menu, please.
ಮೆನೂ ಝ಼ಾಯ್ ಆಸ್-ಲ್ಲೊ. — *me*·noo zaay *aa*·sul·lo

I'd like the bill, please.
ಬಿಲ್ಲ್ ಝ಼ಾಯ್ ಆಸ್-ಲ್ಲೆಂ. — bil zaay *aa*·sul·leng

Emergencies

Help!	ಮ್ಹಾಕಾ ಕುಮೆಕ್ ಕರ್!	*maa*·kaa *ku*·meuk keur
Go away!	ವಸ್!	weuts

Call ...!	... ಆಪೈ!	... *aa*·pai
a doctor	ದಾಕ್ತೆರಾಕ್	*daak*·te·raak
the police	ಪೊಲಿಸಾಂಕ್	*po*·li·saank

I'm lost.
ಮ್ಹಜೀ ವಾಟ್ ಚುಕ್ಲ್ಯಾ. — *meu*·ji waat *tsuk*·lyaa

Where are the toilets?
ಟೊಯ್ಲೆಟ್ ಖೈಂಚರ್ ಆಸಾತ್? — *toy*·let *keu*·ing·tseur *aa*·saat

Shopping

Can I look at it?
ಪಳಯೆತ್ಗೀ? — *peu*·leu·yet·gee

How much is it?
ತಾಕಾ ಕಿತ್ಲೆ ಪೈಶೆ? — *taa*·kaa *kit*·le *peuy*·she

That's too expensive.
ತೆಂ ಏಕ್ಧಮ್ ಮ್ಹಾರಗ್. — teng *ayk*·dam *maa*·reug

Transport & Directions

Where's the ...?
... ಖೈಂ ಆಸಾ? — ... keuyng *aa*·saa

Can you show me (on the map)?
(ಮೇಪಾಚೆರ್) ದಾಕೈಶಿಗೀ? — (*mae*·paa·cher) daa·*keuy*·shi·gee

What time's the first/last bus?
ಪಯ್ಲೆಂ/ಆಖ್ರೇಚೆಂ ಬಸ್ ಕಿತ್ಲ್ಯಾ ವೆಳಾರ್ ಯೆತಾ? — *peuy*·leng/ak·*ray*·cheng bas *kit*·lyaa *we*·laar *ye*·taa

One ... ticket to (Permude), please.	(ಪೆರ್ಮುದೆ) ... ಮ್ಹಾಕಾ ಏಕ್ ಟಿಕೇಟ್ ಝ಼ಾಯ್.	(*per*·mu·de) ... *maa*·kaa ayk *ti*·kayt zaay
one-way	ವಚೊಂಕ್ ಮಾತ್ರ್	*wo*·tsonk maatr
return	ವಚೊಂಕ್ ಆನಿಂ ಪಾಟೀಂ ಯೇಂವ್ಕ್	*wo*·tsonk *aan*·ing *paa*·ting *ayng*·wuk

GLOSSARY

azulejos – glazed coloured tiles

ayurveda – ancient study of healing arts and herbal medicine

baksheesh – tip, bribe or donation

balcão – shady porch at front of traditional Goan house, usually with benches built into the walls

bebinca – Goan sweet made from layers of sweet pancake

betel – nut of the betel tree; chewed as a stimulant

bhaji puri – deep-fried bread with curry

bhelpuri – puffed rice tossed with fried rounds of dough, lentils, onions, herbs and chutneys

cafreal – a marinated chicken dish

caste – four classes into which Hindu society is divided; one's hereditary station in life

charas – resin of the cannabis plant; also referred to as hashish

crore – 10 million

Dalit – preferred term for India's casteless class; see *Untouchable*

deepastambha – lamp tower

dhaba – basic restaurant or snack bar

Dhangars – tribe of Goa's indigenous people

fado – melancholy song of longing, popular in Portuguese colonial era

fish curry rice – fried mackerel steeped in coconut, tamarind and chilli sauce

garbhagriha – shrine room; inner sanctum of a Hindu temple

ghat – steps or landing on a river; range of hills, or road up hills; the Western Ghats are the range of mountains that run along India's west coast, effectively forming the eastern border of Goa

gopuram – gateway tower

GTDC – Goa Tourism Development Corporation

Harijan – name given by Gandhi to India's *Untouchables;* the term is no longer considered acceptable; see also *Dalit* and *Untouchable*

khadi – homespun cloth

Kshatriya – Hindu *caste* of warriors and administrators

lakh – 100,000

lingam – phallic symbol representing the god *Shiva*

maidan – open grassed area in a city

mandapa – assembly hall; pillared pavilion of a temple

mando – famous song and dance form, introduced originally by the Goan Catholic community

Manueline – style of architecture typical of that built by the Portuguese during the reign of Manuel I (r 1495-1521)

marg – major road

masjid – mosque

momo – Tibetan dumpling

monsoon – rainy season between June and October

panchayat – local government; a panchayat area typically consists of two to three villages, from which volunteers are elected to represent the interests of the local people (the elected representative is called the panch; the elected leader is the sarpanch)

pousada – Portuguese for hostel

puja – offerings or prayers; literally 'respect'

qawwali – devotional singing

raj – rule or sovereignty

raja, rana – king

ramponkar – traditional Goan fisherman; fishes the coastal waters from a wooden boat, using a hand-hauled net (rampon)

reredos – ornamental screen behind the altar in Goan churches

salwar kameez – traditional dresslike tunic and trouser combination for women

saquão – central courtyard in traditional Goan houses

sati – ritual suicide of widow on husband's funeral pyre

satyagraha – literally 'insistence on truth'; non-violent protest involving a fast, popularised by Gandhi; protesters are *satyagrahis*

Shiva – Hindu god; the destroyer; also the Creator, in which form he is worshipped as a *lingam*

sitar – Indian stringed instrument

sossegado – see susegad

Sudra – caste of labourers

susegad – Goan expression meaning relaxed or laid-back

taluk – administrative district or region

tank – reservoir

tiatr – locally written and produced drama in the Konkani language

tikka – mark devout Hindus put on their foreheads with *tikka* powder

Untouchable – lowest *caste* or 'casteless' for whom the most menial tasks are reserved; name derives from the belief that higher castes risk defilement if they touch one (formerly known as *Harijan*, now *Dalit* or *Scheduled Castes*)

varna – concept of *caste*

veda – knowledge

waddo – section or ward of a village; also known as a vaddo

wallah – man or person; can be added onto almost anything to denote an occupation, thus dhobi-wallah, taxi-wallah, chai-wallah

xacuti – a spicy chicken or meat dish cooked in red coconut sauce

Behind the Scenes

SEND US YOUR FEEDBACK

We love to hear from travellers – your comments keep us on our toes and help make our books better. Our well-travelled team reads every word on what you loved or loathed about this book. Although we cannot reply individually to your submissions, we always guarantee that your feedback goes straight to the appropriate authors, in time for the next edition. Each person who sends us information is thanked in the next edition – the most useful submissions are rewarded with a selection of digital PDF chapters.

Visit **lonelyplanet.com/contact** to submit your updates and suggestions or to ask for help. Our award-winning website also features inspirational travel stories, news and discussions.

Note: We may edit, reproduce and incorporate your comments in Lonely Planet products such as guidebooks, websites and digital products, so let us know if you don't want your comments reproduced or your name acknowledged. For a copy of our privacy policy visit lonelyplanet.com/privacy.

WRITERS' THANKS

Paul Harding

Thanks must go to the many friends I reconnected with in Goa and the new people I met on this trip. Big thanks to Jack, Ajit and family in Panaji; Ravi in Vagator; John, Jack and Kate in Palolem; and Joanna and Xavi in Patnem. Thanks also to friends in Kochi and Alleppey, Philip, Maryann, Johnson, Shibu and Niaz, and to Joe at Lonely Planet for entrusting me with Goa. Biggest thanks goes to my travelling companions, Hannah and Layla.

Kevin Raub

Thanks to Joe Bindloss and all my fellow partners in crime at Lonely Planet. On the road, Anil Whadwa and Bagpacker Travels, Pankil Shaw, Jas Charanjiva, Khaki Tours, Priyanka Jacob, Roxanne Bamboat, Sanil Kapse, Sudakshina Banerjee, Ashok Tours & Travels, Sakshi Chari, Sheetal Waradkar, Chirag Rupani, Zaid Purkars and Amrut and Aditya Dhanwatay.

ACKNOWLEDGEMENTS

Climate map data adapted from Peel MC, Finlayson BL & McMahon TA (2007) 'Updated World Map of the Köppen-Geiger Climate Classification', *Hydrology and Earth System Sciences*, 11, 1633–44.

Cover photograph: Lamp and *rangoli* (elaborate chalk, rice-paste or coloured-powder design) for the Diwali festival, Puneet Vikram Singh/Getty Images©

THIS BOOK

This 8th edition of Lonely Planet's *Goa & Mumbai* guidebook was curated by Paul Harding, and researched and written by Paul, Daniel McCrohan, Kevin Raub and Iain Stewart. The Mumbai chapter was curated by Anirban Mahapatra; Joe Bindloss curated parts of the Survival Guide. The previous edition was written by Paul, Abigail Blasi, Trent Holden and Iain. This guidebook was produced by the following:

Destination Editor Joe Bindloss

Senior Product Editor Kate Chapman

Senior Cartographer Valentina Kremenchutskaya

Product Editor Kate Mathews

Book Designer Ania Bartoszek

Assisting Editors Sarah Bailey, Judith Bamber, Katie Connolly, Melanie Dankel, Samantha Forge, Carly Hall, Victoria Harrison, Jodie Martire, Lauren O'Connell, Saralinda Turner

Cover Researcher Naomi Parker

Thanks to Patric Colquhoun, Diana Furtado, Antonio Levy, Amanda Williamson

Index

Map Pages **000**
Photo Pages **000**

Map Pages **000**
Photo Pages **000**

Map Legend

Sights
- Beach
- Bird Sanctuary
- Buddhist
- Castle/Palace
- Christian
- Confucian
- Hindu
- Islamic
- Jain
- Jewish
- Monument
- Museum/Gallery/Historic Building
- Ruin
- Shinto
- Sikh
- Taoist
- Winery/Vineyard
- Zoo/Wildlife Sanctuary
- Other Sight

Activities, Courses & Tours
- Bodysurfing
- Diving
- Canoeing/Kayaking
- Course/Tour
- Sento Hot Baths/Onsen
- Skiing
- Snorkelling
- Surfing
- Swimming/Pool
- Walking
- Windsurfing
- Other Activity

Sleeping
- Sleeping
- Camping
- Hut/Shelter

Eating
- Eating

Drinking & Nightlife
- Drinking & Nightlife
- Cafe

Entertainment
- Entertainment

Shopping
- Shopping

Information
- Bank
- Embassy/Consulate
- Hospital/Medical
- Internet
- Police
- Post Office
- Telephone
- Toilet
- Tourist Information
- Other Information

Geographic
- Beach
- Gate
- Hut/Shelter
- Lighthouse
- Lookout
- Mountain/Volcano
- Oasis
- Park
- Pass
- Picnic Area
- Waterfall

Population
- Capital (National)
- Capital (State/Province)
- City/Large Town
- Town/Village

Transport
- Airport
- Border crossing
- Bus
- Cable car/Funicular
- Cycling
- Ferry
- Metro station
- Monorail
- Parking
- Petrol station
- Subway station
- Taxi
- Train station/Railway
- Tram
- Underground station
- Other Transport

Routes
- Tollway
- Freeway
- Primary
- Secondary
- Tertiary
- Lane
- Unsealed road
- Road under construction
- Plaza/Mall
- Steps
- Tunnel
- Pedestrian overpass
- Walking Tour
- Walking Tour detour
- Path/Walking Trail

Boundaries
- International
- State/Province
- Disputed
- Regional/Suburb
- Marine Park
- Cliff
- Wall

Hydrography
- River, Creek
- Intermittent River
- Canal
- Water
- Dry/Salt/Intermittent Lake
- Reef

Areas
- Airport/Runway
- Beach/Desert
- Cemetery (Christian)
- Cemetery (Other)
- Glacier
- Mudflat
- Park/Forest
- Sight (Building)
- Sportsground
- Swamp/Mangrove

Note: Not all symbols displayed above appear on the maps in this book

OUR STORY

A beat-up old car, a few dollars in the pocket and a sense of adventure. In 1972 that's all Tony and Maureen Wheeler needed for the trip of a lifetime – across Europe and Asia overland to Australia. It took several months, and at the end – broke but inspired – they sat at their kitchen table writing and stapling together their first travel guide, *Across Asia on the Cheap*. Within a week they'd sold 1500 copies. Lonely Planet was born.

Today, Lonely Planet has offices in Franklin, London, Melbourne, Oakland, Dublin, Beijing and Delhi, with more than 600 staff and writers. We share Tony's belief that 'a great guidebook should do three things: inform, educate and amuse'.

OUR WRITERS

Paul Harding

Goa As a writer and photographer, Paul has been travelling the globe for the best part of two decades, with an interest in remote and offbeat places, islands and cultures. He's an author and contributor to more than 50 Lonely Planet guides to countries and regions as diverse as India, Belize, Vanuatu, Iran, Indonesia, New Zealand, Iceland, Finland, Philippines and – his home patch – Australia. He's on twitter @phtravel and at paulharding.contently.com.

Kevin Raub

Mumbai Atlanta native Kevin started his career as a music journalist in New York, until he ditched the rock 'n' roll lifestyle for travel writing. He has written more than 70 Lonely Planet guides, focused mainly on Brazil, Chile, Colombia, USA, India, the Caribbean and Portugal, since. Kevin also contributes to a variety of travel magazines in both the USA and UK. Along the way, the self-confessed hophead is in constant search of wildly high IBUs in local beers, and continues pounding the world's pavements with one goal in mind: membership in the Travelers' Century Club before the age of 50. His country count currently stands at 93. Follow him on Twitter and Instagram @RaubOnTheRoad.

Iain Stewart

Beyond Goa Iain trained as journalist in the 1990s and then worked as a news reporter and a restaurant critic in London. He started writing travel guides in 1997 and has since penned over 60 books for destinations as diverse as Ibiza and Cambodia. Iain has contributed to Lonely Planet titles including *Mexico, Indonesia, Central America, Croatia, Vietnam, Bali & Lombok* and *Southeast Asia*. He also writes regularly for the *Independent, Observer* and *Daily Telegraph* and tweets at @iaintravel. He'll consider working anywhere there's a palm tree or two and a beach of a generally sandy persuasion. Iain lives in Brighton (UK) within firing range of the city's wonderful south-facing horizon.

Contributing Writer

Daniel McCrohan wrote the Scams and Women & Solo Travellers chapters.

Published by Lonely Planet Global Limited
CRN 554153
8th edition –October 2019
ISBN 978 1 78657 166 3

10 9 8 7 6 5 4 3 2 1
Printed in China